Cambridge IGCSE®

Business Studies

STUDENT'S BOOK

Also for Cambridge O Level and Cambridge IGCSE® (9-1)

Andrew Dean, Denry Machin,
Mark Gardiner

William Collins' dream of knowledge for all began with the publication of his first book in 1819.

A self-educated mill worker, he not only enriched millions of lives, but also founded a flourishing publishing house. Today, staying true to this spirit, Collins books are packed with inspiration, innovation and practical expertise. They place you at the centre of a world of possibility and give you exactly what you need to explore it.

Collins. Freedom to teach.

Published by Collins
An imprint of HarperCollins*Publishers*
The News Building
1 London Bridge Street
London SE1 9GF

Macken House, 39/40 Mayor Street Upper,
Dublin 1, D01 C9W8, Ireland

Browse the complete Collins catalogue at
www.collins.co.uk

10 9 8

ISBN 978-0-00-825805-4

Andrew Dean, Denry Machin and Mark Gardiner assert their moral rights to be identified as the authors of this work.

British Library Cataloguing in Publication Data

A catalogue record for this publication is available from the British Library.

Commissioning editor: Rachael Harrison
In-house editor: Lara McMurray
Development editor: Alison Silver
Copyeditor: Margaret Levin
Proofreader: Nikky Twyman
Permissions researcher: Rachel Thorne
Cover designer: Kevin Robbins
Cover illustrator: Maria Herbert-Liew
Artwork: Jouve India Private Ltd
Typesetter: Jouve India Private Ltd
Production controller: Tina Paul
Printed and bound by: Replika Press Pvt. Ltd., India

The publishers wish to thank Cambridge Assessment International Education for permission to reproduce questions from past IGCSE® Business Studies papers. Cambridge Assessment International Education bears no responsibility for the example answers to questions taken from its past papers. All exam-style questions and sample answers in this title were written by the author(s).

Contents

Introduction

Many of the topics you will study during your Business Studies course are ones that affect you every day; for example, why do cinema prices vary at different times of day; why do firms use social networking to promote their products; what motivates people to work hard? Business Studies is a very real subject; as you learn about each of the topics in this book, try to relate them to reality – not only will this help you to get a better grade but you will also find the course more interesting.

After successful completion of this course you will understand the different forms of business organisations, the external environment in which businesses operate, and different business functions such as marketing, operations and finance. You will also have an understanding of the important role people play in the success (or otherwise) of a business, and be able to calculate, interpret and use basic business data and basic financial information. You will develop the ability to analyse different business situations and make recommendations about what business actions might be appropriate in different contexts.

The book is laid out into the following sections:

Section 1: Understanding business activity	Section 1 examines the purpose of business activity, what form business ownership can take and what businesses try and achieve. Other topics include: classification of businesses; enterprise, growth and size; types of business organisation
Section 2: People in business	In Section 2 you will learn why people are critical to business success, how firms can motivate and recruit employees, and what laws exist to protect employees. Other topics include: workforce organisation and management; recruitment, selection and training of employees; internal and external communication; employment protection legislation.
Section 3: Marketing	Section 3 examines how businesses attempt to develop relationships with consumers, how they communicate with them and persuade them to buy more products. Other topics include: marketing; market research; marketing strategy.
Section 4: Operations management	Section 4 looks at how products are manufactured, the methods for improving the speed, quality and cost of production, and where businesses locate their operations. Other topics include: scale of production and break-even analysis; achieving quality production of goods and services; location decisions.
Section 5: Financial information and decisions	Section 5 explores basic business accounting tools and examines where businesses get money from. Topics include: business finance (needs and sources); cash flow forecasting and working capital; income statements; statements of financial position; analysis of accounts.

Section 6: External influences on business activity	Section 6 examines how the external environment in which a business operates can affect (both positively and negatively) its activities. Topics include: government economic objectives and policies; environmental and ethical issues; business and the international economy.

Every topic starts by outlining the **Aims** – what you need to know and be able to do for that topic. The content is supported by **Case studies**, giving relevant examples of the theory in action from around the world, and a variety of **Skills activities**. **Did you know?** features highlight interesting facts and figures from around the business world. Each topic concludes with **Knowledge check** questions to test your understanding of the key concepts and a **Check your progress** for you to check your understanding of the topic. Key terms and difficult language are explained throughout, and you can refer to the extensive **Glossary** to double-check your understanding of terms appearing in **bold**. Each section concludes with an **Exam practice** section that will help you prepare for your assessment.

CASE STUDY **Nike is now open**

Vietnam has now overtaken China as the world's largest producer of Nike trainers. Nike has received heavy criticism in recent years for its production methods and lack of communication with customers and other stakeholders. However, Nike now lists its suppliers and factories so that customers can find out where their products were made. This communication has been a positive move by Nike as they look to improve relationships with their stakeholders.

Application **Analysis** **Evaluation**

You will probably experience communication from your school on a regular basis. In pairs, prepare a short presentation that should include:

- A list of all the many different methods that the school uses to communicate.
- Now, identify one example of when the school has communicated with you or your parents. Which method did they use? What are the benefits and drawbacks of the method they used? (Apply this to you and your situation specifically.)
- Do you think this was the most appropriate method to use? Justify your answer.

During your assessment, you will need to think about the following:

Assessment objective 1: Knowledge and understanding	You need to demonstrate knowledge and understanding of the theories and techniques, facts, terms and concepts included throughout this book.
Assessment objective 2: Application	You must relate your knowledge and understanding to specific business problems and issues (for example, you must say how a case study company is affected by a certain situation).
Assessment objective 3: Analysis	You must be able to distinguish between evidence and opinion and be able to interpret and analyse information, whether in written, numerical or graphical forms, as appropriate to a given business context.
Assessment objective 4: Evaluation	You need to present reasoned explanations, develop arguments, understand implications, and make sound judgements, recommendations and decisions based on a business context.

We hope you enjoy the course and that you find this book a useful and valuable companion on your journey of discovery. Good luck!

Every day, people around the world aim to set up and run a business in all industries and sectors, but many do not succeed. While businesses may have different objectives or targets, the key to the success of any business is its ability to meet the needs and wants of its customers.

In this section, you will learn:

- about the purpose and nature of business activity, focusing on the importance of specialisation and adding value to achieve success
- how to classify the sectors in which businesses operate – primary, secondary and tertiary – with examples of each
- how enterprise and entrepreneurship play an important role in making a business successful
- what goes into a business plan and how governments help start-up businesses
- about the methods and problems of measuring the size of a business
- why some businesses grow and others do not, and about the causes of business failure
- about the different forms of business organisation, about unincorporated businesses and limited companies and the concept of risk, ownership and limited liability
- about the need for business objectives, the role of stakeholder groups in business activity and the different objectives of private sector and public sector enterprises.

SKILLS BUILDER

Good progress

Knowledge: You show sound knowledge of the key terminology detailed in the section's glossary.

Application: You demonstrate good understanding of the key terms that you have mentioned through explanations and application to businesses.

Analysis: You develop the consequences of the points that you have mentioned for the type of business in question, commenting on the advantages and disadvantages for the business.

Evaluation: You make reasoned judgements when they are required.

Excellent progress

Knowledge: You define and identify all of the key terms relating to the business environment, using this terminology in your written answers.

Application: You show a clear ability to apply your knowledge to a given business situation, using detail such as the business aims, objectives and classification of the business.

Analysis: You show the ability to classify and comment on information presented in various forms, distinguishing between evidence and opinion.

Evaluation: You make judgements and suitable recommendations justifying your reasoning, where possible using data in your judgements in an accurate and logical manner.

SECTION CONTENTS

1 Understanding business activity

Starting points

You are about to start learning about the purpose and nature of businesses all around the world. To get started, identify your favourite organisation, which you can use as an example. (You could pick a large business such as Apple or a smaller local one near you.) Create a concept map that answers the following questions:

- Which features make this business so successful?
- Why is it your favourite?
- Has it grown in recent years? (Think about the number of outlets or products it sells.)
- What could the business do to improve further?
- What challenges is it facing? How might these affect it?

This business can now be referred to as you work through the section.

Business activity

The purpose and nature of business activity

Aims (1.1.1)

By the end of this section, you should:

- Understand the concepts of needs, wants, scarcity and opportunity cost
- Understand the importance of specialisation
- Understand the purpose of business activity
- Understand the concept of adding value and how added value can be increased.

Needs, wants and scarcity

A successful business will need to create a product or service that people actually want or need. There is a difference here. A need is for a product you could not live without, for example, heating, food or drink. In contrast, a games console is a want: you don't have to have it, nor do you really need it, but you would like it all the same. Usually, essential items (items you must have) are needs, whereas non-essential items are often wants.

Δ A Bugatti Veyron is a very desirable want for some, but not an essential need.

Did you know?

Only 450 Bugatti Veyrons have been made. Each one takes six weeks to complete (compare this with the production time of one day for a normal car) and costs nearly $1 million, so they are truly scarce.

A Bugatti Veyron? Latest mobile phone? Concert tickets? Whatever it is you really want, there will often be a limited amount of it. This is because there is only a limited supply of the resources needed to make it. This could be a limited number of:

- seats in the arena for a concert
- diamonds to make rings
- parts and components that are needed to make a product
- employees with the skills that are needed to make a product.

Scarcity is the shortage of a resource, such as oil, wheat or land. The scarcity of resources can often make products more expensive, as the demand is greater than the supply.

Scarcity of a product is often caused by a limited supply of land, labour, capital or enterprise. These are called the **factors of production**. They are the key inputs that businesses need to produce goods and services.

Key Term

Factors of production: the resources needed to produce a product or service – these include labour, land, enterprise and capital.

Land	The price of land is often more expensive the closer a business is to large cities. This is because land is scarce (in short supply). As businesses often wish to be close to city centres, the land that is available is very expensive. Some businesses also need large amounts of land (for warehouses), which reduces the options available.
Labour	Some parts of the labour force are scarce. For example, pilots are highly skilled employees who have undergone years of training. They are paid high salaries because their skills and expertise are scarce.
Capital	Capital refers to cash or goods that a business uses to generate income. This could be property or money used to purchase materials.
Enterprise	Karachi-born Gulu Lalvani set up Binatone, one of the world's largest manufacturers of cordless phones. His innovative (creative) mind and hard work allowed the product sales to grow. Without his enterprising attitude, it would not have succeeded. This set of skills is rare, and many businesses struggle to find employees who can help improve their performance.

Analysis

Focus on your own needs and wants.

- Identify and then write down your top three wants and your top three needs.
- In pairs, discuss how your wants and needs might differ from those of people in other countries.

What do you notice about wants and needs around the world?

Opportunity cost

Every day people go to work, earning money to help them buy a range of goods and services. There will be some essential items that they need to buy, such as food, but they will also choose to buy other items such as mobile phones, cars and jewellery. They have to decide what to spend their money on.

With so many wants and needs, businesses also need to make choices about what they spend their money on. This may be simply deciding to order a different product from a supplier or a decision about where to spend excess (extra) cash. The decision may be to stop spending money on one part of the business and focus it on another. Every decision has an **opportunity cost**.

Key Term

Opportunity cost: a benefit, profit or value that a firm has to give up in order to achieve or have something else.

Every day businesses experience opportunity costs. For example, a business may invest in a new machine rather than spend that money on a new TV advert. The opportunity cost here is the extra customers that might have resulted from the TV advert. With some resources so scarce, governments have to make the same sort of decisions.

Each year the governments in many different countries have to decide what they are going to spend the money on that they raise from tax or trade. For example, some people may feel that a new hospital is needed in a certain area, whereas the local businesses may feel that a new road system is more important. Whichever decision the government makes will mean an opportunity is missed, therefore creating an opportunity cost.

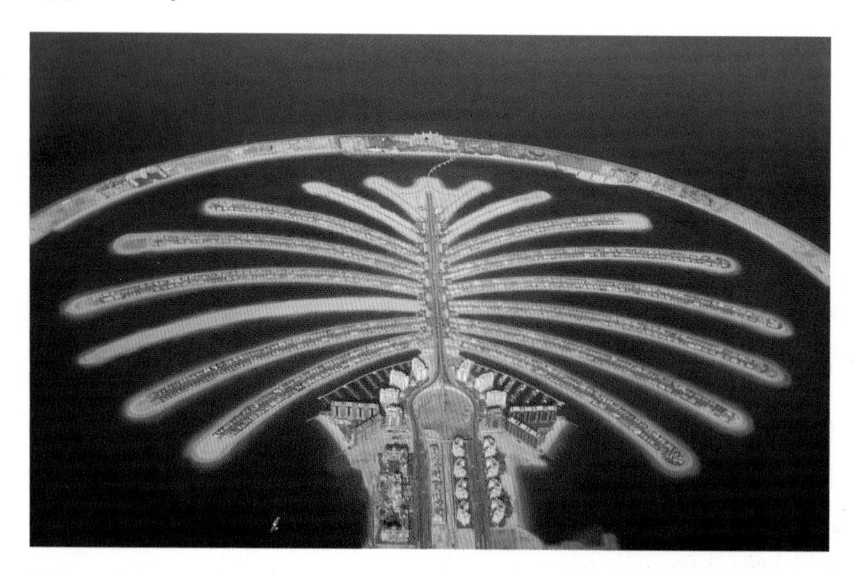

Δ The Dubai government chose to build the palm islands, creating new investment and tourism in the country. The opportunity cost was investment in the country's roads, sewage system and other upgrades. Every decision has an opportunity cost.

CASE STUDY

Change at Nokia

Nokia has seen many changes and decisions over its 150-year history. Having started out as a pulp mill, it became known for producing rubber products such as shoe soles. Over time, it has changed to become one of the of the largest communication businesses in the world. In 2013, it decided to sell its mobile phone business to Microsoft in order to focus on networks and new technology. The opportunity cost here was losing its place in the mobile phone market. However, despite these major changes, it seems Nokia is returning to this market with a new version of its famous 3310 phone. This could be the start of Nokia's return, so changing its long-term priorities.

Analysis

Using your research skills, identify three different businesses or industries that are government-funded. Try to find out the exact amounts of funding and how the level of funding has changed over time.

Try using the following key words to help in your research: public sector, government support for business, government funding and government-run.

- Now analyse them. Discuss whether they are successful. Are they using the funding well? Does the funding achieve its purpose?
- Now try to describe each business or industry to your class, but only give them three clues.

Specialisation

Specialisation is when a person, business, region or country focuses on producing a limited range (small number) of goods or services.

People all have different skills, so different people are best suited to do different jobs. A good business will understand this and will ensure that their employees work on the tasks that best suit their skills. This **division of labour** (dividing up the employees into groups) allows the employee to focus on performing a few tasks. For example, if you went into The Peninsula Tokyo Hotel, there would be a range of employees. Some work on reception, others in the kitchen. Employees are divided up based on their skills and which task they specialise in. This is a very important aspect of business activity, as it allows employees, businesses, regions and countries to focus on the products or services they are best at.

It is not only businesses that focus on one or two tasks – countries do too. Many countries only produce one or two products, because they are very good at making that specific product.

Some examples of specialisation, at the different levels, are shown in the table.

Employee • A skilled carpenter who focuses on producing high-quality violins • A pastry chef who only makes the desserts and cakes for the restaurant • A mortgage adviser for a bank	
Business • Audi specialises in making cars • The local accountants who focus on doing other people's tax calculations • Nestlé specialises in chocolate production	
Region • The Champagne region in France specialises in making ... champagne! • The Santos region in Brazil specialises in coffee production • Nuwara Eliya in Sri Lanka produces some of the world's best tea	
Country • Saudi Arabia specialises in extracting oil • The Ivory Coast specialises in the production of cocoa • Japan specialises in technology and computing	

	Benefits of specialisation	Drawbacks of specialisation
For businesses	✓ By specialising, an improvement in quality and efficiency can lead to larger profits. ✓ Businesses may develop a positive reputation for a particular product or service. For example, a wedding dress shop may become well known because of its specialist products. ✓ A business may be able to charge higher prices if it is one of the only businesses to offer the product or service. ✓ The employees become faster at producing the goods.	✗ Training of employees will often be more varied and expensive. ✗ The employees may become bored with the tasks they do each day, as they tend to be the same. This may cause them to leave the business. ✗ The product or service in which the business specialises can become out of date or no longer required, causing it to close.

	Benefits of specialisation	Drawbacks of specialisation
For employees	✓ Employees may be paid more if their skill is in short supply. ✓ The skills they have may mean they can choose the job they want and the benefits that come with it (for example, a car, flexible working hours).	✗ Machines that can do the same tasks more quickly and cheaply may replace employees. ✗ The employee may become bored with only focusing on one or two skills.
For the world	✓ Scarce resources are used more effectively. ✓ A country that specialises can trade (exchange) with other countries for goods and services that they don't or can't produce. ✓ People benefit from the jobs and incomes that come from producing specialised products or services.	✗ Some countries struggle to produce a product or service that is required globally. ✗ Countries can suddenly become beaten on price, meaning that their entire workforce is no longer in demand.

Top Tip

Specialisation takes place at various levels, from that of a person up to a country. Remember to use examples from all appropriate levels.

Knowledge check

Audi now has a global reputation for comfort and quality. Its range of cars can cost up to $500 000 and is only targeted at the richest customers. Its products include the Audi R8 and Audi RS, two very exclusive cars with only a few thousand of each being made.

1. **Define the term scarcity.** **(2)**
2. **Explain the opportunity costs to Audi of producing the R8 and RS cars.** **(4)**
3. **Explain how specialisation benefits an employee of Audi.** **(4)**
4. **Do you believe that specialisation will benefit Audi when making their cars? Justify your answer.** **(6)**

Total 16 marks

Purpose of business activity

All businesses exist to fulfil a need or want of a customer. Many businesses aim to make a profit from doing this, with the money going to the owners. There are also businesses that invest any profits they make into social activities and projects that try to help society. For example, UnLtd India helps people set up and run businesses.

However, a business cannot exist unless it has customers who want to buy what it sells, whatever this may be.

Some of the purposes a business may have are to:

- create new products
- generate large amounts of sales
- educate the local and global community to reduce pollution and damage to the environment
- create large brands across the world
- listen to the different **stakeholders**
- support community projects and social activities.

Different business structures have a direct impact on the aims and objectives set by a business (see 1.4 Types of business organisation). For example, a **sole trader** will decide on his or her own business aims and objectives, while in a **public limited company**, each business owner, **shareholder** and director will have her or his own ideas and aims for the business. How the business is organised therefore shapes the purpose and activity of the business.

Consider the following examples:

- **Walmart** (USA). Walmart is one of the world's largest businesses, with an estimated revenue of $485 billion. It meets the needs and wants of its customers by selling a wide range of goods in its stores. Its purpose is to provide these goods and make large profits.
- **Divine Chocolate** (UK and Ghana). Its purpose is to sell its chocolate worldwide, but also to boost the Fairtrade production of cocoa and the communities that it works with.
- **UNICEF** (global). UNICEF aims to support children worldwide, through donations and business activities that focus on promoting its cause, rather than generating large profits.
- **Chao Chung** (China). This local family-run restaurant in China aims to support the local community by providing affordable meals. The business makes a profit but not at the expense of losing customers.
- **Tannura** (Japan). Brian Tannura set up a vending machine business in Japan and runs it as a sole trader. His purpose is to generate enough revenue to do this full-time. He plans to bring in a variety of different vending machines and expand his business.

△ Fairtrade Divine ginger and orange dark chocolate.

Adding value

Businesses sell on a product or service in order to add value. The key here is to create a product that is worth more than the cost of making it. If the business can encourage customers to pay more than the total costs, then it will be able to make a profit.

If the production of a new Mazda car costs $6000 and each car is sold for $12 000, then Mazda is adding $6000 value. Once Mazda has paid off all its overheads, marketing, insurance and other costs, the company will make a profit.

Evaluation

In small groups or pairs, discuss the benefits for a business of adding value. You should aim to come up with four different benefits. Write each benefit on a separate sheet of paper.

- Now arrange the benefits in order of importance. Be ready to justify what you think is the biggest benefit.
- How could a business achieve some of these benefits?

Extension: Using your research skills, find out which business has the highest **added value**.

CASE STUDY

Samsung vs Apple

Samsung released the new Galaxy S8 in 2017 in an attempt to rival the iPhone 7. Using its brand image and new features to add value to its products, Samsung hopes to continue its growth in this market with a new range of phones that offer solutions to customer demands such as battery life and screen size.

How to add value

Businesses can add value to their products in numerous ways: by design, quality and efficiency, marketing and convenience.

Design

This can make your product unique and different to the competition. For example, Dyson uses 'cyclone' technology to maintain market leadership due to their innovative and effective product design, which customers will pay a higher price for.

Quality and efficiency

'The better the quality, the higher the price.' Products that are of a high quality can often sell for more. In China, Omnialuo is seen as a luxury clothing range. In contrast, Primark in the UK adds value through efficiency rather than quality. The lower the costs of making the product, the higher the value added.

Marketing

If you think of a product that you want to buy, it will be due partly to the marketing of the product. This has made you more willing to buy the product and perhaps even pay more for that brand. A brand is created through intense (a lot of) marketing, which allows the customer to recognise a product, logo or packaging and associate this with a business. For example, the Van Cleef & Arpels luxury retailer logo is recognised all over the Middle East. This adds value to the product.

Convenience

If you go to a concert or sporting event, such as the Formula One Chinese Grand Prix, the food, drink and merchandise will always be more expensive than elsewhere outside the venue. This is because it is conveniently located for customers to purchase it. This means that those companies can add value because of their location. Customers will be forced to pay higher prices due to the lack of alternative products.

Top Tip

Adding value through their brand is easier for larger businesses that have established and popular products, but it can be difficult for smaller start-up businesses.

Knowledge check

1. **Define the term added value.** **(2)**
2. **Explain two ways in which a business can add value.** **(4)**
3. **Explain why businesses can have different purposes.** **(4)**

Total 10 marks

Check your progress:

- ✓ I can explain the purpose and nature of business activity.
- ✓ I can outline the concepts of needs, wants, scarcity and opportunity cost.
- ✓ I understand the importance of specialisation.
- ✓ I understand the concept of adding value and can explain how businesses can add value.

Classification of businesses

Business activity in terms of primary, secondary and tertiary sectors

Aims (1.2.1)
By the end of this section, you should:
- Understand the basis of business classification using examples to illustrate the classification
- Understand the reasons for the changing importance of business classification, for example, in more and less industrialised countries.

The three sectors

There are three different sectors in which businesses operate: primary, secondary and tertiary sectors.

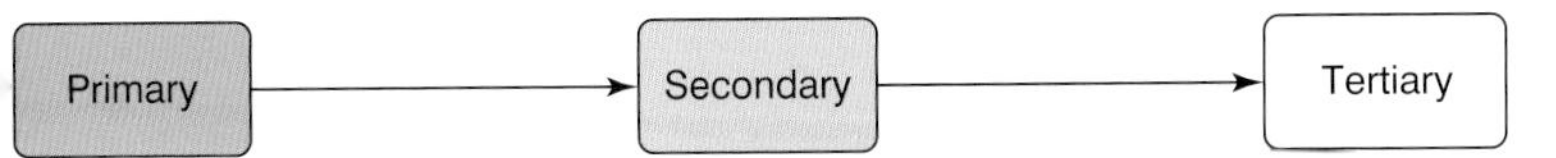

The **primary sector** is made up of businesses that extract raw materials from the land or sea ready to be used by other industries.

For example, Saudi Aramco is the world's largest oil producer, with up to $1 billion revenue each day.

The **secondary sector** takes the raw materials and transforms them into a product. This can be sheets of metal, touch screens, bottles or clothing. A factory that makes a product, and the construction industry that produces a building, are also in this sector.

For example, oil extraction is then refined (changed/cleaned up) and eventually sold at petrol stations.

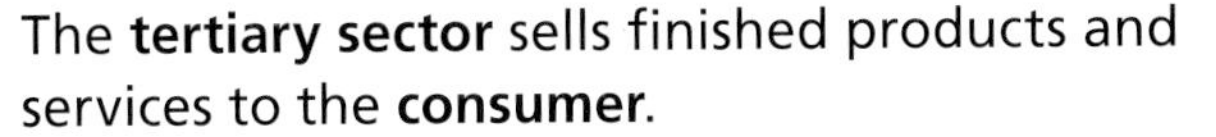

The **tertiary sector** sells finished products and services to the **consumer**.

For example, Chinese fast-food retailer Manfadu and the world's largest department store, Shinsegae in South Korea, are both in this sector. The tourism and entertainment industries are also tertiary.

The number of employees in each of these sectors differs from country to country. Here are a few examples:

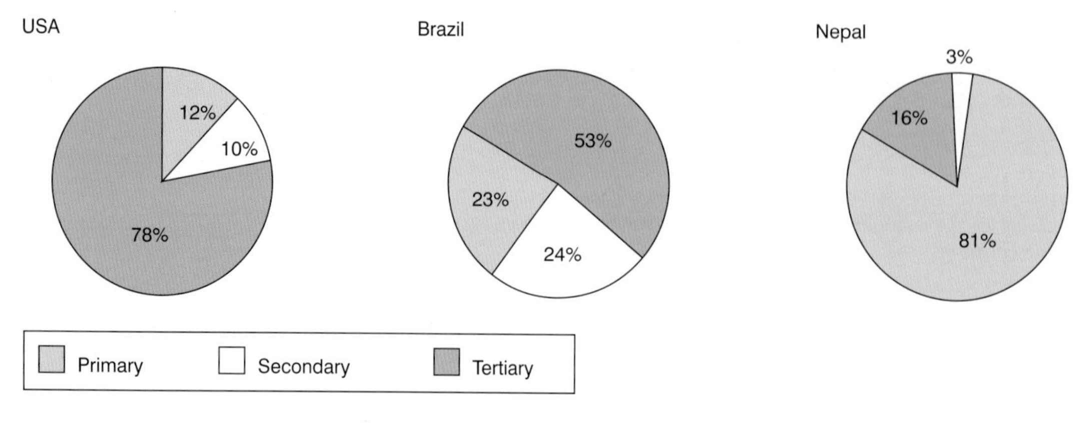

Source: Central Intelligence Agency

It is very important for a country to have businesses in at least one sector that are doing well. Some countries have the majority of employment in one sector. As countries develop, they aim to change the structure of their economy. This will involve developing the tertiary sector, creating more retail outlets and other industries, which increase money being spent. Developing countries are often mainly primary and secondary producers, and so – through investment in airports, tourism venues, and events such as the Olympics – they try to move into the tertiary sector. This helps to boost the countries' revenue and allows them to employ in all three sectors. However, many developing countries also try to increase other sectors, as this will help to secure the long-term production of goods and services.

CASE STUDY

Indonesia's growth is mobile

Indonesia is the fastest growing South Asian economy. With a population of 250 million, its GDP is nearly $1 trillion. It is the third largest mobile phone market in the Asia Pacific region, where 25% of the current population has a mobile phone. This figure is expected to increase to 50% by 2020. This will enable payment platform websites such as eBay, Alibaba and Priceline to help consumers access goods from around the world, supporting Indonesia's growth for years to come.

CASE STUDY

Coca-cola grows in Africa

Coca-cola will pay $3.15 billion for the Anheuser-Busch InBev's stake of 54.5% in Coca-cola Beverages Africa. This move will see Coca-cola gain increased access to countries such as Tanzania, Ghana and Namibia. There is also potential for Coca-cola to own new bottling facilities in Zambia, El Salvador and Honduras. Operating its own secondary sector bottling factories will help the company to have increased control over its whole production process.

Analysis **Evaluation**

Using your own country or one you have chosen, find out how the employment structure in the primary, secondary and tertiary sectors has changed in that country over the past 10 years.

You should then write a short statement, of no more than 100 words, which explains why your chosen country has that particular balance of primary, secondary and tertiary sectors. This statement should be very clear, so that others can fully understand your points.

Be ready to read your statement to the class. You may have to convince some of your classmates, so really emphasise the key points.

Finally, in pairs or small groups, discuss the following questions:

- Why does the number of people in each sector change?
- What does this mean for the economy of the country?

Knowledge check

1. **Define the term primary sector. (2)**
2. **Identify two businesses that operate in the tertiary sector. (2)**
3. **Explain two key differences between the primary and secondary sectors. (6)**

Total 10 marks

Top Tip

You should be able to give a range of different examples for each of the sectors. You should also be able to give examples of countries that operate mainly in one of the three sectors.

Private sector and public sector

Aims (1.2.2)

By the end of this section, you should:

- Be able to classify business enterprises between private sector and public sector in a mixed economy.

Market economy *and* mixed economy

A **market** is where a seller and a customer come together to perform business activity. There are many different types of markets.

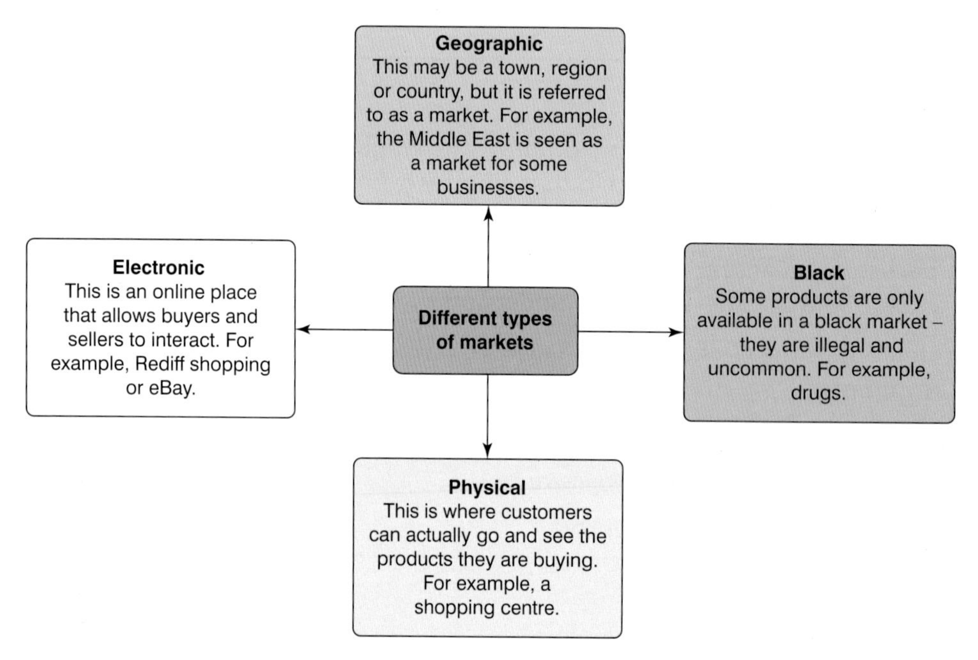

Often, the government will influence the market by creating rules and laws that structure the way in which buyers and sellers meet and interact. The government can do this by:

- imposing a ban on certain products, so there is no market for them
- putting a tax (extra charge) on certain goods or services to limit their supply and demand (for example, cigarettes)
- supplying them itself – for example, governments often supply medical care so that everyone has an equal chance of using it.

The level of government intervention determines in which type of economy the businesses and customers operate.

A market economy	A mixed economy
Here the government has no role at all. It is only the buyers and sellers who determine the price and make trading decisions.	Here the buyers, sellers and government all have an influence. This type of economy is common in nearly all countries.

There are no market economies, as the government often has to intervene. However, the degree (amount) of intervention varies between countries. For example, China and North Korea have a large amount of government intervention, whereas the USA has little. However, the US government has intervened in the motor industry, supporting US-based companies with grants (financial support that does need to be paid back), to help the businesses to continue to trade.

Not all businesses are owned and run by private individuals. This is because some businesses are run by the government or state. This will determine whether they are in the private or public sector.

The private sector

The **private sector** is formed of businesses that are run by private individuals or groups. They often have shareholders (people who own a part of the business) who want the business to generate (make) large amounts of money. Private sector businesses are often profit driven (aim to make large profits).

The following are all types of private enterprise:

- a sole trader
- a private limited company (Ltd)
- a public limited company (PLC)
- a partnership
- a social enterprise
- a charity.

(For more information, see 1.4 Types of business organisation.)

The public sector

The **public sector** is very different. This is often run and funded by the country's government. In India, the government runs the train line, subsidising it (making it cheaper) so more people can afford to use it. Other examples are the police, education and the military. Governments use taxation to help fund these services, so they are often criticised if they are not spending money effectively.

Different business goals

- Pfizer PLC is one of the world's largest pharmaceutical companies, and creates a range of medicines to sell around the world. Its goals are profit and shareholder returns.
- The Indian railway is run by the government as part of the public sector. The organisation's goals are to give affordable access to train travel and to link up the country via the train line.
- VisionSpring is an organisation that sells reading glasses to the developing world. So far, it has sold 3.5 million pairs. Its goal is to help developing countries improve reading.

- Oxfam is a worldwide charity that operates in over 90 countries. Oxfam's goal is to give power to people in developing countries and reduce global poverty.

The reason why businesses have such different goals is mainly due to their structure. A public limited company, such as BP or Microsoft, has shareholders. These shareholders expect a return on their investment (money they have paid to buy shares) and so these companies strive (try hard) to make large profits. A charity or not-for-profit organisation tries to put all of its money into projects that help achieve its aim. Public enterprises such as the National Health Service in the UK are set up by the government to run organisations for the people; therefore they do not have to make a profit.

Δ PLC businesses use markets such as the Shanghai stock exchange to sell their shares.

Private and public enterprises in a mixed economy

A mixed economy has both public and private sector enterprises. The majority of a mixed economy will be privately owned businesses, with the government regulating (monitoring) industries through policies (laws and regulations). Within a mixed economy, the government will often run the education, healthcare and military.

CASE STUDY

Indian government have the power

The Indian government set up the Ghogarpalli Integrated Power Co. Ltd to help support India's energy system. Based in New Delhi, the organisation provides electricity for millions of people. The government set it up so that more people could access this service for a reasonable price. As the government does not aim to make large profits, they can lower their prices. This shows how, in a mixed economy, the government can intervene to run public sector businesses to provide goods or services for the public.

Nationalisation is the process by which the government takes over a privately run business or industry. During the recession of 2009, many countries used government money to support their banking industry but without taking it over fully. Nationalisation usually occurs when an important business or industry starts to fail. This may mean the loss of thousands of jobs and a large amount of income through tax. If the government wants to stop this happening, they take over the business.

For example, the Japanese government put 1 trillion Yen ($12.5 billion) into TEPCO (Tokyo Electric Power Company). This industry has historically been a private one, so this government intervention and nationalisation came as a surprise. The company is now government-run, which means that the government can change the company's board members, policies and aims.

Analysis

Identify two businesses in your country. One should be from the public sector and the other from the private sector. How do the aims and objectives of these two businesses differ? Write these down in two columns – one for similarities and one for differences.

Then carry out research into a social enterprise in your area. What does this business do? How do its aims and objectives differ from those of large private enterprises?

Discuss your findings as a class and see what general conclusions you can draw. Then work in small groups to create a class display based on your research. You will need to think about how best to organise your findings and how to use images, captions and headings to good effect.

Knowledge check

Savages is a leading clothing brand that sells mainly in its own country. However, it is looking to expand into new markets. To do this, Ali, its owner, wants the business to become a public limited company (PLC). Ali is keen to expand the business while maintaining the excellent reputation he has created with his management skills, high-quality products and happy employees.

1. **Explain why Ali is operating in the private sector.** **(4)**
2. **Identify two differences between the public and private sector.** **(2)**
3. **Explain two benefits of Ali's business becoming a PLC.** **(4)**
4. **Explain why a government may nationalise an industry or business.** **(4)**

Total 14 marks

Top Tip

Make sure you can link the different types of businesses with the public or private sector. You should be able to explain the different aims and objectives businesses have and how these relate to the sector in which they operate.

Check your progress:

- ✓ I can outline the different sectors that businesses operate in, in terms of the primary, secondary and tertiary sectors.
- ✓ I can explain the reasons for the changing importance of business classification.
- ✓ I can classify business enterprises between the private sector and the public sector in a mixed economy.

Enterprise, business growth and size

Enterprise and entrepreneurship

Aims (1.3.1)

By the end of this section, you should:

- Know the characteristics of successful entrepreneurs
- Understand the contents of a business plan and how business plans assist entrepreneurs
- Understand why and how governments support business start-ups, for example, grants, training schemes.

Characteristics of successful entrepreneurs

An **entrepreneur** is someone who sets up and runs their own business. Some examples are Carlos Slim Helú of Mexico (telecommunications), Christy Walton of the United States (supermarkets) and Mukesh Ambani of India (energy). All of these successful business people are now on the *Forbes* rich list (which lists the world's richest people). They are all entrepreneurs and got on the list because of their business skills and **enterprise**. As entrepreneurs, they took risks by setting up and growing their own businesses; between them they are now worth over $120 billion!

Did you know?

The world's richest self-made billionaire is Bill Gates. Gates is the founder of Microsoft and has used his estimated $80 billion fortune to fund research into ending poverty and disease around the world.

CASE STUDY

Where to set up?

Malaysia is fast becoming one of the hot spots for start-up businesses. It is much cheaper in terms of cost of living than places such as China and Singapore. Firms are now taking advantage of the investment opportunities that come from registering in Singapore while operating from Malaysia. Start-ups also tend to prefer Malaysia because it is a good test market (larger than Singapore), with three different nationalities. This helps when reviewing and making improvements to products and services ahead of their release in the larger, more profitable nations of India and China.

Many people all over the world are entrepreneurs, but there are only a few who end up making billions of dollars from a business. There are many other private businesses set up and run by entrepreneurs – for example, the local shops, leisure parks and car dealerships in your area.

So what characteristics do entrepreneurs have?

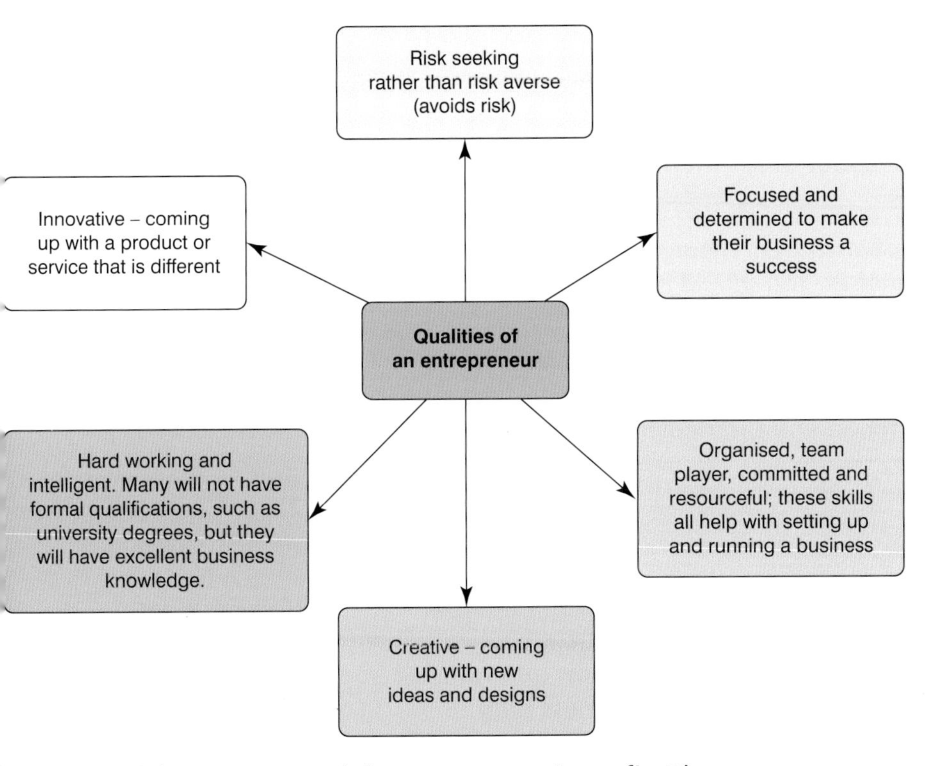

The reward for any successful entrepreneur is profit. The amount of profit will depend on the business, but many successful business people say that, to achieve this, they have to take risks. These risks may be investing personal savings, taking on extra employees or releasing a new or innovative product.

Setting up and running a business requires a large amount of time and effort, and the commitment of the owners. Many entrepreneurs fail and lose large amounts of money because of this. The balance between risk and reward is great and any entrepreneur needs to consider this before starting a business.

CASE STUDY

Alibaba grows

Chinese businessman, Jack Ma, used $60 000 of his own money to set up the Alibaba Group. This is the world's largest business-to-business e-commerce site. Despite the huge risk, he is now worth $1.6 billion. The growth of this business has been impressive – within its first 10 years, Alibaba had 58 million businesses using its site. Last year, Alibaba achieved a 51% increase in its revenue, with its final quarter's results exceeding targets by 30%.

Application **Analysis**

- In no more than 40 words, describe your favourite entrepreneur. Avoid using their name.

Now work in pairs. Read out your description to see if your partner can guess who it is.

- Using the characteristics of an entrepreneur, outline your own strengths and weaknesses. You should be realistic and honest and try to identify two or three of each.
- Now compare yourself to other students in the class. Which skills do most people have? Which characteristic do you think is most important for an entrepreneur?

The business plan

Once someone decides they want to run their own business, they will often produce a business plan. This is a written document that outlines the business's aims and vision (plan for the future). Many entrepreneurs will use their business plan to attract (encourage people to give) finance, whether this is from a bank or investor, and to work out the timeline for the business.

The plan also gives the owner some idea of how the business needs to develop, in line with targets and goals, so that they can measure its success. Having some sort of plan helps keep the business on track and gives other people who are involved in the business – suppliers, customers and employees – some idea of what the business is hoping to achieve.

The business plan is also useful for the stakeholders involved in the entrepreneur's business. A stakeholder is an individual, group or organisation that is affected by, or interested in, a business. Each stakeholder will use the business plan in a different way.

The business plan will be divided up into different sections:

Section	Description of contents
Business summary	This gives a general description of the product or service and the ethos (day-to-day behaviour) of the business. It should give someone reading the plan a good idea of what is to follow. If the business is looking for an investor, then this section should capture their interest and make them want to read more.
Business details	This can be broken down into sub-sections such as business idea, goals, unique selling point (what makes the business different) and recruitment. In this section, there is more information on what the business will actually do on a day-to-day basis. It may also include the legal structure of the business.

Section	Description of contents
Market research	This section describes how the market research was carried out and includes evidence to support the business plan. This could be graphs and tables that demonstrate that the product or service is needed and would be a success. The research will usually involve a questionnaire (primary research) as well as the internet, books and reports (secondary research).
Marketing	This outlines the strategy the business will use to attract customers. This will include the four Ps of the marketing mix (Product design and features, Price choice, Promotion activities and Place of sale) (see 3.3 Marketing mix) and identify any areas the business may struggle with. It may also include pricing methods, promotion examples and costing.
Day-to-day running of the business	This describes areas such as production methods, suppliers, competitors and location choices. This section should also outline any equipment that might be needed – for example, computers, machinery or tools. It gives a more specific idea of what the business and employees do in their roles each day.
Finance	This is a vital part of the plan, especially if the business is looking for investment from an external source. This should show the costs of setting up the business in plenty of detail, as well as the cash flow forecast, predicted profit and loss, and statement of financial position. It is often the hardest part to write, as the owner will need to make informed estimates of the figures. The start-up funding will be clearly outlined, so any investor can see how they will make back their money ... and more.

Analysis

Not all businesses use a business plan to help set out their idea, although it can be much harder without the guidance that a plan gives.

In pairs, create the arguments for and against using a business plan. Try to use some of the business terms you have already learned – for example, opportunity costs.

- Now identify the key point for having a business plan and the key point against having one.

Government support for business start-ups

The governments in most countries offer a wide range of support and finance to start-up businesses. It is in the government's interest to support businesses.

- Businesses reduce **unemployment**, as they create more jobs. This reduces the amount that the government needs to pay in unemployment benefits.
- The country produces more goods and services, therefore increasing its **gross domestic product (GDP)**. (This will be covered in more detail in 6.1 Economic issues.)

- The government receives more money from taxation. If businesses are taking on more employees, it is likely that a lot of their earnings will come back to the government through taxation on goods and services. Also, if the business is doing well and making a profit, in some countries the government will receive **corporation tax** (tax on a business's profits).
- Foreign businesses and investors are attracted to a country that is at the top of enterprise and entrepreneurship. When regions are seeing growth, foreign companies seek to take advantage of this by opening up new offices or shops in these areas. This is because the local people are likely to spend more money in that area, which means extra tax revenue for the government. The business will, in return, have access to higher-quality employees.

Some examples of different ways that a government might support business start-ups are as follows.

CASE STUDY

Taiwan thinking ahead

The Taiwanese government has developed its support of start-up businesses in the ICT industry by creating the Institute for Information Industry (III). This runs as a think tank (that conducts market research and gives advice), which helps ICT businesses to develop products and systems that will drive forward innovation. A new batch of social media and gaming companies has already emerged. Taiwan is now highly regarded around the world as one of the best places to set up and run an ICT-based company.

Grants

These are sums of money that are given to businesses to help pay for set-up costs or expansion. Businesses do not have to repay the money. Finance is often the reason why businesses do not start up, so this method is very important. In China, the National Development and Reform Commission (NDRC) gives money to start-up businesses.

Advice

Having access to sources of advice is important. Many business owners do not understand tax, employee rights or aspects of finance, so they need extra advice and support.

Training schemes

Providing courses for unskilled, unemployed or older people can help to get more of the population into work. Therefore, governments set up training courses, often for free, to help with this. In Bahrain, Tamkeen, the nation's labour authority, has schemes such as grants and training subsidies that support employers, not only to attract top graduates but also to train them.

Loans

At times of economic recession, banks are less likely to lend to smaller businesses or those that are more of a risk. The government can help with this by providing small loans aimed specifically at businesses that are struggling to gain finance. This is risky but it can bring more employment and economic growth to the country.

Tax relief

In some areas of a country, the government may offer tax relief. This allows businesses a set period of time (often a year) when they do not have to pay any tax.

Mentors

Having access to people who have run a successful business is vital for future business growth. Using their advice and knowledge could be the key to a start-up business owner succeeding.

Evaluation

In pairs, discuss why just giving financial support such as grants will not guarantee that a start-up business is successful. Go on to evaluate the other options a government might consider.

Extension: What else could a government do to help start-up businesses? Many businesses such as Google succeed without government support. Do you think that governments should have to provide support to start-up companies?

Knowledge check

1. **Identify two attributes that you would expect a successful entrepreneur to have.** **(2)**
2. **Identify two parts of a business plan.** **(4)**
3. **Explain two reasons why a start-up business should use a business plan.** **(4)**
4. **Outline two forms of support a government can offer a business.** **(6)**

Total 16 marks

The methods and problems of measuring business size

Aims (1.3.2)

By the end of this section, you should:

- Understand the methods used for measuring business size, for example, number of people employed, value of output, capital employed
- Understand the limitations of methods of measuring business size.

Business size

A business's size can be measured in a number of different ways. Choosing the correct method is a difficult task. No one measure can be used on its own – it depends on what you are trying to measure.

CASE STUDY: Is Subway bigger than McDonald's?

It depends on how you measure it! Subway now has 44 702 outlets worldwide compared to 36 899 for McDonald's. However, McDonald's had a profit that was \$9 billion larger than that of Subway. Subway only operates in 107 countries, whereas McDonald's operates in 119. The method used to decide on the size of a business is crucial. With smaller outlets and a wider product range, is Subway going to match McDonald's one day?

It is often hard to calculate the value of a company. To get a good idea of a company's value, many people look at the statement of financial position. This will give an approximate value, but it is not 100% accurate. For example, Google is very hard to value because of the intangible (cannot be touched or seen) assets such as reputation and logo.

The table lists some of the ways that a business can be measured. Each measure of the size of a business has its benefits and drawbacks.

Measure	Benefits	Drawbacks
Capital employed (The amount of money invested in the business)	The value of all the business assets added up shows how much the business could be worth. This gives a value for the business that reflects what it has invested and what it would be worth if sold.	It is difficult to value assets accurately. For example, DHL delivery vans may be worth very little but the business could give a high estimate of their worth in their accounts.

Measure	Benefits	Drawbacks
Market share (The total amount of sales a business has as a percentage of the total sales in that market)	This provides a useful comparison against businesses in the same industry. It shows how much of the money being spent in the market is coming to the business.	You cannot compare one business's market share with that of a business in another industry. For example, you cannot compare Google's market share with Walmart's market share, as they have shares of different markets. The market itself may be very small, so even if a business has a large share, it doesn't necessarily mean it is a large business. This method does not show the other assets a business may have, such as employees, logos or patents.
Number of outlets (The number of shops the business owns and runs)	This gives a geographic idea, as each outlet will take up a certain amount of space. This can then be used to compare it with other businesses.	Outlets are not equal to sales or profit. A business can have lots of outlets but not many customers. Outlets do not show the number of products sold or the value of the products that have been sold. This method does not show how many of the outlets the business owns or rents. It also does not show a monetary value.
Number of employees (Total number of people who work for the business)	Shows the scale (extent) on which the business operates.	You cannot compare industries. For example, a factory may only employ a few people, whereas a supermarket employs a lot. Even if a business only has a few employees, their skills and knowledge could be worth millions of dollars. On the other hand, clothing businesses, for example, may require lots of employees, but still hold little value.
Value of the business (The price another business is willing to pay to own the business)	This can be a good reflection of the true worth in the market place, as many businesses are bought because of their potential to be worth a lot in the future.	This measure can be inaccurate, as sometimes a business will be bought for more than it is worth. For example, Instagram was bought for $1 billion when it had yet to make a profit. The value may be different to a variety of people. Investors may see a lower value compared with a shareholder.

Measure	Benefits	Drawbacks
Value of output (Often called sales or turnover, this is the value of the products or services sold)	This shows how much the business is producing and how much people are willing to pay for these products. It can be easily compared with competitors.	Revenue alone does not take into account the costs of the business. Large revenues are often reduced when costs are taken away. Revenues can vary depending on how well the economy is doing.

Note: Profit is not a measure of size, as it only shows a monetary value. Businesses can be very large and only produce small amounts of profit.

Using your research skills, choose a business from your country. Which method would you suggest for measuring its size?

If possible, produce some information, such as graphs, tables or article evidence, which show the business's size.

Is it difficult to use just one method? Would you recommend using an additional method?

There is no one specific way to measure business size, but applying the different measures to an industry is important. Some industries, such as farming, are better suited to being measured by output. By contrast, supermarkets may wish to use the number of outlets or market share.

The best way to measure the size of a business is to use all of the measures described. This will give a clearer picture of the business size. For example, combining the number of employees and market share gives a more accurate idea of the size. This reduces the problem when measuring the size of businesses that use a lot of machinery.

Knowledge check

1. **Identify two ways in which a business's size can be measured.** **(2)**
2. **Explain why a business should use a variety of methods to measure its size.** **(4)**
2. **Identify two limitations of using the number of employees as a way of measuring the size of a business.** **(6)**

Total 12 marks

Why some businesses grow and others remain small

Aims (1.3.3)

By the end of this section, you should:

- Understand why the owners of a business may want to expand it
- Understand different ways in which businesses can grow
- Understand problems that are linked to business growth and how these might be overcome
- Understand why some businesses remain small.

Why owners may want to expand their business

Imagine you run a small beauty salon. It is producing a profit each year and is well established in the local area. Would you try to grow this business?

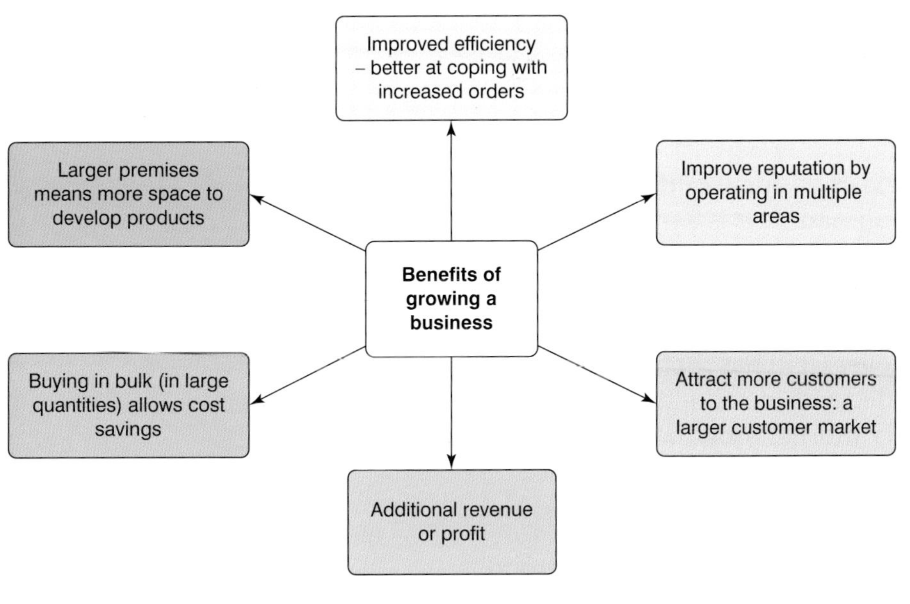

Δ The potential benefits of growing a business

CASE STUDY

Valiram to scale up

Malaysia-based retail group Valiram is planning to upgrade its network significantly this year using its core brands, such as Michael Kors, to help fuel growth across the region. It aims to expand into New Zealand while increasing its presence in Vietnam and Malaysia. Led by the three Valiram brothers, the business now has 343 stores in nine different markets. As well as its home nation of Singapore, it also has stores in Australia, Thailand and Macau. Last year, the business made $647 million, leading to company expansion, more stores and greater influence.

Evaluation

Sammi runs a successful shoe brand in his home country of Iran. His brand has developed a good reputation, and Sammi is keen to see his brand grow by expanding the business into a second factory. This would be located in Egypt and would focus on a new range of products.

Divide a piece of paper into two columns. Create a 'For' and 'Against' list for Sammi's decision.

Now, in small groups, debate whether or not you agree with Sammi's decision.

Tip: Link your reasons to his business, the industry and the different countries to help improve your answer.

Different ways in which businesses can grow

Once a business is up and running, it should naturally start to grow. However, businesses can grow in different ways.

Internal (Organic)

This occurs when the business opens new outlets or factories, or moves into new markets abroad. This is a more natural process, as the business chooses when to open its next outlet or factory. In this case, the growth comes from within the business and is often funded and staffed by existing resources. For example, Jaguar Land Rover (JLR) has seen dramatic increases in sales in China due to its introduction of new models and showrooms. This internal growth has led to greater growth than its competitors.

External (Inorganic)

This happens when a business buys another business through a **takeover**. This is a common practice for larger businesses, normally public limited companies that want to grow quickly by buying smaller firms. Often, the business that is being bought offers a new service or product that the buyer wants or needs.

CASE STUDY

Expanding outwards

India has a large number of small businesses — an estimated 48 million in 2015. Owners grow their business by registering with the online auction site eBay India. Indian sellers are estimated to sell a product through eBay India every 10 seconds, and comprise a third of all sellers on the site.

A **merger** combines two businesses that come together as one. This automatically grows the business. This process can be involuntary for some businesses, as larger businesses buy enough shares to force a takeover. However, mergers are often beneficial for both businesses.

- Split costs allow both businesses to reduce debt or borrowing.
- Sharing the risk between two firms makes it easier to justify decisions.
- The two businesses can share resources such as employees, office space and assets (for example, aeroplanes).

One of the most famous mergers around the world is between Disney and Pixar. Now working together, they have put their separate skills and resources together to improve their product (films). In 2016, the State Bank of India completed a merger with five subsidiary banks to become one of the top 50 banks in the world. It is now worth a combined value of $463 billion and will have a customer base (number of customers) of 370 million people.

External growth is done outside the business and often requires large amounts of money to fund it. Adidas achieved growth by buying rival Reebok for $3.8 billion. This gave it Reebok's products, stores and market share.

CASE STUDY

Tencent invests in games

In 2016, Tencent announced that it had signed a $700 million deal with the NBA (National Basketball Association) to stream American basketball games in China. This year, Tencent has invested $1.78 billion for a 5% stake in the car maker Tesla. These investments in new and growing markets are a sign that Tencent aims to continue its rapid growth and experience markets outside China.

Application

You have been asked by your country's government to create a 'help leaflet' that will explain to business owners the dangers of growth and offer suggestions on how to avoid them.

Try to use images, graphs and tables to show the impact of your tips.

Growth can bring several rewards and boost the potential revenue of a business. However, it does not come without its problems.

Production problems
Eventually the business may struggle with large orders and maintaining stock levels. This can cause costs to go up, reputation to drop and quality to fall.

Communication
Many businesses find this a major problem. The business can get so big that communication between managers and other employees stops. This can cause orders to go unnoticed, decision making to stop and morale to become low.

Morale
Imagine you were one of a million employees. Would you feel valued or listened to? It can be very difficult to maintain motivation and employee happiness when the business grows.

Clash of cultures
If a business merges with another, often they can struggle to work well together. Would Google fit well with Microsoft? Probably not, as they have a very different ethos and working environment.

When Cadbury and Kraft merged, many people thought it would be a huge success. But the clash of cultures, between the employees and the new policies, caused Cadbury to see a drop in its revenue.

There are often problems with both internal and external growth. However, there are ways to overcome these problems:

Training	One of the main problems with growth is that it can cause some employees to be given new roles. They may lack the necessary training to allow them to do their new jobs properly. This could happen to existing employees (internal growth) or employees that the business inherits (external growth through merger or takeover).
Management changes	When a business buys another, it may need to replace or spread its managers to make sure all areas of the business are covered. It may also need to recruit new employees to make sure the two businesses work together.
Incentives for employees	When a business grows, its employees may need to work harder or more efficiently so that the growth is successful. Employee morale is a common problem for businesses when growing. In order to boost employee morale, the business may introduce incentives such as bonuses or extra days off work.
Set realistic targets	When businesses grow, they often set unrealistic targets for future revenue or profit. If this happens it may seem as though the business has not succeeded. By setting realistic targets, a business can be more successful.
Invest in the business	Once a business has grown, either internally or externally, it may need to spend additional money on equipment, training or other assets. This extra investment can help the business to succeed.

Production problems	With the right employees and production methods, a business can maintain production levels. Using IT to monitor stock levels will also help.
Communication	Making sure that the business continues to use all forms of internal and external communication will help to prevent messages from being lost.

Lack of business growth

Some businesses remain small and do not grow. This could be for a number of reasons.

- **Operating at maximum**. Some businesses operate at their maximum, so extra space or outlets will not bring any benefit. In fact, it will only increase their costs and reduce profit. For example, a carpenter will not need to grow his or her premises.
- **Extra cost**. Some small businesses cannot afford to hire new employees or move location.
- **Economies of scale**. The business may be operating at its perfect output and any increase in this may result in **efficiency** dropping (see 4.1 Production of goods and services).
- **Neither time nor desire**. Some business owners do not want to grow their business, as they are happy with its current size.
- **Knowledge**. Some owners do not have the skills or knowledge to expand a business. It is unlikely that they will understand every aspect of running a business, so will need advice on how to do this.

Key Term

Efficiency: the comparison between the output produced and the actual amount that could be made.

Evaluation

'All takeovers will fail because there are no two businesses with the same ethos and work ethic.'

In small teams, use this statement as the centre of a debate. Do you agree or disagree with the statement?

Knowledge check

1. **Identify two reasons why a business might want to grow.** **(2)**
2. **Explain why larger businesses often choose external growth.** **(4)**
3. **Consider why some businesses choose not to grow.** **(4)**
4. **Identify one problem with a business expanding.** **(2)**

Total 12 marks

Why some (new or established) businesses fail

Aims (1.3.4)

By the end of this section, you should:

- Understand the causes of business failure, for example, lack of management skills, changes in the business environment, liquidity problems
- Understand why new businesses are at a greater risk of failing.

Why do businesses fail?

Despite all the hard work, capital and expertise, some businesses do fail. This can happen to businesses of all sizes. It can easily happen to a local takeaway restaurant. In 2017, executive search firm DHR Global's UK operation was forced into liquidation, as it was unable to pay debts of more than £2.3 million. This was because the business had run out of cash to pay its bills on a day-to-day basis. This was a well-established and long-standing business that struggled to maintain sales. So why do businesses fail?

∆ There are various reasons why a business may fail.

Liquidity problems

To make a profit in the long term, a business needs be able to run day-to-day. Regular cash inflows are crucial for a business to pay its daily costs, such as employees, electricity and suppliers. Costs such as those for advertising, running offices or shops, paying employees' wages and making up for production mistakes are often very hard to estimate accurately. This can also be the case for well-known businesses that overspend; for example, a South African business, 1time Airline, filed for liquidation (arranged for closure) because it ran out of money to continue to run the business. The airline was an established business but, because it didn't monitor its expenditure closely enough, it saw its cash flow drop.

Initial errors

Many start-up businesses make mistakes early on, which can cause failure – for example, by choosing the wrong products. These mistakes can often be hard to solve, especially when the business has spent its start-up cash. However, even existing businesses make errors later on. Adidas was criticised for launching a line of new trainers that had 'shackles', which were made to be attached via a chain to the wearer's ankles. Adidas received many complaints from people who said that the shackles were a symbol of slavery.

Lack of management skills

Some businesses, no matter how old, can fail because of the poor decisions of managers. As managers make the more important decisions, they can choose the wrong product, pricing method or market to sell in. An American company, FirstEnergy, was criticised because its managers responded slowly to power failures during Hurricane Sandy in 2012. This can have damaging effects on a business, potentially causing closure if it fails to respond more quickly to future crises.

No reputation

Establishing a reputation can be hard for a business. If a market has well-known brands, start-up businesses may fail. For example, with AirAsia and Malaysia Airlines dominating the Malaysian air travel market, a start-up business may struggle. Yet even businesses that have a strong reputation can lose business very quickly by making errors.

Market conditions

Some markets can be harder to enter than others – for example, the banking market. During the recession in 2008–09, the banking market was targeted as one that needed to reduce its barriers in order to allow more businesses to enter and succeed.

The business environment can cause problems for a business. As the economy moves from **boom** to a recession, people will spend less money. This can cause a business to lose orders and income.

The economy

During a recession, many businesses of all sizes fail. This is due to a lack of customer spending, which causes a reduction in a business's revenue. The South Korean SsangYong Motor Company struggled during the 2008–09 global recession, until it was taken over by Mahindra in 2011.

As governments change, so do their policies on taxation, business support and trade deals. If a government increases the tax placed on businesses' profit, reduces the amount of financial support or increases the cost of employing, then some businesses will suffer liquidity problems and close.

Large competitors

As other businesses grow, smaller businesses can often be squeezed out of the market. This is because larger businesses can often afford to invest in developing new products, reducing their prices or using large advertising campaigns.

Why are new businesses more likely to fail?

New businesses have a higher risk of failure than older, more established businesses. This is because they do not have the reputation or loyal (regular) customers to support them through the early stages. New businesses struggle to compete with larger, more established competitors because of the size of their budgets. Where larger businesses can spend millions of dollars on advertising, smaller start-ups may only have a few hundred dollars to spend.

Customers are very brand loyal. A brand is a name, symbol or feature that identifies a seller or product. For example, many customers will choose Apple if they want an MP3 player. Apple have created an 'i' brand by placing this before its product names; for example, iPhone, iPad and iPod. Once a business creates a reputation, it is less likely to fail.

CASE STUDY

Training needs

During the recession in 2008–09, the Middle East saw a 22% increase in business failures. This resulted in a massive injection of money into training. The governments aimed money at those who had lost jobs in industry, so they could retrain and find new jobs.

Since the recession, global unemployment has increased, with France having around 10% unemployment compared to India's 3%. The change in the market and economic conditions has had a damaging effect on businesses everywhere.

Application

Despite using a business plan and receiving help from the government, businesses can still fail. What are your top three tips for a business owner who is starting up a new business? Produce a poster that highlights these tips.

You may wish to apply these to a specific type of business or industry.

Can you justify why you think these three tips are the most important?

Top Tip

Make sure you understand the key terms used to talk about the economy and business environment: recession, boom, growth, unemployment and stability.

Knowledge check

1. **Identify two reasons why a start-up business may fail. (2)**
2. **Explain why poor management decisions can cause a business to fail. (4)**
3. **Explain why start-up businesses are more likely to fail than established businesses. (4)**

Total 10 marks

Check your progress:

- ✓ I can outline the characteristics of a successful entrepreneur and the different parts of a business plan.
- ✓ I can analyse the methods and problems of measuring business size.
- ✓ I can explain why some businesses grow and others remain small, and the problems they face.
- ✓ I can understand why some businesses fail, what the causes are and why new businesses are more likely to fail.

Types of business organisation

Main features of different forms of business organisation

Aims (1.4.1)

By the end of this section, you should:

- Understand the key features of sole traders, partnerships, private and public limited companies, public limited companies, franchises and joint ventures
- Understand the differences between unincorporated businesses and limited companies
- Understand the concepts of risk, ownership and limited liability
- Be able to recommend and justify a suitable form of business organisation to owners/management in a given situation
- Understand business organisations in the public sector, for example, public corporations.

Unincorporated businesses – sole traders and partnerships

Unincorporated businesses are not legally registered as companies (corporations). The two main types are sole traders and partnerships.

Sole traders

Sole traders, or sole proprietors (as they are sometimes called), are individuals who own their own business. A sole trader does not have to work on their own – they can employ people to work with them or for them – but they are the sole owner of the business. Businesses that are easy to set up and require little start-up finance are often sole traders. A hairdresser requires few items of equipment to get started; therefore being a sole trader is the best form of legal ownership, especially as they require very little paperwork before they can start trading.

◁ A sole trader is the ideal legal ownership for a sole proprietor, as they need very little finance to set up.

Advantages of being a sole trader	Disadvantages of being a sole trader
✓ **Make all the decisions** – Sole traders can make all of the business decisions themselves. This means that decisions can be made quickly and without any conflict of interest.	✗ **Unlimited liability** – This means that the sole trader is personally liable (responsible) for all of their business's debts.
✓ **Keep all of the profit** – As sole traders are the sole owners of their business, they can keep all of the profit for themselves. Larger organisations, such as partnerships and companies, have to split the profit between partners or shareholders.	✗ **Difficult to raise finance** – Although sole traders do not often require much capital, they find it difficult to raise large amounts. This is because they are small, so banks are unwilling to lend them large amounts of money.
✓ **Easy to set up** – Sole traders are often very small operations and therefore require very little paperwork to set up. In most cases, having a bank account and registering with the tax office is enough.	✗ **Long working hours** – Sole traders do not earn money when they are not working, and therefore they often have to work long hours.
✓ **Requires little capital** – As they are small operations, sole traders often require little capital to start their business.	✗ **No holiday pay or paid time off** – When sole traders do not work they do not get paid; also they do not receive benefits such as holiday pay and sick pay.
	✗ **No continuity** – The sole trader and their business are the same, so when the sole trader decides to stop working, the business will also stop unless somebody is willing to take it over.

Partnerships

Partnerships, like sole traders, are unincorporated businesses. This means that, in the eyes of the law, the owners (partners) and the business are the same legal entity. For example, if a partnership of accountants wished to take out a loan to expand their business, the partners themselves would be liable (responsible) for the loan.

Partnerships are small organisations that traditionally used to have between 2 and 20 partners. However, English Partnership Law has allowed businesses to have as many partners as they like. Small local businesses, such as a firm of lawyers, often choose to be partnerships, as they don't have to do as much paperwork as larger companies and can keep all of the profits themselves.

Advantages of being a partnership	Disadvantages of being a partnership
✓ **More expertise** – Partnerships have more owners (partners) than a sole trader, so can normally call on more expertise.	✗ **Lack of capital** – Despite having more access to capital than a sole trader, partnerships still find it difficult to raise large amounts of capital.
✓ **Less financial risk** – Liability or risk is shared among all the partners.	✗ **Sharing the profit** – As a partnership has more than one owner, profits are normally shared out between the different partners.
✓ **More access to capital** – There are more partners to invest in the business.	✗ **Unlimited liability** – All partners, with the exception of sleeping partners, are jointly liable for the partnership's debts.
✓ **Can attract investment** – Partnerships can attract investment from sleeping partners (people who invest in the business but take no active role in running the organisation).	✗ **Conflict of interest** – Partners may have disagreements over business decisions.
✓ **More continuity** – If one of the partners dies or resigns, the business can still continue.	

The deed of partnership

The **deed of partnership** is a legally binding document, drawn up by partners. If a conflict arises between the partners, they can refer to the deed of partnership. A deed will normally include details of the:

- finance provided by each partner
- **salary** entitlements
- percentage of profit to be received by each partner
- holiday entitlements
- registered address.

Key Term

Salary: employees on a salary system are paid an agreed sum for a year's work.

◁ A deed of partnership is a legal document that binds the partnership together.

CASE STUDY

A profitable partnership

In 1934, two electrical engineering graduates from Harvard University, Boston, USA, Bill Hewlett and Dave Packard, started working on a device to test sound equipment. After Walt Disney bought eight devices, they formalised their partnership and formed Hewlett-Packard (HP) in 1939. Throughout the 1940s and 1950s, the business grew. Its innovative approach to providing technological products soon led to an annual (yearly) revenue of over $500 000. By 1960, growth was so large that they formed a company that was listed on the New York Stock Exchange. Now Hewlett-Packard is one of the world's biggest computer companies with an annual revenue of over $100 billion.

Summary: Unincorporated businesses

Sole traders
- Only one owner
- Keeps all the profit
- Makes all the decisions
- The owner is the only source of finance
- Has no continuity

Both
- Normally small businesses
- Unlimited liability
- Difficult to raise finance
- Do not have to release financial information

Partnerships
- Has more than one owner
- Shares profits
- Decision making is shared
- Bound by a deed of partnership
- Can attract investment

Application

Use the internet to research a famous business partnership. Create a presentation describing how their business started and why they might have formed as a partnership. You should aim to make your presentation five minutes long, with at least three slides. Use headings such as: 'How did they start?' 'Why did they become a partnership?' 'Where are they now?'

If they are no longer a partnership, include when and why they changed legal ownership. Try to include terms such as finance, growth, control and continuity.

Incorporated businesses – private and public limited companies

Incorporated businesses, or **companies**, have a separate legal identity to their owners. This means that incorporated businesses are registered with the company registration institute of the country they are based in. The actions and finances of the company are now considered to be separate from that of their owners. For example, when a company such as Fragrance Hotel Management Ltd (a chain of eight hotels in Singapore) wished to take out a loan to open a new hotel, it was the company, and not the owners, that was held responsible for paying back the loan.

CASE STUDY

Where in the world?

Where a company is registered depends on the country in which the company is based. The table shows various authorities around the world where companies have to be registered.

Country	Company registration authority
Brazil	DNRC (Departamento Nacional de Registro do Comércio)
Cambodia	Ministry of Commerce
Germany	Trade Register
Hong Kong SAR	Companies Registry
India	Ministry of Corporate Affairs
Malaysia	Companies Commission
Pakistan	Securities and Exchange Commission
Singapore	Accounting and Corporate Regulatory Authority
United Kingdom	Companies House
USA	US Securities and Exchange Commission

Although there are many differences, there are two main features of incorporated businesses (companies) that differentiate them from unincorporated businesses (sole traders and partnerships): limited liability and the ability to sell shares.

Limited liability

As companies are legally registered, they are **separate legal identities** to the identities of their owners. This means that the company, and not the owners, is liable for all of its debts. If the business was to face legal action, it may lose all of its possessions (assets), including money invested by its owners, but the owners' personal possessions would not be at risk, as they are protected by **limited liability**.

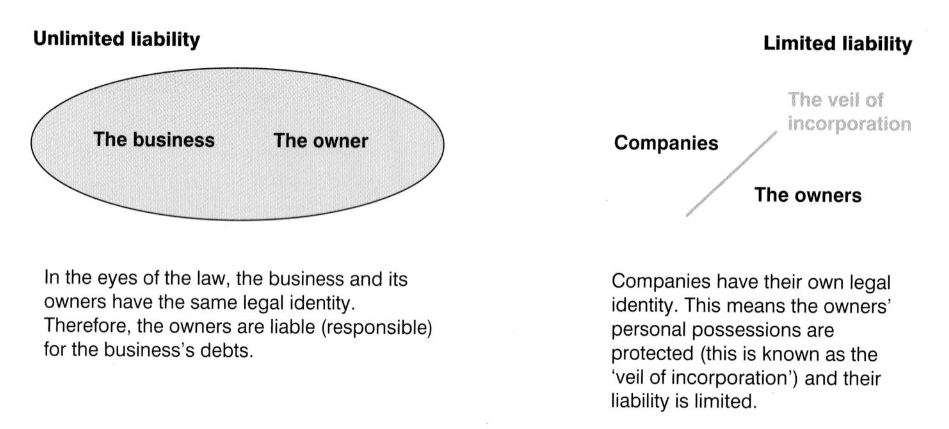

In the eyes of the law, the business and its owners have the same legal identity. Therefore, the owners are liable (responsible) for the business's debts.

Companies have their own legal identity. This means the owners' personal possessions are protected (this is known as the 'veil of incorporation') and their liability is limited.

Issuing shares

As companies have their own legal identity, their ownership is allocated (divided up and given out) by issuing shares. Shareholders invest money in the company and, in return, they own a part of the business called a **share**. The number of shares that a shareholder has determines how much of the company they own. How shares are bought and issued depends on the type of company.

- **Private limited companies** (Ltd) issue their shares to private investors who they choose, which means that the ownership of the business is kept private. They have to prepare two documents, called the articles of association (the legal document detailing the responsibilities of the internal members) and the memorandum of association (the legal document detailing the registered name, address and share structure). In addition, the law requires private limited companies to hold an annual general meeting (AGM), a yearly meeting with shareholders and company directors. Fragrance Hotel Management Ltd is a privately owned company in Singapore. This means that it chooses who it wants to become a shareholder; the price of the share is agreed by both parties; and there is no limit to the number of shareholders it can have.
- **Public limited companies** (PLC) issue their shares to the general public, meaning that anyone can become a shareholder and they are then free to openly trade their share in the business on one of the world's stock exchanges

(depending on where the company is registered). This process is called floatation (also spelled flotation). Nokia PLC, the communications company, is a public limited company. This means that shareholders purchase shares via the Helsinki Stock Exchange (Finland).

CASE STUDY

Floating Facebook

Facebook, the worldwide social media site, floated its shares (made its shares available for purchase) on the Nasdaq Stock Market (based in New York). Each share was initially offered at $38. A few days after floatation, traders must have felt that the business was over priced, as the value of each share fell by as much as 11%.

After the initial public offering, however, Facebook's sale on the Nasdaq Stock Market made its founder, Mark Zuckerberg, an instant billionaire and the 29th richest person in the world.

Advantages of being a private limited company	Disadvantages of being a private limited company
✓ **Shares** – Private limited companies (Ltd) can select shareholders to help them raise more capital. ✓ **More expertise** – Private limited companies are often large enough to have directors who specialise in a particular area (they are often shareholders). ✓ **Maintain control** – Because a private limited company selects its shareholders, it is able to keep control of the business more easily than a PLC. If a shareholder wishes to sell up (sell all their shares), their shares are offered to the existing shareholders first. ✓ **Limited liability** – Shareholders (owners) are protected by limited liability. This means they only risk what they have invested in the company.	✗ **Releasing financial information** – All private limited companies have to register their accounts with the relevant registration authority. The accounts have to be audited (checked and agreed) by external accountants, adding to the running costs of companies. ✗ **Legal restrictions** – Private limited companies have more legal restrictions than unincorporated businesses.

Advantages of being a public limited company	Disadvantages of being a public limited company
✓ **Selling shares to the general public** – Public limited companies (PLCs) can sell shares to any member of the public, both individuals and other companies. This allows them to raise considerable amounts of capital – far more than for any other type of legal ownership. ✓ **Limited liability** – Like those of private limited companies, shareholders of PLCs have limited liability, which limits the risk involved with a potential investment. ✓ **Managerial economies of scale** – PLCs are normally very large organisations that can afford to employ specialist directors to run the business on behalf of the shareholders. These specialists improve the efficiency of the company.	✗ **Releasing financial information** – As members of the general public are shareholders in a PLC, the company has a duty to supply them with up-to-date information about its performance. It has to produce an annual report, which is normally available via its website and therefore visible to competitors. ✗ **Dividends** – PLCs are obliged to pay their shareholders dividends. Finding the right balance between retaining enough profit to reinvest in the business and satisfying shareholders is difficult. If shareholders are not happy, they can vote to replace the company's directors. ✗ **Losing control** – As shares are available to anyone in the general public, existing shareholders can be subject to hostile takeover bids and can lose control of the business if an individual or business purchases 50% or more of the available shares. ✗ **Legal issues** – Public limited companies are bound by more legal constraints than a private limited company, and this can make them more complicated to run.

Summary: Incorporated businesses

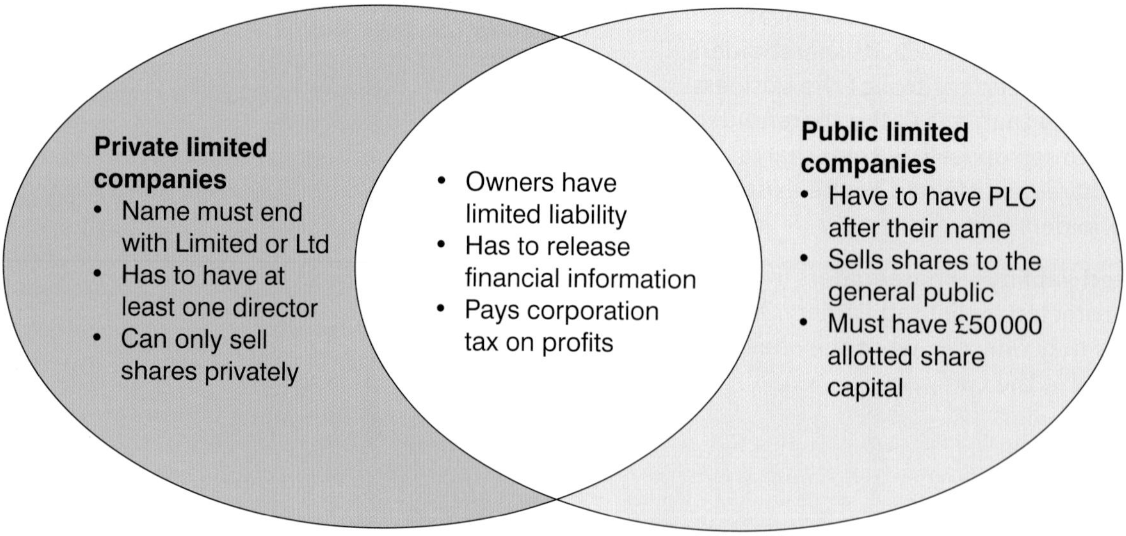

Private limited companies
- Name must end with Limited or Ltd
- Has to have at least one director
- Can only sell shares privately

Both
- Owners have limited liability
- Has to release financial information
- Pays corporation tax on profits

Public limited companies
- Have to have PLC after their name
- Sells shares to the general public
- Must have £50 000 allotted share capital

Knowledge check

1. **Define the term sole trader.** **(2)**
2. **Identify and explain two advantages of being a partnership rather than a sole trader.** **(4)**

Brothers Chahel and Pavel are an Indian-based legal partnership. Since forming the partnership, they have taken on four new partners, each specialising in a different area of law. Chahel is concerned that the partnership is stopping the business from growing.

3. **Define the term unlimited liability.** **(2)**
4. **Explain one reason why Chahel and Pavel might want to draw up a deed of partnership.** **(2)**
5. **Explain one advantage and one disadvantage of being a public limited company rather than a private limited company.** **(4)**
6. **Chahel has recently considered forming a private limited company. Do you think this is the best form of ownership for his business? Justify your answer.** **(6)**

Total 20 marks

Franchises

A **franchise** is an arrangement between two existing organisations, normally a public limited company and a private limited company. A franchise arrangement is when a new business (**franchisee**), although a separate legal entity, trades under the name of an existing business (**franchisor**).

The franchise arrangement

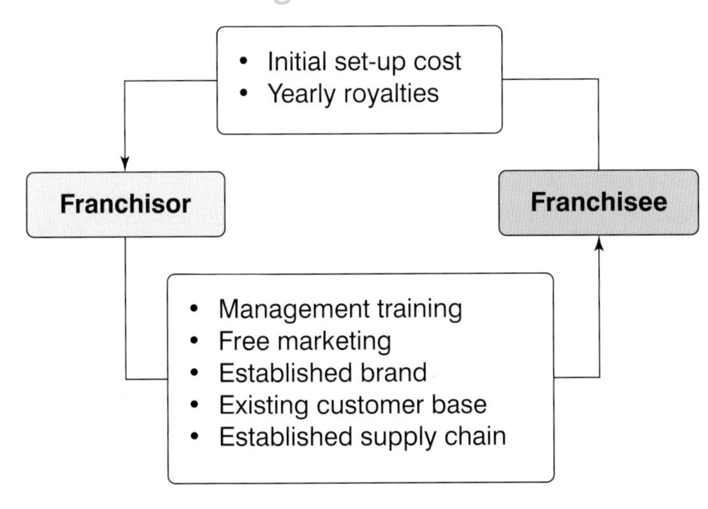

Did you know?

In the United States, franchises contribute 3% of the total GDP (total amount of goods and services in the economy) each year. That is $552 billion!

Entrepreneurs often favour a franchise arrangement, as it allows a new business to trade under an established brand name, which reduces the risk of failure. In return, the franchisee has to pay an initial set-up cost and yearly **royalties** (an agreed percentage of the franchisee's profit).

For example, an entrepreneur wishing to start their own restaurant may choose to enter into a franchise arrangement with an existing restaurant, such as Subway. Although the entrepreneur will have to pay an initial fee and pay yearly royalties, they will have the benefit of the Subway brand and will therefore be far more likely to succeed. This is why many banks are more willing to lend to entrepreneurs entering into a franchise arrangement.

The benefits of a franchise arrangement

Benefits to the franchisee	Benefits to the franchisor
✓ It is much easier to obtain finance, as banks view franchises as less risky than independent businesses. ✓ There is no need to build a customer base by spending heavily on advertising. ✓ Stock control (of raw materials and finished goods) and accounting systems are often provided by the franchisor, which makes the business more efficient. ✓ Being able to offer established products reduces the risk of failure, as there is already an existing customer base.	✓ Franchisors can grow at a much faster rate by allowing people to buy into their business through a franchise arrangement. ✓ The franchisee has to pay the start-up costs, which means the franchisor can grow the business at low cost. ✓ The franchisee will run the franchise on behalf of the franchisor, which reduces the time spent on day-to-day issues by the franchisor. ✓ The franchisor receives yearly royalties from the franchisee.

The disadvantages of a franchise arrangement

Disadvantages to the franchisee	Disadvantages to the franchisor
✗ Being part of a franchise can limit an entrepreneur's freedom to make decisions about how the business operates. ✗ Decisions made on pricing and products offered will be made by the franchisor, yet this may not always suit local market conditions.	✗ The franchisee will keep most of the profit. Although they will normally have to pay a yearly royalty, the franchisee can sometimes keep up to 95% of the profit. ✗ Poorly run franchises can risk the reputation of the franchisor.

CASE STUDY

Fast-food franchise

In 2017, McDonald's shareholders voted against giving franchisees the chance to vote on who should be on the board of directors of the world's biggest fast-food chain. This would have placed considerable power in the franchisees' hands, which is why the shareholders voted against it. Currently 85% of McDonald's restaurants are franchises, and the company is aiming to increase this figure to 95% in the coming years. Franchisees use the products, branding and marketing of McDonald's, and gaining a vote on board nomination would be an added bonus.

Application **Evaluation**

Using the internet, research franchise opportunities available in your area. When you have found a suitable opportunity, make notes explaining the benefits of entering this franchise opportunity. In order to give a balanced argument, you must consider the alternative of setting up a similar business on your own. When you have completed this task, you will need to get into groups of three.

Role play: One of you must act as the entrepreneur wishing to start up the business on his or her own; another person must act as the entrepreneur wishing to enter into the franchise arrangement. The third member of your group should act as the bank manager and choose, based on your arguments, which of you they would lend money to, explaining why. Act out all three examples, changing roles for each one.

Joint ventures

Like a franchise, a joint venture is an agreement between two existing organisations to start a jointly owned third company. A common situation for a joint venture is when a business wants to expand into a new market (such as a new country) and has little knowledge of that market. Rather than setting up on its own and risking failure, it forms a joint venture with a local business that has knowledge of the market and an established brand. Alternatively, some businesses decide to form a joint venture to share resources and expertise.

Advantages of a joint venture	Disadvantages of a joint venture
✓ Risks are shared by both organisations. ✓ Expertise can be offered by both organisations. ✓ Capital is normally invested by both organisations.	✗ There can often be a conflict of interest between the two organisations involved. ✗ Decisions have to be made by both parties, which slows down the decision-making process. ✗ Profits are split between both of the parties involved in the joint venture.

CASE STUDY

Joint venture in China

Jaguar Land Rover (JLR), the British-based car manufacturer, formed a joint venture with Chery Automobile in China to start the production of Jaguar and Land Rover cars in China. The joint venture saw the two companies set up a jointly owned new company, which allowed them to share manufacturing expertise. Chery's knowledge of the local market was the driving force behind the joint venture, and has seen the demand for JLR cars increase in the region.

Public sector organisations

Public sector organisations are different from all the other organisations or arrangements previously mentioned. This is because private individuals (such as sole traders, partners and shareholders) do not own them. Instead, public sector organisations are owned and run by governments. The most common forms of public sector organisations are schools, hospitals, police stations and fire stations.

Differences between the private sector and public sector

	Private sector	Public sector
Ownership	Private individuals own organisations: they can be sole traders, partners in a partnership or shareholders in a company.	The government owns organisations. Central government or local authorities can own them.
Funding	Customers paying for a product or service fund private sector businesses.	Public sector organisations are funded using taxpayers' money.
Objective	Private sector businesses have the objective to make as much profit as possible.	Public sector organisations exist to provide a service to the general public and to provide value for taxpayers' money.

Public corporations

These legal entities are owned by the **state** (government) and act on their behalf. Examples include the Russian Railways, the Nigerian Television Authority and the Bank of China. Unlike privately owned businesses, state-owned organisations have very different goals. Their focus is delivering a necessary service for the benefit of the country. For example, when a government owns and operates a railway network, it may reduce ticket prices in order to help employees travel around the country. Their focus is non-financial, with money raised going back into the running of the business.

Choosing the right type of ownership

Choosing the right ownership depends on a number of different factors, including risk, control, size and ambition.

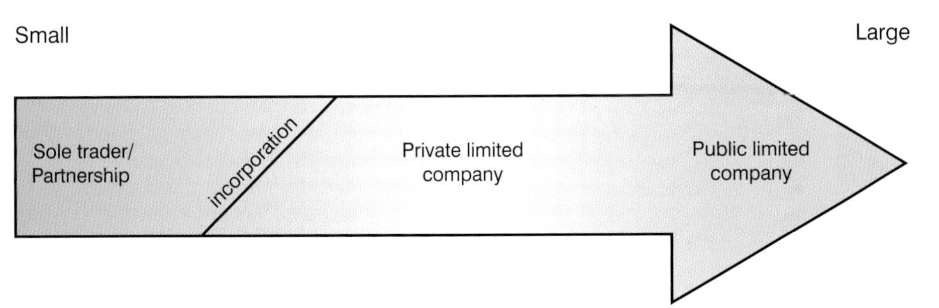

Risk

The smaller the business, the more risk there is involved. Sole traders have to cope with unlimited liability and a lack of expertise. As sole traders are solely liable for the business's debt, one bad decision can mean that their business closes and they lose their personal possessions. Owners of larger companies have more expertise available to them, as they can employ specialist directors who are less likely to make poor decisions and are protected by limited liability.

Δ The smaller the business, the more risk it has. However, some entrepreneurs keep operations small to maintain control.

Control

The more owners a business has, either partners or shareholders, the less control each individual has. However, the more owners a business has, the more access to finance they have. This is one of the problems when deciding to become a public limited company: while the business will raise much more money through selling shares to the public, the original owners will eventually lose some control of the business.

Size

Businesses that wish to grow in size and become large organisations normally have to become public limited companies. Unless the owners have significant private wealth, the ability to borrow large amounts of money from banks and raise millions through selling shares is exclusively available to public limited companies. The larger the business gets, the harder it is to control. As larger businesses branch out into different product lines, with thousands of employees, communication and decision making become harder.

Ambition

Many entrepreneurs want to start a business for more than just financial gain. They gain a feeling of satisfaction and enjoyment from running their business. Therefore, many businesses choose to stay small so that the entrepreneur can control what happens and make their own business decisions.

Size vs ambition

◁ Staying small means the owners can run the business as they want to, for more than just financial gain. Massive businesses such as KFC exist to make profits for their shareholders, often sacrificing their original business principles.

Knowledge check

1. **Define the term franchisor.** **(2)**
2. **Explain two benefits to a franchisee of entering a franchise arrangement.** **(4)**
3. **Explain two disadvantages to a franchisor of entering a franchise arrangement.** **(4)**
4. **Explain the differences between public and private sector organisations in terms of their:**
   a) ownership **(2)**
   b) objectives. **(2)**
5. **Define the term joint venture.** **(2)**

Safesave PLC is a UK-based supermarket wishing to expand into China.

6. **Explain two benefits to Safesave PLC of forming a joint venture with a Chinese business in order to help their expansion.** **(6)**

Total 22 marks

Check your progress:

- ✓ I can outline the main features of different forms of business organisation.
- ✓ I understand the differences between unincorporated businesses and limited companies, and the concepts of risk, ownership and limited liability.
- ✓ I can recommend and justify a suitable form of business organisation to owners or management in a given situation.
- ✓ I can describe business organisations in the public sector.

Business objectives and stakeholder objectives

Business objectives and their importance

Aims (1.5.1)

By the end of this section, you should:

- Understand the need for business objectives and the importance of them
- Be able to outline different business objectives, for example, survival, growth, profit and market share
- Understand the objectives of social enterprises.

Why a business needs objectives

It is important that businesses set objectives, and that everyone involved knows what they are. This is because they act as a target or goal that the business needs to reach if it wants to achieve its overall aims. A business can use the objectives to judge whether it has achieved the targets it set.

For example, a small firm that sells computer parts to large producers sets itself an aim of increasing profit. To achieve this, it sets itself a range of objectives:

Objective 1: Increase sales revenue by 12% by 1 January 2020

Objective 2: Reduce wastage of poorly made components by 2% by 1 January 2020

On 1 January 2020, the business will be able to see if it has achieved these objectives. It can count the revenue and wastage and see whether these objectives have helped the business achieve its aim of increasing profit.

Objectives give employees a sense of direction and a target against which they can be judged. Objectives are also important for different stakeholders to use as a means of judgement. The business owners will be able to judge if the workforce have done what they should have, and perhaps identify where any problems are within the business.

Most businesses have overall objectives that everyone contributes to, as well as separate ones for each department. The diagram on the next page shows an example of how the departmental objectives link in with the overall company objectives.

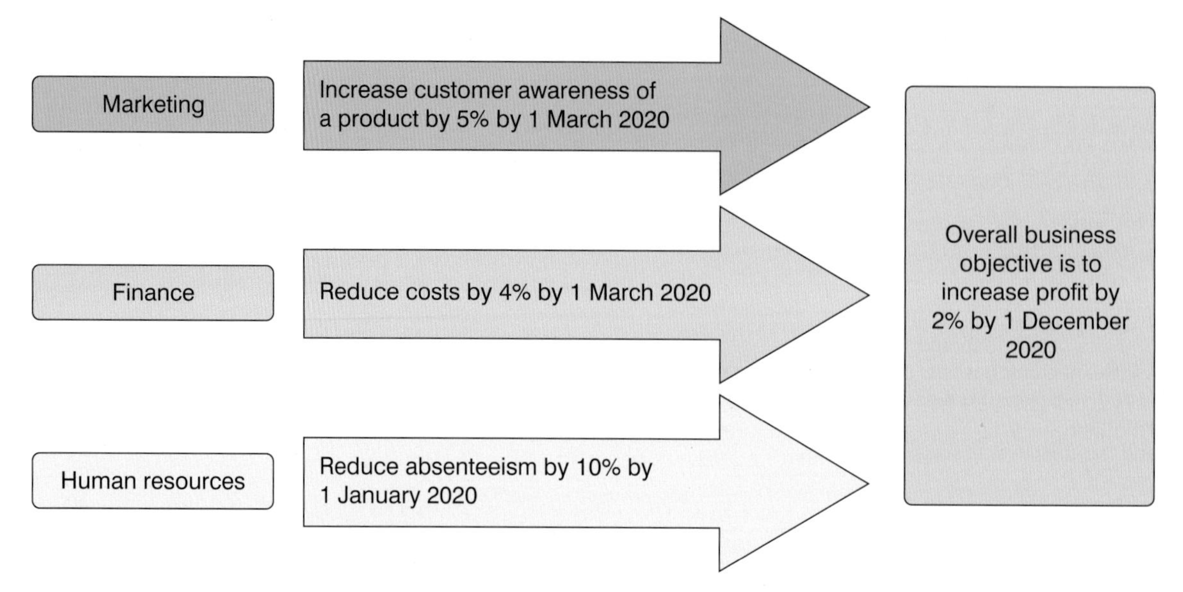

SMART objectives

Businesses should use the SMART approach to set their objectives.

S	**Specific** – The objective should focus on a particular area. For example, a sweet shop may set sales targets for a specific bar of chocolate.
M	**Measurable** – Each objective should have a quantifiable way to measure it; for example, 'Increase hot dog sales by 20% by 1 December'. Normally it is sales, revenue or profit that is measured.
A	**Agreed** – The people involved should agree on the objectives. For example, the sales team agree on their new sales targets.
R	**Realistic** – The objectives should be realistic and actually achievable. There is no point setting targets that could never be achieved by the employees. 'Increase sales by 1000% in two weeks' is an example of an objective that is unlikely to be achieved.
T	**Timed** – The objective should state a clear time frame in which it is to be completed. This means that it can then be measured.

Setting business objectives

There are many different objectives that a business could set. These can change over the business's journey. They can include the objectives of survival, improving the business's image, increasing employee motivation, selling abroad, growth, making a profit or gaining market share.

Survival

Many small businesses will start with this objective. This might involve setting departmental objectives that focus on cost management and sales revenue. These are very important objectives for many businesses, especially those that enter competitive markets.

Improving their image

Some businesses experience problems with the quality of their product, or perhaps they may cause large amounts of pollution. Therefore, they try to improve how stakeholders see them as a business. For example, businesses may set targets to reduce wastage or pollution.

Increasing employee motivation

If employees are motivated and happy, they are more likely to work hard and remain with the business. The business then saves money on recruiting (such as time taken to interview and the cost of adverts). Larger businesses often set these objectives, as employee productivity (how much each employee produces) is very important.

Selling abroad

Larger businesses may set objectives to expand their business into new markets or countries so that they can increase sales. As businesses grow, a key objective may be to continue to increase their market share and sales.

Growth

Businesses may then look to grow in different ways – for example, by increasing sales or the number of employees. Growth is often a key objective for many businesses, as it shows that the business is moving forward. If a business starts to shrink, it could eventually become bankrupt (unable to pay its debts so it has to close down).

Making a profit

Many private sector businesses aim to make a profit. This is because it is often the primary target for shareholders. Without profit, businesses will struggle to stay open. This aim could focus on reducing costs across the business, as well as increasing sales. Businesses may wish to focus on one of these aspects to improve profit.

Increasing their market share

This means increasing the business's proportion of sales within the industry in which the business operates. Some businesses aim, simply, to maintain their share, because the market in which they operate is so competitive, while others try to increase their sales and therefore their market share.

Objectives of social enterprises

Social enterprises have very different objectives. As with many businesses, social enterprises still aim to make a profit. However, they differ from other types of business, as any profits are then used to support parts of the global community. Social enterprises also have objectives that are linked to their moral aims. For example, the business may wish to donate a certain amount of money each year to support a particular cause or initiative.

Social enterprise objectives may focus on social issues such as improving education, health or wealth.

Did you know?

Globally, it is estimated that 50% of social enterprises have posted a profit since their start, with a further 26% breaking even.

CASE STUDY Getting the balance right

Martin Fisher and Nick Moon founded KickStart in 1991. It produces water pumps, irrigation systems and brick presses that help developing countries increase farming yields (amount of crops). The business now turns over $2.5 million. Despite its relatively small turnover, KickStart still follows its principles of giving back to the global community. It aims to help reduce global poverty and to make a profit at the same time. Without this profit, KickStart would not be able to carry out its social activities and would close.

Application **Analysis**

Carry out research into a social enterprise near you.

- What are its objectives?
- Why is it important that it sets objectives?
- How does the business give back to the community?
- Discuss whether you think it achieves its objectives.
- Present your findings as a written report.

Knowledge check

1. **Identify two ways in which a social enterprise is different from a private limited company such as your local shop.** (2)
2. **Identify the ways in which a business might change its objectives over time.** (4)
3. **Explain why it is important to a business to set SMART objectives.** (6)

Total 12 marks

The role of stakeholder groups involved in business activity

Aims (1.5.2)

By the end of this section, you should:

- Be able to describe the main internal and external stakeholder groups
- Understand the objectives of different stakeholder groups
- Be able to explain how these objectives might conflict with each other, using examples.

Main internal and external stakeholder groups

A stakeholder is a person or group who has an interest in the business. Stakeholders can be both internal (within the business) and external (outside the business).

Internal stakeholders

Stakeholder	Interest in the business	Objectives for the business	Example
Business owners These are the people who own the business. They could be the sole owner (sole trader), joint owners (partnership) or shareholder (private or public limited company).	They have money invested in the business so are keen to see it make a profit, or at least break even.	These stakeholders will often want to see the business making increased profit and expanding its sales. Smaller business owners may settle for lower profits and may just look to break even each year while paying themselves a wage.	Petrobras (Petróleo) of Brazil is one of the world's largest oil and gas suppliers. Their owners will want to see an increase in sales so that they receive a large return on their investment.
Employees An employee is someone who works for the business. They could be in a shop, a factory, an office or work from home.	They hold a stake in the business as they earn their living through the business's performance. Therefore, they want the business to do well and continue to employ them.	They will want higher wages, promotion opportunities and to be valued by the owners.	The employees of Burger King will want the business to continue to do well so that they can ask for a rise in wages. They may also look to see if the business offers promotions within it.

∆ Employees are internal stakeholders in a business. It is in their interests for the business to do well so that it can continue to employ them.

External stakeholders

Stakeholder	Interest in the business	Objectives for the business	Example
Customers These are the individuals or businesses who buy a product or service from a business.	Customers do not want to see the business struggle with costs, in case prices increase. Customers will also be keen for the business to continue to trade, so they do not have to travel too far for a product or service.	Customers would like objectives that focus on improving the quality of the product or service, and to receive it at a low price, with value for money.	Customers will want price guarantees and reward cards.
Suppliers These are businesses that sell goods that other businesses use to make their own products. For example, a farmer may supply milk to a food producer.	They want the businesses they supply to do well so that they will receive payment on time.	A business will want to secure long-term contracts with suppliers. Suppliers would like growth and expansion as business objectives.	IBM supplies technology companies all over the world. They would expect to see their invoices paid on time.

Stakeholder	Interest in the business	Objectives for the business	Example
Government/ sovereign The government is in charge of running the country and makes decisions on tax and spending. It is often elected. A sovereign is the head of the royal family of the country.	They expect businesses to treat employees according to the laws and regulations that they have set, to recruit new employees and continue to grow.	They want the business to grow and expand so that they can receive taxation from employee income and business profit.	Governments all over Africa have supported the laying of internet cables to help support other businesses and attract investment from other countries. This should help create jobs and taxation income in the long term.
Local community These are the people who live in the local area that surrounds the business.	They have an interest in the business, as they may rely on the local businesses for jobs and products or services. They will also be interested in the impact of the business on the local area, for example, how the business's activities impact on pollution and transport.	They expect employment opportunities from the business, as well as a reduction in pollution and traffic.	Jaguar Land Rover (JLR) is opening a factory in China and the local community want to make sure they get the jobs in the factory.
Trade unions These groups represent employees in discussions with businesses and the government over pay and working conditions.	Their interest is in the owners and managers treating the employees well. They also have an interest in the way the government sets its employment laws.	They expect objectives that support employees and their wages, conditions and job security (keeping their job).	There have been protests against the government in Prague, Czechia (Czech Republic), because of poor conditions and employees' rights.
Pressure groups These groups try to influence policy in the interest of a particular cause or issue. For example, Greenpeace protests for a cleaner environment.	They have an interest in the business's activities and what its products or processes do to the world. They may also put pressure on the government to encourage them to step in and make changes in the business environment.	They want objectives that aim to reduce any negative effects on the environment or population.	The Urgenda pressure group in Holland is threatening to sue both the government and businesses if they do not start to reduce their CO_2 emissions as promised.

△ Members of the local community are external stakeholders in a business. They are often worried about the impact of business activities on the local environment and show this in a protest. Here the community are protesting against the use of the land by larger businesses.

Objectives of different stakeholder groups

One of the major problems that a business faces is keeping its stakeholders happy. Each stakeholder will have their own needs and wants (their own objectives) in relation to the business. At times, the objectives of different stakeholders will conflict. For example, Chevron has a huge range of stakeholders who have conflicting objectives. Some of these stakeholders, and their conflicting objectives, are described below.

Customers would like petrol prices to decrease. The general increase in prices is a major cause of concern for customers.

Shareholders like high prices, as this means revenues can increase. This will mean they receive a large dividend payment.

The local community wants to see Chevron reduce its impact on the environment by spending more on renewable energy and reducing pollution.

Employees may want an increase in wages rather than Chevron spending the money on renewable sources of energy.

CASE STUDY

Working together

As part of its funding changes, the International Federation of Red Cross and Red Crescent Societies has signed partnership deals with major businesses all over Africa. This is to make it easier to improve services for the most vulnerable people on the continent. The influence of local communities also played a role in the new agreement – they raised concerns that local resources, such as water, were being used to produce alcoholic drinks, which were then sold to other countries. The agreement shows how different stakeholders can work together and not conflict.

Evaluation

You have been given the responsibility of deciding whether your country should build a new airport in the heart of its capital city. This airport will have more runways than the existing airport and will be twice as big.

- Design a table that outlines the different sides of the argument. You should include details of the different stakeholders' positions and outline how they may conflict.
- Assign a stakeholder to each point, to show which stakeholder supports it.
- You should now make a judgement on whether a new airport should be built.

Knowledge check

1. **Define the term internal stakeholder.** **(2)**
2. **Define the term external stakeholder.** **(2)**
3. **Identify a possible objective for two stakeholders of a local convenience store.** **(2)**
4. **Identify two stakeholders of the Exxon oil company.** **(2)**
5. **Using an example, explain why stakeholders will often conflict in their objectives.** **(4)**

Total 12 marks

Objectives of private and public sector enterprises

Aims (1.5.3)

By the end of this section, you should:

- Understand the differences in the aims and objectives of private sector and public sector enterprises.

Defining private and public sectors

There is a huge difference between the private and public sectors:

- The private sector is made up of businesses run by private individuals or groups, often with the aim of producing profits.
- The public sector is made up of government-funded and government-run organisations that often offer services to the public.

Private sector aims and objectives

The aims (overall goals of the business) and objectives (short-term targets) of private sector businesses will be mostly decided by their owners. A start-up business will begin with survival as its aim, as the business has no reputation or customer base. Once this is achieved, the business's aims and objectives may be to increase revenues, profits and market share.

Some of the possible aims and objectives are to:

- **build a strong reputation**, perhaps without even earning a profit – this is how Google started out
- **innovate and develop** – be the first business to produce new products
- **gain customer and brand loyalty** – keep customers coming back
- **increase revenue and profit** – increased revenue and profit become important, especially to the company's shareholders.

Key Term

Brand loyalty: the regular purchase of one brand of a product by a consumer.

The private sector is heavily influenced by the economic climate. This is because, if the economy is doing well, customers have more money to spend on products being sold by private businesses. However, if the economy is doing badly, spending will drop and private businesses will struggle to keep running. This means that they may alter their aims and objectives very quickly.

Application

Produce a poster that clearly shows the aims and objectives of a local private sector business. This can be a small or large business. You may wish to use the internet for research.

CASE STUDY Ethical aims

Ben & Jerry's has been producing ice cream since 1978. The business started as a partnership in the private sector, and grew rapidly.

As Ben & Jerry's is a private business, they have the ability to set their own aims and objectives. While the company's main aim is to make a profit, they have also remained true to the company's social mission, which focuses on the business's role in society and its impact on a local and international scale. They also have to focus on maintaining their customer loyalty, as the ice cream market is extremely competitive. By creating their own product range, Ben & Jerry's have attracted new customers and improved their reputation.

Public sector aims and objectives

One of the key aims of the public sector is to provide jobs. The public sector provides goods and services for the wider community, often without a profit.

Public sector organisations usually run facilities such as:

- hospitals
- police
- army
- ambulance services.

These organisations provide services that many businesses in the private sector would not wish to be in charge of. This is because there may be little profit to be made from them or because the government wants to make the service available to all.

Public sector aims may include:

- providing a service such as healthcare to all citizens
- offering support and advice to the population – for example, advising on taxation
- improving education.

By using government funding, the services can be offered on a large scale without the pressure of making a profit.

Today, some services provided by the public sector are under pressure to improve and meet targets, often without the necessary funding. In countries all over the world, governments are under pressure to account for all the money they have spent. This is money that may have been spent on politicians' personal expenses, wages or activities.

For example, the Penang state government has been heavily criticised for spending millions of dollars on producing magazines that highlight its political agenda. Many people have complained that this is a poor use of the people's money, which has been raised through taxation.

Δ The railway system in China is government-funded and is having a $292 billion investment to maintain its services.

CASE STUDY

Managing water in South Africa

Following the launch of the United Nations World Water Development Report 2017, South Africa started to use private–public sector partnerships to help solve the country's water shortages. Around the world, the private sector supplies over one billion people with drinking water and treats their waste water. The private sector is already developing new initiatives with the government to improve the amount of water available as well as efficiency, so that less water is wasted. For example, a new irrigation system is has saved 55 million m^3 of water each year.

Analysis **Evaluation**

In pairs, debate the following: 'All businesses should be managed by the government in some way.'

Write down at least three key points for each side of the argument, emphasising the most important points.

Knowledge check

1. **Define the term public sector.** **(2)**
2. **Outline why businesses in the same industry set different aims and objectives.** **(4)**
3. **Explain why the government may set up and run businesses.** **(4)**

Total 10 marks

Check your progress:

- ✓ I can identify the different objectives a business may have and explain why they are important.
- ✓ I can explain the role of stakeholder groups and how their objectives can conflict with each other.
- ✓ I can outline the differences in the objectives of private and public sector enterprises.

Exam-style questions: short answer and data response

1. Eduardo set up a magazine business last year. The sports magazine *Global Sport* uses articles written by people all over the world, which helps to give the magazine a global audience. When Eduardo was starting up, he received a small loan from the government. He has seen the number of customers increase by 20% in the last six months. As the sole owner of his private sector company, Eduardo is keen to make a profit in the next two years.

a) Identify two ways in which Eduardo could add value to his product. (2)

b) Identify two characteristics that Eduardo may have as a successful entrepreneur. (2)

c) Explain one reason why the government supports small start-up businesses. (4)

Eduardo wrote an in-depth business plan before setting up his business. He shared this with his journalists and it is displayed on the company's website so that all the other stakeholders can read it.

d) Outline two advantages of Eduardo using a business plan. (6)

The company employs four full-time employees, and sells in over 40 countries. The company's revenue is more than $400 000 and the company has 2% market share. The magazine's success is due to its excellent coverage and specialisation in global sports.

e) Eduardo is now considering expanding the business into new titles such as cars and business news, so it can be more profitable. Do you think Eduardo should expand his business in this way? **Justify** your answer. (6)

2. Top Gym has recently taken over rival company Healthy Place Ltd. Chris, the owner of Top Gym, changed his business objectives from break even to expansion. He wanted to use external growth methods that would give quick results. He decided to take over Healthy Place Ltd, the main competitor in his local area. Healthy Place Ltd has close links with a large number of stakeholders. The local community forms the basis of its workforce.

a) Define external growth. (2)

b) Define the term stakeholder. (2)

c) Explain two reasons why external growth is the best option for Chris if he is to achieve his aim of quick expansion. (4)

A year after the takeover, the business has started to lose money. Chris believes this is because of differences in approach between the two companies. Top Gym has recently spent large amounts of money on new television and radio adverts, in the hope that this will increase its revenue to fund an expansion. The business received advice from mentors who were employed by the government to help local businesses.

d) Explain two possible problems Chris might face when expanding. Explain how could he overcome each problem. (6)

e) With Top Gym not progressing as he would have liked, Chris is considering bringing in a partner and changing the business structure to a partnership. Do you think this will benefit the business? **Justify** your answer. (6)

3. Adam wants to set up his own ballet school. He is looking at two options: Option A, open a ballet school as a sole trader called 'More Ballet'; Option B, open a ballet school as a franchise as part of 'Top Ballet Ltd'. Adam was keen to set up as a sole trader until a friend, Ani, suggested that he should become a franchisee.

a) Define the term franchisee. (2)

b) Define the term sole trader. (2)

c) Outline one reason why Adam should set up his ballet school as a sole trader. (4)

Adam looked into the costs of becoming a franchisee of 'Top Ballet Ltd'. The initial costs would be $10 000, followed by costs of $15 000 each year. However, he would receive national advertising for free, as well as free training and support from 'Top Ballet Ltd'. As a sole trader, Adam would not have to pay these costs, but has been quoted $25 000 per year in advertising, as well as $3000 for each employee he gets trained.

d) Analyse two advantages of Adam becoming a franchisee. (6)

e) Do you think Adam should set up his ballet school as a sole trader or as a franchise? **Justify** your answer. (6)

Note: The exam-style questions, answers and commentary in this book were written by the author; in examination the number of marks awarded to questions like these may be different.

Exam-style questions based on case studies

Horizon Hotels enjoy Dubai's growing market

Horizon Hotels have been operating in Dubai for over 10 years. Because of the large investment in attractions such as the Palm Islands, it has seen its revenues increase from tourists staying at its hotels.

The change in fortunes for its location has come about very quickly – now the economy is very much built on tertiary services and the tourism industry.

Horizon Hotel Group has been one of the businesses to benefit from this increased growth. Owning many of the top hotels, it specialises in luxurious accommodation.

The hotel chain is now considering expanding the business into other countries.

Government advert

The government intends to support businesses of all sizes by offering:

- loans
- advice
- training for employees.

We are here to help boost your business and our economy so that we achieve growth for years to come. Even if you want to enter a new market, we can help!

Contact us today!

Appendix 1: Government advert about supporting business

Memorandum

To: Managing director

From: Sales director

Subject: Growing abroad

Date: 13/4/18

I am currently looking into the new proposed growth into a new country. I believe that opening, as planned, the 5 new hotels will help boost the company's revenue and increase our global reputation. I understand the high costs associated with this project have increased and are now estimated at $12 million. However, I believe that this growth will benefit Horizon Hotels in many ways. Not only will revenue increase, but our global reputation will be improved.

Appendix 2: A memo from the sales director to the managing director outlining the cost and benefits of the expansion into other countries

Option 1: China	Option 2: Japan
Potential revenue per year: $34 million	Potential revenue per year: $23 million
Cost to set up: $12 million	Cost to set up: $10 million
Average wage per year: $23 000	Average wage per year: $12 000
Number of employees needed: 2300	Number of employees needed: 1800
Other issues: Government support is low and Horizon would have to pay 10% more tax	Other issues: The tertiary sector is growing each year in this country by 6%

Appendix 3: The two options for expansion

To: finance@horizonhotels.com

From: managingdirector@horizon.com

Subject: Government loan

Thank you for the information on the government loan that has been offered to help us expand the business abroad. I have had a look over the details and I am a little worried about the length of the loan (paying it back over 5 years). I think this could put a lot of pressure on the business's cash flow. I am also concerned that money is not the issue. Perhaps we should look at alternative ways in which the government could support our expansion plans. I feel that we need help with training and employee recruitment rather than financial aid.

Appendix 4: Email from the managing director to the finance department

1. The managing director of Horizon wants to expand the business into China or Japan.
   a) Using Appendix 4 and the other information, **explain** one potential advantage and one disadvantage of this growth for Horizon. (8)

   b) Using the appendices and the other information, advise Horizon Hotels on the best way to grow. **Justify** your answer. (12)

2. a) Using Appendix 3, **outline** two reasons why the government is encouraging business growth. (8)

   b) Consider the two options for expanding Horizon outlined in the case study. **Recommend** which one of the two options the company should choose. **Justify** your choice using appropriate evidence. (12)

3. a) Using Appendix 3, **explain** two aims Horizon may have after expanding into China or Japan. (8)

   b) Horizon is a registered public limited company (PLC). Is this the most appropriate type of ownership for this company? **Justify** your answer using the appendices and your own knowledge. (12)

Note: The exam-style questions, answers and commentary in this book were written by the author; in examination the number of marks awarded to questions like these may be different.

Exam-style questions based on case studies

Fizzle Ltd dominating the market

Fizzle Ltd is one of Europe's leading TV manufacturers. Based in Turkey, it holds 20% of the market. The company specialises in TVs, personal computers and monitors, and is Turkey's largest exporter. Starting as a sole trader, Fizzle Ltd has grown rapidly and now operates as a private limited company.

Fizzle Ltd adds value through a superior brand and an excellent supplier and manufacturing method. Fizzle Ltd is growing quickly. Employing over 3000 people worldwide, Fizzle Ltd generates over $200 million each year in revenue.

Fizzle Ltd has seen dramatic growth over the past 10 years, mainly through internal growth. The company now has three main offices around the world and has also bought smaller manufacturers.

Fizzle Ltd has recently targeted foreign schools as an area to grow the business. With only 10% of classrooms in Country X using interactive whiteboards, Fizzle Ltd has targeted this market as one for growth. It aims to sell thousands of TVs and whiteboards abroad over the coming years. However, it has come up against conflicting stakeholders.

Dear Board of Directors,

I represent the local community and I am writing to highlight our concerns about your recent expansion into our country. We would like to see our own companies selling the products to our schools, helping to secure jobs for the future.

We are also worried about the damage to the environment and have joined up with 'Fresh Air' pressure group to voice our concerns.

Appendix 1: Part of a letter to Fizzle Ltd from the local community in Country X where Fizzle Ltd is selling its products

Managing director:

I believe we should become a PLC in order to raise large amounts of money very quickly. By doing this, we will not have to pay any interest on a loan, or have to worry about the potential issues with paying it back.

Finance director:

I believe we should use a bank loan to fund the expansion abroad, because we do not have to lose control of the business and we will see bigger financial profits in the future.

Appendix 2: The different viewpoints of the managing and finance directors

1. a) Using the information in the case study and Appendix 1, **identify** two stakeholders who may have conflicting views on the expansion abroad. **Explain** their differing views. (8)

b) Fizzle Ltd is expanding abroad. Identify a problem that Fizzle Ltd may face. **Recommend** a solution that will help Fizzle Ltd to overcome this problem. (12)

2. a) **Identify** and **explain** one benefit and one drawback of Fizzle Ltd being a private limited company. (8)

b) The directors of Fizzle Ltd need to raise $5 million to fund the expansion abroad. Using the appendices, do you believe that Fizzle should become a private limited company? **Justify** your answer using information in the case study and appendices. (12)

3. a) **Identify** and **explain** two methods that could be used to measure the size of Fizzle Ltd. (8)

b) Fizzle Ltd has experienced internal growth. To what extent do you think the company should rely on internal growth to secure its future? **Justify** your answer. (12)

4. a) **Identify** and **explain** two ways in which Fizzle Ltd may add value to its products and services. (8)

b) Fizzle Ltd adds value to its products through marketing. To what extent is marketing the most important method for Fizzle Ltd to add value to its products? **Justify** your answer. (12)

Note: The exam-style questions, answers and commentary in this book were written by the author; in examination the number of marks awarded to questions like these may be different.

Past paper questions

Paper 1

Section 1

Rafa is the Managing Director of Cambridge Fencing (CF), a limited company that makes fences and gates. The business employs 100 workers. They are paid a low basic wage but can earn high bonuses for good productivity. Recently a large number of employees have left to work for other companies. However CF finds it easy to recruit new workers. The business has been successful but last year its sales and profits fell. Rafa wants this to change.

a) What is meant by a 'limited company'?

____

____

____ (2)

b) Identity two reasons why profits are important to CF.

Reason 1: ______________________________________

____

Reason 2: ______________________________________

____ (2)

Cambridge International IGCSE Business Studies 0450 Paper 13, Q1 a & b Nov 2014

Dmit is a partner in a small retail clothing business. The business has been successful, but it is finding it difficult to compete against larger retailers. The partners are thinking of converting the partnership into a private limited company.

Consider the advantages and disadvantages of converting the partnership into a private limited company. Recommend whether the partners should do this. Justify your answer.

Advantages: ____________________________________

____

____

____

Disadvantages: __________________________________

____

____

____

Recommendation: _________________________________

____

____

____ (6)

Cambridge International IGCSE Business Studies 0450 Paper 11, Q5e Nov 2013

Paper 2

Section 1

The following case study is taken from past papers created by Cambridge Assessment International Education. We have only provided extracts of this case study, and it does not reflect the full case study that you may be provided with in your examination.

Rafael's Reliable Motorbikes (RRM)

RRM was set up by Rafael in Downtown, a town 100 km from Main City in country X. Rafael is a sole trader. He started the business 15 years ago. RRM sells new and used (second-hand) motorbikes to local people who live in Downtown. Rafael is going to pass the control of the business to his son next year. He wants to keep the business owned by the family and does not want anyone else to own part of it.

RRM customers are mainly young men. Many of them are married with families and they cannot afford to buy a car. Rafael thinks he could increase his sales by using market segmentation. Rafael imports some of the motorbikes he sells and buys others from local manufacturers. Imported motorbikes are of higher quality than locally produced ones.

Rafael employs 10 workers to repair, sell and deliver motorbikes. They have worked for Rafael for many years. They are paid high wages and receive health and safety training. The leadership style used by Rafael is democratic, but the workers are worried that things may change when Rafael's son takes control. Rafael has told his son that having well motivated workers is important to the business. Rafael is considering opening another showroom in Main City.

Appendix 1
Downtown population data in 000's

Age	0–16	17–40	41–65	66+
Number of people	125	250	500	125

1 a) RRM is a small business. **Identify** and **explain** two reasons why RRM might remain small. (8)

b) Rafael thinks he could increase his sales by using market segmentation. Consider the advantages and disadvantages of each of the following methods to segment the market. Recommend which method he should use. **Justify** your answer. (12)

i) Age

ii) Income group

iii) Gender

Cambridge International IGCSE Business Studies 0450 Paper 22, Q1 Nov 2015

Skills Builder

AO1: Knowledge and understanding

You need to recall the knowledge you have learned. For example, you should be able to define specialisation and its basic advantages and disadvantages. You simply need to outline a point. This may be a benefit or a drawback. Remember to consider the size, industry and structure of the business.

AO2: Application

You need to **apply** your answers to the example given and focus solely on this example. Your answers must relate to the type of business given. When answering questions based on case studies, refer to the information in the case study and appendices, quoting numbers or information where needed. For example, when answering question 1a on the Horizon Hotels case study, the advantage and disadvantage must **apply** specifically to Horizon as a hotel chain.

AO3: Analysis

You need to demonstrate whether you can look at both sides of the argument and then draw a conclusion. In the second case study, question 2b, you need to look at arguments for both sides: 'Yes, Fizzle Ltd should become a PLC because ... However, perhaps it should remain as it is because ...' There will be evidence you can use for both sides of the argument and this needs to be brought out of the case study. Remember, you can't just outline your own personal opinion here – your statements must be based on evidence.

AO4: Evaluation

Evaluation requires you to give a judgement. This means that once you have analysed the points you have mentioned, you should make a decision based on what you have considered. Overall, what is your verdict on the question? Is there one point that you think is more important? Do you have all the necessary information to make a judgement? If not, what other information do you require? It is also useful to look at whether your judgement is likely to change in the short or long term. Whatever you use, you must show a clear judgement.

It is often said that 'there are no business problems, only people problems'. This phrase highlights how important people are to running a business. Without people – whether customers, employees or management – there is no business.

Getting the best out of people (employees) is the role of management. In this section, you will learn:

- why it is important for businesses to have a well-motivated workforce
- how businesses motivate their employees and how they reward employees for the work they do
- how businesses are organised, what the role of management is, the features of different leadership styles and the role of trade unions
- how businesses recruit, select and train employees, as well as why redundancy might be necessary
- why effective communication is important, and the problems of ineffective communication.

SKILLS BUILDER

Good progress

Knowledge: You show sound knowledge of the concepts and ideas related to people management.

Application: You demonstrate an ability to apply your knowledge and understanding to address specific people management issues.

Analysis: You comment on how firms in different industries motivate and reward employees, how different management styles suit different situations, how and why firms recruit employees, and why they may need to make employees redundant. You can explain, as relevant to a given context, the legal considerations associated with people management.

Evaluation: You evaluate and make basic judgements in relation to appropriate people management strategies.

Excellent progress

Knowledge: You demonstrate a thorough ability to define the concepts and ideas related to people management.

Application: You apply your knowledge to draw conclusions about the potential effectiveness of people management strategies in different contexts.

Analysis: You understand that the biggest variable in business success is people: two firms with identical products will perform very differently because of the people within them – you are able to comment on why this might be the case and how people management might affect a given firm.

Evaluation: You are able to accurately evaluate the appropriateness of people management strategies within a given context, recommending reasoned and logical courses of action as appropriate.

SECTION CONTENTS

2 People in business

Starting points

Imagine you have started your dream job. The business wants to know what would motivate you to work even harder.

- Discuss the different ways in which the business could motivate you.
- Could these methods be split into categories?
- Can you think of any businesses that offer some of these methods, to use as examples?

Motivating employees

The importance of a well-motivated workforce

Aims (2.1.1)

By the end of this section, you should:

- Be able to explain why people work and what motivation means
- Understand the concept of human needs, for example, Maslow's hierarchy
- Understand key motivational theories: Taylor and Herzberg.

What is motivation?

Motivation is the desire to achieve a certain result or outcome. The more an individual desires a certain outcome, the harder they will work (the more motivated they will be) to achieve that outcome.

Δ What motivates you?

Did you know?

In the UAE, DHL has been rated the number one business for employee motivation and development. Its mixture of employee development, a fun working environment and family feel have made it a success with its employees for four years in a row.

What motivates you to complete your Business Studies work, or to work hard in your part-time job? What motivates you to want to get out of bed and go to school or work?

Your answers to these questions are the key to what motivates you personally. Your answers are likely to be similar to those given by others around you, but no two people are motivated in identical ways. The challenge facing business is to find ways to motivate each and every one of its employees.

Analysis

Imagine you are a researcher for a magazine aimed at teenagers. Investigate what motivates your friends. Consider the following:

- Are they motivated by high grades?
- Are they motivated by socialising and friendship?
- Does achievement in sports, drama or the arts motivate them?
- Do they have a part-time job? Does money motivate them?

Present your findings as a diagram or image representing the most common answers.

Well-motivated employees are important to businesses because:

- Increased effort results in higher **productivity** (see 4.1 Production of goods and services).
- Pride in the work leads to improved **quality** (see 4.3 Achieving quality production).
- Loyalty to the business reduces **labour turnover** (changes in employees – see 2.3 Recruitment, selection and training of employees).
- Commitment to the business reduces **absenteeism** (absence from work – see 2.3 Recruitment, selection and training of employees).
- Motivated employees are less likely to engage in **industrial action** (see 2.2 Organisation and management).

Above all, if a business can identify what motivates its employees, the end result could be a **competitive advantage** over rivals. That is why motivation theory matters so much.

Key Term

Competitive advantage: the source of a firm's advantage over competing firms. For example, excellent customer service can be a source of competitive advantage.

There is a wide range of motivation theories put forward by business thinkers, managers and psychologists. Three of the most important theories are:

- Abraham Maslow's Hierarchy of Needs
- Scientific management, developed by F. W. Taylor
- Two-factor theory, devised by Frederick Herzberg.

Maslow's Hierarchy of Needs

In 1954, the American psychologist Abraham Maslow put forward his theory of what motivates human beings. He suggested that work fulfils an important role in satisfying human needs.

Maslow suggested that all human beings have similar needs and that these needs have an order of priority. He called his theory the 'Hierarchy of Needs'.

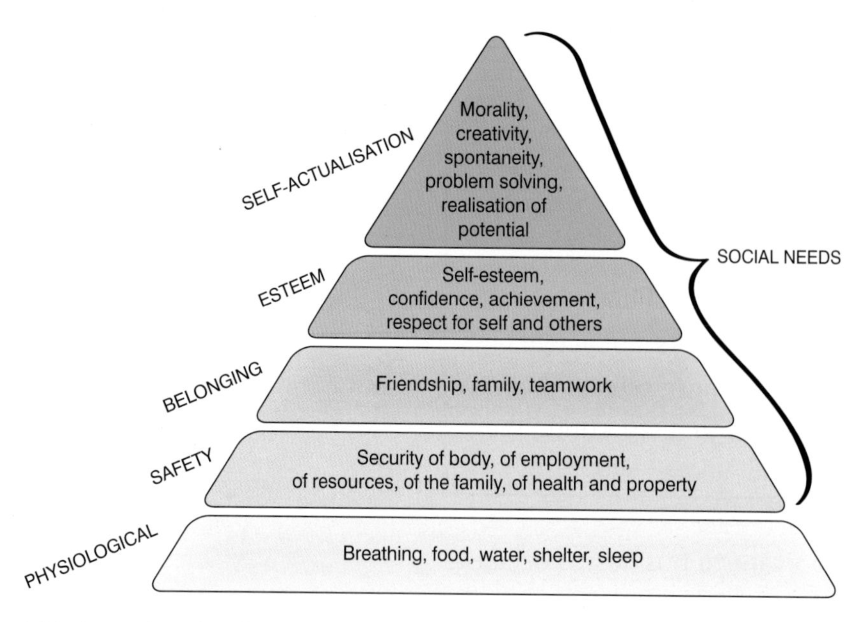

Δ Maslow's Hierarchy of Needs

Need	Example
Physiological At the base of the hierarchy are **physiological needs** – the essentials of human survival, such as food, water, shelter and rest. Maslow placed this type of need at the bottom of the hierarchy because these are the most important needs for any human being: if these basic needs are not met, we simply would not survive. Work helps us to satisfy these needs by providing money to buy food, water, shelter, and so on.	
Safety Once people's physiological needs have been met, they seek the **safety needs** of security, freedom from stress and a sense of stability in their lives. Work helps to satisfy these needs by providing money to 'buy' security. With money, people can afford to live in safe accommodation, they can afford to avoid risk and they may be able to save some money so they feel confident about their future. Freedom from the fear of losing your job (dismissal – see 2.3 Recruitment, selection and training of employees) is also an important 'safety need'.	
Belonging Maslow suggested that once people meet their physiological needs and once they feel safe, they then start to desire a sense of belonging. People like to belong to groups, they like to have friends and they like to be part of a family – Maslow called these **social needs**. Work helps people to satisfy these needs by providing an environment where people can interact and can talk, and by providing a sense of shared purpose (shared aims). For example, if people work on a tough project together, this encourages teamwork and supports relationships between colleagues.	

Need	Example
Esteem Once social needs are met, Maslow argued that people then desire **self-esteem**. When people feel good about themselves, proud of something they have done or when they experience a sense of achievement, their self-esteem grows. How did it feel last time you got a good grade in an assignment? That is an example of self-esteem. Work helps people to achieve self-esteem by setting them targets, giving them projects to work on and providing a sense of achievement when they are successful.	
Self-actualisation The final level of need, **self-actualisation**, refers to people's need to fulfil their potential. Self-actualisation is the ultimate sense of achievement, a feeling that you have achieved something with your life. Many people experience self-actualisation outside of work (through hobbies, and so on), but for some people – teachers, nurses and doctors, for example – the job they do can be a very powerful source of self-actualisation.	

Once all other levels of need are met, it is self-actualisation that continues to motivate people to work harder and to experience new things.

Maslow's Hierarchy of Needs is often split into two levels:

- **lower order needs** – physiological, safety and security/belonging needs
- **higher order needs** – self-esteem and self-actualisation needs.

CASE STUDY

Maslow at work today

A recent Workers and Goodman Management survey examined what motivated employees in New Zealand. They found that 34% of those who responded were motivated by the support of colleagues and a team culture. Acknowledgement of their hard work was considered motivating by 19% of respondents. Only 15% of the people surveyed claimed to be motivated by bonuses and monetary rewards. A third of respondents wanted added responsibility; a quarter wanted a say in strategic decision making; and 17% were keen on being in charge of a special project.

Echoing what Maslow argued over 60 years ago, the survey suggests that money is important, but that teamwork, the chance of promotion and recognition of good work are equally essential in satisfying human needs.

Aldi, the German food retailer, has opened up stores all over Australia. Its rapid growth as a supermarket has been rightly acclaimed in the news but its attitude to motivation and employees' jobs is just as impressive. In all its stores, it pays above the industry norms and looks at employees as long-term investments. Aldi invests in its area managers by putting them through leadership courses, pushing them to be better at their job and giving them the scope and skills to achieve it. This is Maslow at work.

Theory into practice

Maslow's theory has important practical implications for business:

- Satisfying employee needs is not just about money – other things such as teamwork can be equally important.
- Helping people to feel satisfied requires firms to provide opportunities for fulfilment at all levels of the hierarchy.
- Work is important. It gives purpose and meaning to people's lives. If a firm wants to motivate (get the best out of) its people, it must help them find ways to become more satisfied at work.

Ultimately, work provides the means for people to move up Maslow's hierarchy and satisfy more of their needs.

Problems

Maslow's Hierarchy of Needs is only a theory. It does not necessarily fit all people and all situations. Criticisms include:

- There will always be exceptions to any general theory. For example, employees may place little value on gaining praise or developing their potential; artists or musicians may even seek creative needs before financial reward.
- Even if Maslow's theory is true, employees may not seek all levels of need within the workplace. They may be satisfied receiving money from work, while other needs might be met through leisure time.
- Every individual is different, so what motivates one person (money, perhaps) might not motivate someone more concerned with social needs. It could be argued that, in practice, the theory is of little use.

Evaluation

Consider the role of work in satisfying needs for the following people. Which level or levels of Maslow's Hierarchy of Needs might be most significant?

- Olympic athlete
- university student
- rice farmer
- university professor
- airline steward
- teacher
- airline pilot
- bank manager

Apply your knowledge to each person and evaluate what factors might be most significant to these people. Present your findings as a mini role play. Each member of your group should act out one of the roles and explain, in character, what motivates them.

Scientific management (F.W. Taylor)

The work of Frederick Winslow Taylor (1856–1915) shaped the views of managers on motivation for most of the 20th century and remains influential today. Taylor believed that managers could identify the 'best way' to complete a job through a scientific procedure of observation, experiment and calculation. Based on these ideas, he set out a number of recommendations.

- Managers should study the tasks that employees carry out and identify the quickest way of doing each one. Any unnecessary movement or tasks should be eliminated.
- The skills of each employee should be matched to the tasks that need to be carried out. Each employee should be given specific instructions on what to do and how to do it.
- All employees should be supervised and controlled, and those who do not work efficiently should be punished.
- Employees should be rewarded financially for being efficient. Pay schemes should pay more to those who produce more.

Taylor's basic argument was that employees are motivated by money. Taylor suggested that managers should design systems that, in return for hard work, allow employees to maximise their pay – 'a fair day's pay for a fair day's work'.

Taylor's ideas form the basis of the mass-production assembly lines common in many factories today.

Problems

A number of objections have been raised to Taylor's theory:

- It assumes there is a scientific 'best way' to organise production.
- Employees are simply expected to be 'part of the machine', and not to think or contribute to the business.
- The approach suggests managers should control employees. This creates conflict between employees and managers.
- Money is not the only motivator, nor is it the most important one for some people. Taylor's theory ignores the role of work in satisfying an individual's personal and social needs.
- The theory works better with secondary sector jobs, such as production line work. In tertiary (service) industries, such as cinemas, hospitals or even schools, it is difficult to measure 'units' of work and impossible to have rules for how long a task should take.

CASE STUDY

Motivated to serve

The hotel industry is very competitive. With one hotel room (the product) very much like the next, what differentiates hotels is their service. However, good service is very hard to develop and maintain. It requires highly motivated employees who are passionate about looking after customers' needs.

Premium hotel chains – such as The Oriental, Peninsula, Protea (Africa's largest chain of hotels) and six-star hotels such as the Burj Al Arab in Dubai – spend significant sums of money training employees and work hard to ensure they are motivated to provide the best service possible. These motivation incentives include flexible hours, free uniforms, free English language lessons and discounts on hotel products.

Two-factor theory (Frederick Herzberg)

Frederick Herzberg, an American psychologist, conducted research in the 1950s that directly addressed the question of motivation. His results are shown in the illustration.

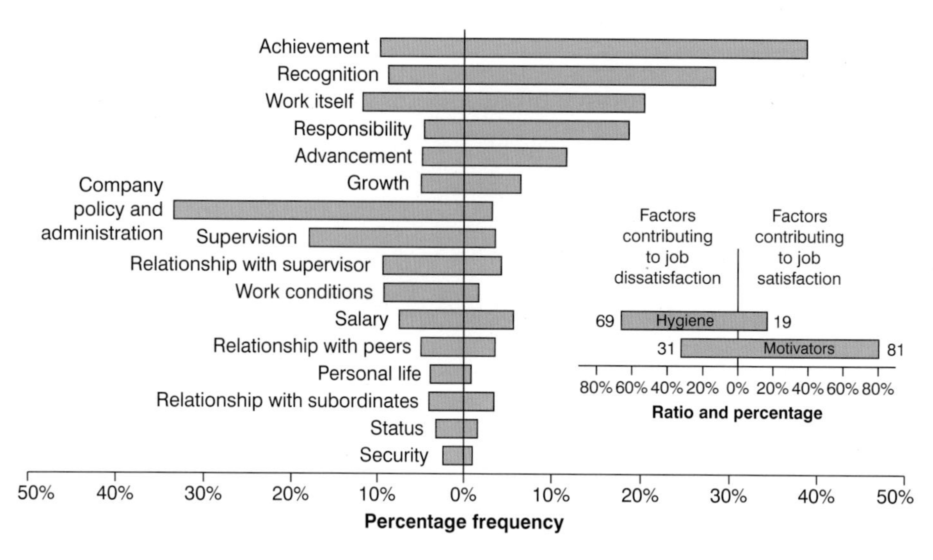

Source: 'One more time: How do you motivate employees' by F. Herzberg

Herzberg used this research to develop his 'two-factor theory' of motivation. This states that there are two sets of factors – motivators and hygiene factors – that are both important in motivating employees, but for very different reasons.

Hygiene factors

Just as poor hygiene can cause illness, Herzberg argued that dissatisfaction with working conditions causes demotivation. The 'hygiene factors' include:

- positive relationships with supervisors or colleagues
- safe and healthy working conditions
- fair pay
- job security.

Herzberg believed that our 'animal' nature leads us to seek the avoidance of pain. If a job can avoid problems in all the areas listed, we won't feel that work is a painful experience. It will prevent dissatisfaction. However, no matter how good these factors are in a job, they will not, by themselves, motivate someone – that is down to the motivators. Good hygiene can stop you getting ill, but it cannot make you happy.

Top Tip

You will notice that many of these factors are similar to Maslow's lower order needs. Being able to analyse how Herzberg's and Maslow's theories are similar and how they are different is an important skill for you to develop.

Motivators

Once the hygiene factors are in place, Herzberg argued that the following factors would motivate employees:

- a sense of achievement
- recognition of effort
- interesting work
- responsibility
- opportunities for promotion and self-improvement.

These factors help to meet the human need to grow psychologically. If a job can provide these motivators, employees will want to work and will enjoy their job.

We can draw several practical conclusions from Herzberg's two-factor theory:

- To motivate a workforce, a business must first make sure that all of the hygiene factors are being met – a fair salary and safe, healthy and pleasant working conditions.
- Jobs must be designed to be meaningful and interesting. The business should train its employees to do their jobs well. They should provide them with the opportunity to develop their skills and offer new challenges and the chance of promotion.

Did you know?

Airbnb, an American business that enables people to lease or rent short-term holiday homes, apartments or hotels, motivates its employees by allowing them to bring their pets to work. It also offers free yoga classes and table tennis at their offices around the world.

Analysis

Identify the motivational strategies of a company familiar to you (perhaps a business that your friends or family work at). Does the firm seem to be aware of the different motivation theories? Analyse which theory the firm seems to be most closely following.

Present your findings as a report to the firm's manager.

Knowledge check

1. **Identify the different levels of Maslow's Hierarchy of Needs.** **(5)**
2. **Explain why 'safety needs' are important to employee motivation.** **(3)**
3. **Identify two problems that arise when applying Maslow's theory in practice.** **(4)**
4. **Explain Taylor's view of employee motivation.** **(3)**
5. **Outline the main points of Herzberg's 'Two-factor theory'.** **(6)**
6. **Explain why having motivated employees is so important to business. Give two reasons.** **(4)**

Total 25 marks

Methods of motivation

Aims (2.1.2)
By the end of this section, you should:
- Understand financial rewards as a method of motivation
- Understand non-financial methods of motivation
- Be able to recommend and justify appropriate methods of motivation in given circumstances.

To motivate their employees, firms use a combination of financial and non-financial methods.

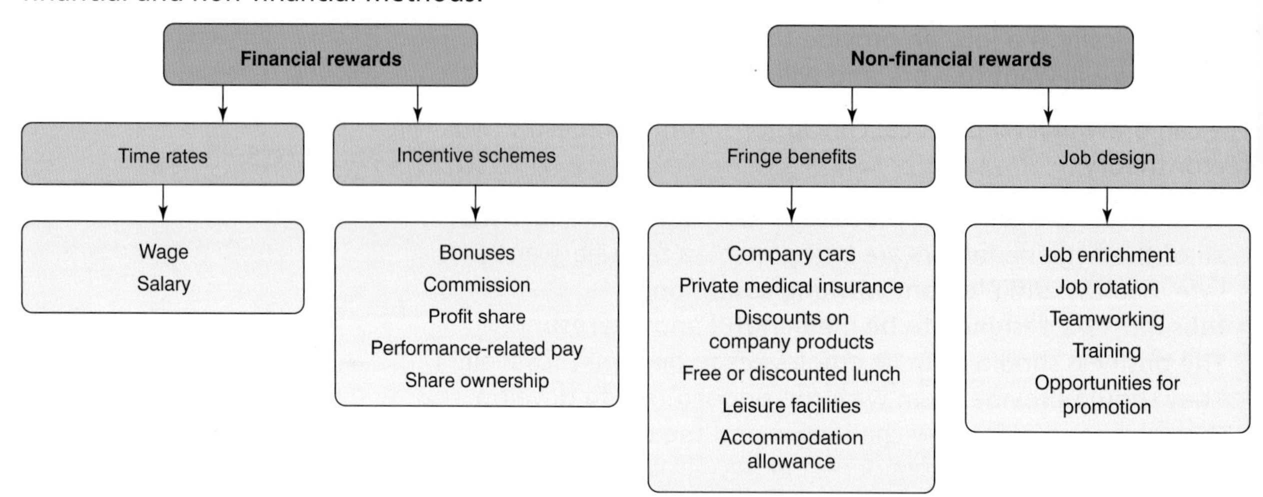

Financial rewards

Businesses reward their employees financially in a variety of ways, all of which have their benefits and their drawbacks.

Wages

Piece rates

A piece-rate system pays employees for each unit of output (each product) they produce. There is no guaranteed level of basic pay, and no sickness or holiday pay. **Piece rates** are used mainly in manufacturing industries, such as clothing factories.

In theory, the harder a person works the more they get paid. Piece rates are, however, criticised for a number of reasons:

- Speed of output becomes more important than product quality (quality may fall as employees aim for maximum output).
- Even employees who work hard have little guarantee of pay levels or job security – if demand falls they will receive little or no pay.
- Employees often resist any changes to work practice (even safety changes) as they slow down production (and therefore reduce their employees' earnings).

A piece rate provides a direct incentive to work harder, but makes no attempt to satisfy any other needs apart from the basic need to earn money (Maslow's safety and security needs).

Time rates

With time rates, employees are paid for the length of time that they work. This may be an hourly rate, common in the retail sector, or a weekly **wage** for completing a set number of hours. **Overtime**, possibly at a higher rate, may be paid for working more than the agreed number of hours.

The main advantage of time rates is that they encourage employees to produce a higher quality of work than piece rates, as there is no focus on the quantity produced. However, there is no reward with time rate for those who work the hardest or achieve the most within the time – so employees may simply do the minimum required.

CASE STUDY

Motivating a million

Working practices at the huge Chinese electronics manufacturer Foxconn Technology Group were widely criticised after a series of suicides among young employees, several workplace accidents and even riots by employees.

In response, Foxconn, which has over 1 million employees, has raised wages by 16–25%. The company also committed itself to providing more training opportunities, as well as better dormitories and leisure facilities, for its employees.

Salary

Employees on a salary system are paid an agreed sum for a year's work. There is more flexibility in terms of when, and how long an employee works in a day, week or month. Schoolteachers are paid a salary for working the normal school year, and for additional time spent marking and preparing lessons. They do not get paid extra for trips, classes after school or running Saturday sports fixtures – such flexibility is the main advantage of salaries.

Like time rates, salaries are criticised for providing no incentive to work hard. Your teachers receive the same salary whether they mark your books or not and whether they run after-school classes or not.

Incentive schemes

Businesses use various ways to improve the financial incentive (motivation) to encourage people to work harder. These include bonuses, commission, performance-related pay, profit share and share ownership.

Bonuses

A bonus is the general term for an additional financial reward given to an employee. Examples include:

- **piece-rate bonus** – additional payment for each unit of output an employee produces above a stated target
- one-off payment – a lump sum paid to an individual, team or whole workforce as a reward for their efforts. It may be a seasonal bonus, such as a holiday bonus, or a reward for attendance, quality or service.

Bonuses act as an incentive because they offer the prospect of reward for additional commitment or for achieving targets. However, if employees expect bonuses as part of their overall payment package, the link between effort and reward is broken. In addition, bonuses can cause conflict due to jealousy between employees.

Commission

Commission is a fee paid to an employee, usually for a sale. It is often used in car dealerships where a percentage of the selling price of the car is paid to the salesperson as a reward for making the sale. This method is used for sales teams all around the world.

Performance-related pay (PRP)

Another type of bonus scheme is **performance-related pay (PRP).** This provides a financial reward to an employee for meeting agreed, individual targets. PRP is closely linked to appraisal. An appraisal is where an employee has their performance reviewed and targets set. If the employee meets the targets, he or she may be awarded a PRP bonus.

PRP is now commonly used for executives (senior management) in both the private and the public sectors. In the sense that PRP provides a financial reward for the 'output' of managers, it represents a management equivalent to the piece rate. However, PRP does have some disadvantages:

- There is potential for conflict between employees and management over the achievement of targets and the level of reward.
- PRP encourages people to work for themselves, not for the team. Imagine a football team where there was a bonus for winning but only for the goal scorers – teamwork would be likely to suffer.
- Performance-related payments need to be large in proportion to salary to have any significant impact. Paying a manager earning over $100 000 a year a $1000 PRP bonus is likely to demotivate rather than motivate.

- PRP ignores the fact that many motivation theorists claim that money is only a very small part of what encourages employees to work harder (see The importance of a well-motivated workforce at the start of this topic).

Profit share

With **profit-share** schemes, employees are offered a share in the annual profits of the organisation. In contrast to PRP, profit sharing encourages employees to work collectively (as a team) for the benefit of the whole organisation. However, the success of profit-share schemes as an incentive for employees depends on how much of the profit is actually shared – and whether there is any profit at all!

Did you know?

American firm Papa Johns shares roughly 30% of its annual profits with employees at all levels of the company. No manager or executive can receive a bonus unless people working under them do — an interesting approach to motivation and collaboration.

Share ownership

Incentive schemes that provide company shares as a reward produce similar benefits to profit-share schemes. As shareholders, employees benefit financially from the success of the business. Issuing shares as a reward is very common in start-up companies or high-tech firms. Some firms pay people in shares only. Steve Jobs, for instance, was paid only $1 per year for his work at Apple. However, he did receive 5.5 million shares in Apple (valued at several billion dollars) and the use of a private plane (a very nice **fringe benefit** – see Non-financial rewards on the next page).

CASE STUDY: Keep the employees happy

Australian farms often give employees monthly bonuses for their hard work, with employees also rewarded with a share of additional profits made on products every season. This helps to keep the employees loyal.

Application

Identify appropriate methods of financial reward and incentive for the following positions:

- teacher
- manual factory employee
- engineer
- car salesperson
- waitress/waiter
- soldier.

Remember to apply your knowledge. Analyse why the types of pay you suggest are the most appropriate for each employee. Present your findings as a visual mind map, with an image of each position surrounded by possible rewards or incentives.

Non-financial rewards

In addition to financial rewards, many organisations offer other forms of non-financial rewards as part of an employee's basic package. These are called fringe benefits, and may include: a company car, private medical insurance, discounts on company products, a company laptop computer and mobile phone, free or discounted lunch, free or discounted childcare, access to leisure and social facilities, an accommodation allowance.

Fringe benefits have become increasingly important as part of the overall payment package given to employees – particularly for management and executive positions. Fringe benefits are significant for a number of reasons:

Status	Receiving fringe benefits can help to give jobs more prestige (status) and helps to provide the 'esteem needs' identified in Maslow's hierarchy.
Motivation	Just as important as money is whether people feel valued at work and the quality of the working environment. Fringe benefits help to meet these additional non-financial motivational needs.
Labour retention	Many fringe benefits, such as access to childcare, help to make life easier for employees. If they have a better-quality working life, they are less likely to look for a job with another company. Good **labour retention** helps to reduce the cost of recruiting new employees and the cost of training. It also helps maintain productivity (new employees will, for a time, be less efficient than experienced employees).
Cost	The value of a fringe benefit is often higher for the employee than the firm. Supermarkets, for example, often allow employees to take food home at the end of the day that is at the end of its shelf-life and cannot be sold. For the firm, this carries virtually no cost, but for the employee it is a valuable perk (benefit).

CASE STUDY

Teacher benefits

International schoolteachers often live many thousands of miles from home. Benefits packages that help teachers feel comfortable and secure (Maslow's 'safety needs') ensure that they are more likely to remain at the school for the long term, reducing labour turnover. The benefits also mean that teachers can focus on their jobs rather than worrying about their lives.

One school in Bahrain listed the following benefits for teachers:

'Annual return airfare home, a shipping allowance of $2000, relocation allowance of $1000, furnished housing, medical/dental and life insurance, free schooling for children, free visa for teacher and dependants, and a retirement plan (10% of base salary).'

Other methods of motivation

△ An employee at a fast-food outlet might be switched between cooking, serving and cleaning duties on different days.

According to Maslow and Herzberg, rewards (whether financial or non-financial) are not by themselves enough to motivate employees. Other needs must also be met. Maslow's 'higher order' needs and Herzberg's 'motivators' suggest that the personal rewards of doing a job are just as important as (or more important than) the direct reward.

Job design is therefore crucial to motivation. A job must be 'designed' to be meaningful and interesting. To achieve this, each employee's job should provide the following:

Job rotation

The process of switching an employee between tasks or jobs over a period of time is called **job rotation**. The variety of tasks should help to prevent boredom, while the **multiskilling** of the employee adds to the flexibility of the organisation.

Another result, however, could be that the employee becomes less practised and so less productive in any one task. Moreover, switching between equally routine tasks does not necessarily make a job more motivating than performing just one routine task.

Job enlargement

Allowing employees to perform more tasks in a production process enables them to see the complete product. This is known as **job enlargement**. The theory is that employees gain greater job satisfaction by performing more tasks and seeing the end result of their efforts.

Job enlargement is not, however, a solution on its own. Giving employees more work to do can cause resentment if they feel they are being asked to work harder without reward.

△ Job enrichment differs from job enlargement, because employees are given more responsibility (not just more work) and may be given more pay.

Job enrichment

To overcome the problems of job rotation and job enlargement, different methods have been tried to make a job more challenging or rewarding. Called **job enrichment**, the methods include:

- allowing employees to use, develop and demonstrate different skills
- enabling employees to take responsibility for their actions and working environment.

Job enrichment is not easy to achieve for all job roles. Unskilled manual jobs, such as a simple production line job, may be limited in scope and difficulty. Once an employee has mastered the basic task, it may be very difficult to find ways to make the job more rewarding. In this situation, job rotation may be more relevant. Equally, some employees might not want their job enriched. Some employees might be happy performing a simple task and resent (dislike) management efforts to enrich the job.

Training

Training employees will help improve the skills they have, as well as add new ones. This could be in two ways:

- **On-the-job training:** this is carried out at the employees' place of work while they are actually doing their job. It could be given by another employee, often more senior, or by an external trainer. It is often used in large fast-food chains such as McDonald's or KFC. This method can be cheaper to offer, as the business uses existing employees while they are at work. However, the increase in skills may be minimal, as the trainee learns only from those employees currently at the business.
- **Off-the-job training:** employees go to a place away from work to undergo training from external trainers. This could be an accountant learning new software or a manager learning new motivation techniques for employees. This requires employees to have time away from work, often costing money. It does, however, give the employee a chance to gain new skills from people outside the business.

Training employees will help improve their skills and efficiency, and can help them to feel valued by the business. This could lead to a greater output from each employee while at work, contributing to larger profits for the business in the long term.

> **Top Tip**
>
> You will notice that the ideas behind Maslow's and Herzberg's theories are very similar – Herzberg's motivators contribute, for example, towards the achievement of Maslow's higher order needs. Both theories suggest that employees are motivated when they enjoy their work and feel that it is allowing them to grow as individuals.

Empowerment

Giving employees the power to make the decisions that affect their working lives is known as **empowerment**. This could include the right to make decisions about how and when work is done, and taking responsibility for those decisions.

Empowerment is at the centre of Herzberg's theory of motivation – giving responsibility, providing opportunities for advancement and making work itself more interesting. Not only can empowerment motivate, it can also get the best out of the workforce by making use of their talents and ideas. If the people who know most about the issues involved make decisions, these might be better decisions than the managers could make.

In practice, empowerment may cause a number of problems:

- The reality may fall far short of the theory, with little power really being given by managers who do not trust the workforce.

- Empowerment may be used as an excuse to cut costs, by removing levels of management and increasing employees' workload.
- Genuine empowerment poses the danger that effective control and coordination may be lost. This could lead to expensive mistakes or a lack of strategic direction.

CASE STUDY

Change in China

Business in China is changing. Not only are Chinese firms growing, they are also changing the way they manage their employees. In the past, Chinese firms treated people as a simple resource. The main objective was business growth. Relationships with people, the softer side of management, were ignored. However, the new generation of Chinese employees, those born in the 1980s and 1990s, are seeking jobs that are fulfilling and meaningful. They expect fair status, more learning opportunities and they want their supervisors to be advisors rather than just bosses. A number of Chinese companies, such as Baidu (China's top search engine), say they have been directly influenced by the open, collaborative and empowered work environments pioneered by companies such as Google and Yahoo.

Teamworking

Teamworking helps to meet employees' social needs for interaction and friendship in the workplace. It involves:

- organising employees into small groups (teams)
- setting objectives for the team to achieve
- giving the team responsibility and rewards for achieving targets, such as improved quality
- training employees to be able to carry out any role within the team.

Many organisations, such as Ford, Levi Strauss and Porsche, have reported benefits from teamworking. These include: increased job satisfaction, higher productivity, improved product quality, reduced labour turnover and absenteeism, and improved employee flexibility.

Opportunities for promotion

All methods of motivation will have limitations in their effectiveness if there are no opportunities for employees to progress up the levels of the business through promotion. Promoting employees internally (from within) helps to keep them, as they believe they can develop a career at the business, rather than leaving to go elsewhere. This can save the business money, as it doesn't need to advertise for new employees. This is vital if a business wants to keep its best employees. However, it does depend on having the jobs available to fill.

Although having motivated employees helps the business succeed, it is not always possible for smaller businesses to offer such a wide range of tasks, training or financial rewards. Therefore, businesses take a different approach to the options outlined, picking the methods that best suit their needs. A smaller firm may find it difficult to profit share and therefore opt to increase bonuses or commission, whereas a large international company such as Volkswagen may look at job enrichment and rotation as key motivators.

Analysis

Identify the methods of non-financial motivation used by a business you are familiar with. Analyse why you think the firm uses these particular methods. Consider how well these methods actually motivate the employees.

Present your findings as a magazine article that analyses the effectiveness of non-financial motivational strategies.

Knowledge check

1. **Identify two methods of financial reward. (2)**
2. **Identify two methods of non-financial reward. (2)**
3. **Explain, using an example, what is meant by the term commission. (3)**
4. **Identify one major advantage of profit sharing as a method of financial incentive. (2)**
5. **Justify appropriate methods of pay for the following: (12)**
   - **a) nurse**
   - **b) freelance graphic designer**
   - **c) lawyer**
   - **d) manual production line employee**
   - **e) production line manager**
   - **f) hotel cleaner.**
6. **Explain, using an example, what is meant by the term fringe benefit. (3)**
7. **Define the term job rotation. (2)**
8. **Define the term job enrichment. (2)**

Total 28 marks

Check your progress:

- ✓ I can explain why it is so important to have a well-motivated workforce.
- ✓ I understand the concept of human needs and can outline the key motivational theories.
- ✓ I can outline the different methods of motivation, both financial and non-financial.
- ✓ I can recommend and justify appropriate methods of motivation in given circumstances.

Organisation and management

Organisational charts

Aims (2.2.1)

By the end of this section, you should:

- Understand simple hierarchical structures: span of control, levels of hierarchy, chain of command
- Understand the roles and responsibilities of directors, managers, supervisors and other employees in an organisation and the inter-relationships between them.

The internal organisation of a business

An **organisational chart** is a diagram that highlights the key roles and responsibilities of a business's employees. It should show the different **departments** within the business and which employees and job roles are included within each department. This organisation chart shows the business's departments (Finance, Operations, HR and Marketing) and the individual roles within the finance department.

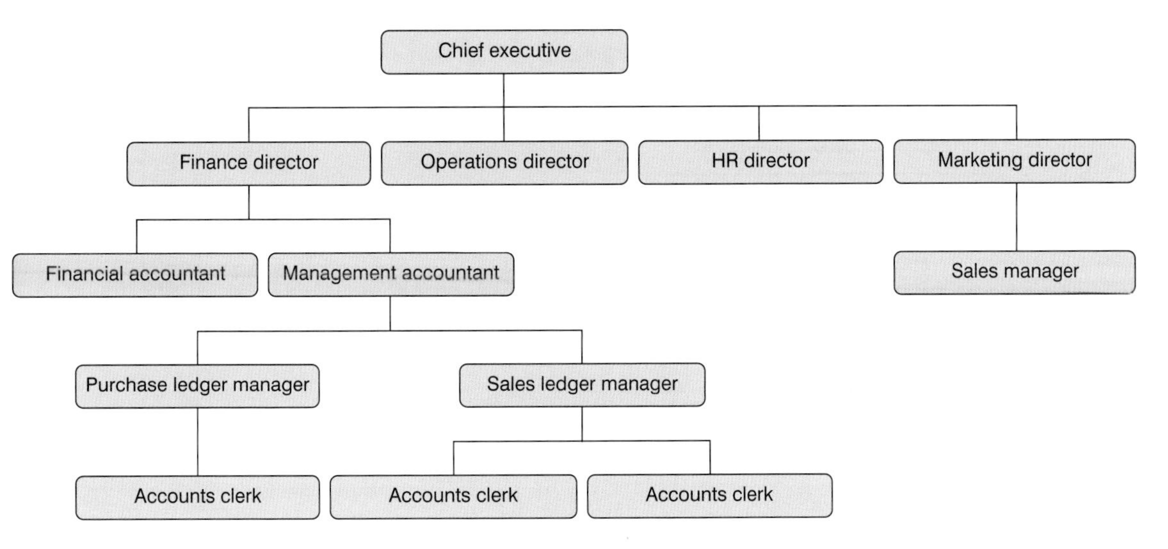

Key features of an organisational chart

Departments. A business is organised into departments. Each department is responsible for a particular function or role; for example, finance, operations, human resources and marketing.

Hierarchy. An organisational chart is also a hierarchy. This means that different positions have different levels of authority. For example, the marketing director, finance director, operations director and HR director are all on the same level, and therefore all have the same authority. The finance director is the level above the financial accountants and management accountants – the accountants have less authority than the financial director and the same amount of authority as each other.

Chain of command. The chain of command shows how communication and tasks are passed down the business from the top to the bottom. For example, the management accountant passes tasks down the chain of command to the sales ledger manager, who in turn might pass them on to the accounts clerks.

Delegation. This means that someone higher up the chain of command can give responsibility to, or delegate the authority to, someone to perform a task. For example, the marketing director might be asked to compile a sales report for top-performing products. He or she might decide to delegate the task to the sales manager, although he or she is still responsible for the completion of the task.

Span of control. The span of control shows how many individuals or **subordinates** are under the control of one manager. For example, the sales ledger manager has a span of control of two: two accounts clerks.

Key Term

Subordinate: an employee who is under the authority of another.

Part of a typical supermarket's organisational chart might look like the one shown.

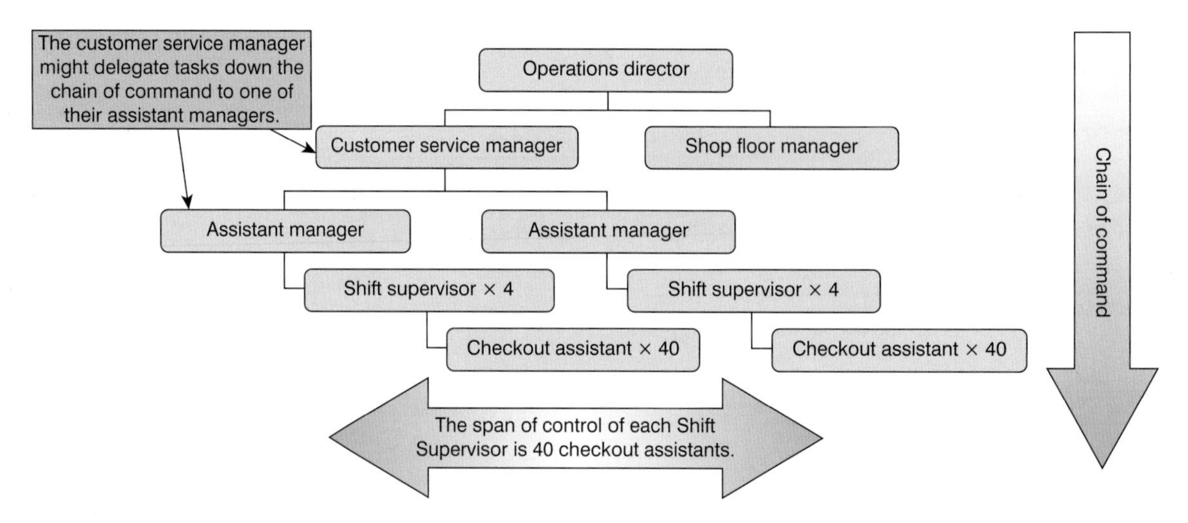

Flat structures

Flat structures tend to have short chains of command and wider spans of control. This is because the organisation has fewer levels of authority.

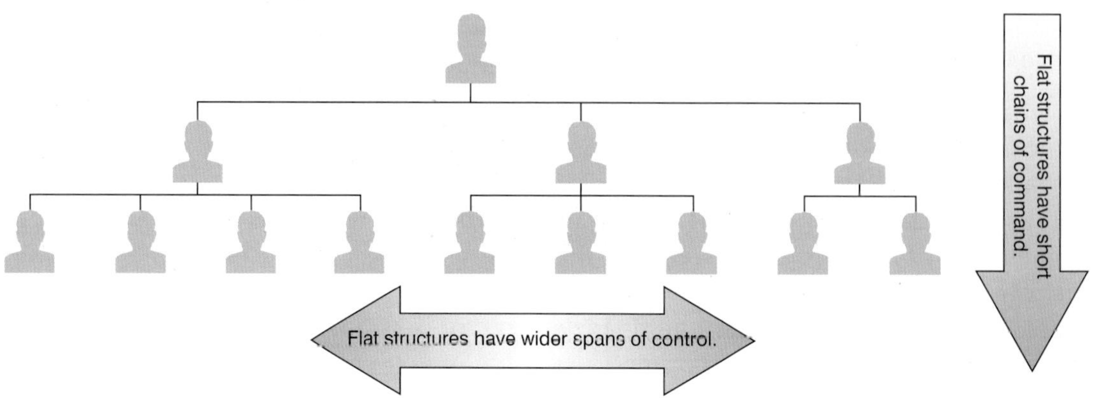

Benefits of having a flat structure	Problems of having a flat structure
✓ Easier communication as the chain of command is shorter, which means there are fewer levels of hierarchy for communication to be passed down ✓ Fewer management roles, which reduces the need for the business to pay high management salaries ✓ Easier for managers to delegate tasks as they have a wide span of control ✓ More delegation to subordinates, which gives employees more responsibility, therefore employees' motivation might increase	✗ Fewer management positions, so employees have little chance of promotion ✗ As managers have such a wide span of control, it is more difficult to monitor the performance of their subordinates, who may make costly mistakes

Tall structures

Organisations that have long chains of command and narrow spans of control are said to have tall structures.

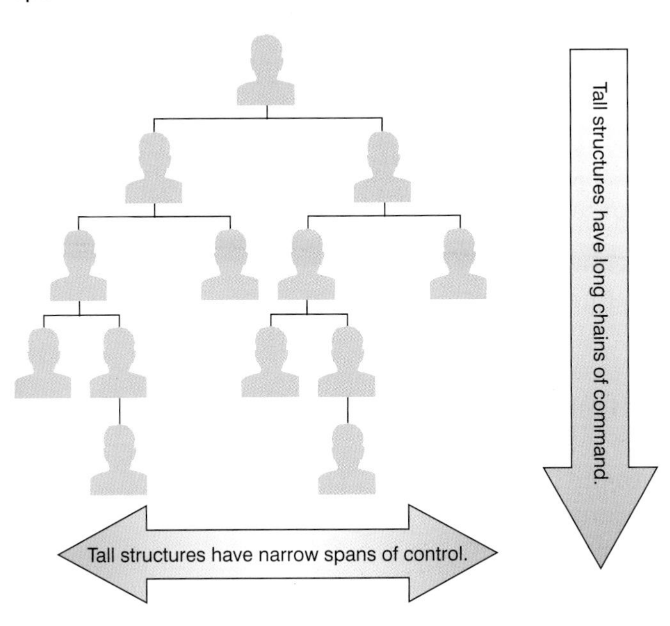

Benefits of having a tall structure	Problems of having a tall structure
✓ More line managerial positions makes it easier to monitor subordinates' performance ✓ More chance of promotion for subordinates, which can be motivating	✗ Communication takes longer, as chains of command are longer ✗ More management positions, which can mean the business has to pay higher salaries, increasing their costs. Businesses can sometimes change this by removing a level of management. This process is called **de-layering**.

CASE STUDY

De-layering

The Tata Group, the Indian-based multinational company, carried out organisational restructuring in all of their subsidiary (minor) companies. The companies included in the group, such as Tata Engineering and Tata Steel, had eight to nine levels in their hierarchy and wanted to reduce the number of layers (levels) to four or five. The de-layering was planned to expand job responsibilities and reduce Tata's overheads. This was achieved by cutting out the number of managerial roles, many of which they thought were underperforming.

Application

Research your school's organisational chart. Using either A3 or A2 paper, draw the school's organisational chart and annotate it to illustrate the teachers' span of control. Highlight the advantages of having either a narrow or a wide span. Try to include key terminology, such as delegation, authority and communication.

Why have an organisational chart?

Organisational charts are vital for individual employees to understand the roles and responsibilities of other employees within the organisation. This has a number of advantages, as it:

- **helps clear communication:** the chart will show how the business is organised, so selecting the right communication channel is easier
- **makes accountability easier:** employees have a clear understanding of who they are accountable (responsible) to and who they have responsibility for
- **shows the inter-relationships between departments:** by establishing the relationships between different departments, the business becomes more efficient, as employees can clearly identify who is responsible for a particular issue.

Roles, responsibilities and inter-relationships

Role	Responsibility	Inter-relationship
Directors	Appointed by the shareholders to act on their behalf and run the day-to-day activities of the business. Each year, an AGM (Annual General Meeting) will be held to review the directors and their success. Directors set the vision, strategy and structure of the business.	The directors have to work closely with the managers and shareholders to make sure the business is acting appropriately, hitting its goals and maintaining standards of practice.

Managers	Managers are in charge of the employees of the business. They assign duties, roles and specific tasks. They then monitor the employees to make sure all standards are being achieved.	Managers have an important role, as they relay messages and progress between employees and the directors. They work closely with supervisors to make sure the vision is implemented and achieved.
Supervisors	A supervisor is normally in charge of a small group of employees who are completing a specific task. For example, within a car factory there will be a supervisor for the employees who are in charge of the interior fittings such as the steering wheel. They have responsibilities, like a manager, but for the standards and output of a smaller number of employees and areas.	The supervisor's role is to work closely with the employees in their specific groups. Their role means that they will feed back to their line managers about progress and report any issues. They have limited interaction with directors.
Other employees	All employees have a responsibility to undertake the duties they have been given when employed. The tasks will vary depending on their role within the business, but all employees should try to complete these to the standards set.	Employees are often the key to achieving a firm's vision and goals successfully. In some businesses, employees are encouraged to work closely with managers and supervisors, even giving feedback directly to directors. However, their main job will be working with their supervisor and manager.

Knowledge check

1. **Outline the term chain of command.** **(2)**
2. **Bolanle is a project manager for a Nigerian building firm, BuildTech. He has a deadline in two weeks' time, so he wants to pass the authority of completing some of his tasks to one of his subordinates. BuildTech has a tall structure, Bolanle is one of many project managers.**

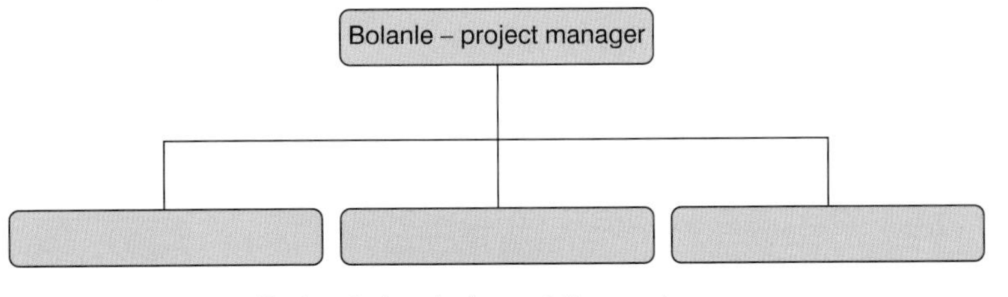

Designated project completion employees

a) Explain what is meant by the term subordinate. **(2)**

b) Identify Bolanle's span of control. **(1)**

c) Explain one advantage and one disadvantage to Bolanle of his company having a tall organisational structure. **(4)**

d) Explain the differences between a tall and a flat structure in an organisational chart. **(4)**

Total 13 marks

Role of management

Aims (2.2.2)
By the end of this section, you should:

- Understand the functions of management, for example, planning, organising, coordinating, commanding and controlling
- Recognise the importance of delegation and trust versus control.

Functions of management

Managers of a business have a responsibility to plan, organise their resources, coordinate, make decisions and control business activity to ensure that the required outcome is achieved. Managers are often held accountable for their actions, so ensuring that they meet all of these responsibilities is vitally important.

Planning: a good manager plans effectively. This means having a clear aim or objective that has to be achieved. However, a good manager will prepare a number of strategies in order to achieve this aim and will draw up (think of or make a record of) a **contingency plan** in case particular strategies are not successful.
Organising: being organised on a day-to-day basis is essential to ensure that the manager uses his or her own time as effectively as possible. However, organisation also means ensuring that the business's resources are used as effectively as possible, including time, money and human resourcing.
Coordinating: achieving objectives often requires that different functions of a business, or different employees, work together. A good manager will coordinate these functions or employees to ensure that they are aware of the common aim and how it can be achieved.
Commanding: a good manager has to have the respect of their employees and be able to direct them on how they are expected to perform. This does not mean that managers simply tell people what to do. A good manager will choose an approach to commanding that best suits their workforce.
Controlling: as a manager is held accountable for their actions and is often responsible if the business struggles, it is important that they are continually controlling and evaluating whether or not the aim or objective is going to be met. Good managers will then have to make decisions if they are not happy with the business's performance.

CASE STUDY

Businessman of the year

Cheng Wei, co-founder and chief executive of China's largest ride-sharing service provider Didi Chuxing (Didi), is Forbes Asia's Businessman of the Year. Didi has 85% market share in China, and has managed to survive and flourish despite the global growth of Uber. Cheng Wei is only 33 years old. He started his career at Alibaba before his entrepreneurial skills helped create a business that operates in 400 cities, attracting over 300 million users. He showed strong leadership during a multi-million-dollar battle with Uber, investing $5.8 milllon in one day to keep the business afloat.

The importance of delegation

Delegating is when a manager gives authority to a subordinate to complete a particular task. Although the manager is still responsible for the completion of that task, the subordinate now has the responsibility of how to complete the task.

A good manager will decide when delegation is necessary, in order to make the best use of the resources at their disposal.

The benefits of delegation

For the manager	For the subordinate
✓ Delegating jobs to somebody else allows the manager more time to focus on other tasks and to keep an overview of what is happening in the business or department. ✓ They can organise their time more effectively. ✓ It gives managers the chance to assess their subordinates' abilities, helping them to make better decisions in the future.	✓ It empowers the subordinate; having more responsibility may increase their motivation. ✓ Taking on more responsibility allows employees to prove their abilities, which could help them gain promotion in the future.

Choosing the right time to delegate

Whether or not the delegation is successful depends on the manager's ability to choose the right tasks to delegate to the right people. If a manager never delegates, they will not be using their resources effectively. Likewise, if they choose to delegate too much, they will have less control over whether the task is completed effectively.

Application

Working in groups of two, interview a manager at your school, such as a head of department or the headteacher. Your task is to find out what makes this person an effective manager.

Plan 5–10 questions that you think will allow you to gain the relevant information on how your chosen person does their job. Report back to your group using either a presentation or a 600-word written report.

Trust vs control

If a manager trusts their subordinates, they are much more likely to delegate tasks. Trust comes when a manager has experienced subordinates who have completed tasks successfully in the past. If a manager has very little trust in the subordinates, he or she is unlikely to delegate much authority.

A risk that managers take with delegation is that they lose some control over the completion of the tasks. This is important because managers are responsible for the completion of the task even if they have delegated it to someone else. The more a manager delegates, the less control they have, which carries a greater risk.

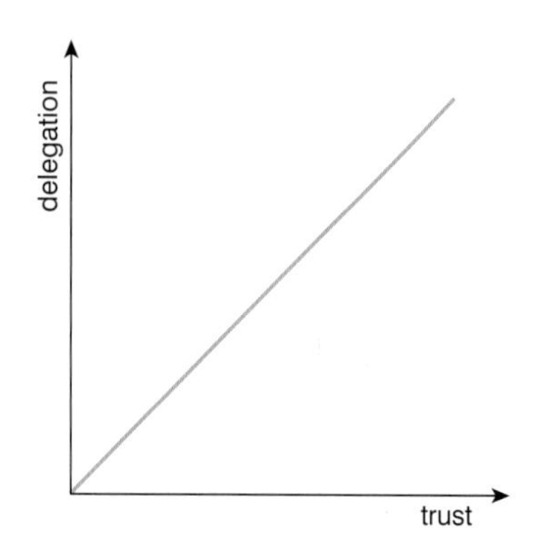

Δ This graph illustrates that the more trust a manager has in their subordinates, the more likely they are to delegate tasks to them

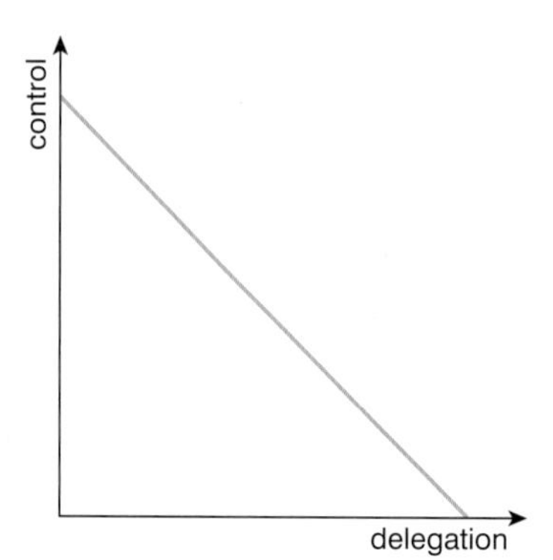

Δ This graph illustrates that the more a manager delegates, the less control they have over the tasks they have delegated

Δ During an operation, surgeons delegate less risky tasks to others.

Top Tip

Delegation, authority, trust and control are quite subtle concepts. Take time to understand the differences between them and ensure you can use the different terms appropriately.

Controlling business activity and organising are both key attributes of a good manager. Therefore, finding the right balance between delegating tasks on the one hand, and completing some themselves in order to maintain control on the other, is essential to ensuring objectives are met.

Knowledge check

Fawaz is a restaurant manager in Dakar, Senegal. The restaurant has 40 employees, 60% of whom work part-time. Fawaz has four shift supervisors who are new to the business. The restaurant is open seven days a week.

1. **Explain two characteristics that would make Fawaz a good manager. (4)**
2. **Explain how coordinating is an important characteristic for a manager like Fawaz. (4)**

Fawaz is looking to delegate some tasks to his supervisors, but he is unsure whether or not he can trust them.

3. **Define the term delegation. (2)**
4. **Explain two benefits to Fawaz of delegating tasks to his supervisors. (4)**
5. **Explain one disadvantage to Fawaz of delegating tasks to his supervisors. (2)**

Total marks 16

Leadership styles

Aims (2.2.3)

By the end of this section, you should:

- Understand the features of the main leadership styles, for example, autocratic, democratic and laissez-faire
- Be able to recommend and justify an appropriate leadership style in given circumstances.

Introduction

Leaders are the people in an organisation who have:

- a vision of the direction in which the organisation should move
- innovative ideas as to how this vision might be achieved
- the commitment and dedication to follow their ideas through
- the ability, self-belief and personal qualities to gain the support of others.

Importantly, leadership is something that anyone, in any position in an organisation, can demonstrate. This is in contrast to management, which is a position of formal authority that an individual holds.

Δ A sports coach has the formal (management) authority to organise and command the players, but there may also be other leaders within the team. The other players may show leadership during a game, in the dressing room or in their general behaviour and attitude.

Leadership styles

Each individual leader adopts (takes on) very different styles and methods in leading others. They range from **autocratic** (the strictest) to **laissez-faire** (the least strict) **leadership**.

Autocratic

Δ Autocratic leadership may make employees feel undervalued.

With an autocratic style of leadership, the leader makes all the decisions. The leader tells others what to do and controls them closely in the way they do it. Autocratic leaders do not seek the opinions of others; they know what they want to achieve and how.

Where circumstances demand the need for swift (fast), determined decision making, autocratic leadership may be the appropriate style. Autocratic leadership is, for example, the normal style of leadership in the armed forces. In business, autocratic leadership tends to be used where crisis situations demand it or where it suits a leader's dominant (controlling) personality. The workforce is more likely to accept autocratic leadership if employees believe it can save their jobs.

Autocratic leadership can cause problems when the dominance (power) of the leader leaves employees feeling ignored, demotivated and resentful of being controlled.

Democratic

The word democratic means that decisions are made by the people and for the people. A **democratic leadership** style is characterised by allowing employees to play a full part in decision making. This may be achieved through:

- **participation** – where the leader seeks opinions from employees on as many decisions as possible. The leader may use suggestion schemes or quality circles (see 4.3 Achieving quality production) to ensure that employees have an input into how the business is managed.
- **teamworking** – democratic leaders delegate (pass on) decision-making power to teams. They do not feel that they have to control every decision. They encourage teamwork and discussion of ideas.

The aim of democratic leadership is to remove conflict ('them versus us') between managers and employees and to replace it with a culture in which all employees, regardless of their position in the organisation, are treated the same.

Democratic leadership ensures that employees feel valued and helps to meet Maslow's higher order need of self-esteem (see 2.1 Motivating employees). A democratic approach may be appropriate in firms with a large number of highly trained employees.

However, democratic leadership can slow down decision making and it may not be appropriate where quick decisions are needed (particularly, for instance, in a crisis situation).

Δ Democratic leadership encourages teamwork and discussion.

In smaller organisations, however, because there are fewer employees, managers often find it easier (and faster) to ask for employees' opinions. Additionally, when employees' motivation is low, giving employees a say in decision making may help increase their motivation.

CASE STUDY

Leadership style

Most successful business leaders use a combination of different leadership styles. However, there are some who are particularly effective using a democratic leadership style.

The CEO and chairman of PepsiCo, Indra Nooyi, is known for taking a personal interest in the lives of her employees, going as far as to speak to parents to get new talent into the company. Muhtar Kent, CEO and chairman of Pepsi's competitor, Coca-Cola, also uses a democratic style and continually asks for input from colleagues on all areas of the business. He has created collaborative management teams to deal with specific issues.

These types of leaders use an inclusive working environment to help encourage employees and ensure their business's success.

Laissez-faire

Laissez-faire literally means 'let it be'. The laissez-faire style is one in which leaders leave employees to get on with their work, with little or no interference. The leader may set broad aims and guidelines, but the day-to-day input of the leader will be limited.

In some situations, employees may enjoy the freedom and respond by taking responsibility and showing creativity. In other situations, employees may lack purpose and direction. They may also take the opportunity to do as little work as possible.

Laissez-faire leadership suits a leader who has a more passive (easy-going) personality. A laissez-faire style is also most appropriate in organisations with highly trained employees, where the production of high quality work is a major motivator. Design or marketing agencies are good examples of situations where a laissez-faire style may be appropriate. However, this style would be inappropriate with low-skilled employees performing routine tasks.

Δ Laissez-faire leadership may result in only highly trained employees getting the work done.

CASE STUDY Very different leadership styles

Steve Jobs, one of the founders of Apple, was widely regarded as an exceptional business leader and well known for having an autocratic leadership style. Employees who worked for him gave examples of Jobs frequently shouting at them and demanding his own way on even the smallest of issues. Given the success of the iPod, the iPad and the iPhone, it is a leadership style that appears to have worked.

Steve Jobs' successor, Tim Cook (Apple's current chief executive officer), has a very different style. He is much more democratic. Employees have reported a greater involvement in decision making and the greater willingness of Tim Cook to listen to employees' opinions. This approach will be put to the test as Apple expands into new markets and products, bringing Apple into competition with companies that adopt different leadership styles with their employees.

Factors affecting leadership styles

There is no single 'best' style of leadership. Different situations demand different leadership styles. The most effective leaders are those who can use all of the styles, at different times and with different people, as appropriate to the current task or situation.

The existing culture of an organisation will be crucial in determining the success of a leader's style.

When recommending and justifying an appropriate leadership style, you will need to consider the following factors.

- **The leader's personality.** A strong-willed, dominant personality will tend to an autocratic style. A more passive (easy-going) person may be more laissez-faire.
- **The type of workforce.** An autocractic style would suit an unskilled and unmotivated workforce. A democratic or laissez-faire style is best for a highly trained, motivated and ambitious workforce.
- **Culture**. A workforce that has become used to a democratic style will resist (refuse to accept) an autocrat's attempts to dominate decision making.
- **Context**. The workforce is more likely to accept autocratic leadership if employees believe it can save their jobs!

Analysis

Investigate and evaluate the leadership styles of two of the following:

- Richard Branson (Virgin Group)
- Sheikh Khalifa bin Zayed Al Nahyan (President of the United Arab Emirates)
- Aung San Suu Kyi (Myanmarese politician)
- Angela Merkel (Chancellor of Germany)
- Sheryl Sandberg (Chief Operating Officer of Facebook)
- Alex Ferguson (former Manager of Manchester United)

1. Identify the leadership style for each person.
2. Comment whether the style is appropriate for the context.
3. Analyse examples of their leadership style.
4. Evaluate whether the style seems to have been successful.

Present your findings as a newspaper article, comparing and contrasting the styles of the two leaders. Use the following heading for your article:

'Whose Style is Better? Recommending Appropriate Leadership Styles'

Knowledge check

1. **Using appropriate examples, outline the differences between management and leadership.** **(4)**
2. **Identify one situation when an autocratic management style might be most appropriate.** **(1)**
3. **Outline the differences between democratic and laissez-faire management styles.** **(4)**
4. **Outline a suitable leadership style for each of the following situations:** **(8)**
   a) creative design agency
   b) law firm
   c) car production factory
   d) hospital surgery.

Total 17 marks

Trade unions

Aims (2.2.4)
By the end of this section, you should:
- Understand what a trade union is and the effects of employees being union members.

What are trade unions?

Trade unions are organisations that represent the interests of employees within a workplace. They are normally a completely separate organisation from the business that the employees work for. The trade union exists to negotiate or bargain on behalf of the employees.

Collective bargaining

Collective bargaining describes the negotiations between an employer and a trade union. The more members a union has, the stronger their bargaining position (the more power the employees have). A trade union's position is also strongest when there is only one union negotiating with an employer: when there is more than one, they often have slightly different agendas (priorities), which makes it harder for all of the unions to get what they want from the negotiation.

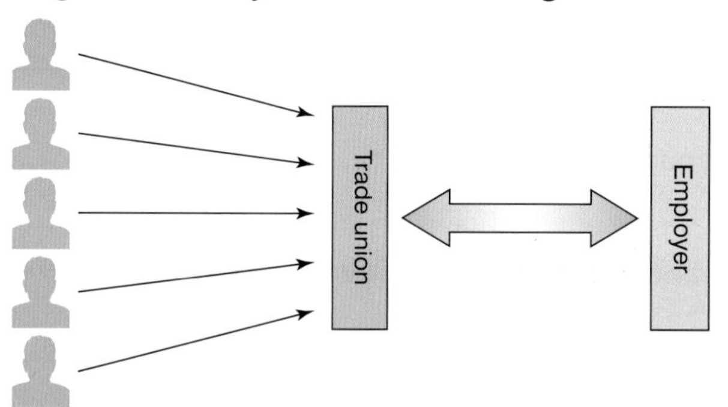

Did you know?

The World Federation of Trade Unions was founded in 1945 to help bring together all the different trade unions around the world. It allows them to be represented by one organisation across the world. It now represents 92 million employees, from 126 countries across six continents.

Benefits to employees of joining a trade union

- Trade unions work to protect employees' pay and conditions.
- Trade unions often provide legal advice and support for their members.
- Collective bargaining gives employees more of a voice when negotiating with their employers.

Analysis

Research two trade unions for employees in your area. What benefits do they each provide for their members, and how much does annual membership cost?

Present your findings to your partners and recommend which of the unions you would join.

Employees have less bargaining power when they have to negotiate their working conditions on their own rather than as part of a union.

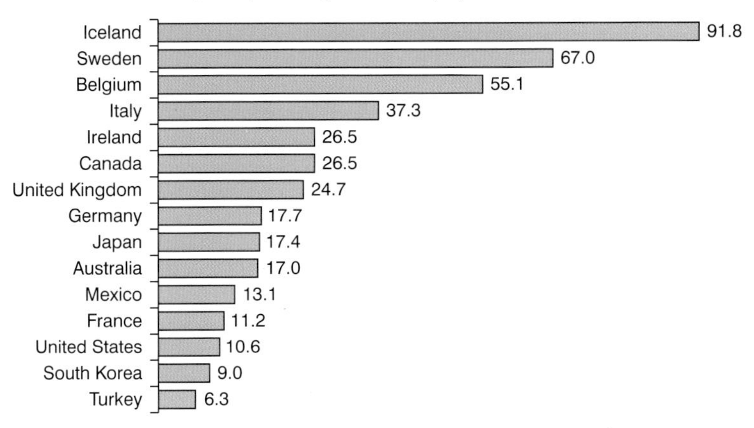

Δ The state of the unions — Labour union membership as a percentage of total employees

Source: OECD

CASE STUDY

NUMSA (National Union of Metalworkers in South Africa)

The National Trade Union of Metalworkers of South Africa (NUMSA) announced that it will continue with its nationwide strike following the news that Eskom (a South African electricity utility) will close a further five coal power stations. It is thought that this closure will affect 30 000 employees within the plants and the connected suppliers. Eskom and the government have been working towards renewable energy sources, the reason behind the closures being an apparent surplus of power. Many members of NUMSA are employees, so collective bargaining power will be used to challenge this decision.

Knowledge check

1. **Explain two benefits to an employee who joins a trade union. (4)**
2. **Outline what is meant by collective bargaining. (2)**

Mutya works for a large and profitable bottling plant in Singapore. Working conditions are poor and very few employees are part of the trade union. She thinks that everyone who works there should join the union.

3. **Explain two reasons why you think it might be beneficial to employees, like Mutya, if everyone joined the same union. (4)**

Total 10 marks

Check your progress:

- ✓ I can draw and interpret organisational charts, and explain the roles, responsibilities and inter-relationships between different levels of management and employees.
- ✓ I can describe the role and functions of management.
- ✓ I can identify the different leadership styles in a business.
- ✓ I can explain what a trade union is and the effects of employees being union members.

Recruitment, selection and training of employees

Recruiting and selecting employees

Aims (2.3.1)
By the end of this section, you should:
- Understand methods of recruitment and selection
- Understand the difference between internal and external recruitment
- Be able to outline the main stages in recruitment and selection of employees
- Be able to recommend and justify who to employ in given circumstances
- Understand the benefits and limitations of part-time and full-time employees.

Finding, selecting and training people is critical to business success. Large companies spend significant sums of money trying to recruit and select the right people and significant time training them to do the best job possible.

The process of finding employees is known as **recruitment**. The recruitment process is:

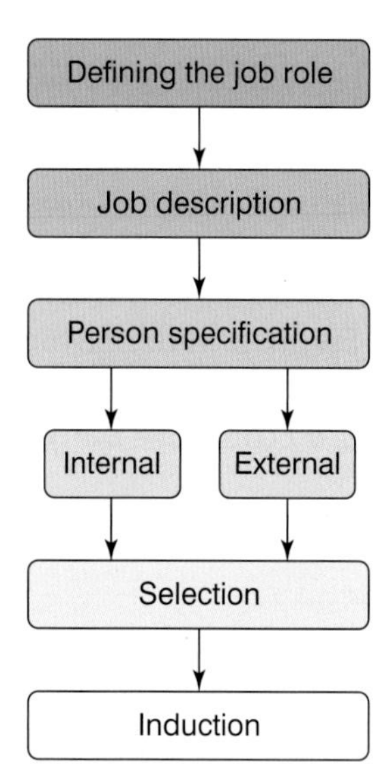

Stage I – Defining the job role

When looking to fill a vacancy (an unfilled position), the first thing a business must do is clearly define the job and the type of person required. This is done by creating a **job description** and a **person specification**.

- **Job description**: provides a description of the job, the tasks involved and the terms (working hours and so on).
- **Person specification**: provides a description of the skills and abilities that the successful candidate will need in order to perform well in the role.

JOB DESCRIPTION

Job title: Children's Nurse

Location: Welltown Hospital

Responsible to: Senior Nurse, Doctors

Responsible for: Patient wellbeing

Roles and responsibilities:

- care for children of all ages on the hospital ward, who may be recovering from operations or staying in hospital to receive treatment
- monitor patients' progress and administer treatment after discussion with the wider medical team, including doctors and other healthcare professionals
- communicate with the patient and their parents or carers about their treatment and condition
- prepare patients and their parents or carers for leaving hospital and advise them on any future treatment needed.

PERSON SPECIFICATION

Job title: Children's Nurse

Attainments:

- five GCSEs/O Levels (or equivalent) at grade A–C, including English and one science, plus A Levels (or equivalent)
- an approved diploma of higher education or degree in children's/paediatric nursing
- professional registration with official Nursing Board.

Experience:

- experience of working with children or young people (preferably in a hospital setting).

Skills

- willing to work shifts and unsociable hours
- good communicator and good at recognising verbal and non-verbal clues about how children are feeling
- calm in a crisis and good at handling people (including parents and carers) in distress
- able to work as part of a team.

Δ An example job description and person specification

Referring to the example on the previous page, create job descriptions and person specifications for two of the following jobs:

- restaurant manager
- chef
- waitress/waiter
- kitchen assistant.

Compare and contrast the role and type of person required for the different jobs.

Part time or full time?

Another decision that a business needs to make about the role is whether it is to be full time or part time. This is particularly important where a firm is seeking to reduce costs, as replacing a full-time position with a part-time employee can be much cheaper.

The advantages and disadvantages of part-time and full-time labour are shown in the table.

	Full time	Part time
Advantages	✓ The employee becomes more familiar with the business and, in theory, more productive. ✓ The employee is likely to be more loyal to the firm. ✓ The employee is likely to have more goodwill (the employee may work additional hours without pay).	✓ The average cost of a part-time employee is lower than the cost of a full-time employee. ✓ Part-time employees can be used flexibly to ensure that employee numbers meet demand (for example, increasing the number of cashiers at a supermarket during busy periods). ✓ Part-time employees spend less time at work and may be more productive (they may be less tired or less bored than full-time employees).
Disadvantages	✗ Full-time employees are entitled to many benefits in addition to their wages/salary. ✗ Full-time employees are entitled to holidays, sick pay and parental leave; there may be costs involved in covering for them during an absence. ✗ Full-time employees may not want to adjust their hours to suit demand (for example, working weekends).	✗ The cost of training large numbers of part-time employees may be high. ✗ Part-time employees may be less loyal (increasing labour turnover). ✗ Part-time employees may be less committed to the firm and less likely to provide good service/produce quality products. ✗ In some countries, part-time employees are being given the same rights as full-time employees; this makes part-time employees expensive.

One other consideration may be whether to allow the employee to work flexible hours. A system of flexible working gives employees choice, perhaps within set limits, about the actual times they work. For example, helping employees avoid rush-hour traffic or allowing them to attend to childcare issues before starting work may have the advantage of increasing motivation. It may mean, however, that employees are absent from work at important times, miss meetings or are not available to serve customers' needs.

Stage II – Internal or external?

Once a firm has a clear understanding of the position to be filled, they must then decide whether to fill the post internally or externally.

Internal recruitment

Internal recruitment might involve:

- **Reorganisation** – sharing the work among remaining employees
- **Redeployment** – moving an employee from another part of the business
- **Promotion** – moving an employee to a position of more responsibility
- **Internal advertisement** – allowing any existing employee to apply.

External recruitment

External recruitment means filling the vacancy from outside of the firm. This might involve:

- **Job centres**. Usually run by the government, job centres help unemployed people to find jobs or get training. They also allow businesses to advertise vacancies for free.
- **Media advertising**. Job advertisements are the most common form of external recruitment. Advertisements may be placed in local or national newspapers, on the internet or in specialist industry magazines.
- **Visiting universities**. Big businesses often visit universities in order to recruit graduate students.
- **Recruitment agencies**. Specialist firms, such as the global recruitment company Adecco, search for suitable candidates on behalf of the firm. They charge a fee for the service, with the rate dependent on the seniority of the position.

△ Newspaper job advertisements are an example of media advertising.

The method of external recruitment chosen will depend on a range of factors:

- **Size of firm**. A small firm might prefer to use cheaper methods such as job centres, and is more likely to have local recruitment needs, making local newspaper advertising an appropriate method.
- **Type of position**. A highly specialised position may require the services of a recruitment agent (a specialist, for example, in recruiting telecommunications engineers). Very senior

positions, such as a managing director position, will be advertised widely (possibly even internationally) to attract the very best candidates.
- **Number of positions**. If only one position is vacant, a firm will want to keep recruitment costs to a minimum (perhaps only advertising locally). If many positions are available, national advertising may be more cost-effective.

The job advert itself is also important when recruiting externally. The firm wants to attract the best candidates possible. The job advert must therefore promote the position and the firm to candidates. A job advertisement usually includes:

- a job title
- a brief description of the job (including tasks, working arrangements and responsibilities)
- a brief statement of the required skills and experience (the person specification)
- an outline of the firm (usually promoting the benefits of working there)
- instructions on how to apply
- an indication of pay and conditions.

Δ Businesses pay specialist recruitment firms considerable fees to ensure they hire the best-quality managers.

Application

Using the example job description and person specification from this section, draw up a suitable job advertisement.

Each approach to recruitment, internal or external, has advantages and disadvantages.

	Internal	External
Advantages	✓ Offers current employees opportunities for promotion and development. ✓ Motivates employees and promotes loyalty by providing opportunities within the business. ✓ Causes less disruption or need for induction training (training of a new employee when they join a firm) because the employee is already familiar with the company and its ways of doing things. ✓ A business will have greater knowledge of the qualities of an internal applicant, so there is less chance of making an expensive mistake in selection.	✓ Can attract a potentially much stronger selection of candidates, compared to internal recruitment. ✓ Can bring new ideas to the business. ✓ Can bring valuable knowledge and experience of the competition. ✓ The successful recruit is likely to be motivated by the freshness of a new job and will therefore work harder in the short term.

	Internal	External
Disadvantages	✘ Another vacancy is created elsewhere in the firm that must be filled. ✘ No new (external) ideas are brought into the firm. ✘ The person recruited may not be the best person for the job, just the most familiar.	✘ Can be expensive and time-consuming. ✘ The new recruit will need induction training and may take some time to become familiar with the firm's operations, so their initial productivity may be low. ✘ There is more risk of recruiting somebody who is not successful in the job.

Stage III – Selection

Once a job is advertised, whether internally or externally, there could be hundreds of applications to select from. Interviewing all of the applicants might be impossible. Usually a shortlist of possible candidates is drawn up, and only those on this list are called for interview. The shortlist will be created by comparing the skills and experience of each candidate (as demonstrated on their résumé or application form) against the person specification and job description.

Candidates on the shortlist will then undergo a series of assessments. The length and number of these assessments will depend on the type of job, but might include:

Interview

Shortlisted candidates will be called for an interview to assess their personality and to verify (confirm) their qualifications, personal qualities and aptitude (ability and skills) for the job. The interview may involve a face-to-face discussion between the interviewer and several interviewees.

△ IQ tests are one type of assessment that candidates may have to complete as part of the assessment process for a job.

Aptitude tests

Some firms require employees to undergo aptitude tests. These tests may range from intelligence (IQ) tests to exercises that assess specific job-based skills. For example, firefighters are tested on physical fitness and suitability for the dangerous nature of the work.

Psychometric tests

Many large firms use psychometric tests to assess candidates' personalities and preferences. These tests assess things such as spatial awareness (ability to visualise objects and spaces), comprehension and writing speed, numerical ability, manual dexterity (ability) and a candidate's personality. Investment banks, for example, often test employees on their numerical ability (and speed) and assess their attitude to risk. (They may reject an otherwise talented candidate if the tests suggest that they are likely to take risks with money.)

Assessment centres

For very senior jobs, candidates may be asked to attend an assessment centre. These centres carry out multiple interviews and tests that often last between one and three days. They also often include role-play situations (such as management meetings or customer complaints), with candidates observed throughout the proceedings.

The selection process is about choosing the right candidate for the job. The costs of selection procedures in time and money can be considerable – for example, the cost of placing advertisements, paying candidates' travel expenses and the opportunity cost (see 1.1 Business activity) of management time.

However, the costs of appointing the wrong person can be even greater. For example, the disruption caused if a new recruit proves to be unsuitable can be significant. The damage to a firm's reputation if the new recruit makes mistakes, and the expense of going through the recruitment and selection process again if the new recruit needs to be replaced, all add to the cost of recruiting the wrong person.

Who to employ

Once a business has completed all aspects of its recruitment process, it has to decide on who to employ. During all parts of the recruitment process, each candidate will have been marked or graded. Once complete, these marks can be added up and discussed by the interview panel (group of people in charge of the recruitment process). They may have different views on whom to employ. However, the decision should be based on which candidate best suits the role, using the job description and person specification. Making this decision is not easy, and sometimes businesses may not hire the best person for a position, because an interview does not always tell you everything about a person and how they will perform once in the role.

CASE STUDY A popular place to work

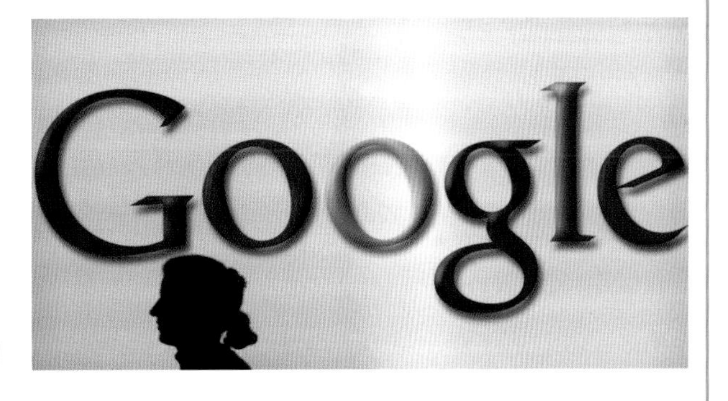

Google receives more than 100 000 job applications per month. With a policy of hiring only the very best employees, Google faces a huge challenge selecting the right candidates.

Potential Google recruits face multiple interviews (often as many as 14) and a series of online personality tests. These personality tests (even asking whether the candidates have neat or messy desks) are designed to assess how well the person would 'fit' with Google's culture. In a process that can often last many months, candidates are also required to solve complex problems and to prove themselves academically gifted and highly motivated.

Before actually accepting a job, there may be negotiation between the company and the individual over the terms and conditions of their employment. Before a formal **employment contract** can be drawn up, there must be agreement on things such as payment, hours to be worked and the exact nature of the job.

Once the employment contract has been confirmed and signed by both the employee and the employer, the individual can begin work. The first few days when joining a new firm are known as **induction**, which is discussed next.

Key Term

Employment contract: a legal contract that a firm gives to an employee, setting out the basic terms and conditions of employment (such as place of work, working hours and salary).

Knowledge check

1. **Explain two differences between a job description and a person specification.** **(4)**
2. **Explain two items that might appear in a job description and two that would appear in a person specification for a teaching position.** **(8)**
3. **Explain why a business might prefer internal recruitment.** **(3)**
4. **Outline two advantages of external recruitment.** **(3)**
5. **Explain what psychometric tests are used for.** **(2)**
6. **Explain the factors a firm will need to consider when selecting an appropriate method of recruitment.** **(6)**

Total 26 marks

The importance of training and methods of training

Aims (2.3.2)

By the end of this section, you should:

- Understand the importance of training to a business and employees
- Understand the benefits and limitations of induction training, on-the-job and off-the-job training.

Why is training important?

Training ensures that a firm's employees are always up to date with the latest ways of working and the latest knowledge about company (or competitors') products. In some professions, such as medicine, ongoing (continual) training is a requirement of the job.

Training seeks to:

- **reduce costs** – through increased efficiency, reduced recruitment costs (reducing the need to recruit new employees with particular skills) or improved health and safety
- **increase revenues** – through improved image, quality or service
- **improve innovation and flexibility** – by developing a workforce that is highly skilled and able to cope with change
- above all, **reduce labour turnover** (the number of employees who leave during a year) – by helping firms to remain competitive.

Training is not, therefore, something that only happens when an employee is new (induction training) – it is something that can (and should) happen at any time.

For an individual, employee training is essential to performing well in a job. Training can help an employee to perform better and thus achieve Maslow's self-esteem needs (see 2.1 Motivating employees). Training is also important to an individual's chances of finding a new job – the better trained they are, the better their chances.

The benefits of training for both the employee and the employer can be summarised as:

Employer	Employee
✓ Increased efficiency, leading to lower costs	✓ Better job performance
✓ Improved health and safety (and fewer workplace accidents, lowering costs of compensation claims)	✓ Higher productivity (and possibly higher pay)
✓ Increased revenues and higher profitability	✓ Higher job satisfaction
✓ Improved innovation and flexibility	✓ Less chance of workplace accidents
✓ Lower labour turnover	✓ Better career prospects (higher chance of promotion)

Induction training

∆ Induction training helps new employees understand the business and their job role.

When a new employee is appointed, specific training will be required to help him or her settle into the new job. This is known as induction. A carefully planned induction programme can last several hours or several weeks, but is likely to include:

- specific training for the job role
- opportunities to meet a range of important individuals within the business
- a tour of the business and its facilities
- explanation of the background to the organisation – its vision, values and ways of working
- health and safety instruction
- discussion of employment, payment arrangements, and so on.

Induction training is crucial in minimising the disruption to the business of having a new employee, and in ensuring that the employee feels secure and positive in his or her new environment. The better the induction process, the more quickly the new employee will become productive.

However, induction training often means that new employees do not actually start work for a few days after joining the firm (because they are being trained). This means the firm is paying the employee but, for the period of induction, is not getting any value from that employee. A danger of induction training is also that new employees learn bad habits from experienced employees.

On-the-job training (internal)

∆ Coaching a trainee helps to develop their skills in the job.

On-the-job training refers to training that takes place while the employee is working. It can be done through:

- **Coaching.** A supervisor or coach guides a trainee through the stages involved in a job or teaches the trainee how to improve the quality of his or her work.
- **Mentoring.** A more experienced colleague offers advice on how best to carry out a job or solve problems. Mentoring can be job-specific or focused on an employee's personal development (perhaps helping to develop the individual's leadership skills).
- **Job rotation.** This involves moving employees from one task (or part of the company) to another, to broaden their range of skills and experience.

Off-the-job training (internal and external)

This form of training often requires an employee to stop working to be trained. The training may still take place within the business, or the employees could go elsewhere to be trained. Off-the-job training methods include:

- **Conferences**. These are the most popular form of off-the-job training. They involve employees attending an event where experts deliver lectures or workshops. Teachers often go to conferences to ensure they are up to date with the latest examination requirements.
- **In-house courses**. This is where a business arranges its own training programmes, often using the expertise of its employees to act as trainers. Larger businesses, such as HSBC, have training centres where they run residential (live-in) courses for employees from other parts of a country.
- **College/university courses**. This is where employees go from the workplace to a local college or university to study for qualifications that are relevant to their job. Employees may also study for qualifications at home through distance learning programmes. A business may support employees by giving them time off to study or by meeting the costs of courses and qualifications.

Δ Conferences are the most commonly used form of off-the-job training.

Advantages and disadvantages of training

	On-the-job training	Off-the-job training
Advantages	✓ Cheaper than off-the-job training ✓ Employees remain productive ✓ Training is specific to the job ✓ Opportunity to learn from experienced, expert employees	✓ A wider range of skills can be obtained ✓ Can learn from outside specialists or experts ✓ May lead to formal qualifications, benefiting both the individual (in career terms) and the business (in marketing terms)
Disadvantages	✗ Quality of training depends on ability of trainer and time available ✗ Learning environment may not be ideal ✗ Bad habits might be passed on ✗ Potential disruption to production	✗ More expensive than on-the-job training ✗ Risk of employees using new skills/qualifications to seek jobs with other firms ✗ May not be specific to the individual's or firm's needs ✗ Productivity may suffer, as the employee is away from the place of work ✗ Research has shown that many people forget 70% of what they have learned on a course within three days

CASE STUDY

Training the Thai Smile

Thai Smile, a Thailand-based Asian airline, needed to recruit and train large numbers of cabin crew. A three-month off-the-job training programme, at a purpose-built training centre, focused on safety, service and language skills. Special attention was also given to the 'human touch', and to making sure employees were well trained in the traditional Thai smile.

Analysis

Use the information in this section to analyse the advantages and disadvantages of off-the-job versus on-the-job training. Working with a partner, imagine you work in a human resources department and present your findings as a report to the human resources manager.

Top Tip

Remember that you need to distinguish between evidence and fact. Consider this in your answer.

Knowledge check

1. **Explain why training is important to employers.** **(3)**
2. **Explain why training is important to employees.** **(3)**
3. **Identify two things that might be included in induction training.** **(2)**
4. **Using examples, outline the differences between on-the-job and off-the-job training.** **(4)**
5. **Discuss two benefits of on-the-job training.** **(4)**
6. **Consider two limitations of on-the-job training.** **(4)**
7. **Define the term induction.** **(2)**

Total 22 marks

Reducing the workforce

Aims (2.3.3)
By the end of this section, you should:

- Understand the difference between dismissal and redundancy, with examples
- Understand situations in which downsizing the workforce might be necessary, for example, automation or reduced demand for products
- Be able to recommend and justify which employees to make redundant in given circumstances.

It is a fact of business life that sometimes a firm needs to reduce the number of people it employs (the **headcount**):

- If the business is not doing very well, it may need to **downsize**. Downsizing means reducing the number of employees (making them **redundant**) to better match the headcount to a firm's current needs.
- If an employee does something wrong, a firm may want to get rid of them (**dismissal**).

Workforce planning

Businesses usually make decisions to increase or decrease (downsize) the number of employees they have on the basis of a workforce plan. The stages involved in a workforce plan are:

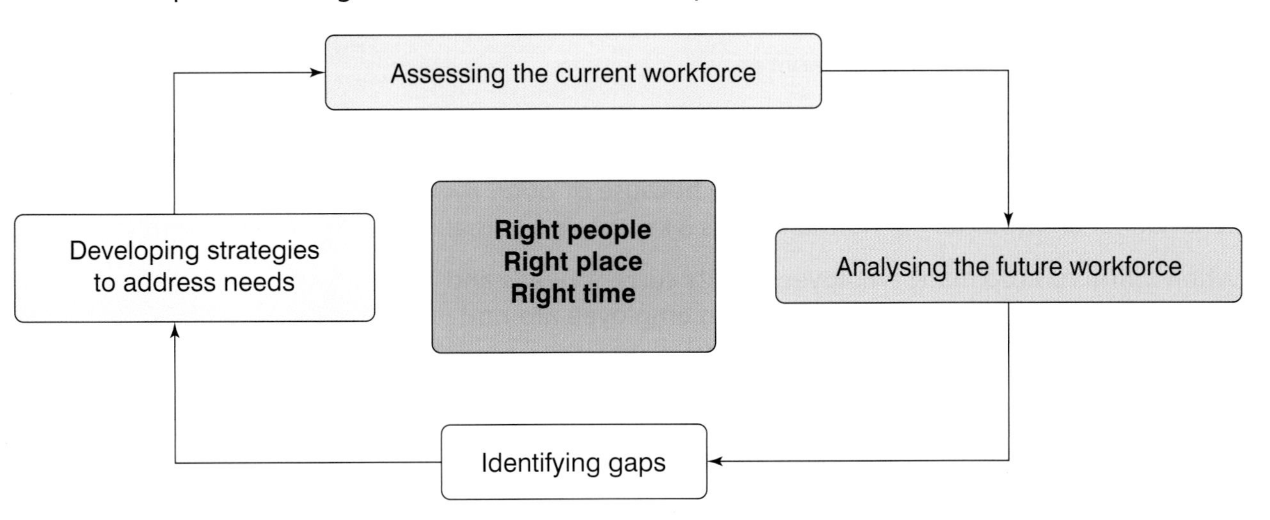

Assessing the current workforce

A firm needs to know how many employees it currently has. It also needs to know what skills and experience the employees have and how old they are. Knowing the age profile of its employees enables a firm to know when employees might retire (leave work due to old age) and helps them to predict employee/labour turnover (the number of employees who leave during a year).

Predict future needs

Taking into account forecasts about the state of the economy and any plans for business expansion (growth) or contraction (reduction in size), a firm will calculate how many employees it needs for the future. The firm may also need to consider the impact of new technology and then decide whether its current employees have the right skills for the firm's future needs.

The balance of these two factors (current employee levels and future needs) will determine whether the firm needs to recruit more employees, or whether they need to downsize (make redundancies).

Reasons for downsizing

A firm may need to downsize for one of the following reasons:

- a business suffering poor sales may want to decrease production and therefore needs to reduce surplus (too many) employees
- a merger (where two firms join together) between firms may result in excess (extra) employees in certain positions
- a firm may move its operations to a new part of the country or even overseas
- a business may close a branch or store
- a firm may automate production (thus reducing the need for employees)
- the firm has **outsourced** some services.

Key Term

Outsource: to use other (external) companies to provide services within a firm.

Dismissal and redundancy

When an employee is told to leave the job because of poor behaviour or unsatisfactory performance, this is known as dismissal.

When a firm has too many employees for its current needs and wants to downsize, or when the skills of an employee are no longer needed, this is known as redundancy.

Dismissal

- Being asked to leave a firm because of poor performance or behaviour

Redundancy

- Being asked to leave a firm where the skills or experience of the employee are no longer needed

Dismissal

The main reasons for dismissal are:

- **Gross misconduct**. Examples of gross misconduct include stealing and breaking a serious company rule (such as those dealing with health and safety).

- **Continual underperformance**. If an employee continually fails to perform at a satisfactory level, the firm can dismiss them. In most countries, the law requires that the employee is given several warnings before dismissal.
- **Breaking the law**. The rules regarding this are quite complex. In simple terms, if an employee breaks a law that is inconsistent with them performing their job, a firm has the legal right of dismissal. For example, if a delivery driver is banned from driving, he or she will no longer be able to perform the job and so can be legally dismissed.

Where an employee is dismissed without good reason, this is known as **unfair dismissal**. Employees can contest (challenge) unfair dismissal and may be able to claim compensation (money) or reinstatement (they may get their job back).

Redundancy

The word redundant means surplus to requirements (more than needed). In essence, this means a firm has too many employees for its needs, or too many employees of the wrong kind.

Making employees redundant saves cost in the long term but is very expensive in the short term. In most countries, employees are entitled to **redundancy pay** (sometimes known as **severance pay**). Redundancy pay is usually calculated on the basis of how many years an employee has worked for a firm. They receive a month's salary (or a proportion of a month's salary) for every year they have worked at the firm. These payments can be very costly in the short term (and can have a significant impact on **cash flow**). They do, however, save a firm money over the long term as they no longer have to pay the employee's salary.

When deciding which employees to make redundant, a firm will consider things such as the employee's skills, their experience, their length of service (and therefore the cost of making them redundant) and their overall performance.

CASE STUDY

Temporary cost-cutting

Hurricane Harvey hit the Gulf Coast of the United States in August 2017 and caused serious damage to homes and local businesses. It is estimated that over 25 000 jobs have been temporarily lost as businesses cut costs whilst infrastructure and tourism recover. This reduction in the workforce should only last a few months as the region recovers and small businesses in the primary and secondary sectors start to see growth in sales.

Evaluation

Using a company you are familiar with (or your school), consider the following questions:

- If 25% of employees are made redundant, what might the impact be on the remaining employees?
- If employees are made redundant, how might the press (or customers) respond?
- What if demand increases? How easy is it for a firm to re-employ people to work for them?

Making employees redundant (or dismissing someone) is one of the hardest decisions a manager may ever have to make. Don't make the mistake of making it sound easy!

Working with a partner, present your findings to the rest of your group. Use presentation software, if available.

Knowledge check

1. **Define the term downsize. (1)**
2. **Identify two reasons why a firm may need to downsize. (2)**
3. **Explain what workforce planning involves. (3)**
4. **Define the term redundancy. (2)**
5. **Explain how redundancy differs from dismissal. (3)**
6. **'An employee can be dismissed if their job is surplus to requirements.' Outline why this statement is false. (3)**

Total 14 marks

Top Tip

When considering how a firm could downsize, take care with your use of terms. Don't use the slang term 'sack' – use the term dismissal. Be careful you don't mean 'make some employees redundant'. Take care not to confuse the terms redundancy and dismissal.

Legal controls over employment and their impact

Aims (2.3.4)
By the end of this section, you should:
- Understand legal controls over employment contracts, unfair dismissal, discrimination, health and safety and the legal minimum wage.

Laws aim to protect the rights of individuals, groups and businesses. If something goes wrong, the law helps people to make sure they are being fairly treated.

While the exact regulations (laws) may be different, most countries have laws relating to employment issues. These laws cover issues such as:

- health and safety
- employment contracts, including unfair dismissal
- discrimination (age, gender, race, and so on)
- minimum wage.

Health and safety

Health and safety is about preventing people from being harmed at work. Health and safety controls might involve things such as:

- providing adequate ventilation (air flow) and light in offices
- fitting safety guards on machinery
- providing employees with suitable safety equipment and clothing
- posting warning signs
- regularly maintaining electrical equipment
- providing employees with suitable desks and chairs.

The main impact of health and safety controls is cost. Ensuring that the working environment is satisfactory (safe, clean and healthy) requires businesses to spend money on methods of prevention. Regulations may also require changes to working practices and could reduce productivity.

Δ Employees in the oil business often complain that safety equipment slows them down and makes doing their job more difficult.

On the other hand, a good health and safety record can be very positive for a business. People may prefer, especially in high-risk businesses, to work for 'safer' companies. Good health and safety controls also reduce costs in the long term because fewer employees are absent due to accidents. Costs are also reduced because firms avoid expensive compensation claims from employees injured at work.

The extent to which health and safety controls impact on the operations of a firm depends on the type of business. A construction firm must, fairly obviously, take health and safety very seriously. A bank will have fewer health and safety issues and thus will be less affected by regulations.

CASE STUDY

Rise of health and safety

The Institution of Occupational Safety and Health (IOSH) estimates that around 2.3 million work-related deaths occur worldwide every year, with the construction industry accounting for about 60 000 of these fatalities. According to researchers, about 50% of all construction site accidents are a result of falls from height, with crane accidents contributing to another 20%.

The United Arab Emirates has some of the fastest-growing cities in the world, and many high-rise buildings, so they have made stricter health and safety regulations in recent years. These laws may have increased short-term business costs, but there have been fewer construction accidents and a reduction in compensation claims.

Employment contracts and unfair dismissal

Employment contract law sets out the basic legal rights (legal entitlement) of an employee. These rights include things such as:

- the right to a written employment contract
- the right to be paid the national minimum wage
- the right to reasonable notice before dismissal
- the right to take statutory (legal minimum) holiday leave
- the right to redundancy payments.

These controls set out the minimum requirements, and instruct a firm's actions when dealing with employees. For example, in the case of dismissal (see Reducing the workforce later in this topic), it is an employee's right to be told in advance (given notice) that they will be dismissed.

In many countries, employees must – except in the case of gross misconduct – also be given warnings and time to improve before they can be dismissed. Failure to provide these minimum requirements would be unfair dismissal. If a firm is found to have unfairly dismissed an employee, it may be required to pay compensation or may even have to give the person their job back.

As with health and safety controls, employment law has the disadvantage of putting additional costs on a business. A firm will need, for example, to allow employees holidays, pay the legal minimum wage and must employ trained employees to produce and manage employment contracts. However, having these controls (and legal rights) in place helps employees to feel more secure in their jobs (see Maslow's Hierarchy of Needs – 2.1 Motivating employees) and can increase **motivation** and reduce labour turnover.

Discrimination

Discrimination is the unfair treatment of one person or group of people as compared to others. Controls against discrimination attempt to protect people from being treated differently because of:

- age
- sexual orientation
- gender
- marital status
- disability
- pregnancy
- race
- religion.

Δ Controls against discrimination at work, such as anti-discrimination laws, aim to protect the rights of individuals with disabilities to fair (equal) access to employment, training, work-related benefits and job promotion.

In most countries, there are different laws dealing with each of these forms of discrimination. Examples of the controls these laws put in place include:

- the right to **equal pay** regardless of race or gender
- fair (equal) access to employment, training or benefits
- equal access to job promotion
- the requirement to ensure disabled people have access to a firm's premises (buildings).

Again, the major impact of these legal controls is cost. For example, the expense of ensuring that a firm's offices are suitable for disabled employees can be significant. More importantly, though, the cost of not obeying these laws could be disastrous – imagine the negative publicity and the impact on sales if a firm was found to be discriminating. The impact for employees is, hopefully, fair treatment and freedom from discrimination.

Key Term

Equal pay: the concept of employees, regardless of age or gender, being paid equally for undertaking the same job with the same level of expertise.

CASE STUDY

Protecting employees from age discrimination

In the Philippines, the Department of Labour and Employment released a new set of rules that focus on protecting employees in the workplace, based on their age. It is now unlawful for businesses to ask for a declaration of age during the recruitment process, to turn down an applicant based on their age or to discriminate against older employees in cases of promotion. Such measures are a positive step forward for employees in the country.

Minimum wage

Many countries specify a legal **minimum wage** – the lowest amount an employee can be paid. Many firms will pay more than the minimum, but the law ensures that employees have the right to at least a set amount per hour or per day.

Of all the laws, paying a minimum wage can be the most costly for a business. When countries raise the level of the minimum wage, businesses complain loudly. However, paying the minimum wage can help improve motivation and reduce labour turnover – obviously, for the individual employee it also means higher pay. Economically, a minimum wage can also increase consumer spending. (If people are paid more, they spend more and all firms benefit.)

Evaluation

Investigate the minimum wage in your country. Examine the following:

- What level is the minimum wage currently set at?
- When was it introduced/last increased?
- How did businesses respond to its introduction/to an increase?

If your country does not set a minimum wage, analyse why not and consider the possible impact of a minimum wage being introduced.

Finally, debate with a partner whether having a minimum wage is a good thing. Consider how individuals and firms are affected, and the overall impact on the economy.

Once you have concluded your debate, write up a summary, with justifications, of your opinion.

In summary, a business must conform to the law if it is to maintain its reputation and its customers and avoid legal penalties. The extent to which any one business will be affected by the law depends on the nature and size of the business. Obviously, a chemical plant may find that health and safety law, for example, has a greater impact on its business than it would have on a small florist's business. Business size is also significant: smaller businesses may find the costs of implementing laws particularly costly.

For employees, legal controls help to protect them from unsafe workplaces and to ensure they are treated and paid fairly.

Knowledge check

1. **Identify two examples of legal controls on employment. (2)**
2. **Explain one factor that may affect the extent to which legal controls impact on a particular firm. (2)**
3. **Consider two positive implications of health and safety law for a business. (4)**
4. **Identify three 'rights' provided under employment contract law. (3)**
5. **Outline, using examples, what is meant by discrimination. (3)**

Total 14 marks

Check your progress:

✓ I can outline the main stages in the recruitment process, adding detail on the different ways in which a business can recruit.

✓ I can analyse the best methods for recruitment, making recommendations for given scenarios.

✓ I can outline the importance of training and the benefits of different methods of training.

✓ I can outline the methods and reasons behind reducing the size of workforce, as well as the legal controls in place.

Internal and external communication

Achieving effective communication

Aims (2.4.1)
By the end of this section, you should:
- Understand effective communication and its importance to business
- Understand the benefits and limitations of different communication methods, including those based on information technology (IT)
- Be able to recommend and justify which communication method to use in given circumstances.

Effective communication and its importance to business

Communication is the passing on or exchange of information (such as a message) from a sender to a receiver. For a business, it is crucial that communication is constant, clear and easy to understand. For communication to be effective, the message must be transferred quickly and without any misinterpretations (errors).

Communication takes place both inside the business and externally with one of its **stakeholders**. However, the communication may not always be effective. For effective communication to happen, the business must consider the following:

- Which communication method best suits the situation – for example, it may be best to inform customers that prices are increasing by writing a letter, because the same message can be sent to a large number of people.
- The needs of the receiver – for example, giving an important message orally, instead of writing it, may mean the receiver forgets it and makes a mistake.
- External influences may alter or slow down the message getting processed – for example, a phone call may end unexpectedly or be interrupted.
- The communication may need following up or duplicating (doing it again) – for example, a business may decide to send a letter to all suppliers and then follow this up with a phone call.

Δ Communication on a building site is very important, because of the large number of people involved and potential dangers.

The communication process is therefore very important. The message will be passed along the chain and, at each stage, care must be taken to make sure it maintains its accuracy.

Message is created by sender

Method or channel used to send message is selected by sender

Message received by receiver

Action taken or feedback given by receiver

Once the message has been delivered, it is very important for a business to check that it has been received and understood. Therefore, the sender should look for some feedback or acknowledgement from the receiver. For example, many businesses prefer to telephone a client, rather than emailing, because they know instantly that the message has been received. As they are speaking directly to the receiver, they can gain some instant feedback.

Getting communication right is a very important task for a business. If communication works well in a business, it may see some huge benefits:

- Employees may enjoy their job and feel valued, as they see their comments and suggestions taken on board (accepted) by the managers and owners.
- Employees will work more efficiently, as they do not have to wait too long for agreements or feedback.
- Customers who receive constant communication may become more loyal, therefore helping the business to secure sales and growth.
- Tasks are completed quickly and on time, allowing the business to seek new customers.

CASE STUDY

Nike is now open

Vietnam has now overtaken China as the world's largest producer of Nike trainers. Nike has received heavy criticism in recent years for its production methods and lack of communication with customers and other stakeholders. However, Nike now lists its suppliers and factories so that customers can find out where their products were made. This communication has been a positive move by Nike as they look to improve relationships with their stakeholders.

Application

Using the three scenarios below, work in pairs to decide what potential problems the senders may face if their communication is ineffective (unsuccessful). These problems may be experienced by the senders or the receivers – for example, the customers or local community.

- Members of the local community write an email to a shoe factory complaining about the increase in noise.
- The local sports shop receives some emails from their suppliers about some poorly made equipment. The suppliers have sent a fax with the product codes on.
- A customer demands to see the manager of the local coffee shop about the service they have received.

You should note down as many potential problems as you can and be ready to give feedback to the class.

Benefits and limitations of different communication methods

Businesses communicate both internally (within the business) and externally (outside the business). With a large range of stakeholders, the quality of the communication is vital for a business to succeed, as is choosing the correct and most appropriate method of communication.

Internal

This could be orders or instructions to employees about product specifications or changes to a service.

Example: the *Daily News* in Egypt may use email and memos as its internal communication methods.

External

Information to the business's stakeholders – for example, a change in the amount needed from a supplier.

Example: Gazprom, the world's largest gas company, may use letters to communicate with its customers.

Formal and informal communication

Business communication can be formal or informal.

A business often chooses to use formal communication when the communication is official and the business needs to present itself in a professional way. Formal communication is often done by the managers and owners, as they need to make sure they are happy with the content. If they were to release some formal communication, perhaps a letter, and it contained errors, this could have a negative impact on the business's reputation.

Formal communication can take place within the business – for example, a manager writing a letter to an employee warning him about his performance. It can also be take place externally – for example, by the owners writing to the local community.

Informal communication is done on a regular basis and can be both internal or external. This form of communication uses less professional language and is often done in shorthand (not full sentences). For example, employees within a business may write emails to each other, which do not need to be written using formal professional language.

Δ Many businesses now use online video conferencing technology to communicate with colleagues or interview job applicants in other parts of the world.

Internal methods of communication

Businesses normally use one of the following methods to communicate internally.

Written methods

Method	Benefits	Drawbacks
Email – these are electronic messages sent via the internet. They are sent within a business by managers and other employees.	✓ These are quick and easy to write and send. ✓ The sender can add a 'receipt' to the email so they know when the receiver has read it.	✘ Some people may not check their emails on a regular basis, so they may not respond to a query or comment quickly enough. ✘ Email can be used too frequently, causing employees to spend too much time answering emails rather than completing other important tasks.
Memorandum (memo) is usually a short message that contains key information. It is often used to remind employees of an upcoming event or change in normal routine. This form of communication is now usually done via email.	✓ Memos can be sent to all employees or can be sent to specific people or departments without being altered. ✓ Memos are very easy and quick to write.	✘ Paper memos can easily be lost. It is difficult to know if the receiver has read the memo. ✘ Emailed memos may not be read by the receiver. The content may become out of date very quickly.
Reports are used to communicate the findings of a project or investigation. They are often produced for new ideas and potential products or services. They communicate the overall findings of the research.	✓ They offer insight into the research topic. ✓ They look professional and can be used in formal situations.	✘ They can be very time-consuming to research and then write. ✘ They offer a lot of information that can be hard to summarise.
Letters are written communications that may contain vital information. An employee may receive one to signal a pay rise, or one may be sent to a supplier to signal an end to a contract.	✓ These can be morale-boosting when used to praise employees, as they are a formal communication that employees can keep and show to others. ✓ A letter can be sent to more than one person, saving the business time.	✘ Letters can be used as evidence of errors – employees may use them as evidence that they are being bullied or that they were promised a pay rise.

Method	Benefits	Drawbacks
Newsletter – a summary of news articles and updates that are of interest to employees. A business may use a newsletter to keep employees up to date with any changes, upcoming events or awards they may have won.	✓ These can be very quick to read but contain lots of information. ✓ They can boost morale by highlighting employee success.	✘ Some employees may not read the newsletter and therefore won't know the latest news. ✘ They can be quite expensive to produce.
Poster – this is a visual method that shows key information in a clear and simple way. The poster should have very few words on it and plenty of images. Businesses often use these to highlight events such as office parties.	✓ These are very quick and easy to produce. ✓ Posters can be seen by lots of people at once, for a very small amount of money.	✘ Businesses cannot guarantee that all employees have seen the poster. ✘ A poster can be confusing if someone doesn't read it properly or if it does not contain enough detail.
Facsimile (fax) allows written documents, images and notes to be sent via a phone line. The receiver's machine will print the document out. This is still used by some businesses, although email communication has all but replaced it in most cases. It is still used to send signed documents that are needed very quickly.	✓ Fax is a quick way to send a hard copy (paper copy) of a document to another person. ✓ It is quick and easy to send, and it can be delivered to places all over the world in a few seconds.	✘ Faxes can often be unreliable, as they may not arrive or may not be read if the receiver doesn't know they have been sent the fax. ✘ Many businesses are no longer equipped to use this method of communication.

△ Businesses are now moving away from paper-based communication methods because of the space and time needed to store them. Methods such as fax and letters have been replaced by email.

Did you know?

The term 'millennials' was given to those people who became young adults in the early 2000s. They think differently from others when it comes to communication. According to the Deloitte Millennial Survey, they would rather text than call other employees and customers. With 63% of those surveyed now able to work from home in their jobs, communication is certainly going to have to adapt.

Verbal methods

Method	Benefits	Drawbacks
Meetings are a very common communication method in a business. When run effectively, a meeting allows a group of people to communicate with each other and make decisions quickly and efficiently. Often an agenda (list of topics to cover) will be handed out and minutes (summary of decisions) produced at the end.	✓ Face-to-face meetings allow people to voice concerns and show emotions, giving quicker decisions and allowing employees to discuss their opinions and ideas.	✗ A few people who want their opinion to be heard can dominate meetings. This means that not all employees get the chance to speak. ✗ Meetings can be time-consuming for businesses and do not always produce an outcome.
Telephones are used a lot in many businesses on a day-to-day basis. They allow the business to communicate both internally (with other employees) and externally (with customers).	✓ The telephone is quick and direct and can be useful for direct communication with colleagues, such as when you need to speak to someone in a different department or office, or to discuss something that is too sensitive to write down. ✓ The phone allows a business to talk to people who are far away – for example, customers in different countries, or who are travelling for work.	✗ The telephone isn't always answered, which means the message may not be transferred. For example, your message to a different department to change a customer's order might be missed.

The growth of the internet has meant electronic communication is now used by millions of people each day to communicate. Whether this is email, Facebook or video conferencing, electronic methods are quicker and cheaper and can reduce barriers such as distance and time. Businesses like Citigroup can use these methods to communicate with their offices situated all over the world.

Did you know?

Every day, 279 billion emails are sent around the world. For people working in offices, this averages 121 emails per day. Many businesses, however, are looking for ways to reduce the number of emails employees receive, to reduce stress and workload.

External methods of communication

External communication methods are aimed at communicating with people outside of the business; for example, suppliers, customers, government and competitors. External communication is used in a slightly different way to internal communication, as it can be seen by a number of people at once. External communication involves:

Public relations
Attract and keep customers by giving the company a good image

Information
Give stakeholders information on products, orders or decisions

Customer service
Speak to customers about problems, orders or to gain feedback

External methods of communication

Method	Benefits	Drawbacks
Email can now be sent as formal documents to speed up the communication process. For example, a business may attach a letter to an email, or write the email as a formal reply.	✓ Businesses often send an email instead of a letter as it is cheaper, but can include the same layout and image as a letter. ✓ Emails allow a business to communicate quickly with external stakeholders. ✓ Emails can be saved for future reference.	✗ Emails are not always written as carefully as letters. ✗ They can be sent to the wrong person / people.
Letters are important for the business's image. A poorly written letter with spelling mistakes can damage the business's image. Letters are used to communicate with customers, suppliers and other businesses. Larger businesses often have a customer relations department that uses letters to respond to complaints and feedback.	✓ Letters give a professional image of the business and show that it values its stakeholders. For example, if a customer writes to a business complaining about its product quality, they may be impressed if they receive a letter, as it shows time and effort has been spent on their complaint.	✗ They are time-consuming to write. ✗ Letters are expensive to send.
Newsletters are another way in which businesses can communicate with stakeholders. Many stakeholders look at the company's newsletter. This is often used to show off new projects, employee achievement or other business-related news.	✓ It is a cheap, cost-effective method to communicate key information to a large number of people. ✓ The newsletter can be used to boost the image of a business.	✗ Not all external stakeholders may read the newsletter, so they could miss important information. For example, shareholders may miss the details of the next meeting.
Advertisement – businesses may place adverts in a range of media (for example, newspapers, television) to inform their stakeholders of important information, new products or offers.	✓ They can be very creative and fun, allowing the business to improve its image. ✓ Putting adverts in the correct places means that businesses can target customers very accurately.	✗ Adverts can be expensive: a 30-second advert during the NFL Superbowl would cost $3.5 million. ✗ They may not be seen by the target audience.

(continued on the next two pages)

Method	Benefits	Drawbacks
Websites – many companies have their own website. Even sole traders may have a small website for their stakeholders to see. Businesses often choose a web domain address that will attract customers; for example, www.QQ.com, www.wikipedia.com and www.baidu.com are all very simple and link in with the business name. Customers are very conscious about internet security, so businesses must make sure their websites are up to date and secure.	✓ These can be quite cheap to develop and allow people to see products, news and contact details. ✓ Businesses can use websites to communicate with their stakeholders and to offer them a variety of ways to contact the business.	✘ Only around 45% of the world uses the internet, so some businesses may miss out on custom. ✘ Websites can 'crash' (stop working) if not updated or there are technical problems, which can cause a loss of custom and a poor image.
Telephone – businesses still use the telephone to contact stakeholders. Businesses can do this internally but also with external groups. Many larger businesses have call centres for customers to ring, whereas smaller firms may have a direct line to the shop or factory.	✓ The phone can be a quick and cheap way to talk directly to someone when face to face is not an option. ✓ The phone can allow a business to speak to suppliers and customers anywhere in the world.	✘ A phone line can have a poor connection, making it hard to hear the person on the other end. ✘ It can often take a long time to speak to someone unless they are available and near their phone at a specific time.
Video is often used to communicate with groups in other countries. Skype, for example, gives people and businesses the ability to talk over the internet. Businesses now operate all over the world, and have offices in multiple cities. Video conferencing allows them to connect and keep the same company ethos and image.	✓ It is direct and is nearly as good as face to face, as it allows the sender and receiver to see each other. ✓ It is cheaper for two offices in different countries to communicate via video conferencing rather than send employees to the other office.	✘ It can be quite difficult to get a time that suits both parties. ✘ Video often requires technology to be available – for example, the internet and some expensive equipment.

Method	Benefits	Drawbacks
Text messages are used by many organisations to contact stakeholders with small updates or important messages. This means the business can contact its stakeholders while they are on the go. This is a direct way of communicating that can target specific people.	✓ This is a cheap way of communicating with stakeholders. ✓ Text messages can include key information, offers and special content, such as prize winners. ✓ The majority of people have access to a mobile phone and can be contacted even when away from a computer.	✗ Like any text message, these can be misinterpreted and misunderstood. ✗ This form of communication relies on the contact numbers being up to date – a lot of time and effort may be needed to keep these accurate.
Social media is the fastest-growing communication method, and businesses use it to inform stakeholders in many different ways. Social networks, online advertising and mobile internet access have made social networking a new communication channel. Many younger customers use their mobile phone to access social media, and this allows businesses instant communication channels.	✓ This communication method is quick, efficient and specific, so it allows businesses to be very accurate with their communication. ✓ Many younger customers have access to social media on their mobile phones. ✓ Social media can be creative and fun, which keeps the business image positive.	✗ Some of the more elderly stakeholders do not access social media and prefer other forms of communication, such as a letter. ✗ Not all customers will use the internet on a regular basis. Therefore websites, emails and social media may not communicate the message to them.
Applications (apps) are used by many businesses as a way of communicating and interacting with their customers. In banking, for example, many banks use an app to help customers access their accounts, as well as up-to-date information and services. Apps are also created by businesses to help provide a medium of exchange where customers can purchase products, review and comment, and find information.	✓ This method is quick and easily accessible by customers who have a mobile phone or tablet device. ✓ This is a relatively cheap way to interact with customers, as an app can be created internally and at a relatively small cost.	✗ Not all customers have a mobile phone or tablet device, which means they can't access an app.

CASE STUDY

Social networks

Not every country uses the same social networks. Indeed, the largest social networks are not available in all countries. For example, Facebook does not exist in China.

Twitter is the ninth-largest social network globally, with 320 million users, yet it is the most popular social network in Japan. Twitter's success there is unique, as its main focus is English-speaking countries. It is also the second-biggest social network in Argentina and Egypt.

Application **Analysis** **Evaluation**

You will probably experience communication from your school on a regular basis. In pairs, prepare a short presentation that should include:

- A list of all the many different methods that the school uses to communicate.
- Now, identify one example of when the school has communicated with you or your parents. Which method did they use? What are the benefits and drawbacks of the method they used? (Apply this to you and your situation specifically.)
- Do you think this was the most appropriate method to use? Justify your answer.

Recommend and justify which communication method to use

Businesses must be very careful when choosing which communication method to use in a given situation. If they choose the wrong method, it may have a negative impact on the business and cause long-term problems. Here are some scenarios that illustrate this.

SCENARIO 1

The local supermarket has been criticised by the nearby community for increasing the number of deliveries it receives each week.

What to consider: The business should consider a communication method that is available to a large number of people at the same time. They also need to make sure they give a professional and positive response which shows respect to the local community.

Recommendation: External method – a letter to the local community.

Justification: A letter shows that time and effort have gone into the reply. The letter is a formal response and shows the local community that the business has acknowledged the complaint and replied in a formal professional way, which can be used in future discussions if needed.

What could go wrong? If the letter contains spelling errors or incorrect details, this could be embarrassing for the business. Also, if the business makes claims or promises to the local community – perhaps to reduce the number of deliveries – and it does not do this in the future, the local community may contact local press (newspapers), which would give the business a bad image.

SCENARIO 2

There has been a major oil spill by a large fuel company.

What to consider: If the public hear about the details first, it may give the business a negative image. They therefore need to make sure they choose the quickest communication method and include the correct information in it.

Recommendation: Internal methods – memo to all employees, email all employees and hold verbal discussions. External methods – news on website, press release to newspapers and a letter to all shareholders.

Justification: This scenario requires both internal and external communications. The external communication must be very well written and contain truthful information so that it cannot be used negatively later on. The internal communication keeps the employees up to date. This allows them to focus on the priority tasks.

What could go wrong? The business could give incorrect details that are used against them in the future. The website will need to be updated regularly; otherwise, stakeholders may feel that the business is not giving out the right amount of information quickly enough.

CASE STUDY Effect on a brand

A survey in the UK has found that 79% of customers will avoid a brand if they have received poor communication or customer service from that company. A lack of customer-focused feedback has made nearly four in every five customers think twice about returning to their original supplier or favourite shop. This loss of custom costs firms over $46 billion in revenue annually.

Application **Analysis**

Create four case studies that describe how businesses of your choice have used communication. You should create two case studies as examples of well-used communication, and two as examples of poorly used communication. Make sure you highlight what went well or what went poorly, and be ready to explain how you would have improved the situation.

Present each case study on a poster for display in the classroom. Remember to use images where possible.

Knowledge check

1. **Identify two reasons why it is very important for a business to communicate effectively.** **(2)**
2. **Explain why feedback from the receiver is an important part of communication.** **(4)**
3. **Outline the reasons behind the success of social media and apps in helping businesses communicate with customers.** **(4)**
4. **Explain one benefit and one drawback of using email to respond to customer questions.** **(4)**
5. **Outline why you think many businesses now use social media to communicate with stakeholders.** **(6)**

Total 20 marks

Communication barriers

Aims (2.4.2)
By the end of this section, you should:
- Understand how communication barriers arise and problems of ineffective communication; how communication barriers can be reduced or removed.

Barriers to communication

Many businesses believe they are very good at communicating with stakeholders. However, there are some barriers that can occur on a daily basis, which they must overcome:

Barrier	Explanation	Example
Method	Some methods do not suit the situation and the incorrect method may upset or annoy people. If a business uses an informal method to pass on a formal message, stakeholders are likely to react badly.	An employee is made redundant via text message rather than a more suitable method – for example, in person or by letter. This upsets the employee, as the method was informal.
Language	If the wrong vocabulary is used, the receiver won't understand key words.	A UK company uses technical terms when speaking to a customer in another country. The customer has only basic English and doesn't understand the technical terms.
Culture	Messages can be misunderstood, as different cultures perceive (understand) things in many ways.	In China, it is considered impolite to reject a suggestion or opinion, so questions such as 'Do we have a deal?' can cause misunderstandings.
Distractions	Noise or bad reception can mean a message is not fully understood by the receiver. There may also be other distractions that stop the receiver understanding the message, such as work pressures or being late for an appointment.	A business telephones its supplier to increase an order. The supplier doesn't hear the message correctly and delivers the wrong order.
Enthusiasm and emotion	These could distort (alter) the original message. Someone who is angry, upset or tired may misunderstand or incorrectly send the message.	An employee who is verbally asked to do something they dislike may stop listening and then make a mistake.
Amount	Too much information may cause the receiver to stop listening or misunderstand.	A waiter forgets a customer's meal, as they received too much information at once.

Barrier	Explanation	Example
Length of chain	If a message is passed through various people before finally ending up with the receiver, it may change slightly, as each person puts their own interpretation on the message. Words may be changed or the meaning altered.	A manager passes on a message for all employees. This may be changed slightly as it goes through each level in a business, as managers summarise the message or alter it slightly.
Losing messages	Some messages may be lost in the process. For example, faxes, emails and memos may be accidentally deleted, misread or fail to arrive (for example, if the fax machine was not turned on).	Some email systems do not deliver messages that contain rude words or large attachments. This means they could be lost.
Technical problems	Some office equipment may not be working, which stops a message being sent. Machines are also likely to break or wear out over time, meaning messages could be lost or slowed down.	If there is a power cut, computers will not be able to work, meaning some methods of communication won't be available.

These barriers can all be solved if the business is willing and able to dedicate time and resources to overcoming them.

- Many businesses encourage employees to communicate regularly with all stakeholders, including managers and customers.
- Businesses need to train employees in how to communicate and which method is the best to use in a certain situation. This should reduce mistakes as employees become better at choosing the correct method and producing a response that solves the initial issue.

The example below shows how training can help solve a communication barrier:

The owner of a small café needs additional stock for the weekend. They telephone the supplier to make the order. However, the order was misintepeted over the phone and the correct items are not delivered.

→

With training: The owner of a small café needs additional stock for the weekend. They telephone the supplier to place (make or give) the order. However, to make sure the order is correct, they also send it by email. The employee has received training in choosing the best communication method. They have been taught to follow up supplier orders with a phone call to check it has been received, and to check the details again.

Businesses also have to invest heavily in their communication tools, buying new technologies, equipment and systems and then training employees to use them. This is expensive, but the long-term benefits can be far greater than the costs.

CASE STUDY

The world's local bank

HSBC prides itself on being a 'global bank' and its adverts focus on addressing cultural barriers. It uses its managers from various countries around the world to run training sessions for employees in other offices. This is to help bridge the cultural gaps between employees and their customers. The world's local bank is aiming to eliminate any cultural barriers by training its employees in a wide range of global traditions. Businesses may back up their emails in case they need to check they have been sent. A business may also have a system in place that helps to avoid misinterpretation, for example, sending a summary email after every telephone discussion, or by recording calls.

Problems of poor communication

Communication problems can cause major damage to a business in both the short and long term. The short-term issues may include missing payments to the suppliers, reducing wages and losing customers. In the longer term, the business may lose so many customers and suppliers that it is forced to close.

Other consequences of poor communication are:

- **Employees are unhappy with their managers, as they feel they are not listened to**. If employees cannot communicate with their managers or the business owners, they may feel the business does not value them or their ideas. This is not good for a business's employee retention (keeping employees) or morale.
- **Customers do not get a quick enough reply and the business develops a poor reputation**. Many businesses invest in their customer service department, as this is very important in keeping existing customers. If a customer has a problem or issue, businesses need to make sure it is solved as quickly as possible, otherwise the customer may move to a competitor.
- **Orders are missed or are incorrect**. If a global business places an incorrect order, this may cost the business millions of dollars. A smaller business may also suffer large costs if they misread communications or do not communicate clearly with suppliers or other stakeholders.

In pairs or small groups, design a role play set in a business environment of your choice.

The role play should involve a form of communication, either internal or external, which fails. For example, a business owner wants a meeting with a supplier so he sends a fax to the head office, or an employee replies to a customer complaint with a letter that she sends by post.

The class should then identify the reasons behind the failure and comment on how to correct it.

Knowledge check

1. **Define the term barrier.** **(2)**
2. **Identify one way in which a business can overcome a language communication barrier.** **(2)**
3. **Consider the likely impacts of bad communication for a relatively new small business.** **(4)**
4. **Explain two barriers to communication that may stop a message being delivered.** **(4)**

Total 12 marks

Check your progress:

✓ I can explain why effective communication is important and the methods used to achieve it.

✓ I can analyse different communication methods, giving benefits and drawbacks of the methods used.

Exam-style questions: short answer and data response

1. Steve is the senior principal of a large for-profit international school. He is a democratic leader. He believes that motivating his teachers is very important if the students are to get good examination results. He also believes that money does not motivate teachers and pays them all the same salary regardless of their experience.

   a) **Define** the term democratic leader. (2)

   b) **Define** the term motivation. (2)

   c) **Explain** one advantage and one disadvantage of all teachers being paid the same salary. (4)

   d) Recruiting teachers to work in international schools is highly competitive and expensive. **Explain** two factors that Steve should consider when recruiting new teachers to his school. (6)

   e) Steve has a policy of recruiting vice principals from outside the business (externally). As a result of pressure from a trade union, Steve is changing this policy so that internal recruitment will be used for senior employees in the future. Do you think that the change will benefit the school? **Justify** your answer. (6)

2. The school has a high labour turnover, with a large number of teachers leaving their job each year. All employees at the school have an employment contract and must complete training on the school's communication systems as part of their induction programme.

   a) **Explain** what is meant by an induction programme. (2)

   b) **Identify** two pieces of information in an employment contract. (2)

   c) **Explain** two possible problems of poor communication within a business. (4)

   X and Y are two catering companies that reward their employees in different ways. Figures 1 and 2 show how the two pay systems operate.

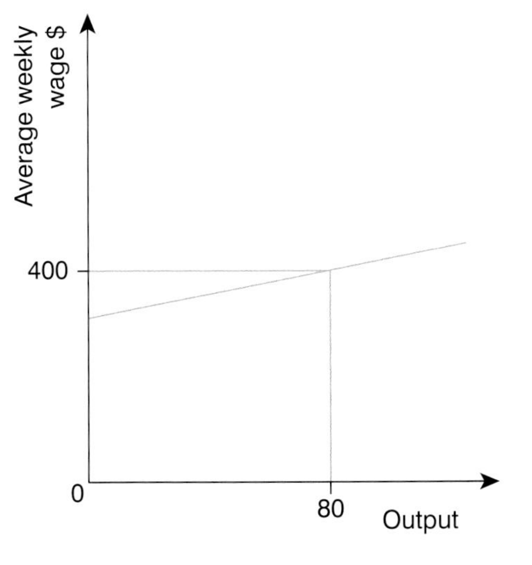

Δ Figure 1: Company X

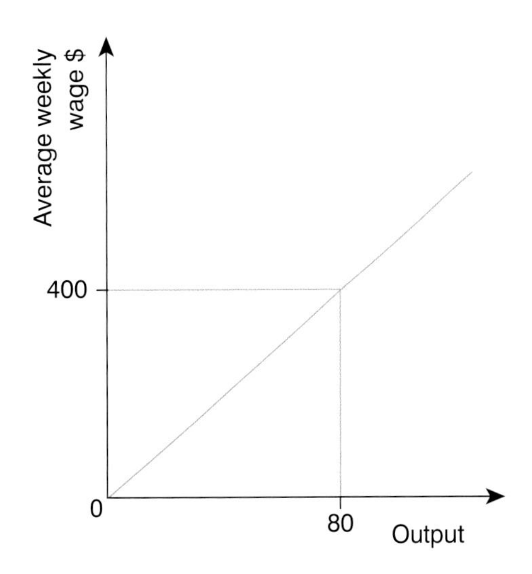

Δ Figure 2: Company Y

a) **Explain** three main differences between the two pay systems. (6)

b) Steve believes that money does not motivate his employees. With reference to an appropriate motivational theory, **explain** what evidence Steve may have based his judgement on. (6)

3. Steve is well liked by the teachers at his school and is considered to be a good manager. He is known for effective delegation and for his caring nature. As a result of his good management, few employees in the business feel the need to belong to a trade union.

a) **Outline** what is meant by the term trade union. (2)

b) **Define** the term delegation. (2)

c) **Identify** and **explain** two disadvantages to Steve of delegation. (4)

d) **Explain** two characteristics, other than delegation, that might make Steve a good manager. (6)

While working at the school, there are many rules and regulations that Steve has to follow. Many of these rules concern employment of teachers.

e) **Consider** the implications of two pieces of employment legislation that Steve will need to follow. (6)

Note: The exam-style questions, answers and commentary in this book were written by the author; in examination the number of marks awarded to questions like these may be different.

Exam-style questions based on case studies

Pearson–Harmann

Pearson–Harmann is a large firm of architects based in Brazil. They specialise in designing modern shopping centres. They currently have 800 employees and have offices across South America, North America and Europe.

Pearson–Harmann is about to complete the takeover of another company, SkyHigh. Specialising in skyscrapers, SkyHigh has struggled in recent years due to global recession and a slow-down in the number of large-scale projects (mega projects). The takeover was an opportunity for Pearson–Harmann to buy SkyHigh's impressive office buildings and to benefit from their employees, expertise and their strong relationships with the construction companies.

Henrique is the human resources manager for the company. He is responsible for all recruitment, for employee morale and for ensuring that the company follows the correct employment law in all the countries in which it operates. It is also his job to ensure that the takeover does not affect employees' motivation.

Company	Number of employees	Primary locations	Years in operation
Pearson–Harmann	800	South and North America Europe	23
SkyHigh	1000	Asia	67

Appendix 1: Details of each company

Pearson–Harmann

Union 1
Union 2
Union 3
Union 4
Union 5

SkyHigh

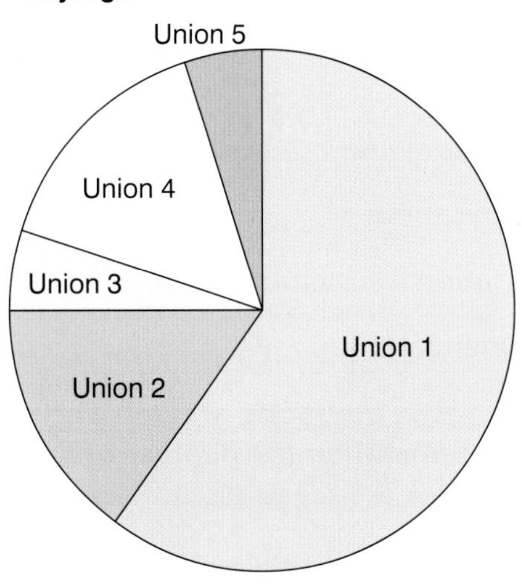

Appendix 2: The percentage of employees in each company that belongs to each trade union

1. To avoid the firm becoming too hierarchical, Henrique has been asked to draw an organisation chart for Pearson–Harmann after its takeover of SkyHigh.

   a) **Identify** two reasons why firms use organisation charts and **explain** two issues for a firm if its organisational structure is too hierarchical. (8)

b) As part of the takeover, it was agreed that a new (external) chairperson would be appointed. **Outline** three elements of the recruitment and selection process that Pearson–Harmann may go through as it recruits a new chairperson. (12)

2. Governments often pass laws to protect employees. After the takeover, Pearson–Harmann wants to reduce the total headcount to 1200 employees. Henrique is worried about the threat of industrial action from trade unions as a result of this downsizing.

a) **Explain** two pieces of employment legislation that Pearson–Harmann will need to follow when deciding which employees to make redundant. (8)

b) Do you think employees need legal protection from business activity? **Justify** your answer. (12)

3. Henrique is responsible for all recruitment and, with his team of human resources employees, conducts job interviews.

a) **Identify** four questions Henrique should ask when interviewing applicants for these jobs. **Explain** why he should ask each question. (8)

b) Henrique is responsible for ensuring that employees are motivated. Which leadership style do you think might be most effective in motivating employees? **Justify** your answer. (12)

4. The trade unions have found evidence that many mergers are unsuccessful. Based on this, they are suggesting that Henrique reconsider his decision to merge with SkyHigh.

a) **Identify** what is meant by the term trade union and **explain** two possible impacts on Pearson–Harmann of trade union action. (8)

b) Focusing on the following issues related to people management, **outline** the problems the merger may cause and **explain** whether you think the merger should go ahead. (12)

i) Motivation

ii) Communication

iii) Organisational structure

iv) Recommendation

Note: The exam-style questions, answers and commentary in this book were written by the author; in examination the number of marks awarded to questions like these may be different.

Exam-style questions based on case studies

ComputeIT

ComputeIT is an IT firm located in New Town (Country X). The business is a partnership owned by Simon and Katherine Kinthuia. They provide IT repair and consultancy services for Country X's growing technology industry. The firm is well known for the quality of its service and expertise.

ComputeIT currently employs 10 employees. Simon does the accounts and marketing for the firm. Katherine provides the consultancy service and manages the employees who provide repair services.

The technology industry in Country X is growing at 20% per year. ComputeIT is struggling to get enough employees to meet this demand. A major problem they face is training. Few colleges in Country X have the equipment to train employees to the level ComputeIT needs. Katherine estimates that it takes her three to six months to train new employees. Most of this training is currently done off the job.

Another issue ComputeIT faces is labour turnover. More than half of the 10 repair employees have worked for ComputeIT for less than one year. Faced with a small budget (see Appendix 3), ComputeIT cannot afford to pay the employees higher salaries.

Business	Average prices (price per hour)
ComputeIT	$10
ITu	$5
FixIT	$10

Appendix 1: Comparison of the repair fees of ComputeIT and its competitors

Business	Average complaints (per month)
ComputeIT	12
ITu	15
FixIT	12

Appendix 2: Comparison of complaints received by ComputeIT and its competitors

Revenue	$500000
Cost of sales	$100000
Gross profit	**$400 000**
Expenses	
Salaries	$200000
Training costs	$150000
Rent	$15000
Utilities	$10000
Other	$5000
Net profit	**$20 000**

Appendix 3: ComputeIT's basic accounts

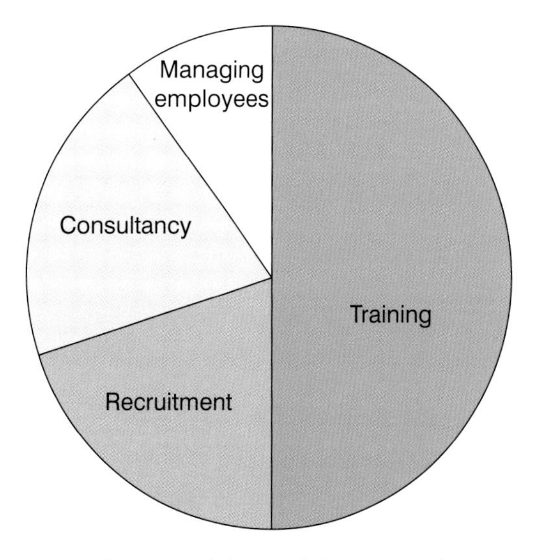

Appendix 4: Breakdown of the time Katherine spends on different tasks

1. Katherine and Simon currently pay their employees using piece rate.

   a) With reference to the appendices, **outline** one advantage and one disadvantage of them using this method. (8)

   b) Katherine thinks that using non-financial methods of reward will be effective. Advise Katherine on what methods she might use. **Justify** your recommendations. (12)

2. Katherine and Simon recognise the need to reduce their labour turnover.

   a) With reference to the appendices, consider whether ComputeIT's current off-the-job training is effective. **Justify** one alternative method of training they may use. (8)

   b) With reference to appropriate motivational theories, **outline** and **justify** three non-financial methods Katherine and Simon might use to address their labour turnover. (12)

3. a) **Explain** why it is important for ComputeIT to recruit skilled IT employees. (8)

   b) Advise Katherine and Simon on the best ways to recruit and select new employees. **Justify** your recommendations. (12)

4. a) None of ComputeIT's employees belong to a trade union. **Consider** two benefits to the employees if they joined a trade union. (8)

   b) To help address their employee needs, Katherine and Simon are considering employing a number of part-time employees. Advise Katherine and Simon on the advantages and disadvantages of this approach. **Justify** whether you think they should employ part-time employees or not. (12)

Note: The exam-style questions, answers and commentary in this book were written by the author; in examination the number of marks awarded to questions like these may be different.

Past paper questions

Paper 1

Section 2

NCE manufactures cars in 4 factories using flow production. NCE's Human Resources Director thinks good induction training helps achieve high productivity. Factory X is its most efficient factory. Last year the size of the new car market fell by 20%. NCE now has to make 400 workers redundant at one of its other factories. 'I am pleased NCE is a large business', said the HR Director, 'I think a small business cannot survive in this competitive market.'

Table 2: NCE operations data for 2014

Number of cars made	Number of employees
168 000	2800

c) Identify and explain two ways in which induction training might benefit NCE.

Way 1: ______________________________

____

Explanation: ______________________________

____

Way 2: ______________________________

____

Explanation: ______________________________

______________________________ (4)

d) Identify and explain two factors that NCE would need to consider in deciding which workers to make redundant.

Factor 1: ______________________________

____

Explanation: ______________________________

____

____

____

Factor 2: ______________________________

____

Explanation: ______________________________

____

____

______________________________ (6)

Cambridge International IGCSE Business Studies 0450 Paper 12, Q3 c & d, Nov 2015

Past paper questions

Paper 2

Section 2

The following case study is taken from past papers created by Cambridge Assessment International Education. We have only provided extracts of this case study, and it does not reflect the full case study that you may be provided with in your examination.

ACE Engineering (ACE)

ACE is a public limited company located in country Z. It makes large ovens which are sold mainly to restaurants and hotels in many different countries. The main components used to make the ovens are metal. There are also rubber components which fit around the oven doors and electrical components for the temperature controls. Only the electrical components are imported. All other components are purchased locally.

ACE employs 200 production workers in its factory and 50 office workers. A high proportion of the workforce leaves each year and the Human Resources department has frequently to recruit and train new employees. All employees are members of a trade union. The directors of ACE have held meetings to discuss how to manage the employees effectively. They want to improve the employees' motivation.

The managers expect workers to follow instructions and the workers are told they will be dismissed if they do not follow orders.

Appendix

To: Operations Manager of ACE

From: Managing Director of ACE

Date: 4 October 2014

Re: Efficiency improvements

We need to be efficient to remain competitive. We should be using lean production methods. All our competitors use lean production methods such as just-in-time and waste reduction. Please research this for me and let me know what you think.

1 a) **Identify** and **explain** **one** advantage and **one** disadvantage to ACE of all of its employees being members of a trade union. (8)

b) Consider the advantages and disadvantages of **two** management styles which could be used by managers at ACE. Recommend which would be the best style for the managers to use if they want to improve motivation. **Justify** your answer. (12)

Cambridge International IGCSE Business Studies 0450 Paper 22, Q2 a & b, Nov 2014

Skills Builder

AO1: Knowledge

The People in business topic contains a lot of different theories. You need to **understand**, for example, the different motivation theories and the different leadership styles. You need to be able to use this **knowledge**. Remembering Maslow's Hierarchy of Needs is not enough; you must be able to demonstrate that you can use the concept.

AO2: Application

Using concepts requires you to **apply** them to different contexts. Different leadership styles might be appropriate in different contexts – for example, a crisis situation might require autocratic leadership. Different types of jobs require different types of recruitment and selection strategies. Always ensure that you do not just write everything you know about a concept or theory (for example, leadership styles, recruitment, communication or motivation), but also make sure this knowledge **applies** to a particular context.

AO3: Analysis

People in business has close links with many other topics. You need to be able to **analyse** the importance of these links. Good management of employees in a hospital is essential if patients are to get the best service possible. In an internet firm, people management may be less important than product management (though it will not be unimportant). You must be able to **distinguish** between what is important in different contexts and **assess** how a firm might respond. A balanced discussion of different viewpoints or decisions is an important skill.

AO4: Evaluation

People are not easy to manage. They do not always do what you want them to. Just because a theory sounds good in a textbook does not mean it will work in practice. More motivation does not automatically mean more business success. Even with highly motivated employees, a firm might fail due to a poor product, poor marketing or a bad location. You must acknowledge the implications of complex human behaviour in your answers and consider that the most logical outcome might not be the most realistic. You must be able to make reasoned recommendations, but you must recognise that these solutions might not work. When people are involved, nothing is certain. To evaluate successfully you should try to consider as many angles of the discussion as you possibly can.

Marketing is the business process responsible for anticipating, identifying and satisfying customer needs. Without marketing, a firm would have to guess who its customers are, where to sell its products and even what products to make. Without marketing, a firm would be invisible to its customers and would quickly fail.

In this section, you will learn:

- to analyse the role of marketing and how the market changes, looking at the concepts of niche and mass marketing and how and why market segmentation is undertaken
- about market research, the methods used, and how market research results are presented and used
- how firms use product, price, place and promotion (known as the 4Ps or the marketing mix), and how technology is used in the marketing mix
- about marketing strategies, the nature and impact of legal controls, and the opportunities and problems of entering new foreign markets.

SKILLS BUILDER

Good progress

Knowledge: You show sound knowledge of the concepts and ideas related to marketing.

Application: You demonstrate an ability to apply your knowledge and understanding to address specific marketing issues, strategies and situations.

Analysis: You can distinguish which marketing strategies and activities might be appropriate to a given firm, commenting on the implications of those strategies.

Evaluation: You evaluate and make basic judgements on the appropriateness of different marketing activities in different contexts.

Excellent progress

Knowledge: You demonstrate a thorough ability to define the concepts and ideas related to marketing.

Application: You apply your knowledge to draw conclusions about the potential effectiveness of different marketing activities and strategies in different contexts and to make judgements about how cost-effective different marketing activities are.

Analysis: You comment accurately on how various marketing activities and strategies impact on a given firm.

Evaluation: You accurately evaluate the appropriateness of marketing activities and strategies within a given context, recommending reasoned and logical courses of action.

SECTION CONTENTS

3 Marketing

Starting points

Marketing is all around you. Businesses are competing for your money, hoping that through their careful marketing planning they can convince you to spend on their product or service.

Consider a product or service you have bought recently.

Now, think about the four areas below. For each one, give information on the product/service you have chosen.

- Product: What is the product? Does it come in different sizes/colours/variations? What does it do? What is it for?
- Price: What does it cost? Does the price differ depending on where it is bought?
- Place: Where is it sold? How does it get to the customer?
- Promotion: How do customers find out about the product/service, for example, through a local newspaper ad or on the radio? This may be on a local, national or international scale.

Marketing, competition and the customer

The role of marketing

Aims (3.1.1)

By the end of this section, you should:

- Understand the role of marketing in identifying customer needs
- Understand the role of marketing in satisfying customer needs
- Understand the role of marketing in maintaining customer loyalty
- Understand the role of marketing in building customer relationships.

Identifying customers' needs and building customer loyalty

There are many different ways of defining marketing. For example, consider these definitions.

Marketing is ...

... the activity, set of institutions, and processes for creating, communicating, delivering, and exchanging offerings that have value for customers, clients, partners, and society at large.

American Marketing Association

... the social process by which individuals and groups obtain what they need and want through creating and exchanging products and value with others.

Philip Kotler

... the management process responsible for identifying,anticipating and satisfying customer requirements profitably.

Chartered Institute of Marketing

Whatever the exact definition of marketing, it is clear that, above all else, marketing is about being customer-focused. The role of marketing is to ensure that a business's product meets customer needs – if it doesn't, customers won't buy it. This simple fact makes effective marketing essential to business success.

Focusing on the needs of customers is known as **market orientation**. A market-orientated business starts by asking what consumers need from a product. They then try to develop products that meet and satisfy those needs. An analysis of what consumers want will shape decisions about product design, pricing, promotion and distribution (place). For example, McDonald's responded to changing customer needs by introducing salads and healthier meal options.

The opposite of market orientation is known as product orientation. This is where a firm designs a product independently of known customer needs, and then uses marketing to convince customers to buy the product. This approach is common with technology products such as 4K televisions.

Modern marketing is not just about getting new customers, it is also about maintaining customer loyalty and building relationships with those customers. Relationship marketing involves communicating with customers regularly and encouraging repeat purchases (**brand loyalty**). Building relationships means not just selling a product to customers and then forgetting about them. Firms need to engage their customers with (remind them of) the brand regularly.

Businesses build relationships with their customers through personalised promotions and rewards that encourage the customer to keep coming back. Supermarkets and airlines often use loyalty cards and points to reward customers, as well as specific promotional emails outlining deals and offers. Businesses will also build a strong customer service department, to help deal with any queries or issues raised by customers. This helps keep customers happy and creates a positive image for the business.

Many firms use Facebook and Twitter to communicate with customers in an attempt to develop trust and loyalty. This kind of two-way marketing allows firms to listen to customers and respond to their needs quickly. By engaging with customers through websites, live TV text-ins, retail/store loyalty cards and even through internet games, firms can build **brand image**, strengthen relationships with customers and improve brand loyalty.

CASE STUDY

Building customer relationships

Magazines such as Seventeen, CosmoGirl, TeenVogue and Men's Health use their websites and email newsletters as a way of frequently communicating with customers. The websites run daily articles, ask readers to participate in surveys, run competitions and manage chat forums. Supported by podcasts and online videos, fresh daily content encourages customers to engage with the brand as often as possible. This means that when it comes to buying a magazine, the customers are loyal to the brand. It also means that customers talk to their friends about the latest 'news' or celebrity gossip and even forward links to the sites (further promoting brand awareness).

Satisfying customers' needs

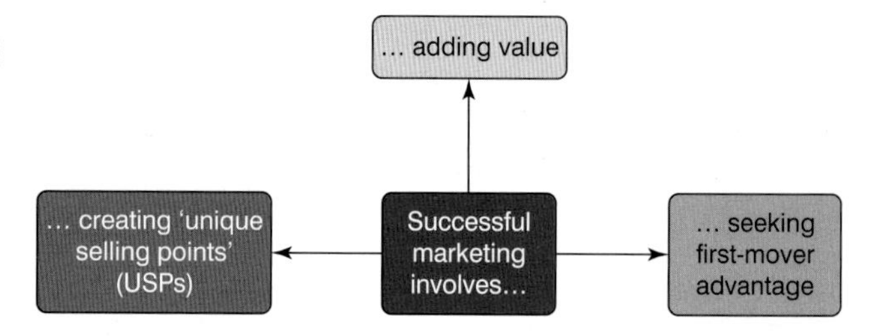

Adding value

To 'add value' is to be able to sell a product for more than it cost to make (see 1.1 Business activity). The business can then sell the product for profit. Marketing is crucial for achieving **added value** because it creates willingness to pay for a product. In the case of Nike trainers, for example, customers are willing to pay high prices (much higher than the cost of production) because of the brand image created by Nike's marketing.

> **Did you know?**
>
> Dyson, a British technology company, is most famous for its Cyclone technology vacuum cleaners, which sell worldwide. James Dyson (the founder) had to create 5127 prototypes (models) before he was happy it would have a working USP and meet customer needs.

Creating unique selling points (USPs)

It is not enough for a business just to meet customer needs. It must meet those needs better than the competition.

In order to achieve **competitive advantage**, a business should identify its **unique selling point (USP)** – a feature of either the product, its image, price, promotion or distribution (place) that is superior to the competition.

A successful USP will enable consumers to identify the main reason why they should purchase a specific brand and will encourage them to do so. A USP can therefore help a business add value and achieve profit.

CASE STUDY

A very unique selling point

A good example of a USP is the packaging (and shape) of Pringles potato chips (crisps). In essence, Pringles are just the same as any other potato chip. The USP is that they are packaged differently (in a tube) and therefore the shape of each potato chip is unique to Pringles.

Pringles have consistently used the USP as the basis for their marketing (promoting, for example, the opening of the Pringles tube as part of the overall eating experience).

Even if a product is not unique, it is the job of marketing to ensure that it is differentiated from competitors' products. There are many social network sites as well as Facebook, and there were many that existed prior to Facebook's launch. In the case of Facebook, **differentiation** is achieved through its simple design (the product), its features (such as the Timeline and Facebook games). Facebook is also differentiated by its vast (1.86 billion) membership; to compete, other social networks need to offer a similar membership base – an almost impossible task.

Seeking first mover advantage

Successful marketing must anticipate future market trends. It must also enable a business to be the first to meet a new or previously unrealised (not yet met) consumer need. By being first with a new product, a business can achieve much greater success – it is estimated that being the first to enter a new market can double a product's profitability. This is known as **first mover advantage**.

For example, Apple dominates the tablet computer market because it was, arguably, the first to market one. The iPad was not only a great product technically, it also anticipated a trend for tablet-style computers. When the iPad was launched, people didn't quite know what it was for, but Apple has since sold over 60 million of them.

Top Tip

The customer is king. Remember to think not just about what marketing is, but also about the role of marketing in identifying and satisfying customer needs.

Analysis

Investigate one of the companies listed below. Then, using the information in this section on the role of marketing, analyse why you think their marketing is successful.

- Adidas (sports clothing)
- Uber (taxi service)
- Mac (cosmetics)
- Ducati (motorbikes)
- H&M (clothing)
- Apple (technology)

Present your findings as a poster, using both visual images and words to outline the marketing activities and why you think they are successful.

Knowledge check

1. **Explain how marketing is used to develop/maintain customer loyalty.** **(6)**
2. **Define, using a suitable example, market orientation.** **(4)**
3. **Identify one example of how marketing adds value.** **(2)**
4. **Define the term unique selling point.** **(2)**
5. **Explain the term first mover advantage. Why is being 'first mover' considered an advantage?** **(3)**
6. **Explain how marketing helps a firm to identify customer needs.** **(3)**

Total 20 marks

Market changes

Aims (3.1.2)

By the end of this section, you should:

- Understand why customer/consumer spending patterns may change
- Understand the importance of changing customer needs
- Understand why some markets have become more competitive
- Understand how businesses can respond to changing spending patterns and increased competition.

Markets do not stay the same; over time, the number of customers and competitors within a market will change. New technology and shifting fashions will change the type of products sold. To remain successful, a business must respond to these market changes.

Consumer spending patterns

The products that consumers buy today are not the same as they bought last year or last decade, nor are they the same as they will buy in a hundred years' time. A variety of factors affect how much consumers spend and what they spend their money on.

- **The economy.** During times of recession (see 6.1 Economic issues), consumers may switch to cheaper, better-value products. During times of economic growth, consumers may be more prepared to spend money on luxury items.
- **Technology.** Consumer spending patterns change to reflect current technology. For example, mobile phones were once a luxury good but are now so popular that there are more mobile phones in the world than people! The fast pace of developments in mobile phone technology also means that existing phones are quickly replaced with more sophisticated models.
- **Fashion.** Who would want to be seen wearing last year's fashion? The whole fashion industry relies on using marketing to shift consumer spending from one trend to the next. Moreover, fashion is not restricted to clothing.

Δ There are trends in many different markets that firms must follow to remain relevant. The current trend, for example, is for larger screens on smartphones.

For the individual consumer, spending might be affected by the following.

- **Age.** As we age, the products we buy change. The older the average age of a household, for example, the lower the spend on housing products. Young adults purchase furniture as they buy their first home, and perhaps later if they move to a larger second home (buying more furniture as they do so). The older people get, the less they move house and the less furniture they buy.
- **Life stage.** Single people, young couples and adults with children all spend very different amounts on very different things. For example, adults whose children have left home (so-called 'empty-nesters') may spend more money on overseas holidays than parents with children still living at home. Dinkies (Double Income, No Kids) may spend money on luxury and technology products.
- **Income.** A person's income has a clear impact on his or her spending patterns. The lowest-income earners spend more of their household budgets on necessities such as housing, food and fuel. Higher earners spend proportionally more on clothing, footwear, recreation and transport.

CASE STUDY

Research results

Credit Suisse conducted a survey in India into the average monthly expenditures of Indians on various categories, as shown in the chart.

As the Indian economy has grown over recent years, some Indians are finding they have more disposable income to spend on non-essential items such as personal care and entertainment. These changes have seen the launch of many Western brands, such as Tesco, Sony and Coca-Cola, across India.

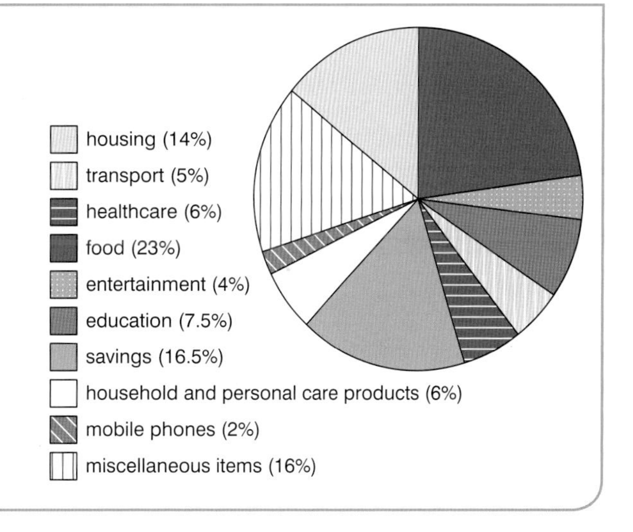

Source: Credit Suisse Research Institute

The importance of changing customer needs

An awareness of consumer spending habits is essential if a firm and its products are to remain competitive, especially for a market-orientated business (see The role of marketing earlier in topic 3.1). On the one hand, you can gain competitive advantage by understanding current spending patterns and being able to predict new ones. On the other hand, failure to spot changes can lead to falling sales and even business failure. Knowing what customer needs are and being able to predict how they might change are therefore vital for a firm's long-term success.

A business might respond to changing spending patterns by:

- adapting its products
- launching new products
- selling its current products to new markets
- closing down unprofitable products/locations.

Both the newspaper and music industries, for instance, were slow to spot changes in the way that people 'consume' news and music. With music and news available online and now on mobile devices, CD and newspaper sales fell significantly. Numerous music companies and newspapers, such as the French newspaper *France Soir*, have closed as a result. Companies that spotted this trend – for example, the world's most popular online newspaper, the *Daily Mail* – have enjoyed strong sales and healthy profits.

Competitive markets

Competitive markets exist when there is wide choice for consumers of both products and suppliers. If a consumer is able to compare products and prices and can switch between brands easily, the market may be intensely competitive.

Competition in a market might increase because of:

- changes in technology making it easier for more firms to enter a market
- changes in technology making it easy for customers to compare prices and product benefits
- changes in regulations making it easier for more firms to enter a market
- changes in regulations that affect operating costs (lower costs might, for example, attract more firms into the market, increasing competition)
- a decrease in the number of customers in a market.

For consumers, competitive markets have several advantages:

- lower prices
- wide choice
- frequent promotions
- a faster pace of invention and innovation (leading to better products)
- improvements in the quality of service.

How businesses respond to increased competition

For businesses, competitive markets can be tough. Profit margins may be low and the firm may have to work very hard to stay ahead of the competition. It will also have to invest significant amounts of money in market research (see 3.2 Market research), new product development and promotion (see 3.3 Marketing mix).

The strategies firms use to respond to competitive markets include:

- investing in employee training to improve quality of service
- improving operations management to speed up delivery times
- conducting research to develop new products
- launching a promotional campaign to increase sales
- using relationship marketing to develop brand loyalty
- using pricing strategy to increase competitiveness.

Above all, a firm operating in a competitive market will need to use market research in order to understand its customers, their changing needs and its market.

Application

The online retailer Amazon and the popularity of e-books (and e-book readers such as the Kindle) have made the publishing industry very competitive.

Examine the book publishing industry. Consider the following:

- How easy is it for consumers to compare prices across book retailers?
- Are there significant additional costs involved for customers when purchasing from one retailer rather than another?
- Are the products the same across retailers? Do any retailers try to differentiate the product in any way?
- What seems to be the main focus of book retailers' marketing efforts?

Use your answers to analyse the competitive nature of the book industry and to evaluate what a firm might do to ensure its survival. Present your findings as an article written for the business section of a newspaper or magazine.

Knowledge check

1. **Identify two reasons why consumer spending patterns change.** **(2)**
2. **Explain, using an example, how life stages change consumer spending patterns.** **(3)**
3. **Explain why a competitive market may benefit consumers.** **(3)**
4. **Outline, using examples, two ways in which a firm might respond to a competitive market.** **(6)**
5. **Explain why knowledge of changing consumer spending patterns is vital to business success.** **(6)**

Total 20 marks

Niche marketing and mass marketing

Aims (3.1.3)
By the end of this section, you should:
- Understand the benefits and limitations of niche and mass marketing.

Businesses have to choose their marketing strategy based on whether they want to:

- sell a small number of goods at a high price
- sell a large number of goods at a lower price.

This choice of strategy determines whether a firm will sell its products to the **mass market** or to a small **niche market**.

Mass marketing

Mass (large-scale) marketing (also known as **undifferentiated marketing**) aims for a high sales volume (amount) at low prices. It is an attempt to appeal to an entire market with one basic marketing strategy using mass media and mass distribution. Mass markets are characterised by:

- low prices
- similar customer needs across the market
- undifferentiated products
- a wide range of sales outlets/wide availability
- extensive promotion
- high sales volume.

> **Did you know?**
>
> To help maintain its mass market position, Coca-Cola spends an estimated $4 billion a year on advertising. This may seem like a lot of money, but the world's 27th most valuable brand does sell its products in over 200 countries.

◁ Coca-Cola and Pepsi are examples of mass market products.

The benefits of mass marketing

The main advantage of mass marketing is **economies of scale** (see 4.2 Costs, scale of production and break-even analysis). The average cost of production, marketing and distribution will all be lower if products are sold in large volumes. These lower costs can then be passed on to the consumer in the form of lower prices. Selling at lower prices helps the firm to generate a high sales volume and the potential for large profits overall.

The limitations of mass marketing

The main disadvantage of mass marketing is that the products may not be suitable for sale in all countries. Customers may prefer a product made specifically for their needs. When Procter & Gamble launched its brand of disposable diapers (Pampers) in Japan, they were a failure (see 3.3 Marketing mix). As soon as Procter & Gamble changed the product to suit Japanese needs, they became the market leader in Japan.

Another disadvantage of mass marketing is that, because of the volume of production, any mistakes with products can be very costly.

CASE STUDY

Product recall

Ford has had to recall over 570 000 vehicles across North America and Europe, in order to fix separate issues that have caused engine fires and doors to fly open. When firms request that customers return products because of safety reasons (for replacement or refund), it is known as a product recall. The size of this recall, and the cost to Ford, is an example of the risks for mass market businesses when things go wrong.

Niche marketing

Niche (small-scale) marketing (also known as **focused marketing**) involves selling goods to small, clearly identifiable segments of a market. Niche markets are usually characterised by:

- premium prices
- small sales volumes
- highly differentiated products
- a high skills base – it is often difficult for large companies/competitors to easily find the skilled labour to produce the product.

Examples of niche markets include: the market for expensive tailor-made clothing, the 'rent-a-pet' services available in Japan, and six-star hotels such as the Burj Al Arab in Dubai.

Niche marketing has a significant effect on the type of marketing activities that a firm will use. Promotion will have to be very specific, the product clearly differentiated and the outlets (stores) where it is sold must clearly reflect its image.

The advantages of niche marketing

Targeting a product or service at a niche market has several benefits:

- less competition
- a clear focus on a small target group (making marketing more accurate and cheaper)
- the firm becomes an expert in the segment
- niche markets usually attract premium prices
- customer loyalty is often high
- profit margins are often higher.

The disadvantages of niche marketing

The main limitations of niche marketing include:

- few economies of scale (see 4.2 Costs, scale of production and break-even analysis)
- a risk of over-dependence on a single product or market
- the threat of competition (especially due to small market size)
- a vulnerability to market changes.

Analysis

Consider the past global trend for fish spas. Starting life in Asia, these spas were once a niche product. Growing in popularity, with branches found in many cities throughout the world, they quickly became mainstream. However, their mass market status was threatened by health scares and negative publicity.

Use the fish spa example to prepare a poster that compares and contrasts the features of niche and mass markets.

Knowledge check

1. **Identify two characteristics of a mass market.** **(2)**
2. **Identify one advantage of mass marketing.** **(1)**
3. **Explain one disadvantage of Coca-Cola's mass marketing approach.** **(3)**
4. **Explain, using an example, what is meant by niche marketing.** **(2)**
5. **'The toothpaste market is a good example of a niche market.' Explain this statement. To what extent do you believe it to be true?** **(6)**

Total 14 marks

Market segmentation

Aims (3.1.4)

By the end of this section, you should:

- Understand how markets can be segmented, for example, according to age, socio-economic grouping, location, gender
- Understand the potential benefits of segmentation to businesses
- Be able to recommend and justify an appropriate method of segmentation in given circumstances.

The purpose of market segmentation

Few goods are truly mass market products (see the previous section on Niche marketing and mass marketing). In most markets, products are differentiated to some degree. Sectioning large markets into smaller segments (parts) helps businesses to differentiate products and market them effectively.

Through market research (see 3.2 Market research), businesses try to discover a huge range of information about customers (and potential customers). They might find out:

- what TV programmes they watch and what magazines they read
- how much they earn
- where they do their shopping and who does it
- what other products they use and why.

They can then use this information to develop products and marketing strategies that appeal directly to specific **market segments (target markets)**. For example, the market segment interested in the BMW Mini is young, fun-loving, usually lives in cities and has a sense of humour. Marketing for the Mini reflects this market segment.

Effective segmentation allows businesses to:

- use marketing budgets effectively
- target marketing campaigns accurately
- identify gaps in the market and new opportunities
- differentiate products from those of their competitors (allowing higher prices to be charged).

In short, knowing and understanding market segments makes marketing activities more likely to succeed.

Δ A promotional electric car covered in fake grass. Quirky (unusual) advertising can appeal to some market segments.

How markets are segmented

Businesses use many different criteria to segment markets.

Geographical segmentation

Geographical segmentation is a way of grouping consumers according to the area in which they live. This could be quite broad, such as targeting customers in large cities, or it may be quite specific – for example, many insurance companies segment customers according to crime rates in their immediate area, charging those who live in high-crime areas more.

Demographic segmentation

This is the broadest of all segmentation methods and includes a wide range of different criteria.

Criterion	Example
Age	Movies aimed at under-10s
Gender	Hair products aimed at females
Ethnic group	Food products aimed at different religious groups (for example, halal meat adheres to Islamic law)
Income	Credit cards aimed at people earning over certain amounts
Family characteristics	Multi-packs sold at supermarkets, often aimed at large families
Education	*The Economist* aimed at well-educated people
Occupation	Magazines, such as *Management Today*, aimed at specific professions

Socio-demographic segmentation

Markets may also be segmented according to social class (socio-demographic segmentation). The most common classification of social groups is shown in the table.

Group	Social status	Description
A	Upper middle class	Higher managerial, administrative or professional (doctors, lawyers, company directors)
B	Middle class	Middle management, administrative or professional (teachers, nurses, managers)
C1	Lower middle class	Supervisory, clerical or junior management (shop assistants, clerks, police officers)
C2	Skilled working class	Skilled manual employees (electricians, service engineers, technicians)
D	Working class	Semi-skilled and unskilled manual employees (agricultural employees, production line employees)
E	The poorest in society	The elderly, casual employees, the unemployed

Products can then be aimed at specific groupings such as ABs or DEs. Mercedes cars, for example, are aimed at ABs. Most businesses use a combination of all of the segmentation methods to accurately segment their markets. The starting point of marketing success ('know your customer') is an essential part of segmentation. Segmentation involves clearly defining who these customers are and developing a detailed understanding of their needs.

CASE STUDY

Anyone Guess?

Guess jeans are Guess's main product, but it also segments its market into clothing and accessories for women, men and children. It even has a line of clothing for babies. Guess has stores in over 80 countries throughout North America, South America, Europe, Asia, Africa and Australia. Each country carries different Guess products, depending on local trends and the particular segment's needs. For example, warmer South East Asian countries carry lighter-weight clothing; the size ranges also reflect the smaller body sizes of Asian customers.

Application

1. Identify which types of segmentation are used in the following statement:

   Car magazine

   Our average reader is male, aged 14–24. He watches motorsport on TV and attends motorsport events. He drives a performance car (and if he doesn't, he wishes he did). He is passionate about cars and spends his time reading about modifications. He lives in the city and is socio-economic group B/C1/C2. He is highly image-conscious and buys branded products.

2. Choose one of these products. Create a segmentation statement (like the example given) and justify appropriate methods of segmentation.
   - A fashion magazine
   - A business newspaper
   - A fast-food restaurant
   - Expensive make-up for women

   Apply your knowledge to make your statements specific to the example. Present the statement (and your reasons) to the rest of your group.

Knowledge check

1. **Explain, using an example, what is meant by a market segment. (2)**
2. **Explain the key advantages of market segmentation. (4)**
3. **Identify two examples of markets that might be segmented by age. (2)**
4. **Identify two examples of markets that might be segmented by gender. (2)**
5. **'Segmentation is especially important for large firms.' Explain why this might be the case. (3)**

Total 13 marks

Check your progress:

- ✓ I can explain the role of marketing and customer needs, loyalty and relationships.
- ✓ I can explain the factors that cause market changes and how businesses can respond to market changes.
- ✓ I understand the concepts of niche and mass marketing and can identify their benefits and limitations.
- ✓ I can explain how markets are segmented and can recommend and justify the best method of segmentation for a particular market.

Market research

The role and methods of market research

Aims (3.2.1)

By the end of this section, you should:

- Understand market-orientated businesses – uses of market research information to a business
- Understand the benefits and limitations of primary research and secondary research
- Understand different methods of primary research, for example, postal questionnaires, online surveys, interviews, focus groups
- Understand the need for sampling
- Understand the methods of secondary research, for example, online, accessing government sources, paying for commercial market research reports
- Understand the factors influencing the accuracy of market research data.

Market-orientated businesses

> Twenty or thirty years from now, I predict that instead of carrying stylish smartphones everywhere, we'll wear stylish glasses. Those glasses will offer VR, AR and everything in between and we'll use them all day.

Michael Abrash, the chief scientist of Facebook-owned Oculus Research

To maximise their chances of success, many firms do not just create products and hope customers will buy them. Instead, they investigate what customers want before designing the products. This approach is known as **market orientation,** as it focuses on customer needs. The quote above highlights the work Facebook is undertaking to listen to customers and create products that provide what customers want (orientation means the direction in which something is focused, and market orientation means a focus on the customer – the market).

A market-orientated approach will attempt to:

- create products based on what consumers want
- develop brand loyalty by ensuring (making sure) customer needs and wants are satisfied
- secure competitive advantage over rivals by targeting and meeting the needs of a specific group of consumers
- identify changes in the market and changes in the needs of customers, allowing the business to be the first to react.

An essential part of market orientation is **market research**.

What is market research?

If market orientation is all about meeting the needs of customers, market research is the key to understanding what those needs are. Market research is the process of collecting and interpreting data about customers and competitors. Firms can then use this research to make more reliable business decisions.

If a firm implements market research effectively, it can:

- help the business to identify the wants and needs of customers
- allow the business to spot a gap in the market that it can profitably fill
- help the business to design its **marketing mix** (product, price, place and promotion) to target the needs of different market segments
- allow the business to respond quickly to changes in customer needs
- help the firm to design, develop and launch new products with greater confidence in their success
- help the business to reduce the wasted expense of products or promotions that are unlikely to be successful.

Both new and existing businesses use market research to investigate:

Market size and trends	A business will investigate: • whether the number of customers is growing or shrinking • what the potential size of the market might be • what the firm's own sales and **market share** are and the potential for growth.
Market segments	A business will try to find out: • who their current and potential customers are • the needs, habits and lifestyles of different groups of customers.
Customer preferences	A business will try to understand: • what customers want from the product • what price they are prepared to pay • what methods of promotion might be most effective • where (the place) customers are likely to buy the product from.
Competition	A business will want to identify: • who their main competitors are • their competitors' market share • their competitors' strengths and weaknesses.

How is market research done?

Types of data

There are two different types of information that market research can generate:

- **Quantitative data.** This is data from a large group of people (respondents) showing numbers, proportions or trends within a market (such as related to quantities). An example of quantitative data is the number of bottles of water sold per day, per week or per month at a particular supermarket.
- **Qualitative data**. This is in-depth research into the reasons why consumers buy or don't buy products (such as related to qualities). Qualitative research gathers information from a much smaller group of people, but uses detailed discussions and interviews to explore the attitudes of consumers in depth. An example of qualitative research is an examination of the reasons why consumers purchase one brand of bottled water rather than another.

There are two types of market research: primary research and secondary research.

Primary research

Primary research (also known as **field research**) is the gathering of new and original, first-hand information. It can be done through observation, experimentation, questionnaires or interviews.

Observation

Supermarkets and large retail stores often use observation: watching consumers as they shop, measuring pedestrian flows in a shopping mall or looking at how rival products are packaged and displayed. Firms try to draw conclusions about shoppers from observing their behaviour – such as where they go first when they enter a store or how long they spend selecting a product. They can then use this data to improve the marketing of products, including store and shelf layout or point-of-sale promotions (promotional displays of goods in stores, often near the checkout tills).

△ A common strategy is to move popular products to the back of the store, forcing customers to walk through the store and therefore increasing the chance that they might purchase other items on the way.

Focus groups

Firms often ask groups of consumers (known as **focus groups**) to give their opinions on a product. They give these groups products to test, taste or try, and observe the consumers' responses and record their comments. Firms often use focus groups when they are introducing a new product.

Experimentation

Manufacturing companies often build prototypes (examples) to test new product ideas. Alternatively, they might launch a product in a small part of the market – such as a region or just a few stores – in order to see how consumers react to it. This is known as **test marketing**. In the internet era, prototyping is often done in the form of A/B split testing. For example, Twitter created two prototypes of web pages and encouraged users to sign up. Users then tested the two prototypes and Twitter chose the page that generated the most sign-ups as the permanent page.

∆ A snack company might give customers a range of new snacks to taste; they then launch the product that is most popular with the focus groups.

Questionnaires

A questionnaire can be carried out face to face, by telephone, by post or, more commonly, via the internet.

- Face-to-face questionnaires allow an interviewer to explain questions that the respondent (interviewee) doesn't understand. However, there is the possibility of bias in the way questions are asked or explained.
- Telephone surveys are quicker and cheaper to carry out than face-to-face surveys, but many customers resent (dislike) this method.
- Internet and postal surveys rely on customers completing and returning the questionnaire – this is a cheap method that avoids questioner bias but suffers from very low completion rates. For example, Twitter offers a questionnaire service for companies. A tweet is sent, inviting a company's followers to complete a short questionnaire.
- SurveyMonkey is an online research tool that helps gather primary research through surveys. It is used by businesses of all sizes, with some larger firms such as Virgin, Samsung and Kraft Foods using it for data collection and analysis to help develop their brands. Last year it received 90 million survey responses per month.

Interviews

To gain more detailed, qualitative information from a smaller group of people, interviewers use personal interviewing. The interviewer may spend a long time with each respondent, asking them a wide range of questions and exploring their responses more deeply.

Advantages and disadvantages of primary research

The main advantages of primary research are:	The main disadvantages of primary research are:
✓ **Timely** – Primary research is up to date. ✓ **Specific** – Primary research focuses on the particular topic the business is interested in. ✓ **Unique** – Primary research collects data that no other business has access to (and the results are confidential). ✓ **Fast** – Some types of primary research (online surveys, for example) can yield (give) very quick responses.	✗ **Cost** – Primary research can be very expensive to collect. ✗ **Time** – While online surveys might be fast, other methods of primary research, such as interviews, can be very time-consuming. ✗ **Expertise** – Good primary research relies on the people doing it. Choosing the most appropriate method and carrying out the research effectively is not easy. Mistakes and poorly conducted research are common.

CASE STUDY

Satisfied with our service?

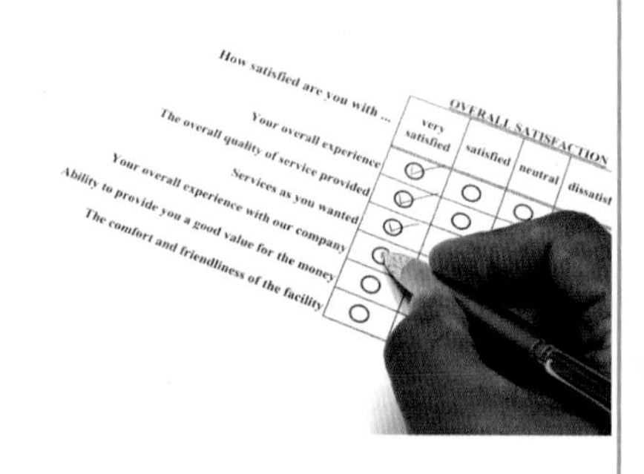

Have you ever been presented with a survey at the end of a meal in a restaurant or at the end of a flight? These customer satisfaction surveys are a form of primary research.

The benefit to the companies is that they are cheap and can address the exact questions they want answering. Response rates can also be much higher than other methods.

The disadvantage is that people who fill in these surveys are already the firm's customers. It may be even more useful to find out information from people who don't use the firm's services.

Analysis

Imagine you work for a market research company. Write a short report to your manager outlining the most appropriate methods of primary research for the following products:

- a new brand of female cosmetics
- a magazine for IGCSE students
- a new tablet computer
- a new Pixar movie.

Sampling

Whatever the method of primary research chosen, it would be too expensive and time-consuming to survey all of a firm's customers. To avoid this problem, the firm chooses a **sample. Sampling** means a smaller group is selected from a bigger population. The sample needs to be large enough to provide data that is reliable and representative (typical) of the attitudes and characteristics of the total population, but small enough to make research cost-effective.

As well as the correct sample size, the business must also choose a sampling method. The sampling method determines how research participants (interviewees) are to be selected. Some common sampling methods are:

- **Random sampling.** This involves selecting individuals in such a way that anyone in the total population has an equal chance of being chosen. For example, a supermarket might use **systematic random sampling** by interviewing every 10th person who walks into a store.
- **Stratified sampling.** Here the business first selects the market segment it wants to research. If, for example, a supermarket wanted to research the type of hair care products used by females in their twenties, it would only conduct surveys with people in that specific segment (group).
- **Quota sampling.** This method involves building the sample group so that it reflects the proportions of a total population. For example, if 60% of cinema audiences are male, then 60% of the sample questioned should be males. If half of these males are under 18, the sample should also reflect this.
- **Cluster sampling.** This method draws a sample from a single, specific geographic area. For example, a school may only want to conduct research with people who live within travelling distance.

Secondary research

Secondary research (also known as **desk research**) is the process of gathering data that has already been collected or published. **Secondary data** may exist within the business or be gathered from elsewhere, often online.

◁ Secondary research is a relatively quick and inexpensive way for a business to gather market data.

Within a firm, secondary data may exist in the form of:

- **Sales records.** Identifying sales trends over time or sales patterns around a country.

- **Customer information.** The firm may have records of customers' spending habits. For example, Apple's iTunes is able to suggest new music based on a customer's previous purchases (every purchase made is essentially research for Apple on the customer's music tastes).

There are also published sources of information available from outside the business. The growth of the internet has made a large volume of secondary information easily accessible to firms. Such sources include:

- **Government data.** Government departments collect, collate (put together) and publish a huge variety of information about all aspects of the economy and society.
- **Information about competitors.** Examining rivals' websites will reveal much about their products, prices and promotions.
- **Commercial data.** Organisations such as Mintel specialise in market research. Their reports are expensive but they provide detailed, up-to-date and accurate information on markets of all types. (For example, it is possible to receive a monthly Mintel report that, among other things, examines people's pizza-eating habits.)
- **Other sources.** Newspaper or journal articles, magazines and even social networking sites can all be useful sources.

The main advantages of secondary research are:	The main disadvantages of secondary research are:
✓ **Cost** – The main advantage of secondary data is that much of it is available free of charge and is easy to access. ✓ **Time** – Because it is easily available, using secondary data can save a business a significant amount of time. ✓ **Access** – For small firms, secondary research offers access to professionally collected data that they would not otherwise be able to afford.	✗ **Amount of data** – The large amount of secondary data available is often a problem in itself. A firm would need to sort the data carefully in order to extract the useful information that it needs. ✗ **Reliability** – Depending on the source, secondary data may or may not be reliable. Government data, for example, may be very reliable; data from other sources may, by contrast, be unreliable and potentially misleading. ✗ **Specificity** – Secondary data may not be specific (directly related) to a firm's needs. If a firm has particular questions it needs answering, it is unlikely to find answers in generally published secondary data.

While the accessibility and cost of secondary information can be seen as a strength, it can also be viewed as a limitation. This is because competitors have access to exactly the same information. To gain an advantage over the competition, a firm may need to carry out its own, specific, first-hand research.

Factors influencing the accuracy of market research data

Good market research data can be invaluable for a business. However, simply because a business carries out research, it does not mean that the information will be accurate or useful. There are many factors that affect the accuracy of market research data.

Sample size	The size of the sample used will determine how accurately the research represents the overall market. A smaller sample size may be easier and cheaper, but with fewer people actually surveyed, the results may not be as statistically accurate as with a larger sample.
Interviewer and interviewee quality	The type of questions asked and the skill of the interviewer will determine the quality of the answers. People may give responses that they think will please the interviewer, or they may not understand the questions. Some respondents may even give false answers.
Research design	Using the wrong research method can result in weak data. For example, a postal survey used to research teenage online gaming habits is likely to yield a very low response rate.
Time	Secondary data is often out of date or not focused on exactly what the business wants to know. For example, using secondary data to research internet habits is not likely to yield accurate results, as tastes change so rapidly. Primary data avoids these problems, but can be expensive to collect and analyse.
The human factor	Careful market research is behind almost all product launches and yet 90% of all new products end in failure. It is clear, then, that while market research findings can prove of great benefit in guiding business decisions, human behaviour is unpredictable and no amount of research can allow for this.

Knowledge check

1. **Identify the differences between primary and secondary research, supporting your answer with examples.** (4)
2. **Explain the difference between quantitative and qualitative data.** (4)
3. **Identify two key advantages of secondary research.** (2)
4. **Define the term sampling.** (2)
5. **Outline one limitation of primary research and one limitation of secondary research.** (4)
6. **Outline two reasons why market research may not be useful for a firm selling technology products.** (4)

Total 20 marks

Presentation and use of market research results

Aims (3.2.2)
By the end of this section, you should:
- Be able to analyse market research data shown in the form of graphs, charts and diagrams, and draw simple conclusions from such data.

Presentation and use of market research data

Being able to present and interpret data is an important skill. Quantitative market research data is usually presented in graphical form. The main ways of presenting data include:

<table>
<tr><td>Table/tally chart</td><td>Tally charts can be used when collecting information (they act as an aid to counting) and to present data in a very simple form. However, they are very basic and the information should be converted into other forms if it needs to be understood or analysed carefully.</td><td><table><tr><th>Number of vehicles</th><th>Tally</th></tr><tr><td>Cars</td><td>|||</td></tr><tr><td>Motorbikes</td><td>|||</td></tr><tr><td>Lorries</td><td>||</td></tr><tr><td>Buses</td><td>𝍸</td></tr></table></td></tr>
<tr><td>Bar chart</td><td>Bar charts are one of the most common ways of presenting data. They are normally used to compare two or more sets of data. They can be visually simple and easy to understand, but can be limited in how much information can be easily presented.</td><td>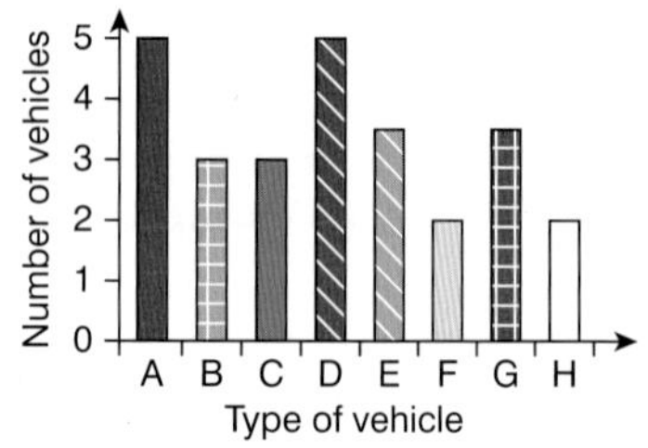</td></tr>
<tr><td>Line graph</td><td>Line graphs show the relationship between two variables. They can be drawn as straight lines or curves, or each point can be joined. They are usually used to compare things (perhaps sales) over time and help managers to identify trends.</td><td>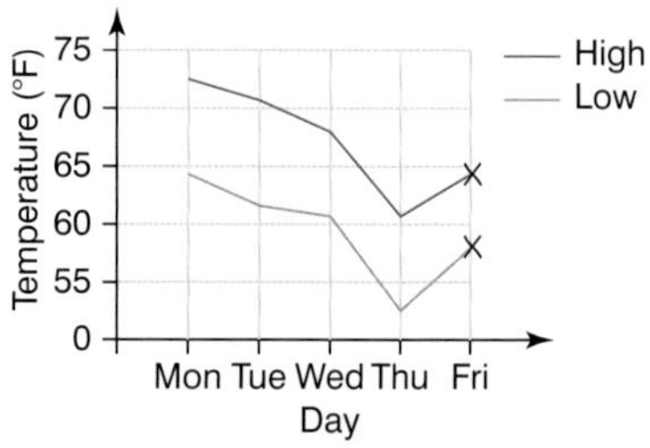</td></tr>
<tr><td>Pie chart</td><td>Pie charts show the proportion that each result takes up compared to a total. They are quick and easy to understand, but can be complicated to draw up.</td><td>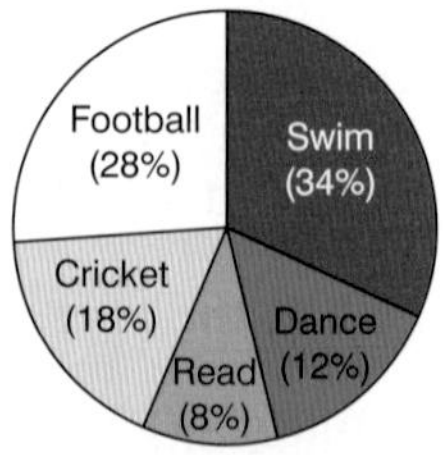</td></tr>
<tr><td>Pictogram</td><td>Pictograms are similar to a bar chart but use symbols instead of columns. They are useful when the data is simple and the audience needs to quickly grasp its meaning (they are often used on TV news shows, for example).</td><td></td></tr>
</table>

Analysis Evaluation

Present this data in a suitable format (other than a table).

Product/$	June	July	August	September	October	November
A	125000	125000	125000	125000	125000	125000
B	300000	280000	260000	255000	265000	278000
C	140000	160000	200000	180000	180000	185000
D	0	20000	40000	45000	35000	22000
E	160000	140000	120000	120000	130000	145000

- Describe what the data shows, making specific numerical references to the data.
- Explain and give reasons for any patterns in the data. Explain possible links between the data.
- Consider the implications that the data set might have for Product B and for Product D. What further questions might help in understanding the impact of these implications?

Knowledge check

1 **Identify when a pictogram might be the most appropriate form of data presentation. (1)**

2 **Identify appropriate methods of presentation for the following:**

a) the sales of a product over time

b) a comparison of multiple product sales for one month

c) percentage responses to questions about movies viewed in the last month. (3)

3 **Present the following data in a suitable format (other than a table) and identify any conclusions that can be drawn from the data. (8)**

Sales projections	Month 1	Month 2	Month 3
Sales @ $1000	400000	1200000	2400000
Sales @ $750	300000	900000	1800000

Total 12 marks

Check your progress:

✓ I understand the role of market research and the methods used.

✓ I can give examples of primary and secondary research methods and explain the need for sampling and the factors that influence the accuracy of data.

✓ I understand how market research results are presented and used and can analyse market research data.

Marketing mix

Introduction

The methods by which a product is promoted, where (the place) that product is sold and at what **price** it is sold is known as the marketing mix. It is this combination (mix) of product, promotion, price and place that a firm uses to make its product/service appealing to customers. The marketing mix is also referred to as the 4Ps.

The marketing mix involves making decisions on things such as:

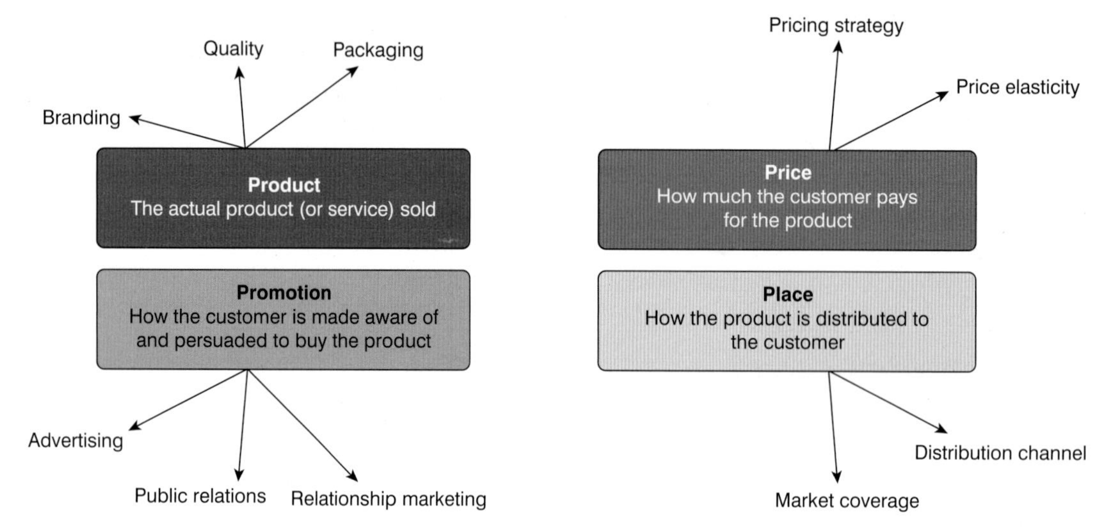

A successful marketing mix is one that:

- **meets customer needs** – persuades customers to buy the product
- **is consistent** – gets elements of the mix to 'work together' (for example, premium-priced products such as Louis Vuitton handbags must be sold in premium locations and must be of premium quality)
- **secures competitive advantage** – creates a unique selling point (USP) to differentiate the product from those of competitors.

It is known as a mix because, while each element is important, for some businesses one or two elements of the mix may be more important than others. It is the skill with which the business mixes the different elements together that can determine business success.

Consider the marketing for your school or institution. Analyse how each element of the marketing mix is used. Evaluate whether you think the marketing is successful.

Work in pairs and present your findings to the rest of the group.

Product

Aims (3.3.1)

By the end of this section, you should:

- Understand the costs and benefits of developing new products
- Understand brand image and its impact on sales and customer loyalty
- Understand the role of packaging
- Understand the product life cycle: the main stages and extension strategies; draw and interpret a product life cycle diagram
- Understand how stages of the product life cycle can influence marketing decisions, for example, promotion and pricing decisions.

Getting the product right is an essential part of the marketing mix. It is the part of the mix that customers will use. Developing products or services that customers actually want is vital to marketing success.

New product development

New product development is expensive. For example, the cost of bringing a new pharmaceutical drug to market can be billions of dollars. For many companies, though, constantly bringing out new products is essential to survival. The benefit of new product development is competitive advantage – the ability to stay one step ahead of the competition by offering a better product. Imagine what would happen to BMW if it stopped launching new models. Very quickly the competition would be selling better products, and BMW would soon go out of business.

Spending money on new products is known as **research and development (R&D)**. R&D brings together science, imagination and marketing with the aims of generating ideas, inventing completely new technologies, making prototypes (models of the product) and testing products with consumers.

Branding

Branding refers to the use of a name, symbol or design to identify a particular product and to help maintain or increase its sales. Some of the most popular brands are Tata, Nadec, Manchester United, Sony and Apple. Even Lady Gaga is a brand.

Brand image is the personality given to a product through marketing activities. A product's brand image is deliberately created to appeal to a specific market segment. Lady Gaga's eccentric (unusual) image was created to differentiate her from other pop stars and was designed to appeal to young people.

Branding is used to:

- **Create and maintain loyalty.** When Coca-Cola, at great expense, changed its unique recipe, customers were very angry (despite the new product tasting better). Coca-Cola had significant brand loyalty and its customers did not want change. Brands create familiarity and encourage long-term repeat purchasing (protecting and helping to grow sales).
- **Expand product ranges.** Consumers are much more likely to try a new product if they trust the brand. Porsche, for example, was able to successfully enter the kitchen appliance market because people trusted the brand.
- **Differentiate products.** In crowded markets, branding may be the only thing that makes one product different from another. In fact, this was the original purpose of brands. The Cadbury's chocolate brand was originally created to differentiate Cadbury's from other chocolates on the market.
- **To aid recognition.** The presence of a distinctive brand logo can help products stand out in shops. Customers will instantly recognise their favourite brand and will be less tempted to try out the competition. Chanel No 5 perfume, for example, has an instantly recognisable colour, bottle shape and design.
- **To gain price flexibility.** The fact that the product is 'different', and has established brand loyalty or has a desirable brand image, allows firms to charge higher prices. Adidas, for example, may be able to increase the price of its sports trainers without affecting sales to a great extent (this concept, known as price elasticity, is discussed later in this topic, under Price).

Such is the power of brands that children as young as 36 months are able to distinguish between different brands.

CASE STUDY

Great design

There are many reasons for Apple's success, but a very important one is design. Great design is central to the Apple brand. Where other companies may compromise on design in order to make functions work, Apple engineers are pushed to make the product function perfectly and look great. The all-metal case of the MacBook Pro has, for example, changed our idea of what computers can (and should) look like. For Apple, design is a major feature of its products; design differentiates the brand from the competition.

Packaging

Packaging is sometimes referred to as the fifth 'P' (after product, price, promotion and place). Packaging is used to:

- promote the product
- differentiate the product
- protect the product from damage
- communicate information (for example, about ingredients or usage)
- make the product convenient to use (such as easy-pour caps)
- make the product easy to store/display.

Packaging can be extremely important in the purchase decision. The initial purchase of a food or drink item may be driven entirely by its packaging or appearance.

∆ Pringles: a brand of potato snack chips in a can – simple, distinctive and recognisable.

Application

Consider the following brands. Examine what features of the brand or packaging make them successful:

- Mercedes-Benz
- Justin Bieber
- Hilton Hotels
- LUXE travel guides
- Kellogg's breakfast cereal
- Real Madrid football shirt.

Present your findings as a poster. It could show images of the different brands surrounded by text that explains what you think makes each brand successful.

The product life cycle

The concept of the product life cycle is based on biological life cycles. For example, we are born (introduction), we grow (growth), we become adults (maturity) and after a period as an adult we die (decline). In theory, it is the same for products.

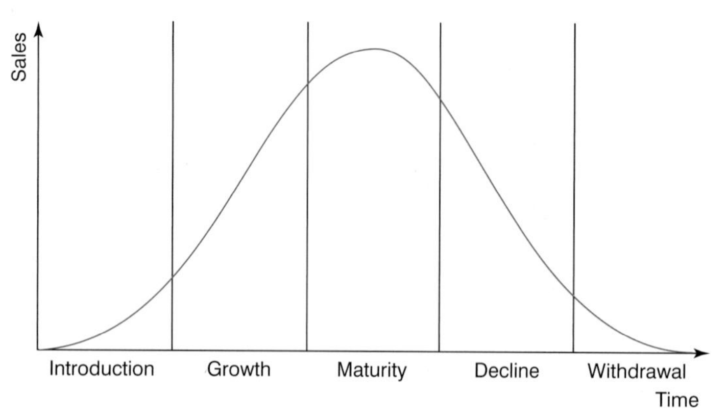

Δ Typical product life cycle

> **Did you know?**
>
> The Snickers bar is the world's best-selling chocolate bar, with sales of over $2 billion a year. This product has stayed in the maturity stage of the product life cycle for many years.

After development, a product will be introduced to the market. Hopefully, its sales will grow and eventually the market will stabilise, become mature and eventually saturate (the market is, in essence, 'full' – there is little room for continued sales growth). Then, as new products are launched, sales for the original product will start to decline.

Stages of the product life cycle

Stage 1: Introduction

After research and development, the product is launched on to the market. Costs incurred (the costs adding up over time) in launching the product will be high and sales will be low. The product is unlikely to make any profit at this stage. Customers will be early innovators (people who 'have' to buy the latest products) and marketing will focus on awareness.

Δ Virtual reality headsets are in their introduction stage.

Stage 2: Growth

Sales begin to grow and competitors enter the market. Having covered its development costs, the product may become profitable. Marketing will focus on brand preference and new features may be added to the product (new features are added to mobile phones almost constantly throughout the growth stage). Tablet computers, such as the new Apple iPad, are in their growth stage.

Stage 3: Maturity

Sales grow at a decreasing rate and then stabilise as the market saturates (no new customers enter the market). Marketing focuses on brand loyalty and producers attempt to gain market share by differentiating products. With competition at its peak, price also becomes an important factor (see the section Price later in this topic). Mobile phones are currently in the maturity/saturation stage.

Stage 4: Decline

Sales for most products eventually fall. New, more innovative products may be introduced or consumer tastes might change. Marketing expenditure (money spent) is reduced and the product will be simplified to cut production costs. Products that reach this stage are often withdrawn from sale. For example, the market for DVDs has declined rapidly over the last few years.

The different features and marketing implications of the product life cycle are considered in more detail in the table.

	Introduction	Growth	Maturity	Decline
Features of stage				
Sales	Low	Growing	Slow growth	Declining
Profits	Low	Highest	High but declining	Low
Cash flow	Negative	Positive	Positive	Positive, but falling
Competitors	Few	Growing	Many	Falling
Marketing strategy				
Marketing expenditure	High	High (cost per sale falling)	Falling	Low
Price	Skimming or penetration strategy used	Price cut/ increase depending on introduction strategy	Competitive pricing strategy	Low
Product	Basic	Improved	Differentiated	Basic
Promotion	Focus on awareness	Generate brand preference	Retain brand loyalty	Targeted promotions
Place (distribution)	Few outlets	Number of outlets increasing	High number of outlets	Number of outlets falling

Knowledge of the product life cycle allows managers, in theory, to 'adjust' marketing strategy according to the stage they believe a product is in.

Extension strategy

Often, while individual products may go into decline, the market itself continues to grow. For example, sales of Nokia phones declined while the mobile phone market in general continued to enjoy good sales. Brand managers often respond to this by introducing a variety of life cycle **extension strategies:**

- **Encourage increased usage.** For example, Doritos tortilla chips were marketed under the slogan 'friendchips' in an effort to encourage people to share them with friends (and thus buy more of the product).
- **Find new users.** Gillette, once a brand focused solely on men, now sells a range of successful products aimed at women.
- **Find new uses for the product.** O'Neill, Quiksilver and Caterpillar all managed to increase brand awareness and extend the life of their specialist clothing by promoting it as fashionable.
- **Change the product.** This may involve tangible changes to the product (for example, new features every time a new iPad is launched) or intangible changes to the product's image (for example, BlackBerry changed its marketing in an effort to appeal to users beyond its usual business customers).
- **Increase promotion.** In the short term, a promotional campaign might help to boost sales.

Different types of life cycle

Not all products follow the classic life cycle described in this section. The following graphs represent some of these different life cycles:

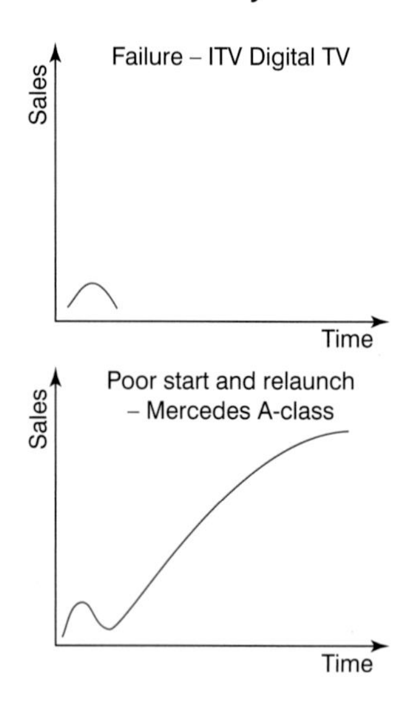

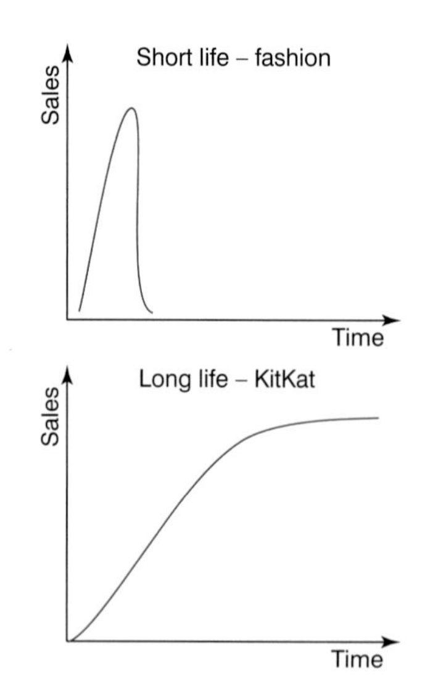

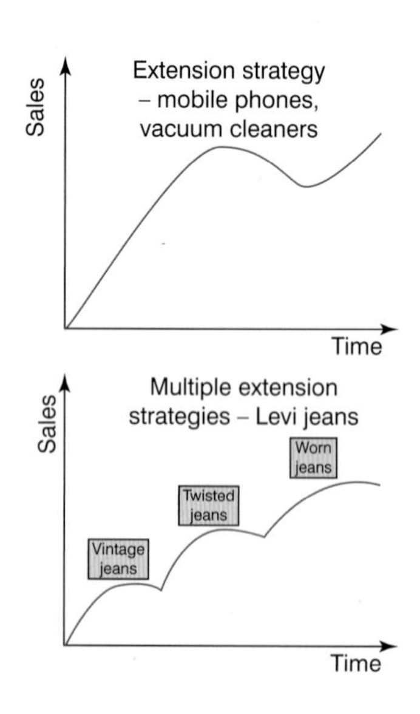

Criticisms of the product life cycle concept

When evaluating how useful product life cycle analysis is to a firm, it is important to consider the following:

- In reality, very few products follow the classic life cycle.
- The length of each stage varies enormously between products.
- It is difficult to identify exactly where a product is in its life cycle.
- It is impossible for managers to know, with any degree of certainty, when a product will enter the next stage of its life.
- Knowledge of the product life cycle does not allow managers to predict what might happen to a product; it just guides their reaction once a product has obviously moved into the next stage. Any changes to marketing strategy are therefore going to be reactive. If they could predict the future, their plans could be proactive.

Application

Investigate sales of the following products and draw suitable product life cycle diagrams:

- PlayStation 4 (PS4)
- iPad 3
- skinny jeans
- DVD players
- Mars bar.

Knowledge check

1. **Explain, using an example, what is meant by the term brand image.** **(2)**
2. **Identify one advantage of 'brand loyalty'.** **(1)**
3. **Identify the main stages of the product life cycle.** **(4)**
4. **Outline the details and draw product life cycle diagrams for the following:** **(4)**
   a) a failed product
   b) a successful extension strategy.
5. **Identify one reason why packaging is an important additional element of the marketing mix.** **(1)**
6. **Outline how the promotion of a product might be different in each stage of its life cycle.** **(4)**
7. **Explain, using an example, what is meant by the term R&D.** **(3)**

Total 19 marks

Price

Aims (3.3.2)

By the end of this section, you should:

- Understand pricing methods, for example, cost plus, competitive, penetration, skimming, promotional and their benefits and limitations
- Be able to recommend and justify an appropriate pricing method in given circumstances
- Understand the significance of price elasticity: difference between price elastic demand and price inelastic demand; importance of the concept in pricing decisions.

Introduction

A variety of factors will influence the price of a product:

- the cost of production
- the type of customers being targeted (market segment)
- the amount of competition in the market
- the objectives of the business
- where the product is in its life cycle (see the previous section under Product).

With these different factors in mind, a firm will set its price based on a particular pricing method.

CASE STUDY No-frills travels

AirAsia is Asia's largest low-cost, no-frills (basic) airline. AirAsia operates flights to over 400 destinations across 25 countries. Its main hub is Kuala Lumpur's Low Cost Carrier Terminal. The product is no-frills: no free food or drink, small seats and no extras. Price, while not the only element of AirAsia's marketing mix, is arguably the most important.

Pricing methods

Businesses can adopt a range of pricing methods.

- **Cost plus**. This is the most commonly used pricing method and forms the basis of all pricing decisions. The average cost of one item is calculated (total cost ÷ number of units) and then a **mark-up (profit margin)** is added to give the final **selling price**.

WORKED EXAMPLE

A business produces headphones for personal music players. Total costs of production are $500 000; the business produces 100 000 units.

$$\text{Average cost per item} = \frac{\text{total cost}}{\text{number of units}} = \frac{\$500\,000}{100\,000} = \$5 \text{ per unit}$$

If the business then decides its mark-up will be 150%, the selling price will be:

$5 + ($5 × 150%) = $12.50 selling price.

- **Competitive pricing.** In this pricing method, the price charged is set at the same level as other products in the market and at a level customers expect/are willing to pay.
- **Penetration pricing.** When a product is launched into an established and competitive market, for the first few weeks/months its price may be set low to attract customers.
- **Price skimming.** Where a product is first to market, a high price is often charged. New technologies are often launched at a high price to recoup (get back) development costs as quickly as possible. A firm can also benefit from high profit margins when a product is new and desirable. Blu-ray used a price skimming strategy when first launched.
- **Promotional pricing.** Reducing the price of a product or service to attract customers is known as promotional pricing. Methods include the BOGOF (buy one get one free) promotion, money-off coupons and introductory offers.

Top Tip

Once you have calculated the mark-up, remember to add the original cost of production in order to calculate the final selling price.

CASE STUDY

New market, same strategy

Both Tide, the laundry detergent, and Coca-Cola chose to launch their brands in India at the same price as their nearest competitors. Price skimming may have put price-sensitive Indian consumers off, and penetration pricing risked immediately reducing the brands' value in the market. The best strategy was a simple competitive one.

Other types of pricing strategies include:

- **Premium pricing.** A high price approach is used where a product has significant competitive advantage or is clearly differentiated from the competition. It might also be used where a strong brand image has been developed. Gucci clothing is premium priced.
- **Discriminatory pricing.** Different prices are charged to different groups of people at different times. Cinemas, for example, charge different prices for daytime and evening showings.
- **Geographical pricing.** Prices vary according to the location of the store or outlet. Petrol, for example, is often cheaper in city centres than in the countryside.

Benefits and limitations of pricing methods

Method	Benefits	Limitations
Cost plus	✓ Simple ✓ Easy to use a set percentage for all products ✓ Easy to set price according to profit targets	✗ If the same percentage is used for all products, customer expectations or geographic differences are ignored ✗ Some products may be more expensive than those of competitors' products
Competitive pricing	✓ Price matches customer expectations	✗ The firm gains no advantage in terms of price
Penetration pricing	✓ Helps a firm to gain sales in competitive markets	✗ Once a low price is set, customers may expect it to remain low ✗ The low price may not fit with the overall brand image and may therefore damage sales
Price skimming	✓ Helps the firm to gain maximum profit early in the product's life ✓ Can help to establish a premium/high-quality image	✗ The price may be too high for some customers ✗ A price reduction early in the product life cycle because low sales can damage brand image
Promotional pricing	✓ Can increase sales in the short term ✓ Can increase brand awareness ✓ Can stop consumers buying competing products if they have already 'stocked up' on a firm's products	✗ Reduces profit margins for the period of the promotion ✗ Customers may not purchase the product unless it is 'on promotion' ✗ May harm brand image

Application

Imagine you work for a marketing department. For each of the following products, consider and justify an appropriate pricing strategy. Present your findings in the form of small group presentations.

- A new magazine aimed at teenagers
- A new concept mobile phone with a strong USP
- A breakfast cereal relaunching in new packaging
- A hair care product manufacturer with excess (too much) stock

How important is price?

Price, to most customers, is very important. Yet people will not always buy the cheapest product available. A wide range of factors affect the price customers are willing to pay:

- degree of product differentiation/USP
- brand image/reputation
- product quality (perceived and actual)
- customer service
- speed of service and/or delivery
- availability.

CASE STUDY

A cheap night in

Following the low-cost airline model, Tune Hotels offer no-frills (basic) hotel rooms. With hotels in places such as Malaysia, Indonesia, Thailand, London and Australia, Tune offers some of the cheapest hotel rooms on the market. Toiletries, 12- or 24-hour air conditioning, TV and internet access are all charged for as additional services.

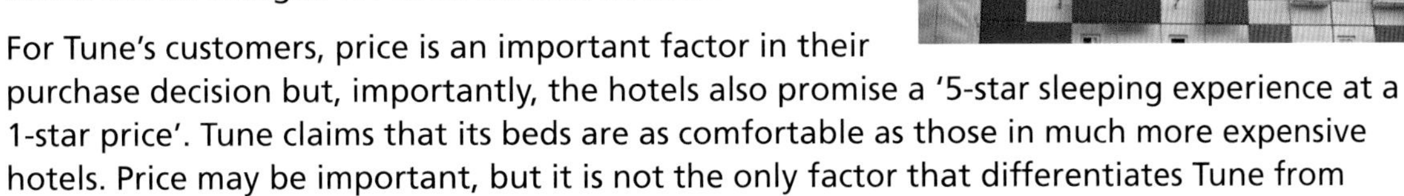

For Tune's customers, price is an important factor in their purchase decision but, importantly, the hotels also promise a '5-star sleeping experience at a 1-star price'. Tune claims that its beds are as comfortable as those in much more expensive hotels. Price may be important, but it is not the only factor that differentiates Tune from the competition.

The importance of price in a consumer's buying decision can be measured using the concept of **price elasticity** of demand.

Price elasticity of demand

Businesses need to measure how sensitive (responsive) demand for a product is to changes in price. For example, a product that is very price sensitive might suffer a big decline in sales if the price is put up by only a small amount. A firm selling a product that is not very sensitive to price changes may be able to put its price up significantly with little impact on sales.

This price sensitivity is known as **elasticity** (something that is elastic can change readily, responds to forces, is not fixed). A product that is sensitive to price changes has **price elastic** demand. A product that is not very sensitive to price changes has **price inelastic** demand.

Demand for cigarettes is price inelastic. Despite continually rising prices, smoking remains a popular habit in many countries. The purchase of cigarettes is not very sensitive to price changes.

Goods in competitive markets where there are many substitutes tend to have price elastic demand. If, for example, the price of Starbucks coffee went up significantly, customers could easily switch to other brands.

How sensitive a product is to changes in its price is affected by:

- **Availability of substitutes.** The more choice consumers have, the greater the price sensitivity. Breakfast cereal is likely to be price sensitive, as lots of alternative brands are available.
- **Buyers' knowledge.** The more buyers know about alternatives (prices, sales locations, and so on), the more price sensitive a product will be.
- **Ability to switch costs.** If the cost of switching to a substitute product is high, the product may not be sensitive to price changes. Where, for example, customers are locked in to mobile phone airtime contracts (and therefore not able to change easily), they are less sensitive to changes in the price of calls. On the other hand, where customers can switch easily, the product may be very price sensitive.

Δ Fast food – price elastic demand?

Δ Petrol – price inelastic demand?

The concept of price elasticity is important because businesses need to know how responsive demand for products is to price changes so they can analyse the potential impact of special offers and other price changes. Firms can use price elasticity of demand to predict:

- The impact of a change in price on total revenue – if a price rise causes demand to fall significantly, then revenue will also fall. In such a case, the firm should reconsider the price change.
- The effect of a change in a government tax (see 6.1 Economic issues) – tax changes alter a product's price and therefore affect demand for it, so a firm will want to know whether the business is able to pass on some or all of a tax on to the consumer.

Information on the price elasticity of demand can also be used to support **discriminatory pricing**. For example, a firm could calculate the different price sensitivities of weekend and weekday cinema-goers and adjust prices accordingly.

Top Tip

Always remember to use precise knowledge from your Business Studies course to make your point. For example, state clearly that a firm's pricing strategy might depend on a product's price elasticity of demand.

Evaluation

Consider how sensitive to changes in price demand the following products might be. Identify whether demand for each is likely to be elastic or inelastic and justify your answer.

- unbranded rice
- BMW cars
- Prada clothing
- iTunes music tracks
- headache tablets
- IMAX cinema tickets

With reference to your responses, consider how important knowledge of price elasticity of demand might be for a firm.

Present your findings as a mini-report, outlining the concept of elasticity and evaluating the possible elasticity of each product.

Knowledge check

1. Identify three factors that will affect a firm's pricing decision. (3)
2. Explain when a firm might use price skimming. (2)
3. Explain an advantage and a disadvantage of using competitive pricing. (4)
4. Identify which pricing strategy a firm might use when trying to gain a foothold in a competitive market. (1)
5. Explain what the term price elasticity measures. (2)
6. Identify two types of goods that might be price inelastic. (2)

Total 14 marks

Place – distribution channels

Aims (3.3.3)

By the end of this section, you should:

- Understand the advantages and disadvantages of different channels, for example, use of wholesalers, retailers or direct to consumers
- Be able to recommend and justify an appropriate distribution channel in given circumstances.

Distribution channels

Place (or, more properly, distribution strategy) is the way in which a product is distributed – how it gets to customers. The product must get to the customer at the right time, in the right quantities and in good condition. Place is not about a business's actual physical location.

A **distribution channel** refers to the **intermediaries** (stages in the distribution chain) a product passes through before it reaches the consumer. The main channels of distribution are as follows:

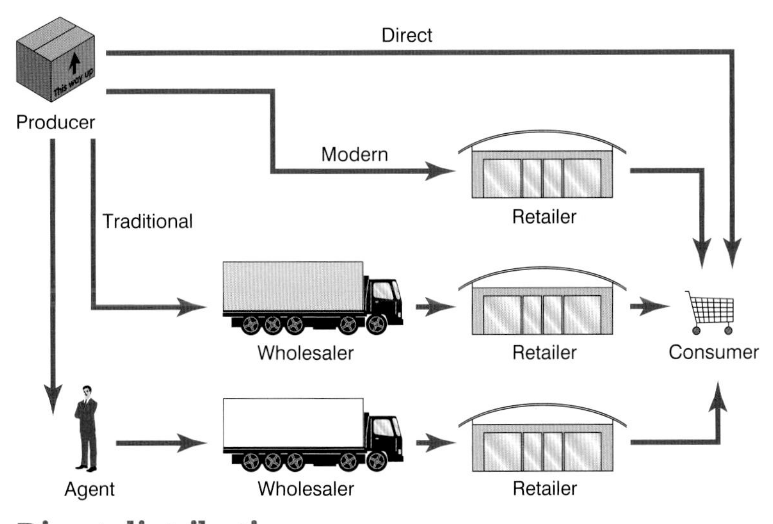

Direct distribution

This is when the producer sells goods directly to the end consumer. No intermediaries are used. A small local baker (bread-maker), for example, distributes products directly to customers.

Due to the introduction of the internet, direct distribution has become much more common. Products traditionally sold through long distribution chains have undergone a process of **disintermediation** (removing the intermediaries). Producers are now able to sell directly to large numbers of consumers at relatively low cost. Niche products can be sold to much wider audiences (for example, specialist skateboard equipment can be purchased very easily via the internet, even in countries where it is not sold in stores). Online retailers such as Dell Computers have become successful by exploiting the advantages of direct selling.

Advantages	Disadvantages
✓ By cutting out intermediaries (who add their own mark-ups), the product can be sold at a lower price, aiding competitiveness. ✓ Producers benefit from direct customer feedback and can respond to changing customer needs quickly. ✓ A direct relationship with the customer can lead to increased customer loyalty.	✗ The retail outlet may not be close to potential customers. When products are sold at a physical location, the extent of distribution is limited to customers within a reasonable distance of the store. ✗ It may be impractical, or difficult, to send items ordered over the internet by post (for example, household furniture). ✗ The firm does not share the cost of distribution with retailers.

Retail distribution

Even though direct selling is very popular, the majority of consumer products are still sold via retailers. Global online retail sales are growing every year. In terms of country, the UK has the highest retail e-commerce sales as a percentage of total retail sales (15.6%), followed by China (13.8%), Norway (11.5%), Finland (10.8%) and South Korea (10.5%).

- Retailers allow producers to achieve wide distribution and can help to support or develop brand image (for instance, designer clothing is usually sold in small boutiques).
- Some retailers may have a strong brand image themselves (such as the Harrods department store in London), helping to boost the image of products sold there.
- Retailers can also help to promote and sell a producer's products (for example, through point-of-sale display and special offers).
- Retailers might offer credit to customers for big purchases. Large department stores, for example, often offer customers interest-free credit.

Advantages	Disadvantages
✓ Wide distribution is possible. ✓ Selling through specialist retailers can ensure that customers receive product advice. ✓ Selling through premium retailers can help a product's brand image.	✗ Retail stores often sell more than one brand of the same product. The wide choice attracts customers to retailers, but at the same time exposes them to competition; brands have to fight against the competition for customers' attention. ✗ Retailers add their own mark-up, making the product more expensive at the point of sale. ✗ There can be loss of control of product (quality, presentation, environment) at the point of sale.

CASE STUDY Coffee contained

Increasingly, businesses around the world are looking to use container boxes previously used by container ships as their premises. Old container boxes have been recycled for use as storage sheds, swimming pools, offices, indoor gardens and even homes.

Container Coffee is a new coffee shop in Dublin, Ireland, that sells coffee from an old container ship. The company's unique approach to direct selling enables it to compete with some of the largest brands in the world.

Wholesale distribution

Wholesalers buy in large quantities from manufacturers and then sell these products in smaller quantities to retailers (this is often called breaking-bulk). Where a retailer does not have the purchasing power to buy directly from a manufacturer, they buy from a wholesaler. For example, the Chinese firm Global Sources buys large quantities of products from Chinese manufacturers and sells these in smaller quantities to retailers all over the world.

Advantages	Disadvantages
✓ Wholesalers ensure that products are available to both large and small retailers. ✓ Wholesalers reduce the cost of distributing products to a large number of retailers. ✓ Wholesalers hold stock, thus reducing stockholding costs for the seller.	✗ Wholesalers add their own mark-up to the product's price, which may make the product uncompetitive. ✗ The additional stage in distribution increases the time a product takes to reach consumers. ✗ Increased handling as products are processed by retailers increases the chance of product damage. ✗ The producer loses control over product storage (potentially leading to mishandling and damage).

Wholesalers provide a way for small producers to get their products into retail outlets. A large supermarket chain may be unwilling to buy directly from the manufacturer until certain production volumes are reached or until sufficient demand has been established. Wholesalers provide an alternative route to market.

Where a business sells many products and cannot afford the distribution costs of shipping these products to thousands of retailers, they may use a wholesaler. Wholesalers can also provide storage facilities and can reduce a producer's stockholding costs.

CASE STUDY

Disintermediation

The development of downloading online music has transformed the way music is sold. Traditionally, music was sold in a physical format (CDs) and through retail stores. Apple's iTunes, Spotify and other online streaming websites have changed that. Music still goes through an intermediary (iTunes, for example), but many of the warehouses that used to store CDs and the retail stores that used to sell them have closed as a result of disintermediation (removing the intermediaries). However, vinyl music has seen a 1225% increase in sales in the last decade.

Distribution through agents

In contrast to wholesalers, agents never actually own the product. Agents simply connect buyers and sellers and manage the transfer of the goods. Agents usually take a commission on sales or charge a fee for their services.

Agents are most often used by businesses involved in import/export. Differences in local product laws, language and procedures can make exporting very challenging. Agents specialise in managing complex customs procedures and can provide a range of advice services. Businesses with little experience of foreign trading often find that agents offer a relatively safe way of entering new markets.

Δ Agents can help businesses to sell their products in foreign markets.

Advantages	Disadvantages
✓ Agents know and understand the best methods of distribution/transport within their own country and can ensure that products get to customers quickly and easily. ✓ Agents understand the language, culture and tastes of the local market. ✓ Agents understand the laws and regulation involved with importing and selling goods within a particular country.	✗ The producer loses a degree of control over how and where the product is sold, so there is a risk of damage to brand image. ✗ Agents add their own mark-ups, so the price charged to customers may be high and uncompetitive.

What determines how a product is distributed?

A product's distribution channel will be determined by a number of factors:

- **Marketing aims.** A business aiming to increase sales volume is likely to attempt to secure as wide a distribution as possible.
- **Product characteristics.** The cost of the product, its shelf life and product type will all affect how it is distributed. A product with a short shelf life (a product that expires quickly, such as a fresh food item) needs to get to customers as quickly as possible.
- **Market coverage.** The number of outlets a product is sold in will also affect the distribution method. Getting products into thousands of convenience stores (such as 7-Eleven stores) requires many different stages in the distribution channel.
- **Cost considerations.** The longer the distribution channel, the more costly the distribution (and the product price) will be.
- **Customer expectations/brand image.** Customer perceptions about retail outlets and a desire to create/maintain brand image may affect distribution. Many premium brands, for example, will not allow their products to be sold in shops that do not have a high-class brand image.
- **Product life cycle.** Different channels can be used at different points in the product life cycle. Coffee used to be available only in a dedicated coffee shop on the high street. However, the huge increase in coffee consumption worldwide has led to leading brands such as Costa Coffee having make-it-yourself machines in a whole range of retailers, including petrol stations and department stores.

The choice of distribution channel will reflect a balance between these considerations. Essentially, this means that a business has to balance its own needs (a desire for cost efficiency, for example) against the needs of the consumer. This balance is represented in the diagram on the next page.

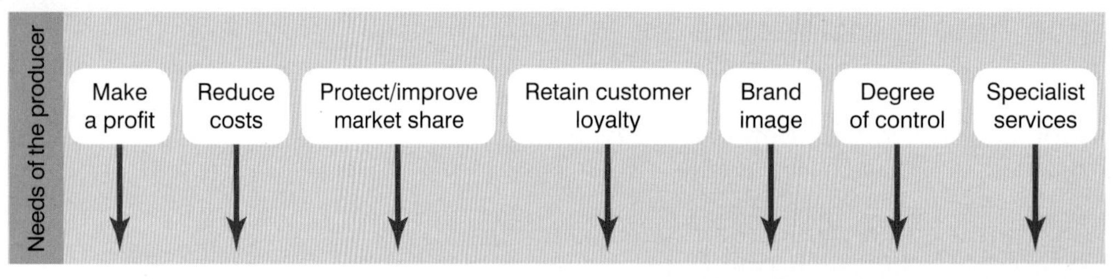

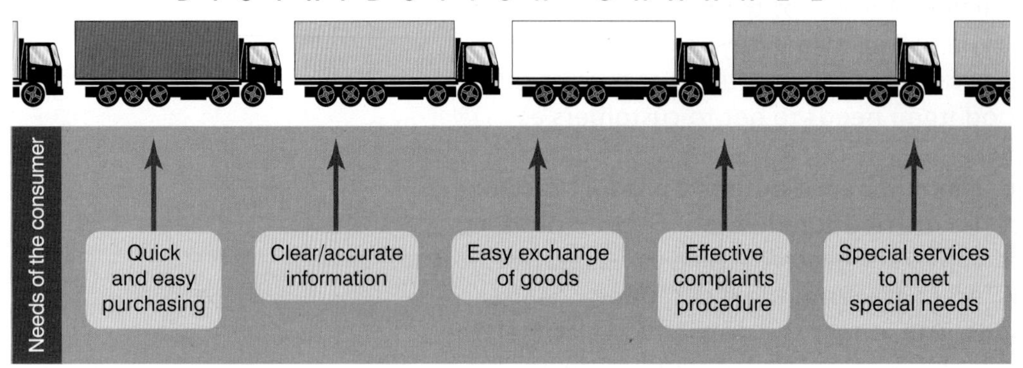

Recommend and justify an appropriate distribution channel for the following:

- a new breakfast snack
- a new book
- a Vietnamese firm exporting Vietnamese art
- a Honda motorbike.

Present your findings as a sketch of the appropriate distribution channel. Include text that evaluates, with reference to the needs of the consumer and producer, why it is an appropriate channel.

Knowledge check

1. **Define the term intermediary.** **(2)**
2. **Explain two factors that influence the choice of distribution channel.** **(6)**
3. **Explain the role of a wholesaler.** **(2)**
4. **Identify one disadvantage of using a wholesaler.** **(1)**
5. **Explain the role of a distribution agent.** **(2)**
6. **Explain two benefits of using direct distribution methods.** **(4)**
7. **Identify and explain the impact of the internet on distribution.** **(5)**
8. **Identify the relationship between cost of distribution and product price.** **(2)**

Total 24 marks

Promotion

Aims (3.3.4)

By the end of this section, you should:

- Understand the aims of promotion
- Understand the different forms of promotion and how they influence sales, for example, advertising, sales promotion
- Understand the need for cost effectiveness in spending the marketing budget on promotion.

Introduction

Promotion is the part of marketing that most people are familiar with. Promotion is about communication with customers and potential customers. Through promotion, a business might aim to communicate:

- who they are (developing a brand image)
- what they sell (informative promotion)
- why consumers should buy their products (persuading)
- the brand image of a product (reminding/reinforcing)
- where customers can get the product (informative)
- how much the product costs (informative).

CASE STUDY Eye-catching promotion

At first glance, this looks like an advert for sunglasses. It is in fact a promotion for one of Lebanon's most famous hotels, the Riviera Hotel. This campaign of massive vinyl stickers was used in the bathrooms of Beirut's trendy hangouts (bars, nightclubs, and so on) to draw attention to the hotel. By associating itself with popular hangouts, using cool images and the clever placement of stickers, the hotel reinforced its image as a cool and exclusive brand.

The aims of promotion

The aims of promotion are to:

- increase demand for products
- establish a price for products
- create, enhance or maintain a brand image
- raise awareness, emotion or concern for an issue or product
- maintain, protect or increase market share.

Ultimately, promotion is essential because, with consumers facing so much product choice, it is often the business that 'shouts the loudest' that gets noticed.

How important is promotion?

The extent to which promotion is important, relative to other aspects of marketing, might depend on:

- the degree of competition in the market
- the market segment (for example, a niche product may need little promotion)
- the marketing emphasis (Is the product differentiated? Is this difference physical – a feature of the product? Or is it emotional – related to the strength of the brand? Emotional, brand-based differences might require heavy promotional support)
- stage in the product life cycle (established products may need little promotion)
- the extent of supply (a product that is widely available may need little promotion).

Methods of promotion

The choice of promotion method might depend on the answers to the following questions:

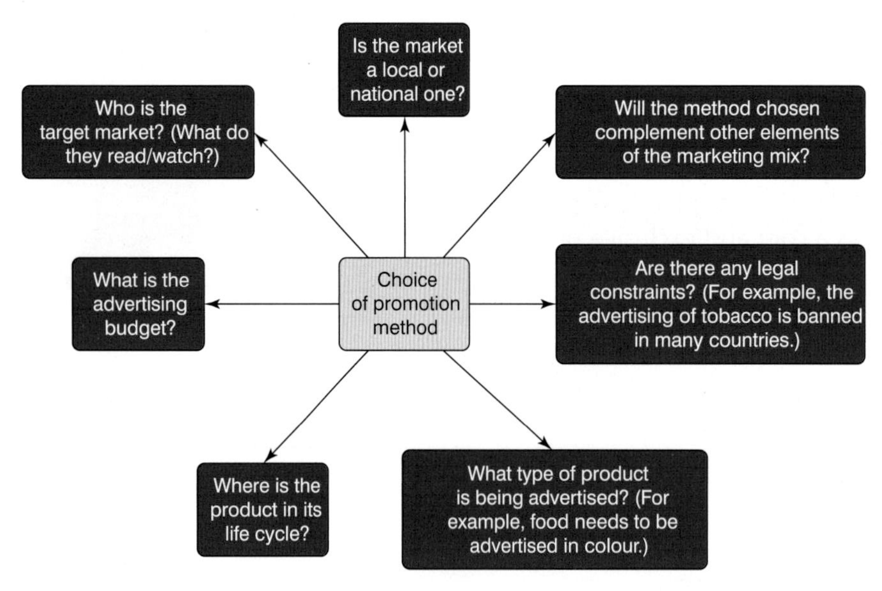

A firm with a small marketing budget promoting a product to local teenagers will, for example, select cheaper methods of promotion that closely target young people – such as in the form of posters placed at a local school.

Examples of different methods of promotion are described in this section.

Television

TV is the most familiar face of advertising. Because of its wide reach, most mass market consumer goods are advertised on television. Television is relatively expensive, but should be looked at on a 'per viewing' basis.

Δ Over 100 million people watch the US Super Bowl championship game. When you can reach that many people, for companies that can afford the large initial fees, TV advertising can be very cost-effective.

Internet

Expenditure (money spent) on internet advertising has grown faster over the past decade than for any other media type. It is estimated that internet advertising spending has now overtaken television advertising, with Google AdWords and Facebook Adverts the two most popular forms of this. Internet advertising allows very precise targeting of market segments (for example, on specific websites viewed by the target group). Internet adverts are, however, often ignored (or removed by ad blockers).

New media

The adverts you see when you play a computer game such as Minecraft, Tetris or Candy Crush, adverts via SMS and promotions on Twitter are all forms of new media marketing. These new forms of advertising allow very precise targeting and help firms to develop two-way relationships with customers (the firm and the customer can interact, sending messages to each other, via media such as Facebook or Twitter). This type of relationship marketing is very powerful, as it allows firms to tell customers about products and listen to what customers have to say.

CASE STUDY Nike – just gets it

Realising that its core customers have traded television for the internet, Nike has cut its spending on TV advertising by 40% in recent years. Nike still creates thrilling advertising campaigns, but they are more likely to debut online than on TV. For example, Nike unveiled a 90-second, star-studded online campaign called Equality before it launched its TV advert a week later. It also used other methods of advertising, including magazines and newspapers, to help spread awareness of the new advert. By releasing the video online, Nike could track the number of people who viewed the advert and who were interested in Nike's products.

Newspapers

Newspaper advertising has the benefit of being able to target specific audiences. Different types of people usually read different types of newspapers. This makes newspaper advertising attractive to companies looking to reach specific market segments. The main disadvantages are cost and declining newspaper circulation (news is now often accessed online). Newspapers are also considered 'busy' advertising spaces – because they include lots of adverts, it is hard to capture customer attention.

Magazines

Magazine publishers, like newspapers, also have a clear idea of who their readers are. Advertisers can use this information to target specific markets. Magazines are also useful for building brand image. For example, clothing that is featured in fashion magazines such as *Vogue* or *Elle* gains fashionable status simply by appearing in these magazines. The main disadvantage of magazines is that they are published infrequently (usually only monthly) and, like newspapers, they are very 'busy' with advertisements.

Radio

The main advantages of radio advertising are its low cost and ability to target specific regions. The main disadvantages are that consumers cannot see the product and that radio adverts are often ignored (not listened to).

Cinema

Cinema advertising is often used to reach young audiences who are difficult to communicate with via other media. The main disadvantage of cinema advertising is that its effectiveness depends, to some extent, on the success of the movie industry – if people don't go to the cinema, they won't see the adverts.

Outdoor

Bus stops, bus sides, taxis, billboards and posters are all common types of outdoor advertising. The benefits of outdoor advertising are the possibility of national coverage or regional targeting, the ability to use colour and the possibility of innovative marketing campaigns. However, the message must be very short and customers, having perhaps only seen the advertisement briefly, may not be able to recall important information if they want to make a purchase. As a result, outdoor advertising is most often used to build brand image rather than to give product information.

Δ Advertising on bus sides is eye-catching but may only be visible for a short time.

Viral marketing

Modern marketing campaigns often use what is known as viral marketing. This involves small-scale publicity stunts (planned events designed to attract the public's attention) targeted directly at key market segments. The aim is that news of the stunt goes viral (spreads around the internet rapidly). With videos or images of the stunt shared over the internet, some of the best viral marketing videos generate millions of hits within the space of only a few days. For a relatively low cost, if it is successful, viral marketing can be very effective at creating customer awareness about a product.

Did you know?

When Pokémon Go launched, very little money was spent advertising it. Instead, the company spread viral adverts among gamers and online. Within the first week of the launch, Pokemon Go broke the App Store's record for most downloads within the first week.

CASE STUDY Viral videos

In 2012, the Belgian TV station TNT staged a dramatic (but obviously fake) shoot-out scene in a town square to promote a new TV channel. Passers-by were shocked to see a fist fight between a cyclist and an ambulance medic and a shoot-out between (fake) police officers and bank robbers. The scene also included a 'rescue' of one of the actors by an entire American football team. Video of the stunt received thousands of hits (web page views).

Public relations (PR)

PR involves a business communicating with different stakeholders (see 1.5 Business objectives and stakeholder objectives), often at very little or no cost to the business. Businesses might use press releases or press conferences, and so on. PR can be seen in action all of the time. Think of the media coverage generated when a pop star is launching a new album – they will be seen on TV, in magazines and as 'VIP guests' at special events arranged to ensure that newspapers and magazines report on the star's clothing and even their hairstyle! All of this media coverage is good PR for the star and helps to sell whatever product (often their own music or movie) they are promoting.

Sponsorship

Sponsorship is where a business pays to be associated with a particular event, individual star or even a TV programme. For example, Beats, Delta Air Lines, IBM and Audemars Piguet sponsor the world's highest-paid female athlete, the tennis player Serena Williams.

Direct mailing

Many firms send out promotional fliers to customers and potential customers; this is now most commonly done via email. A lot of information can be included in direct mailing, but the receiver often ignores this kind of material.

Merchandising

Retailers often use a range of tactics such as point-of-sale displays (promotional displays of goods in stores, often near to the checkout tills) and free samples to promote products and improve sales. This is known as merchandising (displaying goods, also known as merchandise, in the most attractive way possible).

Analysis

Working in a small group, choose one product you are familiar with and recommend appropriate methods of promotion. Present your findings, if possible, in the format of that promotion. (For example, for TV and radio, you could act out your justification in the form of an advert.)

Marketing budgets

Firms need to ensure that their marketing is cost-effective. The marketing budget outlines how much money is allocated (given) to the firm's marketing and on what types of marketing it will be spent. For example, estimates suggest that over $35 million was spent on TV advertising alone for the release of the *Batman vs Superman: Dawn of Justice* film.

Δ Luxury brands often use Hollywood films and celebrity endorsement to promote their products. This can take up a significant portion of their marketing budgets.

The effectiveness of its marketing budget is one of the hardest things for a firm to judge. Analysing whether a rise or fall in sales is due to a successful promotion, the right price, a great product or is the result of other variables is very difficult. A product's sales can be affected by many things outside of a firm's control (the competition and even the weather, for example).

CASE STUDY

Budget cuts

Firms in India have been cutting their marketing budgets as the economy starts to slow down. Due to poor economic conditions and low sales, firms across India have found that marketing, particularly promotion, has been less effective. Some of India's biggest companies have been cutting back on advertising campaigns, opting instead for short-term sales promotions and point-of-sale discounts to persuade consumers who have less money to buy their products.

As it is difficult to measure how effective marketing is, it is difficult for a firm to decide how much to spend on marketing (the marketing budget). A firm obviously does not want to spend too much, as the cost of marketing may then exceed the additional sales revenue it generates. Equally, it does not want to spend too little, as it will not experience a large enough increase in sales.

A firm will therefore set its budget at a level it feels is the most **cost-effective** (providing enough profit in return for the money spent/invested).

Ultimately, the size of the marketing budget will be the basis on which a firm makes its promotional decisions. A large marketing budget will give the firm flexibility to use a range of marketing strategies, whereas a small budget will restrict its decision making and, therefore, the range of its marketing activities.

The size of the marketing budget is determined by:

- **The firm's marketing objectives.** A mass market product will require a larger budget than a niche one (see 3.1 Marketing, competition and the customer).
- **How much competitors spend.** If competitors spend large sums of money on marketing, a firm may feel that it needs to spend similar amounts.
- **The market.** Changes in the market may require a firm to increase marketing spend. For example, illegal downloading of music has required record companies to spend more money on marketing and to increase the range of promotional strategies they use to attract buyers (such as offering discounts on concert tickets or merchandise).
- **How much money the firm has.** A business with little money or that is suffering from cash flow problems will obviously spend less on marketing than a business with large cash reserves.
- **The cost of different promotion methods.** The price of different promotion methods varies over time. Newspaper advertising, for example, has fallen in price in recent years. Firms once unable to afford newspaper advertisements may now be able to access this method of promotion.
- **Where a product is in its life cycle.** A product in the introduction stage of the product life cycle may require lots of promotion and therefore a large marketing budget. A product in the decline stage may require very little marketing and therefore a small budget may be sufficient (enough).

Knowledge check

1. Identify the aims of promotion. (3)
2. Identify three methods of promotion. (3)
3. Explain, using an example, one of the benefits offered by TV advertising. (2)
4. Explain the role of public relations. (2)
5. Explain why promotion might be important early in a product's life cycle. (2)
6. Explain why new media advertising might be important to a firm targeting teenagers. (4)
7. Identify and justify appropriate methods of promotion for the following: (12)
   a) a new brand of shampoo
   b) a new smartphone aimed at teenagers
   c) holidays for the over-60s
   d) the latest James Bond movie.
8. Define the term marketing budget. (2)
9. Explain two factors that determine how much a firm allocates to its marketing budget. (4)

Total 34 marks

Technology and the marketing mix

Aims (3.3.5)

By the end of this section, you should:

- Be able to define and explain the concept of e-commerce
- Understand the opportunities and threats of e-commerce to business and consumers
- Understand the use of the internet and social networks for promotion.

Defining e-commerce

E-commerce is the buying and selling of goods or services over the internet. This form of selling is relatively recent and today generates a large amount of sales for businesses of all sizes. Since the late 1990s, businesses of all sizes have set up web pages allowing customers all over the world to view and buy their product or service range. Today more than 3.7 billion people have access to the internet, which represents around half of the world's population.

> **Top Tip**
>
> Like many things, the way that firms do their marketing has changed substantially in recent years. Technology has created new ways to reach customers, new ways to sell products and new ways for consumers to buy products. No firm, large or small, can afford to ignore technology – imagine how strange it would be for a firm of any size not to have a website or email address. These changes should prompt you to **analyse** the implications of technology and market forces (both the costs and the benefits) – it is this kind of critical thinking that will help you develop your business skills.

Types of e-commerce

Within e-commerce, there are two main types:

- Business to business buying and selling (B2B)
- Business to consumer selling (B2C).

Business to business (B2B) buying and selling

Business to business (B2B) is the process of one business selling to another – for example, a computer repair shop buying spare parts from a manufacturer.

Businesses of all sizes can now trade with each other over the internet. This method of buying and selling allows even smaller businesses to access the cheapest materials by searching the internet for the most competitive prices. This helps reduce costs, as businesses can find the parts and materials they need for a cheaper price. Most transactions in a production process are business to business, as products are put together using parts and components.

Business to consumer (B2C) selling

Business to consumer (B2C) is where a business produces a product or service and sells it directly to a customer. In the past, customers visited their local shops to buy the products they needed. Today, e-commerce allows the customer to visit the retailer's virtual shop by going to their website. This allows the business to access customers in all parts of the world.

For this form of e-commerce to happen, a business needs to develop a website. Websites can vary greatly in size, quality, ease of use and speed. Therefore, it is very important that a business has a website that is acceptable to its customers. For example, a small painting and decorating company may only need a small site, which includes some pictures of its work and the company's contact details. However, a large PLC, such as Siemens, needs a much larger site with a vast amount of information for its stakeholders.

∆ Electronic components companies in Guangzhou, China, use e-commerce to supply various local businesses, which then assemble the components to make electrical goods.

A good website is:

- good-looking, clear and easy to use
- updated regularly with new products, information and offers
- attractive to new and repeat customers
- informative – it gives customers all the information they need to make a decision
- accessible to all users (some websites have large videos or graphics that make it hard for low-speed internet users to view them).

CASE STUDY

Amaz-ing!

Amazon has grown at a fast pace over the years. In 2010 its revenue was $34 billion, whereas in 2016 it was $107 billion. The company now employs 268 900 employees worldwide compared to 33 700 in 2010. Amazon is expected to sell 7.2 billion items in 2017. By 2020, that number is expected to grow to 12.6 billion items. Amazon's founder, Jeff Bezos, puts the company's massive success down to low running costs and availability to a global audience through e-commerce. Amazon is a great example of the power of the internet and e-commerce to attract customers.

Consumer to consumer (C2C)

Since the development of eBay, Alibaba and OZtion, a new method of e-commerce has evolved. **Consumer to consumer (C2C)** is a growing market in which consumers try to sell old or unused products to other consumers. Although the internet business that hosts the transaction charges an advertising/ selling fee, the selling is from one consumer to another.

For example, Airbnb.com allows people to rent out their homes to holidaymakers and travellers from all over the world. The website simply connects the people who want to rent their home out with people who are looking for somewhere to rent.

Opportunities and threats of e-commerce

The table describes the various opportunities for both businesses and consumers created by e-commerce, as well as the potential threats.

Opportunities of e-commerce to businesses	Threats of e-commerce to businesses
✓ Businesses can access customers all over the world, allowing sales to increase for relatively low costs.	✗ There is increased competition, as businesses with lower costs can charge even lower prices. For example, a business in Thailand may have lower running costs and lower taxes to pay, which means it can charge lower prices than businesses elsewhere.
✓ Costs are much lower for a business, as they have no shops to run. This means they can afford to spend more on advertising and on the website.	✗ Websites may cost large amounts to design and set up, and it may take months to start earning the money back. This can be difficult for smaller businesses to afford.
✓ The business can provide in-depth information on each product that it sells, giving reviews, links to other related products and showing the product in action. This can give customers a much better understanding of the item than if they saw it packaged in a shop.	✗ If a website breaks or needs updating, the website may need to be temporarily closed. This may mean the business loses out on sales and damages its reputation.
✓ With internet usage increasing, the business can now use mobile, tablet and computer technology to sell its products.	✗ When buying via a website, customers expect fast and efficient service throughout the ordering and delivery process. For example, delivery must be on time and customers will expect to be able to speak to someone about their order or to register a complaint.
✓ Businesses are now reviewed online – for example, through TripAdvisor. This can help promote and increase a business's reputation at little cost to the business.	

Opportunities of e-commerce to consumers	Threats of e-commerce to consumers
✓ Consumers can now search the internet for the lowest prices. ✓ The internet is a fiercely competitive market place, so businesses have to offer acceptable prices and quality. This means customers can access higher quality for less money. ✓ The internet allows customers to access reviews and feedback about the businesses that are selling and also about products and services. This means they can make an informed decision. ✓ Consumers can buy products from all over the world without having to actually visit that country or business.	✗ Consumers may lose money through fraudulent (fake) payment. Illegal companies may set up fake websites that appear to sell products at amazingly low prices to attract customers. ✗ Consumers cannot try on or touch the products or services they are buying, which increases the chance that they will not fit or will not satisfy the customer. ✗ The time it takes for a product to be delivered can be very frustrating. E-commerce allows a consumer to buy from all over the world, but that can mean delivery time increases from days to weeks. ✗ If there is a fault or issues with a product, it can often be very hard to speak to someone. Many e-commerce businesses try to reduce costs by having minimal employees allocated to customer service.

Evaluation **Application**

Working in pairs, identify the key features of your favourite e-commerce websites. These may be the colours, layout and range of activities or products.

Based on this research, produce a leaflet for businesses of all sizes on what they should remember to include when setting up their own e-commerce website. Arrange your key points in order of importance, and ensure that you justify each point that you make. You may want to refer to some websites by name and perhaps use images to highlight your points.

The internet and social networks for promotion

Many businesses see the internet as a low-cost way of promoting their business and products to a global audience. The diagram summarises the many different ways in which a business can use internet promotion to help increase sales.

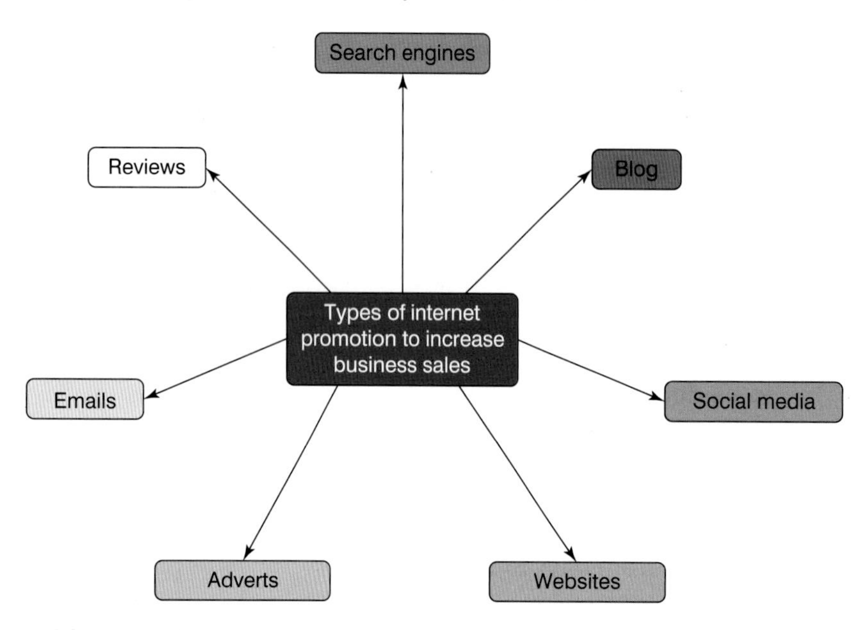

A **blog** is a discussion or information site that anyone can contribute to. Businesses use blogs to gain customer feedback and to release information, images or competitions. Many blogs are linked to the company's website, which helps generate a community feel, as customers have a wider experience rather than just viewing products.

Once customers visit a website, they are often encouraged to 'sign up' or 'register' to the business. This allows the business to send out emails or newsletters to help promote the business.

There are many benefits to internet promotion:

- It is often cheaper to use and set up. For example, a business can set up a four-week advertising campaign on Google for as little as $2000. This allows the business to appear when individuals enter key words in the search engine that match the business's products.
- It saves time. Off-line (non-internet-based) promotion may need to be different depending on the newspaper or magazine it is in, for example. However, online promotion can be targeted specifically at the correct type of people. This saves time designing and then accessing the appropriate off-line method.

> **Did you know?**
>
> The Huffington Post blog is the most-visited blog in the world, with over 110 million visits each month. Sharing news stories and reviews has made it a popular site for those seeking a different approach to news reporting.

CASE STUDY Online promotion

Social media and internet use in Africa are still developing, but many African businesses have seen the benefits. Kenya Airways has seen an increase in sales since it started to focus on online promotion and social media. Its online promotions include a new website that aims to make it easy for passengers to book and check in. The website is the first step in engaging with customers who have very different internet access and quality.

- An online advertisement can be altered quickly and easily if required. This means a business can keep up to date with customer demands and fashions.
- Online promotion can be measured easily. For example, a business can accurately measure the number of times a customer clicks on the advert to take them to the website.

∆ Samsung uses its own mobile phones to allow customers to access social media sites faster and more easily. It then runs online forums and competitions to boost sales.

The use of social media is a key promotional tool for businesses. Customers can now access social media sites, such as Facebook, Netlog and Orkut, on their mobile phones and tablets, as well as on their computers. This means that businesses can attract customers at any point in the day. For example, with over 1.3 billion Chinese people and 90% of the Japanese population using mobile phones every day, businesses know that promotion on the internet and social media is crucial to success. The computer firm Dell has trained more than 10 000 of its employees to be able to connect with customers online. It uses well-placed adverts, pages on over 15 social networking sites and competitions to attract customers.

CASE STUDY Y is it doing well?

YY.com is a new social media website in China that is achieving the highest growth in the market. It has recently reached 400 million users. YY.com uses a combination of techniques to promote itself and other businesses. It allows other businesses, such as gaming or mobile apps, to advertise themselves on its website. It also runs various competitions and blogs to engage the user.

Application

Design an online promotional campaign for an e-business of your choice. You should consider the following methods:

- blog
- emails/newsletters
- adverts
- competitions.
- videos

You should also consider the business size and financial capability before you design the campaigns – the costs should be realistic. Produce drawings, images or written detail for all the methods you use.

Produce a poster to display the details of your campaign.

Knowledge check

1. **Define the term e-commerce.** **(2)**
2. **Explain two benefits to a business of e-commerce.** **(4)**
3. **Explain two potential threats to a customer from e-commerce.** **(4)**
4. **Identify two important features of a successful website for a business.** **(2)**

Total 12 marks

Check your progress:

✓ I can outline the four different parts of the marketing mix: product, price, place and promotion.

✓ I can recommend and justify the most appropriate marketing mix for a given business.

✓ I can outline the concept of e-commerce and the potential opportunities and threats to business and consumers.

Marketing strategy

Appropriate marketing strategies

Aims (3.4.1)

By the end of this section, you should:

- Understand the importance of different elements of the marketing mix in influencing consumer decisions in given circumstances
- Be able to recommend and justify an appropriate marketing strategy in given circumstances.

A firm might have a range of marketing objectives. These might include:

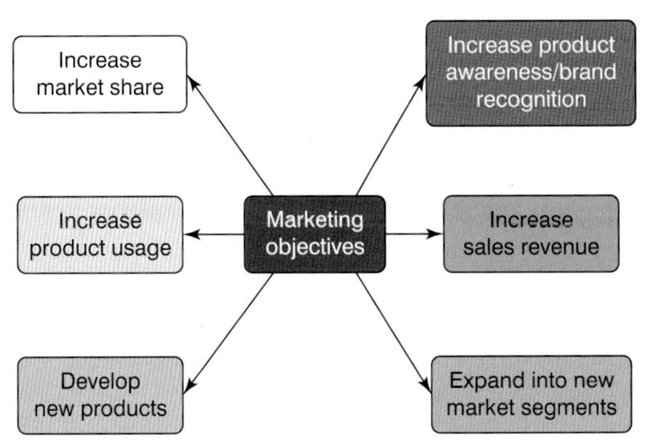

The firm's marketing objectives will then determine which elements of the marketing mix (product, price, promotion and place) are most important and thus will determine **marketing strategy**.

The importance of different elements of the marketing mix

The aim of marketing is ultimately to influence consumer behaviour. Firms want consumers to purchase more of their products, and they use the marketing mix (a particular combination of price, product design, promotion and place) to persuade them to do so.

The challenge for a business is to decide which element (or elements) of the marketing mix is most important for a particular product. Sometimes one element may be more significant than others (price is, for example, the most significant factor for low-cost airlines). For other products, a blend of the different aspects of the marketing mix may be important. (For example, Beats earphones use a combination of product design, promotion and price to establish themselves as the 'must have' earphones for teenagers.)

Marketing strategy refers to how a business decides which elements of the marketing mix it will prioritise (put first) to influence consumer behaviour. Different marketing strategies might involve:

Price	A supermarket may focus on price to distinguish it from competitors.
Product	Sony uses the latest technology and most fashionable designs to make its products highly desirable.
Promotion	Louis Vuitton uses expensive promotions in high-class magazines, often using famous movie stars, to establish itself as a premium brand.
Place	Coca-Cola is distributed as widely as possible to ensure that the product is always placed 'within arm's reach'.

It is important to remember that firms do not just use one element of the marketing mix. For Apple, product design is the priority, but price, brand and promotions also play an important part in reinforcing the premium nature of Apple products.

Different marketing strategies

As discussed in 3.1 Marketing, competition and the customer, a basic principle of Business Studies is the decision between high volume/low price and low volume/high price. Businesses essentially have to base their marketing strategy on one of these positions.

Δ Stonemasons offer a service targeted at a very small range of customers. They charge high prices for their unique skills.

- A **niche marketing strategy** suggests a differentiated product and high prices. It might also require exclusive distribution (place) and promotion in specialist media that targets small groups of customers.
- A **mass marketing strategy**, on the other hand, requires wide distribution (place) and low prices. Promotion is likely to use mass media such as TV, newspapers or the internet, and the product itself may be undifferentiated (the same or similar to other products).

If the product a business sells is undifferentiated, the business may need to pursue a strategy of **cost leadership**. This is where the business uses price to differentiate itself (make itself different) from the competition. The aim is to be the lowest-

▷ A branded shirt may be identical to an unbranded one in quality (it may even have been made in the same factory), but the presence of a well-known logo and brand name helps to differentiate the branded shirt and justify a higher price.

price seller in the market. Ikea, the Swedish furniture retailer, is arguably a cost leader within the home furnishings market.

The danger of cost leadership is that, for many firms, prices are often so low that it can be difficult to make a profit. (African farmers growing coffee beans to sell to coffee chains such as Starbucks face this problem.)

Because cost leadership is difficult to achieve and can result in low profitability, most businesses differentiate their products. Businesses offer customers something different from that of competitors. In the case of Ikea, not only are they often the cheapest but they also differentiate themselves from the competition by focusing on modern design and convenience.

Some products rely on perceived (how customers see the product) differentiation rather than tangible (physical) differences.

Evaluation

Compare and contrast the marketing strategies of two different products. Examine how each product uses the different elements of the marketing mix and evaluate whether the approaches are appropriate for the products in question.

Work in pairs on this activity and present your findings (using presentation software, if available) to the rest of your group.

Choosing appropriate marketing strategies

A wide range of factors will influence a business's choice of marketing strategy:

- **Corporate objectives.** Most importantly, marketing objectives must directly reflect overall corporate objectives, such as the objective to increase the company's total global sales revenue.
- **Stage of life cycle.** As discussed in 3.3 Marketing mix, different types of marketing are appropriate at different stages of a product's life cycle.
- **Competition.** Perhaps one of the most important influences on marketing strategy is competition. For example, a business seeking to grow market share will use appropriate marketing strategies to meet this aim – for example, a price cut, special offer or promotional campaign.

Top Tip

Remember that promotion is just one part of marketing. Promotion might be the bit of marketing we recognise the most, but without a product to promote, or a place to sell it, promotion would be pointless. Questions about marketing are unlikely to refer to promotion only – don't forget the rest of the marketing mix.

CASE STUDY Challenge the leader

Marketing strategy is determined by a business's competitive environment. Intel is the market leader in microchip production, but over recent years AMD has challenged that dominance. As a result, Intel has been forced to defend its market share. Intel differentiates itself by focusing on the product – making ever-faster microchips.

AMD, as a **market challenger**, uses price to attack Intel's leadership position. AMD claims that its microchips are just as fast as Intel's but significantly cheaper – AMD promotes this fact heavily.

- **Type of product.** Industrial goods are likely to require different marketing strategies to consumer goods. Industrial markets often have small numbers of buyers and sellers. Products are also often very specialised. Increasing market share in an industrial market can be difficult, so a business might concentrate on developing new products in related markets (for example, Rolls-Royce's entry into the marine engine market).
- **The market.** Highly changeable markets demand flexible marketing strategies. Clothing retailers, for example, have to constantly adjust their strategies to cope with new fashion trends and new influences (such as what the latest pop star is wearing), often even adjusting promotions related to the weather (for example, discounting cold-weather clothing as temperatures rise).
- **Finance.** Marketing can be very expensive. The amount of money a business can afford to spend on marketing will determine its marketing strategy.

Knowledge check

1. **Identify two examples of marketing objectives.** **(2)**
2. **Outline, using appropriate examples, two factors that might affect a business's choice of marketing strategy.** **(6)**
3. **Justify the element or elements of the marketing mix that might be most appropriate for:** **(12)**

   a) a new magazine aimed at teenagers

   b) a laptop aimed at graphic designers

   c) a plain chocolate bar

   d) a new book in a popular series.

Total 20 marks

Legal controls related to marketing

Aims (3.4.2)
By the end of this section, you should:
- Understand the impact of legal controls on marketing strategy, for example, misleading promotion, faulty and dangerous goods.

Marketing strategy and legal controls

When a business produces a marketing strategy, it must make sure that it does not purposely mislead or misinform the consumer by telling them something that is untrue. For example, a car dealership would not be able to promote a faulty product or offer it at a price that is below the real asking price.

Businesses therefore need to think very carefully about the way they organise their marketing strategy. While the business will want to encourage consumers to purchase its product or service, it cannot promote these in a misleading way.

Consumer protection laws are designed to stop businesses making such false claims and promises. The key legal requirements on businesses when marketing goods and services are described in this section. Each country has its own specific laws, so companies may have to alter their marketing depending on the country in which they operate.

Misleading the customer through promotion

A business must not mislead the customer by suggesting that the product or service does a task that in truth it doesn't. An advert or publication that suggests a product can carry out a job that it cannot is illegal.

Δ US company POM Wonderful, which produces pomegranate-based health foods and drinks, claimed in a marketing campaign that its products contained antioxidants. The company was criticised and later fined by the Federal Trade Commission for making false claims.

A business must make sure it has terms and conditions that are clear and visible to the customer. For example, a supermarket that advertises a promotion where customers receive a $5 voucher for every $50 spent must make clear any terms and conditions.

Businesses must also make sure that any marketing contains accurate and truthful prices. In addition, prices should be consistent across all of the marketing. For example, airlines all over the world have come under heavy pressure from consumers over hidden charges on flights.

Faulty or dangerous goods

A business must provide a product or service that meets certain standards and expectations – for example, the product sold is expected to be of a good quality and fit for purpose (good enough for the job it was designed to do). A marketing strategy should highlight any dangers or limits of the product. Now that cigarette packaging must highlight the health risks of smoking, many countries have also banned cigarette packs from being visible in shops.

A faulty (damaged) or dangerous product can damage a company's reputation and image. The reputation of car manufacturers Hyundai and Kia suffered after consumers reported faulty cars.

Organisations representing customers' rights

Marketing laws work in partnership with consumer organisations that represent consumers. Some examples of consumer organisations are described in the table.

Consumer organisation	Description
The Better Business Bureau (BBB) – USA/Canada	This not-for-profit organisation works with over 100 businesses and organisations across the USA and Canada to provide reviews and advice for customers of businesses of all sizes. They work hard to report businesses for running misleading marketing campaigns.
The African Consumer Protection Dialogue – Africa	This organisation brings together companies and government organisations to help reduce damage to consumers' rights from the sale of products.
All India Crime Prevention Organization (AICPO) – India	Set up in 1990, AICPO works hard to help businesses produce and sell products and services that do not break laws or damage consumers' rights.

Analysis

Laws that try to stop businesses being untruthful in their marketing campaigns protect customers in most countries.

You have been asked to advise the marketing department on their marketing campaigns for the products below. Discuss in pairs which legal controls are most important for the business when marketing each product.

- A car
- A can of fizzy drink
- A computer game

Knowledge check

1. **Identify two ways in which a business might mislead customers in its marketing campaign.** **(2)**
2. **Explain why there are laws to protect consumers when buying a product.** **(4)**
3. **Explain two possible impacts of a business selling faulty or dangerous goods.** **(4)**

Total 10 marks

Entering foreign markets

Aims (3.4.3)
By the end of this section, you should:
- Understand the growth potential of new markets in other countries
- Understand the problems of entering foreign markets, for example, cultural differences and lack of knowledge
- Understand the benefits and limitations of methods to overcome such problems, for example, joint ventures, licensing.

The growth potential of new markets in other countries

In the past, businesses used to grow to a national scale before looking to expand overseas. However, the fast growth of the internet and computer technology means that businesses of all sizes can access global markets, selling in countries that are hundreds of miles away. This means that many companies are now experiencing the benefits of operating in new markets in other countries.

Δ Amore Pacific produces a range of high-price, high-quality skincare products and has an expanding global market. Net sales in 2011 were $600 million.

Did you know?

UK supermarket giant Tesco failed famously to enter the US market in its new form, 'Fresh & Easy', despite spending over $1 billion on researching the US market. Its new US stores were sold off after only five years.

The benefits of going into new markets

Going into new markets has a number of benefits:

Benefit	Description
✓ Increased sales	Selling into another country increases the number of potential customers. This will boost the number of sales and sales revenue. For example, UNIGLOBE, an international business travel company, has started to sell in Poland and has seen sales increase steadily.

Benefit	Description
✓ Increased customer base	The new market will increase the number of customers a business can sell to. For example, a business expanding to sell in Africa could increase their customer base by one billion!
✓ Culture-specific products	Some businesses can alter their existing products to sell to new markets where customers want different things. This increases their customer base. For example, in Indonesia, McDonald's meets the needs of the Muslim population by selling burgers made from halal meat (prepared according to Muslim law).
✓ Product differentiation	Different products sell better in different countries, so when a business goes into a new market it may see sales of some of its products rise. In more affluent countries, products such as trainers tend to be of higher quality and a certain type. For example, Diadora receive most of their sales from southern Europe and the Middle East.
✓ Spreading risk	The more countries a business sells in, the less risk it faces from external problems. For example, Greece and Spain have suffered poor economic conditions and businesses there have seen sales drop. Greek and Spanish businesses that also sell in other countries may have been able to maintain their sales revenue, despite falling sales in home markets.

A business will often look for a new market in a growing economy. This means that the country experiences an increase in its gross domestic product (see 6.3 Business and the international economy). This shows that trade within the country is growing, and that people are spending money.

The Côte d'Ivoire (Ivory Coast) is Africa's fastest-growing economy, according to the IMF's latest World Economic Outlook. The West African nation's GDP is expected to grow by 8.5% in 2017. A business that is looking to expand into foreign new markets may be interested in the short-term gains from extra customers, as well as the longer-term benefits, such as increased market size, that will come as the Ivory Coast's economy grows.

Analysis **Evaluation**

Many countries look to sell into new markets. Often the main benefit for the business is the increase in revenue.

Using the five benefits discussed in the table, research a business that has expanded into a new market in your country. Produce a poster that explains the benefits to the company of doing so. Try to find evidence of these benefits. For example, if you find a business that has expanded into a new market because of the increase in potential customers, find evidence to show this increase. Decide which is the key benefit.

The problems of going into new markets

There are various problems to overcome when entering a new market. Many businesses, both larger multinationals and smaller businesses, can struggle with entering markets they are not familiar with.

Problem	Description
✗ Cultural differences	Opening in a foreign country with a different culture can be difficult. Without understanding the country and its culture, a business can offend customers by not taking on board the local culture. If a business fails to engage with local people, its marketing efforts will fail.
✗ Language	If a business opens up in another country, it may struggle to communicate with customers if it does not speak the local language. This will make customer service and marketing very difficult.
✗ Different laws	In some countries, laws are very different. These can be laws on product quality, taxation or employment. There may also be laws on when a business can operate. For example, in some countries businesses do not open on Mondays.
✗ Lack of knowledge	A business may not have done enough market research and therefore lack knowledge of the market it is going into. If the business does not know how local businesses are expected to operate, or what customers want, it will struggle to increase sales.
✗ Market decline	Sometimes external factors can threaten a business when it enters a new market. If the economy of the new country starts to decline, it may mean a business cannot afford to continue to trade there.

Entering a new market can be a costly and difficult task for any business, but many larger businesses do this every year. A larger business will be more likely to succeed in a new market because:

- They are likely to have access to more money. This means they can afford to pay for extra research, increased advertising and a larger amount of working capital (day-to-day money used to pay bills).
- They may have experience in entering a new market and will understand what they need to do to make it a success.
- They may be able to allocate specific employees who have the skills or experience needed to make it a success. For example, employees who can speak additional languages may be very useful when entering a new market abroad.

△ There can be language problems when entering new markets. The baby food company Gerber sells in many international markets but not in France, as the French word 'gerber' means 'to vomit'.

CASE STUDY

Business smells good

Eurofragance is a successful Spanish business that specialises in design and production of fragrances for the food and perfumery industries. By 2009, 70% of its revenue came from exporting to Europe. More recently, Eurofragance moved into a new market: the Middle East and Asia. With the Muslim market representing 23% of world sales, Eurofragance was keen to enter the market, and has now seen its revenues increase by 60%. The key to this success was the in-depth company research that Eurofragance carried out, which highlighted the cultural and legal differences in these new markets. One such difference was that Eurofragance needed to make sure their products for these markets were certified halal (prepared according to Muslim law).

The size of a business is not the only deciding factor on whether the move into a new market succeeds or not. Some smaller businesses are often very successful in new markets because they appeal to very specific customers.

Did you know?

Despite a huge increase in methods to stop piracy, the value of cross-border fake items, such as headphones, mobile phones and clothing, is estimated at over $500 million a year. This figure is disappointing for many global firms.

Ways to address the problems of entering new markets

There are various methods that businesses can use to overcome the problems of entering a new market abroad.

Method and description	Benefits	Limitations
Joint ventures: working with another business when entering a new market	✓ This spreads the risk across two businesses. Often, the costs will be split as well, so if the entry into a new market fails, each individual business will have lost less money. ✓ One business may have expertise and experience that the other business will benefit from, which means the venture is more likely to succeed. ✓ The businesses do not have to commit as many resources (for example, employees, time and money) to the project.	✗ The potential revenues and profit will now be split with the other business. ✗ The two businesses may have different ideas about certain situations and decisions that need to be made. This may make it difficult for a business to run the expansion in the way it would like.

Method and description	Benefits	Limitations
Licensing: when a business gives the right for others to produce or sell its product/ service in another country	✓ No investment is needed by the business that owns the rights to the product/service. ✓ The business creates revenue from new markets without the risk of losing money invested. ✓ It is a quick way to increase sales, as new customers are created in a new market.	✗ Piracy (illegal copies) of products from foreign firms in this market can often occur and be hard to stop. ✗ Not all the profits go to the original firm (licensor), with much of this going to the licensee.
Investment: investing in training, new equipment and advertising	✓ The business may invest in employee training, so they are more comfortable in and knowledgeable about the new market. This improves employee morale, the skills available to the business and the chance of the expansion into a new market being a success. ✓ This type of investment keeps the business ahead of competitors and makes sure they have the most up-to-date equipment and skills.	✗ The large expense may be difficult for the business to fund, especially if they have invested a lot in the expansion already. ✗ The investment does not guarantee success. For example, training may not be specific enough and it may not give the employees enough knowledge of the new market.
Testing: having a test period in the new market to see if customers like the product	✓ By testing the product, the business can see how the new market responds to it. If the product is not popular, then the business can choose not to go ahead with the expansion. ✓ The business can use initial comments and feedback to improve the product or service before its full launch.	✗ Testing may waste time, meaning competitors release their product or service in the new market first. ✗ The testing may be a failure and the business may lose money.
Sell in many different markets: when businesses sell their product or service in many different markets	✓ By selling in many different markets, a business: • can reduce the risk of potential failures in new markets (provided sales in other markets are strong) • may be able to fund a move into a difficult new market.	✗ A business may try to expand into too many new markets. This may cause cash flow problems and put the future of the business at risk.

CASE STUDY

Two is better than one

Even businesses as large as Shell use joint ventures to gain experience and knowledge of new markets from other companies. Saudi Basic Industries Corporation (SABIC) and Shell have announced that they will be buying the remaining 52% stake in the joint venture with Shell Arabia. Having undertaken the joint venture, SABIC have decided to buy the whole entity from Shell due to its success. The venture, known as SADAF, started in 1980; at its peak it has produced 4 million tonnes of chemicals per year.

Analysis

In pairs, discuss the following scenario:

You own a medium-sized car company. A larger competitor has suggested a possible joint venture into a new market. The proposed plan is to produce a new car that runs on renewable energy. The other company has offered to pay 60% of the costs but has asked for 70% of the profits.

- What would be the benefits and drawbacks of this proposal for you and your business? Why would a larger competitor want to join with a smaller business in this way? Make a judgement on whether you would recommend this proposal.
- Produce a presentation for the stakeholders of your business on the benefits and drawbacks of the proposal.

Knowledge check

1. **Define the term cultural difference. (2)**
2. **Identify two potential reasons why a business would want to expand into a new market. (2)**
3. **Explain two reasons why a business might not succeed when moving into a new market. (4)**
4. **Explain one way in which a business may overcome problems when entering a new market. (4)**
5. **Explain one potential benefit and one potential limitation of a joint venture for a business. (6)**

Total 18 marks

Top tip

Businesses of all sizes will often want to grow, so understanding which limitations they would face is important. For a specific business, you must make sure you apply the best solution, given its size, resources and other assets.

Check your progress:

- ✓ I can outline the different marketing strategies used and the impact of legal controls.
- ✓ I can justify which marketing strategies are appropriate for different businesses.
- ✓ I can outline the benefits and drawbacks of entering new foreign markets.

Exam-style questions: short answer and data response

1. StreetBeat makes premium-priced fashion clothes. Its target market is teenagers. It sells its products through its own chain of shops. The management knows that the market is very competitive, with lots of other companies selling similar products.

StreetBeat is, however, the current market leader in teenage fashions. It has achieved this position through a market-orientated approach and a USP – every item of StreetBeat clothing is designed to making listening to music on the go easier (special pockets for MP3 players, loops to hold headphones, etc.).

a) Define the term market-orientated. (2)

b) Define the term market leader. (2)

StreetBeat is about to carry out some primary market research. It intends to use sampling to research the market.

c) Explain two methods of sampling that StreetBeat might use in its research process. (4)

The internet has changed the way that people shop and the way that teenagers spend their leisure time. StreetBeat is thinking of changing its channel of distribution so that it sells directly to its customers via the internet.

d) Do you think that StreetBeat should start distributing their clothes via the internet? **Justify** your answer. (6)

e) Explain three problems that StreetBeat might face if it exported its clothing to other countries. (6)

2. StreetBeat believes that its main USP is fashionable and functional design and that its marketing mix helps to sell its products.

a) Identify two possible elements of StreetBeat's marketing mix. (2)

b) Outline two benefits to StreetBeat of using secondary data. (2)

c) Explain two important factors that StreetBeat should consider when deciding on the packaging of its products. (4)

d) Identify two methods of promotion StreetBeat might use. **Justify** your choices. (6)

e) Outline two problems that StreetBeat might face if it attempted to market its clothing to other countries. (6)

3. StreetBeat's management is considering using promotional or dynamic pricing for items bought on its website. Secondary research suggests that demand for its products is price inelastic.

a) Define the term promotional pricing. (2)

b) Define the term price inelastic. (2)

c) **Explain** two reasons why demand for StreetBeat's products might be price inelastic. (4)

d) Would you advise the management of StreetBeat to use dynamic pricing? **Justify** your answer. (6)

Governments sometimes pass legislation designed to make markets more competitive.

e) Does competition always benefit consumers? **Justify** your answer. (6)

Note: The exam-style questions, answers and commentary in this book were written by the author; in examination the number of marks awarded to questions like these may be different.

Exam-style questions based on case studies

SunnySide up

Sunny runs a small coffee shop (called SunnySide), based in Addis Ababa, the capital of Ethiopia, and located near a university campus and several high schools. The shop is frequented by young people.

The shop serves coffee, tea, fruit shakes, cakes and sandwiches. The majority of Sunny's customers (see Appendix 1) use the take-away service. The small indoor eating area is very busy in the mornings and during lunch, but is quiet once the university and schools have closed. During school and university holidays, demand is very low.

There are several other coffee shops and restaurants in the area. Sunny's business is popular because of its location (close to the university), but there is lots of competition. As most of his customers are students, Sunny has to keep his prices low.

To improve sales (especially during school and university holidays), Sunny is thinking of offering a sandwich/cake delivery service. He is also thinking of catering for parties and special events (baking special cakes for the party and delivering on the day).

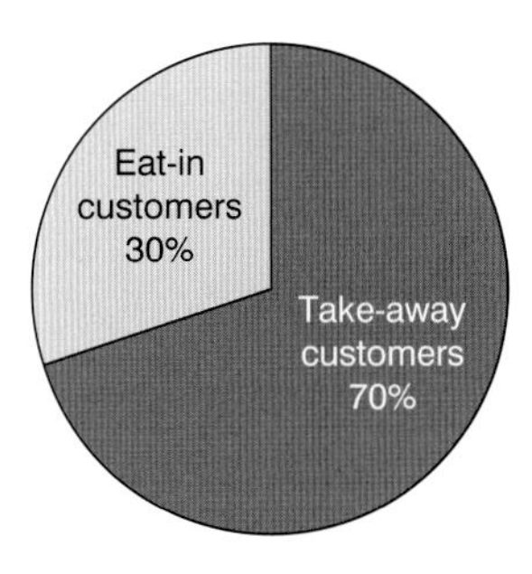

△ *Appendix 1: Proportion of eat-in and take-away customers at SunnySide*

	Average coffee prices	Seating area	Food	Holidays	Delivery service
SunnySide	$1.99	Yes (small)	Yes	Open	
Starworld	$2.19	Yes (large)	Yes	Open	No
Coffee Been	$1.99	Yes (medium)	Yes	Open	No
Coffee @U	$1.89	No	No	Closed	No

△ *Appendix 2: Market research – competitor analysis*

1. SunnySide is currently targeted at young people.

a) Using relevant information from the appendices, **justify** a suitable marketing mix for SunnySide. (8)

b) Sunny decides to trial-launch his sandwich and cake delivery service during a school holiday. **Explain** three methods of promotion that Sunny could use. **Outline** which one you think would be the best method to use. **Justify** your choice. (12)

2. To improve sales, Sunny is thinking of targeting new markets, particularly during the quieter summer months.

a) **Identify** one alternative target market for SunnySide and **outline** what changes Sunny may need to make to his marketing mix to appeal to that market. (8)

b) There are many legal controls that SunnySide must follow, especially because it is a food business. **Identify** three legal controls on SunnySide's marketing activities and **explain** the impact of each. (12)

3. Sunny currently uses competitive pricing. To improve profits, he wants to use a different pricing strategy.

a) **Explain** two alternative pricing strategies Sunny could use. (8)

To help him identify new market segments, Sunny intends to do some market research.

b) Should Sunny use primary research or secondary research into possible new market segments? **Justify** your choice. (12)

4. SunnySide currently only sells its products directly to consumers through its shop.

a) Using your knowledge of distribution channels, **explain** two alternative ways Sunny might increase sales of his products. (8)

b) Sunny is considering using the internet to take orders for his delivery service. Do you recommend this strategy? **Justify** your answer. (12)

Note: The exam-style questions, answers and commentary in this book were written by the author; in examination the number of marks awarded to questions like these may be different.

Exam-style questions based on case studies

uSmile

Sudha has won several national photography competitions.

When Sudha graduated from university, she decided on a career in photography. Sudha had noticed that the photographs people posted on Facebook and other social networking sites were often of poor quality. She developed a website (uSmile) that included tips, tricks and techniques that people could use with even the most basic cameras. Users can access the site for free, but can also pay a small fee to register and receive a weekly newsletter.

The site's unique selling point is its auto-improve feature. Sudha allows users, for a premium fee, to upload photographs to the site which are then automatically cropped, recoloured and adjusted to look as good as possible. The results are not always perfect, but the small number of people who have used the service love it. Sudha's problem is that, with so many other photography sites available on the internet, she is struggling to get noticed.

Site	Hits per week
Photo Weekly	10 000 000
Photography	13 500 000
Lens Life	5 000 000
uSmile	450 000

Appendix 1: Comparison of website traffic

Asia	6%
Europe	2%
Middle East	90%
USA	1%
Africa	1%

Appendix 2: Location of traffic to uSmile

The following summary comes from Sudha's original business plan:

Product – Sudha designed the website herself using a template from the internet. The interface is clear but basic. Through secondary market research, Sudha believes that her auto-improve feature is unique.
Price – Access to the website is free. A small fee is charged for a weekly newsletter and a premium price is charged for the auto-improve feature.

Place – Her product is web-based only. Sudha works from home. uSmile has no presence in any physical locations.
Promotion – So far Sudha has done little promotion. She mailed a link to her site to friends, created a Facebook page and managed to get a small news report in a printed Middle East photography magazine.

Appendix 3: uSmile marketing activities

Sudha operates in a highly competitive market.

1. Sudha currently uses a mass marketing approach. Her product is aimed at anybody who is interested in photography.

a) **Explain**, using examples, how market segmentation may help Sudha to better target appropriate customers. (8)

b) Using relevant information from the appendices, **consider** three possible consequences of operating in such a competitive market for a business like Sudha's. (12)

2. Currently Sudha's website is mainly accessed by customers in the Middle East. She is planning to expand usage to Europe, Asia and, eventually, to the USA.

a) With particular reference to Appendices 1 and 2, **consider** whether uSmile might benefit from a niche marketing approach. **Justify** your answer. (8)

b) **Consider** the potential benefits and drawbacks of entering these new markets. Should Sudha expand or not? **Justify** your recommendation. (12)

3. a) Sudha could expand into the market for online videos. She wants to carry out primary market research using online questionnaires. **Explain** how she should carry out this research. (8)

b) Sudha's website is currently mainly visited by young people. **Identify** a different market segment she could target and **outline** a suitable marketing mix to appeal to that segment. **Justify** your choices. (12)

4. a) Sudha wants to increase the number of times her auto-improve feature is used. **Identify** two types of promotion she could use to attract customers to this service. **Justify** your choices. (8)

b) Sudha needs to be aware of various legal controls on marketing activities. **Identify** three legal controls Sudha needs to consider and **explain** the implications of these controls on her marketing activities. (12)

Note: The exam-style questions, answers and commentary in this book were written by the author; in examination the number of marks awarded to questions like these may be different.

Past paper questions

Paper 1

Section 3

Walt owns a company which has developed a new computer game for adults. A focus group report shows customers like it. Walt has been considering the marketing mix, including the packaging for this product which is likely to be sold in many countries. 'I don't want to use a wholesaler as it would affect my profit margin' he said.

Identify and explain two advantages to Walt if he decided to use a wholesaler to distribute his products

Advantage 1: ____________________

____

Explanation: ____________________

____

____

____

Advantage 2: ____________________

____

Explanation: ____________________

____

____

____________________ (6)

e) Consider two possible methods of promotion that Walt could use for the new game. Recommend which method he should use. Justify your answer.

____

____

____

____

____

____

____

____

____

____

____

____________________ (6)

Cambridge International IGCSE Business Studies 0450 Paper 13, Q1 d & e, Nov 2015

Paper 2

Section 3

The following case study is taken from past papers created by Cambridge Assessment International Education. We have only provided extracts of this case study, and it does not reflect the full case study that you may be provided with in your examination.

Celebration Biscuits (CB)

Chris is qualified as a chef and baker. He was made redundant from a restaurant after it closed. The Government provides advice to unemployed people to help them start their own business. Chris has had an idea for a business known as Celebration Biscuits (CB). He wants the business to be a partnership and thinks this will be better than a sole trader or a private limited company.

His idea is to make and sell large biscuits with messages on them such as 'Happy Birthday' or 'Congratulations' with the name of the person on them.

Chris has many things to do before he can start trading. He needs to find suppliers of the ingredients and test his recipes. He intends to start by using his own kitchen and oven to bake the biscuits. Chris will have to ensure that each biscuit is always of the highest quality and any broken biscuits will have to be thrown away. Chris could buy a new larger oven for his kitchen and then he would need an employee to help him produce more biscuits.

Marketing will be very important to CB and Chris will need to decide on a marketing mix for his biscuits to improve the chance of the business being successful. His target market is mainly parents giving a celebration biscuit to their children on their birthday.

Appendix
Proposed newspaper advert for CB

Celebrate a birthday or other happy event by giving a biscuit with a personal message on it. This gift will be unique to the person. Buy them for birthdays, graduation, weddings or any other event you want to celebrate.

1. a) **Identify** and **explain** two reasons why marketing is important to CB when Chris starts his new business. (8)

   b) Chris has to decide on the 'place' part of his marketing mix. Consider the advantages and disadvantages of the three following methods of distributing his biscuits to the target market. Recommend which will be the best one to use. **Justify** your choice. (12)

   i) Selling through his own stalls in shopping malls
   ii) Selling through a website
   iii) Selling to large supermarkets

Cambridge International IGCSE Business Studies 0450 Paper 23, Q2 a & b, June 2015

Skills Builder

AO1: Knowledge

When discussing marketing make sure that you always use specific business terms, not just general terms. Develop your **knowledge** so you know what the right terms are and use them correctly – remember, businesses do not sell 'things'; they sell **products**.

AO2: Application

Marketing is everywhere. **Apply** your knowledge of marketing to the things you see around you every day. Why does your local cinema charge the prices it does? Could it charge more? Why? Why not? Do this regularly and you will find that applying knowledge to specific case studies will become easier.

Marketing strategy will be focused on the specific circumstances a business faces. Similarly, your answers must be **applied** to context.

- What industry is the business in?
- Is it a small or large firm?
- Is the market growing or shrinking?
- Where is the firm's product in its life cycle?

These and many other questions will be important in understanding context.

AO3: Analysis

Marketing is not just relevant to profit-driven private sector businesses. Every organisation, whether it is a school, hospital or local charity, has 'customers' whose needs it must serve. You need to analyse which aspects of marketing might be most important to them. Identifying the advantages and disadvantages of the different promotional methods will be vital, as will putting together a balanced view.

AO4: Evaluation

Marketing is just one of the many important factors of business success. More market research, more promotion or more distribution will not (on their own, at least) secure success. Business history is littered with failed marketing campaigns. You must judge what other factors might affect the success of a marketing strategy. How will the competition react? How will the state of the economy affect any decision? What legal considerations are there?

The business world – and especially marketing – is full of trends, fashions and 'buzz' words. Judging a business's marketing decision requires careful consideration of the business's circumstances and finances.

Operations management includes the production of goods and services, the management of costs, quality of production and decisions about location. For a business to be successful, effective management of all its resources is essential. Productivity and labour skills need to be increased, costs must be analysed, high quality must be achieved, and change is driven by new technology.

In this section, you will learn:

- about the meaning of production, the main production methods and how technology has changed production methods
- about costs, scale of production and break-even analysis, identifying and classifying costs and analysing economies and diseconomies of scale
- why quality is important and how quality production may be achieved
- about the main factors that influence the location decisions of a business.

SKILLS BUILDER

Good progress

Knowledge: You show sound knowledge of the key terminology.

Application: You demonstrate good understanding of the key terms that you have mentioned through explanations and application to businesses.

Analysis: You develop the consequences of the points that you have mentioned for the type of business in question, explaining the advantages and disadvantages for the business.

Evaluation: You make judgements when they are required.

Excellent progress

Knowledge: You define and identify all of the key terms relating to operations, using this terminology in your written answers.

Application: You show a clear ability to apply your knowledge to a given business situation, using detail such as the type of product or service it sells, the market it sells to and the financial resources available to the business.

Analysis: You develop the consequences to the business in question, explaining the advantages and disadvantages for the business.

Evaluation: You make judgements and suitable recommendations, justifying your reasoning. Where possible, you use data in your judgements to make reference to the business's overall profit.

SECTION CONTENTS

4 Operations management

Starting points

- For a business to produce goods and services, it must take resources (inputs) and use them to create its finished product (outputs).

Think about a business near you that produces a product or service. What inputs do they need to create it?

- One of the inputs needed by a business is labour (employees). Labour can vary depending on what the business produces; however, it is often regarded as a vital element.

How can a business increase the productivity (amount a person makes) of its employees? Make a list.

Production of goods and services

The meaning of production

Aims (4.1.1)

By the end of this section, you should:

- Understand how to manage resources effectively to produce goods and services
- Understand the difference between production and productivity
- Know the benefits of increasing efficiency and how to increase it, for example, increasing productivity by automation and technology, improved labour skills
- Understand why businesses hold inventories
- Understand the concept of lean production and how to achieve it, for example, just-in-time inventory control and Kaizen, benefits of lean production.

Managing resources effectively

The role of the production department within a business is to provide the service that the business offers or to physically produce the product that the business makes. It is an essential department within a business, as the three other functional areas (marketing, human resources and finance) all work to support the production or provision of the product or service.

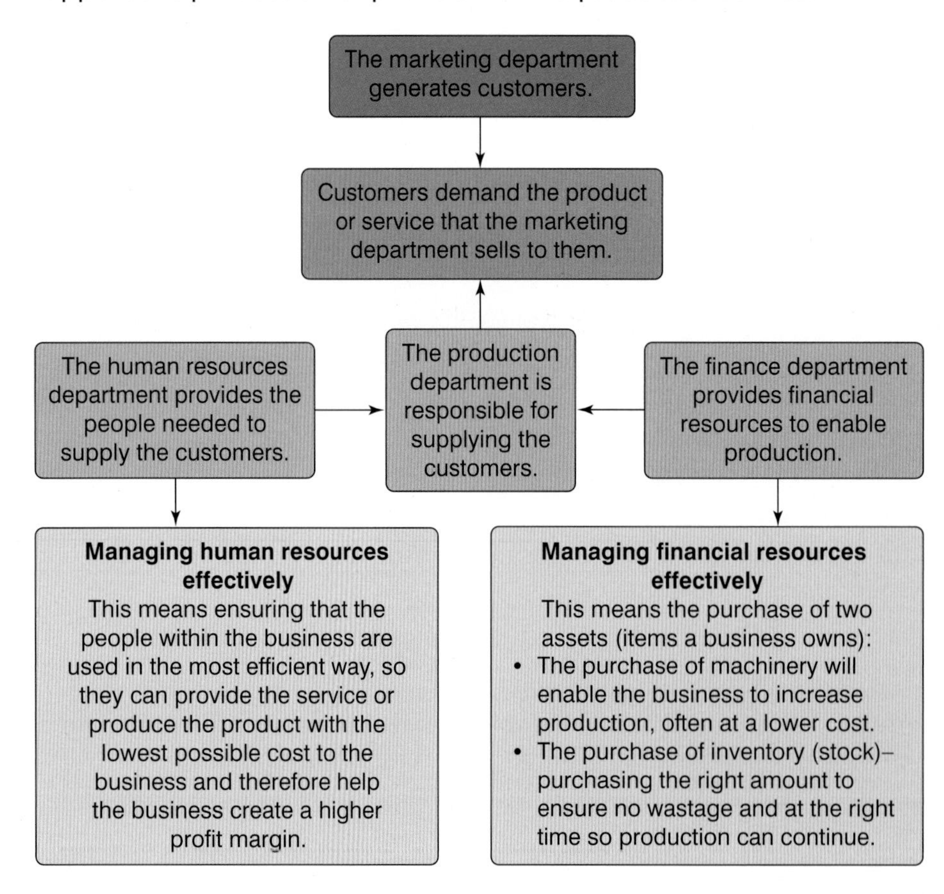

Difference between production and productivity

Δ Houses can take a number of months to complete, so it would be better to monitor production over a two- to three-month period.

Production

The amount or level of production (**output**) simply means how many products are produced or how many customers are served. This can be measured over a working shift (for example, between 9am and 5pm), a day, a week, a month or a year. Different businesses have different timescales over which they measure how much production has taken place. This will depend on the type of product or service that they produce or provide.

Productivity

This measures how much a business has produced in relation to its resources. Its resources are normally the people the business employs (human resources), so this is known as **labour productivity**. Labour productivity enables a business to compare its level of production with that of competitors who have different resources available to them.

Δ Productivity can be measured by looking at how a business uses its resources, in this case its employees.

How to measure labour productivity

$$\frac{\text{Output (the amount of production)}}{\text{Number of employees}}$$

WORKED EXAMPLE

Vaas Drinks Ltd has 100 employees and its output is 1000 litres per week. So productivity per employee is:

$$\frac{\text{Output}}{\text{Number of employees}} = \frac{1000}{100} = 10$$

How to improve productivity (efficiency)

Productivity is the best way a manager can measure the performance of their production department. Improving the level of productivity will mean that a business is making more efficient use of their resources and are therefore reducing their costs. There are several ways a business can improve its productivity. The type of product or service they offer will determine the most appropriate method.

- **Investing in more automation (mechanical production) or better technology.** Regardless of whether the business manufactures (makes) a product or provides a service, having a more automated approach to production should improve efficiency. This can mean buying new technology or making better use of the existing technology.

Benefits of using technology to improve productivity	Drawbacks of using technology to improve productivity
✓ Unlike people, technology does not require additional costs such as wages. ✓ Technology can enable a business to work for longer hours, as machinery can run 24 hours a day, seven days a week. ✓ Having a more automated process can mean that fewer people are needed, which significantly reduces the business's costs.	✗ Although technology can require low running costs, it normally requires a large initial cost. ✗ A more automated approach takes responsibility away from employees, which can often reduce motivation. ✗ Technology can become out of date very quickly, so it may have to be updated to meet the changing needs of customers.

- **Improving employee motivation.** Improving the level of motivation among a business's employees can often improve the level of output for each employee. This therefore improves the business's productivity.
- **Improving the employees' skills.** Improving the skill level of the employees through training can reduce the number of mistakes they make and help employees produce more quickly.
- **Effective management.** One role of a good manager is to coordinate a business's resources. Having a good manager will increase employees' motivation and ensure that resources are used efficiently through good organisation.

Benefits of improving a business's efficiency

The benefit of improving a business's productivity is that it reduces the cost of producing each unit and therefore increases the **profit margin** for each item made.

Application **Analysis**

Using the following data, calculate the cost per unit and the productivity per employee at the moment.

Number of employees	10	Cost of cocoa per bar	$0.50
Average wage per employee	$7.50	Number of bars produced	150
Total cost of employees per day	**$75**	**Total cost of cocoa**	**$75**
Total cost for the day	**$150**		

Now calculate the cost per unit and the productivity per employee if the following changes were introduced.

The company sends their employees on a training course. When they return, each employee produces double the amount of chocolate.

The business invests in technology to make the production process more automated. Only half the number of employees are needed per day, but the business produces three times as many bars in the same time.

Write a 250-word report to the production manager outlining the benefits of increasing productivity. Ensure that you use data to back up your argument.

How can holding the *right* level of stock improve efficiency?

Holding the right amount of inventory (stock) can have a significant impact on a business's efficiency and the cost of production. Businesses that manufacture a product need to buy stock or raw materials from their suppliers. They can then manufacture the raw materials and sell them on to their customers at a higher price. However, if they order too much stock, they will have to hold (store) that stock until it is ready to be used. Ordering too little stock will mean they cannot produce the amount needed or demanded by their customers.

◁ Companies that manufacture food items using fresh ingredients need to take care to order in the right amount of stock each day.

Consider the following example for a business that manufactures computers.

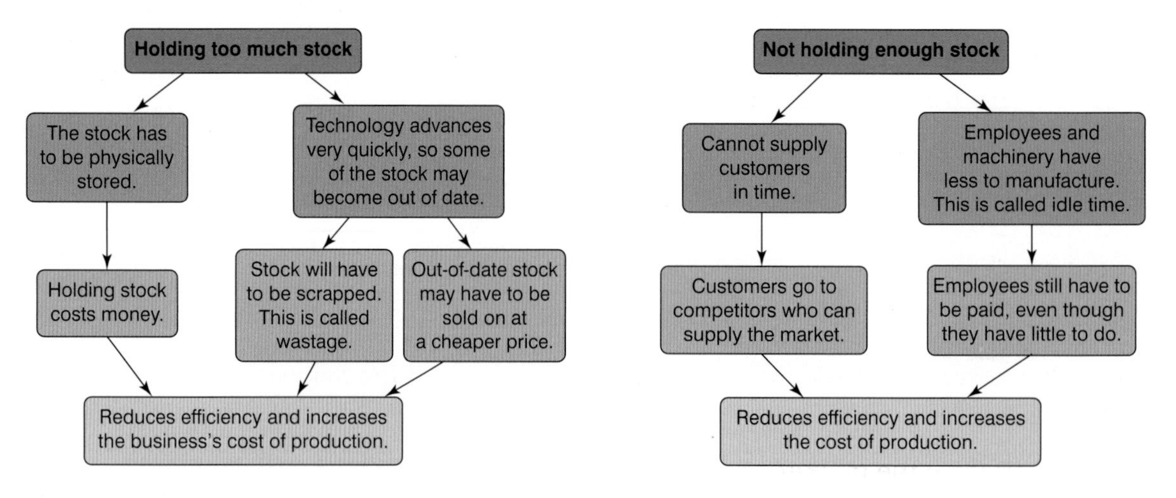

The concept of lean production

Lean production is a philosophy (a way of doing things) that reduces the amount of a business's key resources within production – for example, reducing the amount of time, money, people or materials needed within the production process.

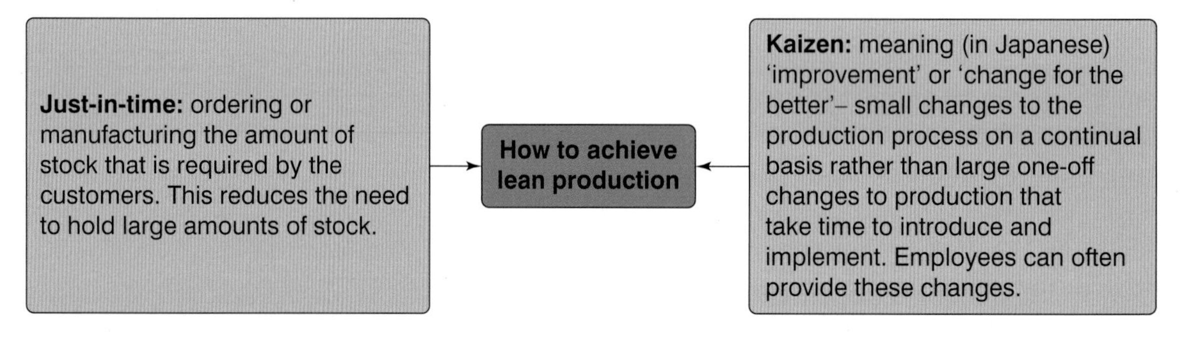

The benefits of lean production

There are various advantages of applying these philosophies:

- They can result in higher labour productivity, which reduces the production cost per unit.
- They can require less stock, which reduces high stock-holding costs.
- Asking employees to suggest improvements can empower employees and increase their motivation.
- They can improve the quality of the final product and reduce the amount of wastage, as fewer of the business's resources are needed in production.

Did you know?

Toyota uses Kaizen and just-in-time as part of its production process. However, it has 12 other 'pillars' it follows, starting with Nemawashi. This involves planning or building a consensus before production starts.

CASE STUDY Perfect Toyotas just-in-time

Toyota, the Japanese car manufacturer, was one of the first businesses to implement a lean production philosophy within its production department. Toyota has refined its production system over a number of years by making continuous improvements. The objective is to produce the vehicles ordered in the quickest and most efficient way, so that they can be delivered as quickly as possible. The current Toyota Production System (TPS) is based on two core philosophies: only producing the amount of parts needed (just-in-time) and stopping production as soon as a defect is noticed. This enables Toyota to keep its production costs down, giving it a competitive advantage within the market.

Knowledge check

1 **RM Sweets Ltd has the following production data available for two weeks' production of sweets.**

	Week 1	Week 2
Number of employees	40	50
Output of sweets	30000	35000

a) Calculate the productivity per employee for week 1 and week 2. **(4)**

b) With reference to your answers in part (a), explain the difference between production and productivity. **(4)**

c) Explain two ways in which RM Sweets Ltd could improve their efficiency. **(4)**

2 **Identify and explain two benefits of RM Sweets Ltd making their production process more automated.** **(4)**

3 **Identify two ways in which a business can manage resources to produce goods.** **(4)**

4 **Define the following terms:**

a) just-in-time **(2)**

b) Kaizen. **(2)**

Total 24 marks

The main methods of production

Aims (4.1.2)
By the end of this section, you should:
- Understand the features, benefits and limitations of job, batch and flow production
- Be able to recommend and justify an appropriate production method for a given situation.

Different methods of production

Businesses use three main methods of production. The method most suitable for each job depends on the type of product, the resources available to the business and the skill levels of the employees.

Job production

Job production is where each product is produced individually. This occurs when each individual finished product is different. This method of production is commonly used for items of clothing, such as a made-to-measure suit, and within construction, where buildings, stadiums and bridges are built to specific requirements.

◁ The Al-Bayt Stadium, in Al-Khor, is planned to be built in time for the 2022 FIFA World Cup – it will be the only stadium in the world like it.

Benefits of using job production	Limitations of using job production
✓ The product can meet the exact requirements of the customer; this can give the business a competitive advantage. ✓ Tasks are often different for the employees, which can give them more motivation. ✓ Businesses that use job production can often charge far higher prices than for mass-produced goods.	✘ Job production often requires a lot of employees, which makes the process very costly. ✘ As products are made to order, they can often take a long time to produce. ✘ As businesses produce one item at a time, they often do not buy their raw materials in large quantities, so they cannot reduce the cost per item (see 4.2 Costs, scale of production and break-even analysis).

Batch production

Batch production means businesses produce small amounts of similar products often at the same time, then the whole batch (group of products) can be moved on to the next stage of production together.

△ A bakery can produce different batches of products (breads or cakes) at the same time by having more than one oven.

Benefits of using batch production	Limitations of using batch production
✓ Batch production is flexible and allows a business to offer a range of different products in the same production time. ✓ It offers employees a variety of tasks, which can help motivation.	✗ This method of production often requires a range of machinery to allow the different products to be produced. ✗ Businesses are required to hold a wide range of raw materials (stock). ✗ A manufacturing defect will result in the whole batch being ruined.

Flow production

Flow production, or mass production, is where identical products are mass produced (produced in large quantities) in a continuous flow on an assembly line. Most products for a mass market, such as televisions, cars, soft drinks and most packaged foods, are produced in this way.

△ Mass production of soft drinks

Benefits of using flow production	Limitations of using flow production
✓ Machinery increases the business's productivity. ✓ Businesses can order large quantities of raw materials, which enables them to negotiate cheaper costs per unit. ✓ High productivity and cheaper costs for raw materials enables a business to have low costs and higher profit margins. ✓ Businesses can lower their selling price if they need to increase sales and maintain a good profit margin. ✓ Goods are produced quickly for market.	✗ Flow production is mainly done via automation and machinery, which can lead to repetitive and boring tasks for employees, resulting in poor motivation. ✗ The machinery required to produce the goods is often very expensive and requires a significant capital investment. ✗ Machinery can break down, which means all production has to stop. ✗ The production process is fixed (inflexible): all products are standardised (the same), which makes it difficult to meet any changes in consumer demand.

Choosing the most suitable method of production

Choosing the most suitable method of production depends on a number of different factors.

The type of market the business operates in

If a business operates in a mass market (products that are aimed at lots of people), then flow production is the most suitable. This is because customers of mass market products want cheap prices, so businesses need to keep their unit costs low. Although the profit margin on each product will be small, they will sell a lot of products.

Businesses that operate in a niche market (smaller market with specialised products) may choose to batch produce or job produce to make their product stand out. Although the cost of production is higher, this cost can be passed on to the customer.

> **Did you know?**
>
> Lego, the Danish toy company, has produced over 600 billion pieces since it opened in 1949. It now produces 1140 pieces per second at its factories around the world.

The skill level of the employees

Some businesses pride themselves on their 'handmade' products. This requires a less automated approach to production. Depending on the quantities, batch production or job production might be the most appropriate.

◁ A high level of skill is needed to make handmade pots.

The business's resources

Some businesses do not have the capital (see 5.1 Business finance: needs and sources) or the space to flow produce their products. This means they have to choose a method that allows them to produce smaller quantities, such as batch production.

The nature of the product

The product that the consumer demands will ultimately determine the type of production. Custom-made products have to be job produced, whereas standardised products are almost always flow produced.

CASE STUDY Handmade crisps

Lisa's is a new organic crisp brand from Tyrells that has been launched in the UK. Tyrells bought Lisa's – an Alps-based firm – in a bid to move into the organic crisp market. The process of making these crisps is much more expensive than the mass-produced crisps you find in the supermarket.

Analysis **Evaluation**

Choose four products that you use on a regular basis. Try to choose products that you think might have been job produced, batch produced and mass produced. Carry out some research into how they are produced.

Create a poster that includes images of all four products, detailing the production method used and why they are produced in that way.

Knowledge check

1. **Explain one advantage and one disadvantage to a business of using job production. (4)**

African Book Publishers (ABP) Ltd produces a range of factual books for children. Although none of their books sell in large quantities, all of the books in their range on natural geography have a steady demand. At the moment, ABP uses batch production but is considering using flow production.

2. **Identify the main features of flow production. (2)**
3. **Explain two advantages for ABP of using batch production. (4)**
4. **Outline one limitation of using flow production. (3)**

Total 13 marks

How technology has changed production methods

Aims (4.1.3)

By the end of this section, you should:

- Understand how technology has changed production methods, for example, using computers in manufacturing and design.

Technology and the production process

Technology has revolutionised production over the past 30 years. Technology reduces manufacturing costs, making many products cheaper for the consumer. Technology becoming cheaper and more accessible to businesses has resulted in a more consistent quality of product and a higher level of production. Technology has also reduced the number of employees needed because of increasingly automated manufacture and design processes.

The three main technologies that have had the most impact on production are **computer-aided design (CAD), computer-aided manufacture (CAM)** and **robotics**.

Computer-aided design (CAD)

Rather than hand-drawing designs, CAD allows designers, architects and engineers to produce images electronically.

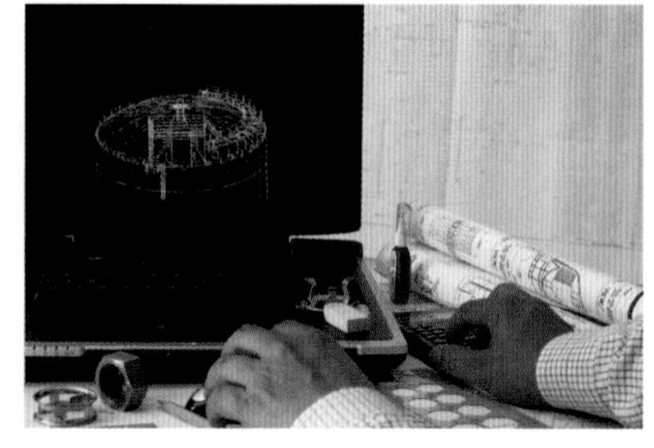

Δ CAD has reduced the need for designers to produce hand-drawn images.

Computer-aided design has several benefits:

- It increases designer productivity, as it is easier and quicker to reproduce and amend designs. Designers can change the size of designs and images without using complicated mathematical formulas, so they can spend more time on design innovation rather than redrafting.
- Designers can rotate three-dimensional images to show how a product will work before it has been manufactured. They can view an image from multiple angles, instead of having to draft several two-dimensional views of the same product from different angles.
- Design quality is higher, because the images are more accurate and easier to change to improve the product.

Computer-aided manufacture (CAM)

CAM uses computers to control and manage the production process.

Δ Computer-aided manufacture allows identical products to be made.

The benefits of CAM are that:

- it allows for a consistent (always the same) output on a large scale
- it increases productivity, as more products are made without the need for human involvement
- exact measurements can be achieved with every production.

Robotics

In robotics, computerised arms are used to manufacture products such as cars and electrical goods.

The benefits of robotics are that:

- tasks can be carried out with 100% accuracy
- although expensive to buy, robotics are cheaper to run than employees are to pay
- they can work long hours and so increase productivity.

Δ Robotic arms have made production safer, cheaper and more accurate.

CASE STUDY

CAD cartoons

In 1995 Pixar Animation Studios released *Toy Story*, the first computer-animated feature film. Before *Toy Story*, animators drew the images of characters by hand, so the films were two-dimensional. However, Pixar decided to design their characters and create their movement using computers, which made a three-dimensional animated film possible. Computer-aided design improved the quality of the animation because the characters could easily and quickly be refined, improved and consistently made the correct size throughout.

Analysis **Evaluation**

You are a business advisor for a firm of architects in South Africa, which employs 20 architects to work on designs for commercial buildings. Profit margins have been falling. Manual design processes are used and 20 to 30 different drafts of each building are produced before construction starts.

Research a suitable CAD software package that might be suitable for your firm. Discuss all the potential benefits and drawbacks of using this software.

Recommend whether they should implement the software you have researched. Justify your choice.

Knowledge check

1. **Explain two benefits of using robotics to help production. (4)**
2. **Identify two products that might use robotics in their manufacture. (2)**
3. **Outline two benefits to a business using CAD when designing their products. (2)**
4. **Explain two ways that technology has changed production. (4)**

Total 12 marks

Check your progress:

- ✓ I can outline the difference between productivity and production, and give suggestions on how to increase efficiency.
- ✓ I can explain the concept of lean production and give examples of just-in-time and Kaizen.
- ✓ I can outline the main methods of production, including the features, benefits and limitations of job, batch and flow production.
- ✓ I am able to explain how technology has changed production methods.

Costs, scale of production and break-even analysis

Identify and classify costs

Aims (4.2.1)

By the end of this section, you should:

- Be able to classify costs using examples, for example, fixed, variable, average, total
- Understand how to use cost data to help make simple cost-based decisions, for example, to stop production or continue.

Classifying costs

The production department of a business splits costs (see 5.3 Income statements) into:

- costs that are directly linked with production (**variable costs**)
- costs that are not linked with production (**fixed costs**).

Variable costs

Variable costs are the costs that are directly linked with producing a product. These are costs such as raw materials, power, packaging and direct labour. So, the more a company produces, the more variable costs it has to pay.

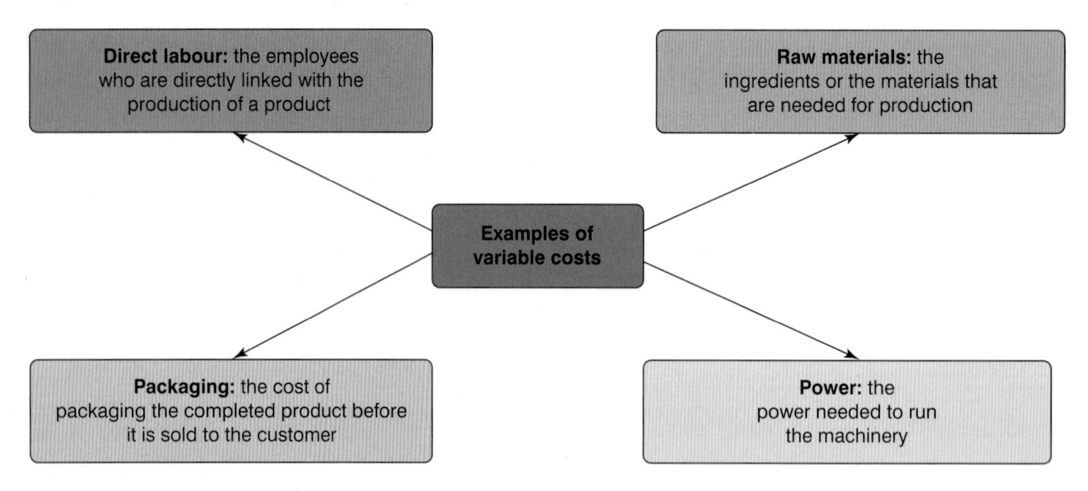

Fixed costs

Fixed costs are all of the other costs that a business has to pay. These costs are fixed in the sense they do not change with production. Regardless of (not considering) how much a business produces, the fixed costs will remain the same.

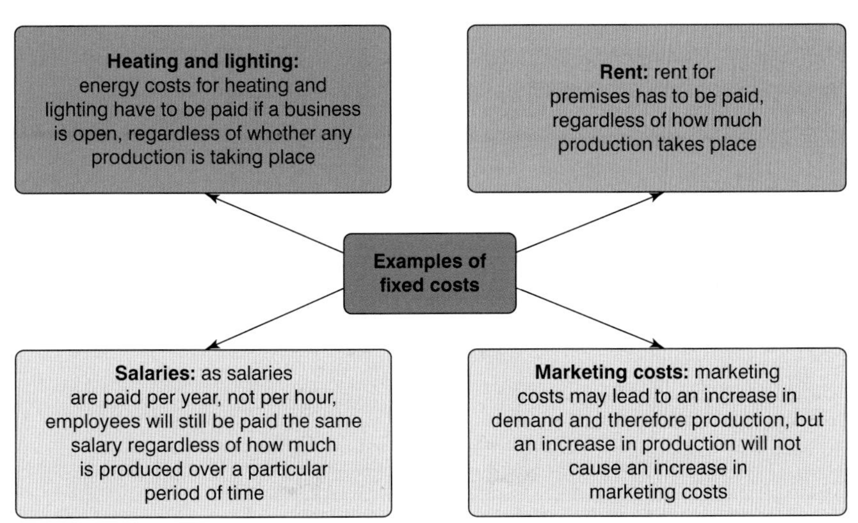

Total cost

The **total cost** of production is the sum (total) of the fixed costs added to the variable costs for each unit of production.

If a business has fixed costs of $10 and variable costs of $1 per unit, their total costs will be $11 after 1 unit has been produced, $12 after 2 units, and so on.

Average cost

The **average cost** is the total cost of producing a certain number of units, divided by how many units have been produced. By calculating this, a business can determine how much they wish to charge for a product and set targets for production in order to keep their costs down.

$$\frac{\text{Total cost}}{\text{Number of items made}} = \text{Average cost}$$

△ The average cost of a product falls as the business produces more of them. When a business produces only a few products, the average cost is a lot higher. A mass-produced school uniform is much cheaper than a uniform produced for just one school.

Application **Analysis**

A clothing manufacturer produces silk shirts in its factory. The employees are paid $1.50 for each shirt they produce and the cost of silk is $3.00 per shirt. The monthly fixed costs include salaries of $3000, heating and lighting of $150 and rent of $2500, plus a marketing cost of $350 per month. The business sells each silk shirt for $6.00.

Copy and complete the following table. Alternatively, if you have access to ICT, create a spreadsheet and complete the table.

(*continued on next page*)

Units produced	Fixed costs	Variable costs	Total cost	Average cost
1				
100				
250				
500				
1000				
2000				
5000				
10000				
15000				

Add an additional column to your table and calculate the profit or loss made after the production of 2000, 5000, 10000 and 15000 shirts.

Using graph paper or spreadsheet software, create a graph of your data to show the units produced and the average cost per unit.

Analyse the impact on profit per garment as the units produced increases.

CASE STUDY

BT comes home

BT (British Telecommunications plc) is a British multinational telecommunications company and in 2003, BT moved its call centres abroad, mainly to India. However, with complaints increasing, BT decided to hire 1000 new employees for its call centres in the UK, with 80% of calls going to these centres. While the move to India was made to reduce costs such as salaries, it actually cost BT more money, as customer complaints increased dramatically. This resulted in BT losing many of its customers to competitors.

Using cost data to make decisions about production

Businesses can use cost data to help make decisions about whether they should continue to make a product or not.

WORKED EXAMPLE

A Korean car manufacturer has overseas operations in the UK and Azerbaijan. They have decided to close one of the factories, as they want to move some of their production back to Korea. They have the following data available to them for the last year's production. All costs are in British pounds.

	£ (000s)	
Variable costs (per car)	**UK**	**Azerbaijan**
Labour	2	0.6
Materials	2	2
Power	0.3	0.2
Shipping	0.2	0.2
Total variable costs	4.5	3

Fixed costs (per year)		
Salaries	1000	250
Heating and lighting	800	500
Rent	50	25
Total fixed costs	1850	775

Selling price per car £ (000s)	20	20
Production per year (number of cars)	200	150

From the data in the table, we can determine which of the two factories to keep open by calculating the average cost of production at each factory:

	£ (000s)	
	UK	**Azerbaijan**
Variable costs per car	4.5	3.0
Cars produced	200	150
Total variable costs	900	450
Fixed costs	1850	775
Total cost	2750	1225
Average cost per car	**13.75**	**8.17**

From the data, we can see that closing the UK factory would be the best option because the average cost of production in Azerbaijan is much lower (£5580 cheaper).

Knowledge check

1 **Identify one example of a variable cost and one example of a fixed cost.** **(2)**

2 **Using examples, explain the difference between fixed costs and variable costs.** **(4)**

Variable costs	Factory 1	Factory 2
Bike parts	90	90
Labour	10	10
Total	100	100

Fixed costs		
Salaries	10 000	15 000
Marketing	3000	3000
Heat and power	2000	4000
Rent	5000	7500
Total	20 000	29 500

Selling price per bike	150	150

3 **Calculate the total cost at Factory 1 of producing the following numbers of bikes:**

a) 500 **(2)**

b) 1000 **(2)**

c) 2500. **(2)**

4 **Calculate the average cost at Factory 2 of producing the following numbers of bikes:**

a) 500 **(2)**

b) 1000 **(2)**

c) 4000. **(2)**

5 **Explain why the average cost falls as Factory 2 makes more bikes.** **(4)**

6 **If Factory 1 makes 2600 bikes and Factory 2 makes 3000 bikes, consider which factory produces the most profitable bikes. Use average cost data to justify your answer.** **(6)**

Total 28 marks

Economies and diseconomies of scale

Aims (4.2.2)
By the end of this section, you should:

- Understand the concepts of economies of scale with examples, for example, purchasing, marketing, financial, managerial, technical
- Understand the concept of diseconomies of scale with examples, for example, poor communication, lack of commitment from employees, weak coordination.

Economies of scale

When businesses grow in size, or increase the level of their output (production), they tend to become more efficient. This means they lower their costs per unit. When this happens, we say they have benefited from economies of scale.

Businesses that use flow production have very low costs per unit produced because of economies of scale.

A business can benefit from a number of different economies of scale. Try to think of them as the advantages of a business growing in size. Better technology reduces the cost of production, while buying products in bulk reduces the cost per item.

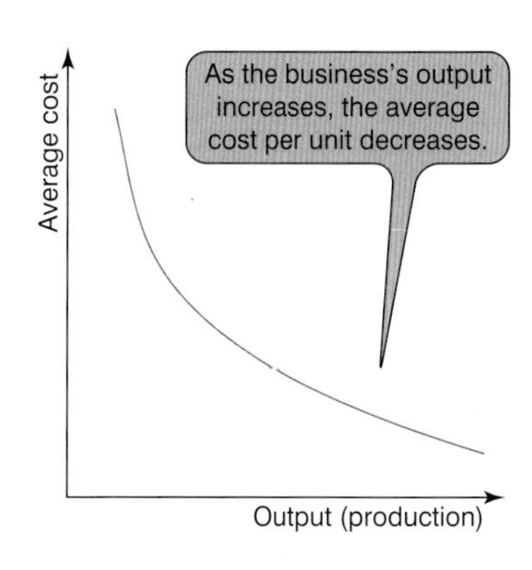

Economies of scale	Description
Technical	Businesses that produce more can invest in better technology that increases productivity and reduces waste (products that have gone wrong). This reduces the average cost.
Purchasing	Larger businesses can place bigger orders for raw materials. The bigger the order, the cheaper the cost per item. This is the same as when you buy products in a multi-pack rather than on their own.
Managerial	Bigger businesses can employ specialist managers to make better decisions.
Financial	Larger businesses can borrow more money than smaller businesses and negotiate a cheaper rate of interest (finance cost) as banks know that large firms can pay them back.
Marketing	A large business can spread its total marketing spend over a larger output. For larger chains, national marketing strategies costs can be spread across many outlets or stores, making it an efficient way of marketing the business.

Δ Better technology reduces the cost of production.

Δ Buying products like eggs in bulk reduces the cost per egg.

Diseconomies of scale

If economies of scale are the advantages of a business growing in size, then **diseconomies of scale** are the disadvantages of a business growing in size. Diseconomies of scale occur when a business gets too large. This often happens when a business expands rapidly and is not ready for the growth.

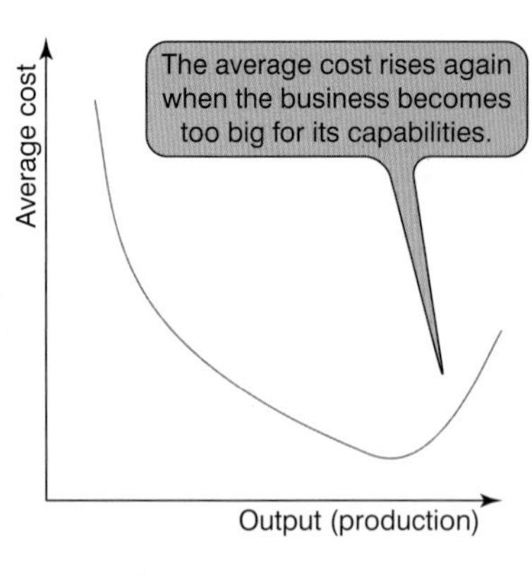

Diseconomies of scale increase the **cost per unit**.

Examples of diseconomies of scale include:

Diseconomies of scale	Description
Poor communication	As the business expands, it becomes harder to communicate effectively with its employees. This can result in employees carrying out tasks incorrectly, which can result in a waste of the business's resources.
Lack of commitment from employees	As the business grows, employees lower down the organisational chart have less contact with management and therefore feel less important. This can lead to lower productivity and a lack of commitment to the businesses goals.
Weak coordination	Larger businesses find it harder to coordinate their employees and resources in the most efficient way. This can result in not allocating the right number of employees for shifts or jobs.
Increased need for delegation	As management have more work to complete, there is a greater need to delegate tasks to other employees who might not make the right decisions or might take longer, which can lead to inefficiencies.

CASE STUDY

HSBC continues to cut costs

HSBC continued its ongoing programme for reducing its global workforce by 25 000 by making 120 employees redundant in its technology department in Hong Kong. Banks all over the world are looking to cut costs as they struggle with profitability. HSBC has already confirmed it believes it will miss its return-on-equity target (10%), which is a measure of a bank's profitability. HSBC aims to reduce its overall costs by $5 billion by the end of the year.

Application

Consider economies of scale that affect businesses that you use.

Visit a local supermarket and carry out some research into the cost of products that are sold individually and as part of a multi-pack. Working in pairs, analyse the other economies and diseconomies of scale that might affect a supermarket. One of you should look at the economies while the other looks at the diseconomies.

Present your findings to the class.

Top Tip

When looking at purchasing economies of scale, remember to show the cost per unit.

Knowledge check

Car Accessory Components Ltd (CACL) sells flat-packing crates that can be easily fitted to and removed from car boots (trunks); they act as a boot organiser. After originally starting as a partnership, they now have over 100 employees, including 10 specialist managers.

Their supplier has the following pricing information for boot crates.

Number of crates	Cost ($)
10	60
50	250
100	400
250	950
500	1800
2000	7000
10000	30000
50000	125000

1. **Define the term economies of scale.** **(2)**
2. **Explain which of the economies of scale CACL is benefiting from.** **(1)**
3. **Outline two other economies of scale that CACL might benefit from now that the business has grown.** **(4)**
4. **Define the term diseconomies of scale.** **(2)**
5. **As CACL continues to grow, explain one possible diseconomy of scale that might affect the company.** **(2)**

Total 11 marks

Break-even analysis

Aims (4.2.3)

By the end of this section, you should:

- Understand the concept of break-even
- Be able to construct, complete or amend a simple break-even chart
- Know how to interpret a given chart and use it to analyse a situation
- Be able to calculate break-even output from given data
- Be able to define, calculate and interpret the margin of safety
- Be able to use break-even analysis to help make simple decisions, for example, about the impact of higher prices
- Understand the limitations of break-even analysis.

The concept of break-even

The concept of **break-even** is crucial to businesses when they make decisions regarding production – for example:

- how much they need to produce
- how much to spend on marketing
- how much they want to charge for the product
- finance (ensuring their costs are kept to a certain level).

The term break-even refers to the point where a product's income is equal to its costs (fixed and variable). This is known as the **break-even point**.

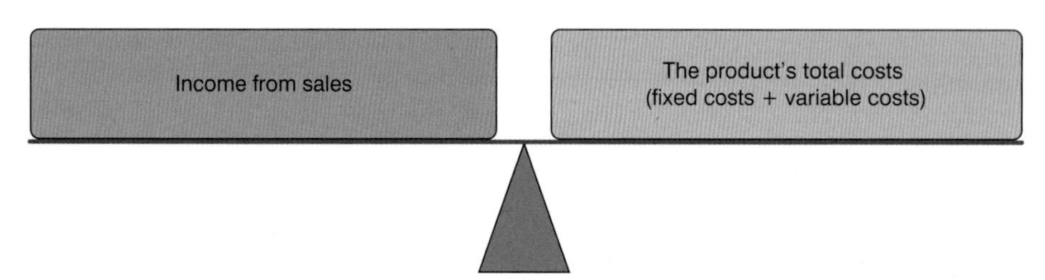

∆ The break-even point occurs when income from sales revenue generated by a product is equal to the total costs (fixed and variable) of production.

How to calculate the break-even point

To calculate the break-even point, you need to know the product's selling price, the variable costs (the costs directly linked to production) and the fixed costs (the costs not directly linked to production).

Top Tip

You must work out the calculation in the brackets first. Otherwise, you will get the wrong answer.

$$\text{Break-even point} = \frac{\text{Fixed costs}}{(\text{Selling price} - \text{Variable costs})} = \frac{100}{(2-1)} = 100$$

Using break-even analysis to make decisions

A business will use a break-even chart to visualise (show) its potential costs and revenue at different levels of **output** (production). It can therefore use the break-even chart to make decisions about the selling price and to assess the impact of a change in costs (for example, due to an increase in costs from its suppliers).

Did you know?

Despite not breaking even for the first nine years, Facebook finished last year with 1.86 billion monthly active users, a 17% increase from the previous year. This caused a 54% jump in revenue to $27.6 billion, and a 171% increase in net income to $10.2 billion.

WORKED EXAMPLE

In order to see how break-even works, we need to consider a simple product, such as a sandwich.

Calculating the break-even point:

$$\text{Break-even point} = \frac{\text{fixed costs}}{(\text{selling price} - \text{variable costs})}$$

$$\frac{100}{(2-1)} = \frac{100}{1}$$

$$= 100 \text{ sandwiches to break-even}$$

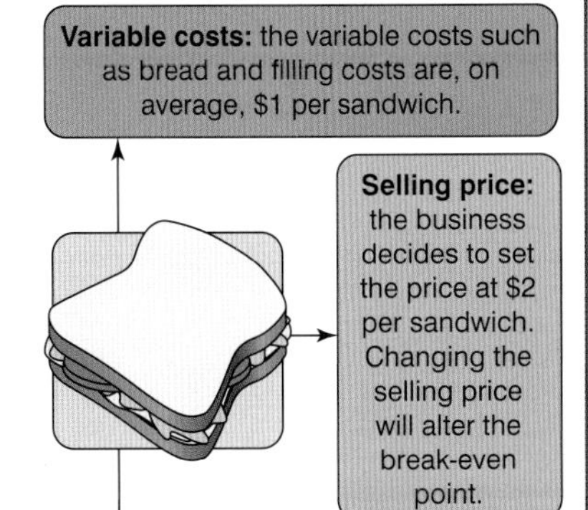

Fixed costs: in order to sell this product, the business has to pay costs not related to each sandwich – such as rent, employee wages and electricity. These costs are $100 per day.

CASE STUDY Ed Sheeran break-even tickets

With music concerts and artist tours all around the world, organisers have to make sure they, at least, break even. Costs range from hiring trucks and pyrotechnics to video costs and catering. The bands have to consider all these costs when setting a suitable price for customers to ensure that they break even for the tour. However, the artist wants to make a profit on the tours and concerts as well.

In his previous tour, Ed Sheeran was reported to earn over $80 000 per concert. With his new tour already sold out, it will definitely have broken even.

How to construct a simple break-even chart

Businesses often decide to show information about break-even graphically, as it is easy for managers to visualise the break-even point and use the graph to make simple decisions.

WORKED EXAMPLE

Using the same example as in the previous worked example, we can plot this data on a break-even chart to show the break-even point visually.

	$
Selling price	2
Variable cost per sandwich	1
Fixed cost per day	100

Step 1. Add the fixed costs

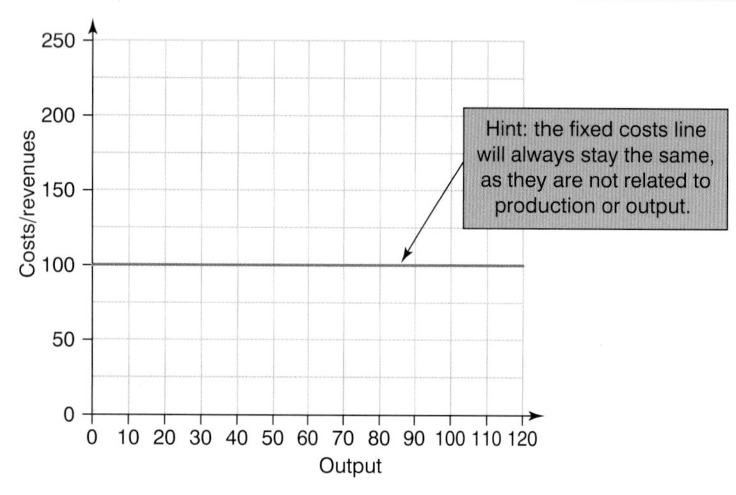

Step 2. Add the total costs (fixed costs + variable costs)

In order to add the total costs, you will need to add the fixed costs and the variable costs at different levels of output.

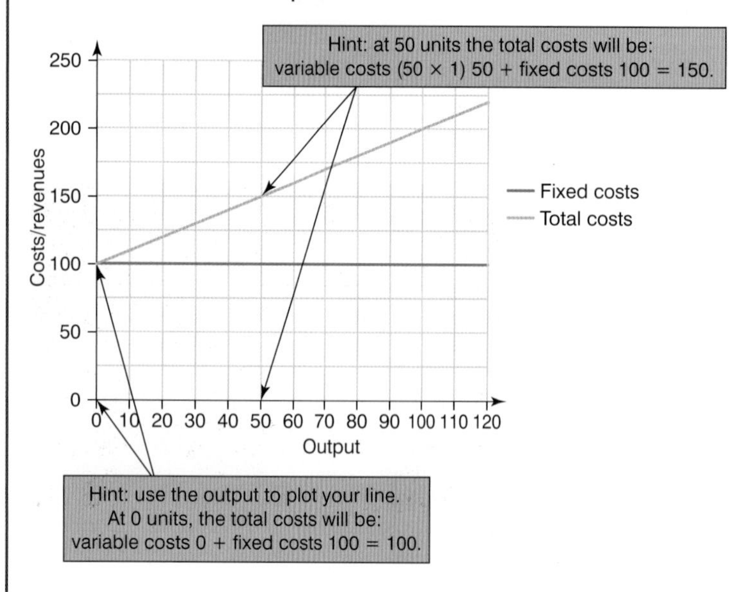

Step 3. Add the revenue line (selling price × number sold)

In order to add the revenue line, you will need to plot some figures by using the output. For example, calculate the revenue (selling price × quantity sold) at different levels of output, e.g. 0 and 50.

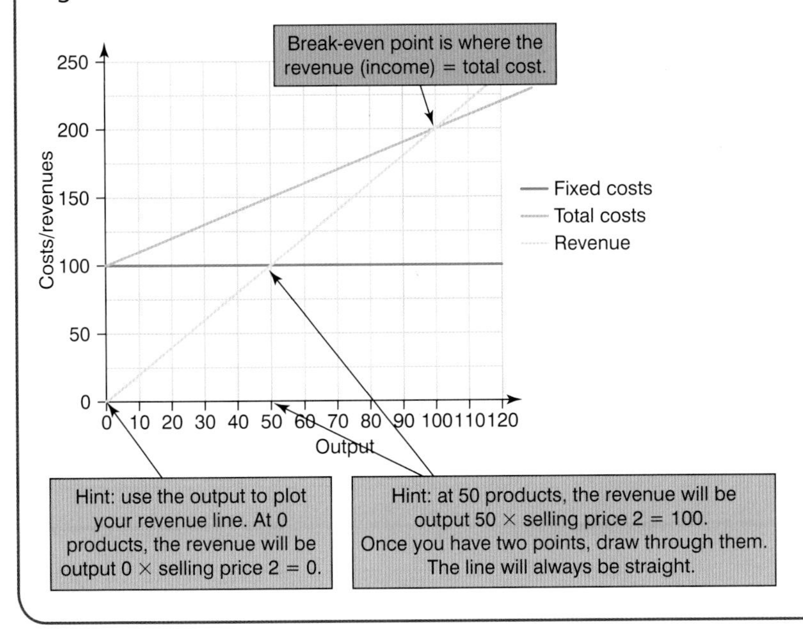

Interpreting a simple break-even chart

A break-even chart can help a business make certain decisions, once it has analysed and interpreted the graph to fully understand what it shows.

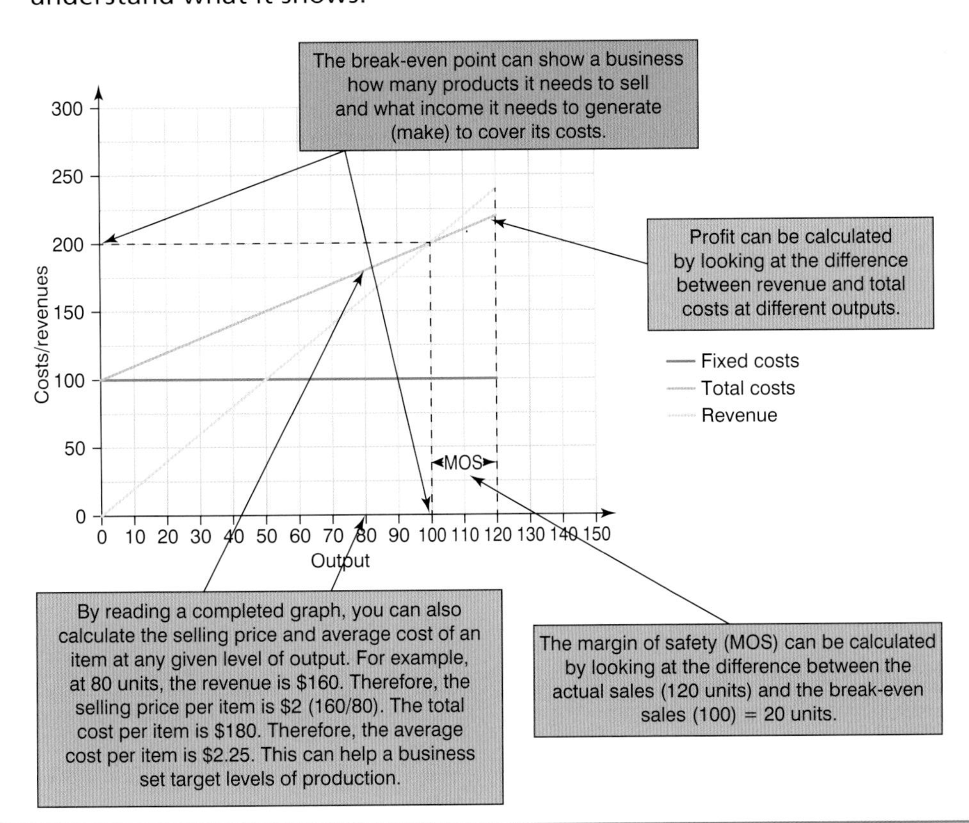

The margin of safety

The margin of safety (MOS) is used to indicate the amount of sales a business has above the break-even point. Put simply, it shows the number of goods or services a firm can afford not to sell before they move into a loss:

margin of safety = actual sales − break-even sales level

For example, if a business was to achieve sales of 6000 units but the break-even point was 5000 units, it would have a margin of safety of 1000 units. This means it could afford to see its sales drop by 1000 units before it would drop below break-even and into a loss.

WORKED EXAMPLE

The graph below uses the price and cost data from the worked examples. However, this time the selling price has changed from $2 to $2.25. Notice the difference in the break-even point.

	$
Selling price	2.25
Variable cost per sandwich	1
Fixed cost per day	100

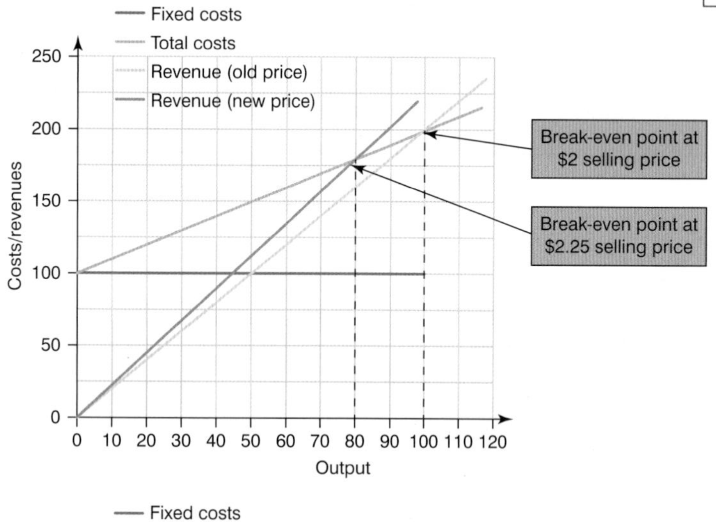

The graph shows us that the break-even point has been reduced, as it has moved from 100 units to 80 units, 20 units fewer than before.

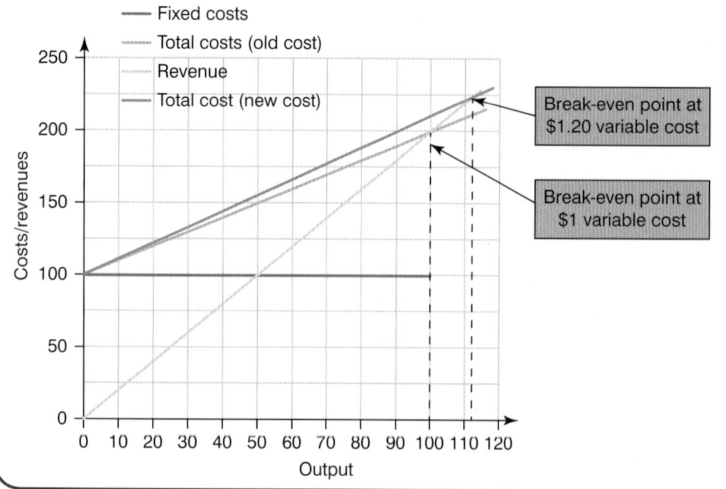

Keeping the selling price at $2 per item, we can now see the impact on the break-even point if the suppliers decided to increase the cost of their ingredients from $1 per sandwich to $1.10 per sandwich. The break-even point has increased from 100 units to 111 units.

Application **Analysis** **Evaluation**

A small business that makes designer satchels publishes the following information:

Selling price $120

Variable costs $70

Fixed costs $2500 per month.

Construct a break-even graph using the following data, clearly labelling your graph.

When you have done this, draw a new revenue line on the same graph, illustrating the impact on the break-even point if the selling price was to increase to $130. Underneath your graph, list the advantages and disadvantages of raising the selling price.

Using the data from your graph and your knowledge of cost and profit data, recommend whether the business should increase the selling price to $130.

Top Tip

Work out the two different break-even points mathematically using the formula given in the worked example for the sandwich business. This will help you find a suitable scale for your graph.

Limitations of using a break-even chart

There are some drawbacks to using a break-even chart:

- A break-even chart assumes that variable costs stay the same. However, we know that businesses benefit from economies of scale when they produce more, which reduces the cost per item (see the earlier section in this topic on Economies of scale).
- There is also an assumption that the selling price will remain the same for all products sold. This ignores products that are sold at a discount, or seasonal products that might be sold at a different price at different times during the year.
- The revenue and cost lines both assume that only one type of product is being sold. Most businesses have more than one product line or service, which have different prices. In this case, they cannot use a break-even chart.

Δ Break-even charts are not possible when a business sells more than one product at different selling prices.

Knowledge check

1 A business selling handbags has the following information:

Selling price $40 Variable costs $25 Fixed costs $2000

a) Define the term break-even. (2)

b) Calculate the break-even point based on the above data. Show your working. (4)

c) Calculate the break-even point if the selling price was to increase to $50. (8)

2 Irum Hussain, a sole trader selling jewellery, has produced a break-even chart for her business. Her fixed costs are $200.

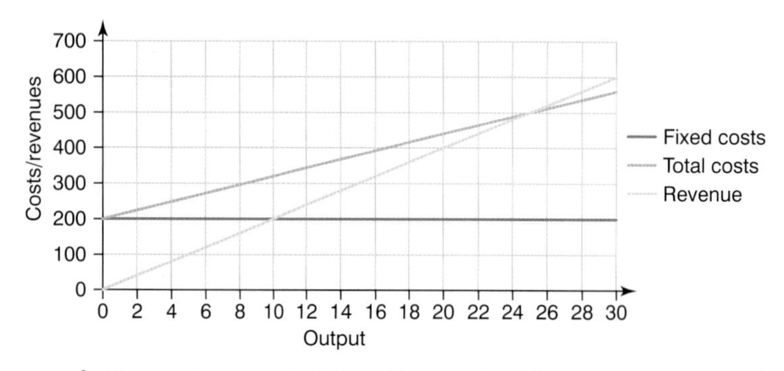

a) Using the graph, identify the break-even point. (1)

b) Using the graph, calculate the margin of safety if sales are 30 units. (2)

c) Using the graph, calculate the following:

i) the selling price per bag (2)

ii) the average cost per bag at 14 units (2)

iii) the average cost per bag at 24 units. (2)

d) Amend the graph to show an increase in fixed costs to $250. Outline the impact on the break-even point if the fixed costs increase. (6)

3 Explain two limitations of a break-even chart to someone like Irum. (4)

Total 33 marks

Check your progress:

- ✓ I can identify and classify the different types of costs a business has.
- ✓ I can calculate cost data to make simple cost-based decisions.
- ✓ I can explain the difference between economies and diseconomies of scale, and give examples of both.
- ✓ I understand the concept of break-even and am able to construct, complete and amend a break-even chart.
- ✓ I can interpret a break-even chart and calculate the margin of safety.
- ✓ I can use break-even analysis to help make simple decisions for a business.

Achieving quality production

The importance of quality and how to achieve quality production

Aims (4.3.1)
By the end of this section, you should:
- Understand what quality means and why it is important for all businesses
- Be able to explain the concept of quality control and how businesses implement quality control
- Understand the concept of quality assurance and how this can be implemented.

Why quality is important

Quality means meeting and exceeding customer expectations. Quality (high standards) in a finished product or service is vital for all businesses as it keeps customers happy. A satisfied customer is likely to use the business again and can often generate good publicity through word-of-mouth promotion.

All businesses should aim for high-quality output (production). However, this is even more important for businesses that charge a high price for their product or service. This is because customers associate good quality with a high selling price.

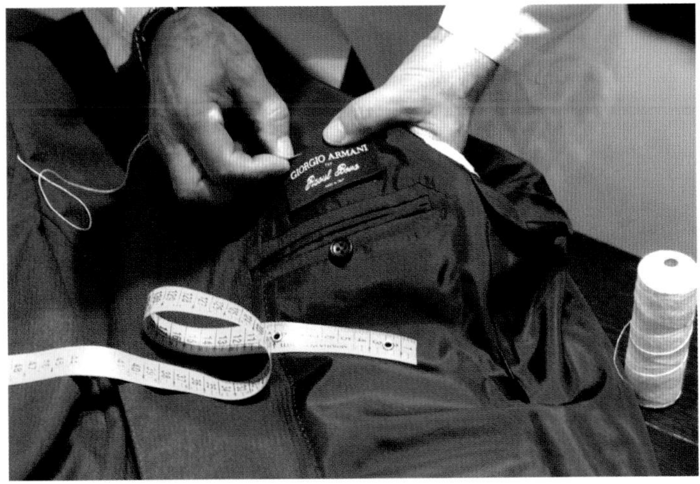

∆ Customers often associate expensive products with good quality.

> **Did you know?**
>
> FedEx is one of the most trusted global delivery firms because of its quality service. Its ability to deliver what it promises is a key aspect that customers look for in that market.

Methods of ensuring high quality

Quality control

Quality control is the traditional approach to ensuring that the product offered by a business meets the expectations of customers. Quality control occurs when an individual or a department checks random products at different intervals throughout the production process.

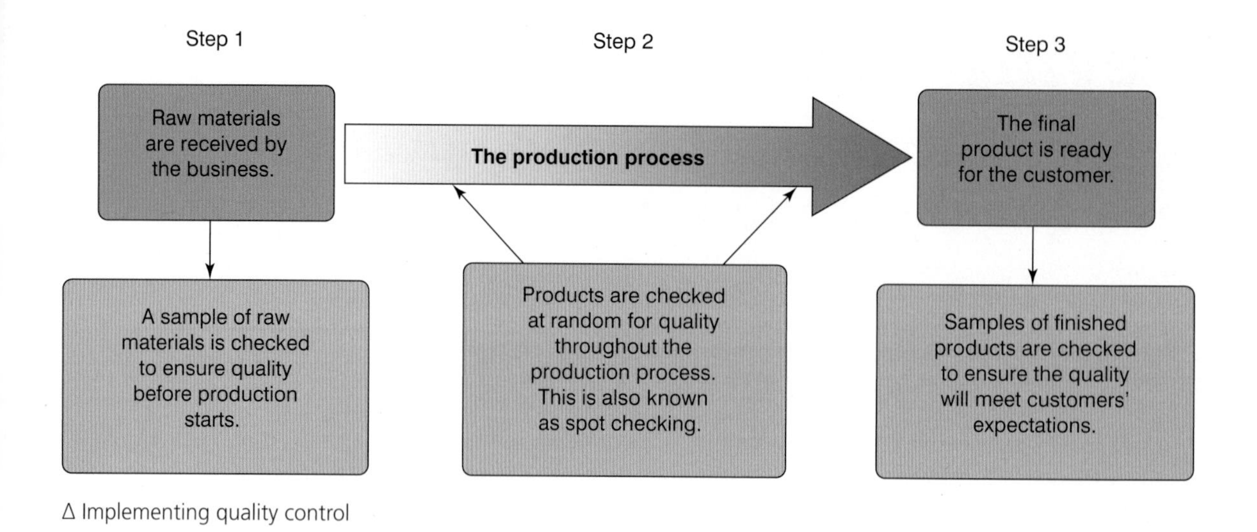

∆ Implementing quality control

Advantages of using quality control	Disadvantages of using quality control
✓ Can help ensure that products meet the requirements of customers, helping to generate more sales and a better reputation. ✓ Can identify poor-quality products before they become finished goods, which reduces the chances of selling poor-quality products to customers.	✘ Can be expensive, as it requires people and time and can lead to waste of raw materials. ✘ Does not improve quality; instead, quality control reduces the chance of selling poor-quality products. ✘ Does not check all products, so there is still a chance of poor-quality products reaching the customer.

Quality assurance

Quality control as a method of checking quality is now considered outdated and not cost-efficient by many businesses. Instead, they are choosing to implement **quality assurance** to improve the quality of their products.

Quality assurance means that checks are carried out within the production process to prevent mistakes ever happening. To implement quality assurance successfully, all employees must support the system and be prepared to self-check to ensure that quality control is not needed.

For example, Samsung has invested in quality assurance testing for all parts of its phones. It undertakes an eight-part check of its batteries. This is carried out by machines, as well as employees, to check the reliability and safety of the batteries. In farming, robotic machines are being used to measure the crop strength, soil acidity and other factors, to make sure the quality of produce is acceptable for sale.

Advantages of quality assurance	Disadvantages of quality assurance
✓ Making quality a key aspect of everyone's job rather than the role of an individual or department should ensure that quality improves. ✓ Quality assurance does not require employing additional quality checkers, so it is cheaper than quality control.	✗ The whole workforce must support the system; otherwise, it will not work. ✗ Employees may require additional training to ensure they produce the highest-quality products.

CASE STUDY Technology reduces manual checking

Ravenwood Packaging, a food packaging company, has unveiled its latest game-changing technology, the VXR, which combines vision, X-ray and seal check technology. With supermarkets demanding superior quality products, Ravenwood decided it needed to invest in additional quality assurance. The new technology will reduce the need for manual checks that are costly in terms of labour and time-consuming when production deadlines are tight. X-raying the food as it is packaged can reduce the chance of any contaminated or poorly packaged food making its way on to the shelves.

Evaluation

Your company is based in the UK and supplies soft toys to large supermarkets in Europe. The soft toys are made in bulk in China and are then shipped to the UK for sale. Recently there was a problem with toys being of poor quality and the stitching (sewing) coming undone. How can your company ensure high quality if the toys are manufactured in China?

Make your recommendations in a formal report written to the operations director.

Knowledge check

1. **Identify two reasons why quality is important for a business. (2)**
2. **Outline two benefits to a business of using a quality control system. (4)**
3. **Identify two differences between a quality control system and quality assurance. (2)**
4. **Analyse one benefit for a business of implementing a quality assurance system. (2)**

Total 10 marks

Check your progress:

- ✓ I understand why quality is important to a business and how quality production can be achieved.
- ✓ I can explain what quality assurance is and how businesses implement it.
- ✓ I can explain what quality control is and how businesses implement it.

Location decisions

Factors influencing location and relocation decisions

Aims (4.4.1)

By the end of this section, you should:

- Understand factors relevant to the location decision of manufacturing businesses and service businesses
- Understand factors that a business could consider when deciding which country to locate operations in
- Understand the role of legal controls on location decisions
- Be able to recommend and justify an appropriate location for a business in given circumstances.

Location of businesses

Choosing the right location for a business depends entirely on the type of business in question. Most businesses will want to stay close to their market (customers), whether they operate on a local or a global scale. The type of business activity – for example, whether the company manufactures a product or provides a service – is also important, as businesses' requirements vary when choosing the right location.

Factors affecting the location of manufacturing businesses

- **Scale of production:** a business that uses flow production will need a location that is big enough to store their machinery. Businesses that use job production will often need a far smaller location.
- **Proximity to raw materials/components:** proximity (closeness) to raw materials will enable a business to lower its transport costs and increase the speed of delivery, especially when using just-in-time stock ordering.
- **Cost of site:** the business's budget will have the biggest impact on the chosen location. Businesses have to choose a location that is affordable and within budget.
- **Government influence:** a government can influence a business's choice to choose one location over another by offering them grants (financial support) to attract a business to a particular area. For example, areas with high unemployment might provide grants to businesses wishing to locate in that area to boost the local economy.
- **Availability of labour:** although manufacturing businesses often require less labour, they still need a location that can supply them with that labour, preferably at the cheapest cost to the business.

- **Infrastructure:** the infrastructure (or transport links) are important, as businesses will need easy access for their suppliers. Even more importantly, good transport links will ensure easy delivery of goods to their customers, especially if they export. These include access to motorways, airports and seaports.

Factors affecting the location of service businesses

Service businesses have many of the same requirements as manufacturing businesses. However, because their business often requires interaction with their customer, they often choose their location to meet the requirements of the customer rather than the business.

- **Cost of site:** although premises will often be smaller than manufacturing bases, the cost of a site has a big impact on the choice of location. The size of the business and its budget will determine the premises a business can afford. City centre premises are normally far more expensive due to the footfall (number of potential customers).
- **Customers:** proximity (closeness) to customers is often vital for service industry businesses, as customers often choose local businesses that are the most convenient. However, this is not a requirement for some service businesses, such as the growing number of online businesses.
- **Government influence:** like manufacturing businesses, service businesses may receive government grants to set up in a particular area so they support the local economy, especially as service businesses often provide more jobs than manufacturers.
- **Accessibility for customers:** very similar to infrastructure for manufacturing businesses, businesses providing a service need to be easily accessed by their customers. This could mean adequate parking for customers who drive or having suitable transport links such as being on a bus line or a train line.
- **Availability of skilled labour:** service industries are normally far more labour-intensive (requiring a lot of employees) than manufacturing businesses, so they will need to locate where there is a ready supply of skilled labour.

△ A developed infrastructure will enable better access to the business for suppliers and customers.

Relocating to a different country

As businesses grow into global enterprises, they often choose to relocate to a new country. This could be for a number of reasons, including cheaper labour, more skilled labour or the opportunity that emerging markets (growing economies) bring. Brazil, Russia, India and China have seen a vast and steady increase in businesses wishing to take advantage of their growing economies. Likewise, markets such as Mexico, Indonesia, South Korea and Turkey are predicted to be the new 'big four' emerging markets. There may therefore be a rise in the number of businesses choosing to locate in these countries.

Factors that influence a business's decision to relocate abroad include:

- **Saturated domestic market.** When a business's demand in a local or national market starts to fall, they may wish to seek new markets. This often results in a business relocating to a new country.
- **Cheaper labour.** The minimum wage varies enormously from country to country, so many businesses choose to relocate to take advantage of cheaper labour. For example, in the Indian capital of Delhi, the minimum wage is $207 a month, compared with the USA, where it is $1160 a month. Cheaper labour can significantly reduce a business's costs and therefore improve their profit margin.
- **Cheaper rent.** Businesses that require a lot of space, such as large manufacturing businesses, might choose to relocate to a new country if they can purchase or rent much cheaper land. This allows them to reduce their costs.
- **Proximity to raw materials.** For manufacturing businesses, moving closer to raw materials reduces transportation costs and time, which allows for more efficient production. Countries like Brazil have vast amounts of raw materials and may therefore be a popular choice for some manufacturing businesses.

Did you know?

In India, the minimum wage is split into different categories, such as unskilled, semi-skilled and skilled, and there is a higher wage for graduates. Wages differ from region to region, with Delhi the highest-paying region.

CASE STUDY

Offshoring? No, reshoring

In the past, many businesses moved their production 'offshore' to countries that offered cheaper employees because of lower pay expectations. Countries such as China, and more recently, Vietnam and Indonesia, have attracted many UK and European firms. However, with the emergence of cheaper robotic machinery, businesses are now 'reshoring' (going back) to the original country as production becomes easier and more efficient. The location is still a key factor for business production, but, with changes to production methods resulting in cheaper alternatives to human employees, many firms are seeking new destinations yet again.

The role of legal controls on location decisions

All businesses, wherever they locate, have to abide by (obey) local trading laws, which can limit their business activity. Knowledge of these legal controls will have a big impact on where a business chooses to locate.

- **Legislation.** Different countries have different laws regarding business activity, such as health and safety, data protection and marketing laws. A business must ensure that it follows these laws. This is particularly applicable for manufacturing businesses that use a lot of machinery, as there will be more legal constraints affecting how they operate.
- **Trade barriers.** Some countries put barriers, such as **quotas**, on the number of imports into the country. A quota is a limit to the number of goods that a country will allow to be imported. To overcome these barriers, businesses may choose to relocate to that country so they are no longer exporting to them and are therefore not affected by the quotas.

Recommending an appropriate location

In order to recommend a suitable location for a business, you should consider the following questions before making your decision:

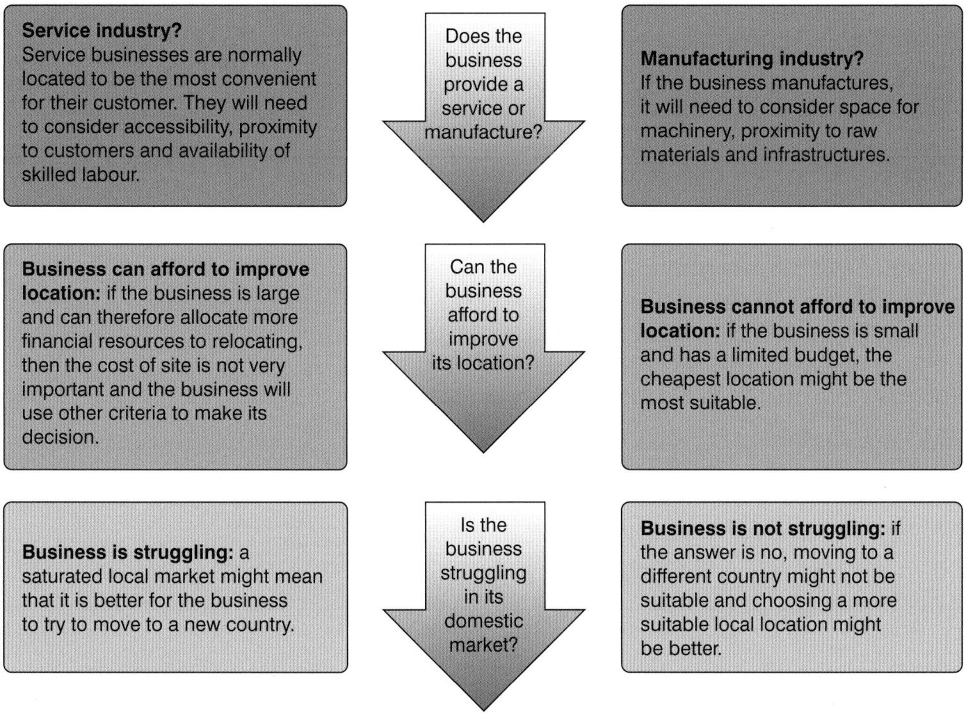

Service industry?
Service businesses are normally located to be the most convenient for their customer. They will need to consider accessibility, proximity to customers and availability of skilled labour.

Does the business provide a service or manufacture?

Manufacturing industry?
If the business manufactures, it will need to consider space for machinery, proximity to raw materials and infrastructures.

Business can afford to improve location: if the business is large and can therefore allocate more financial resources to relocating, then the cost of site is not very important and the business will use other criteria to make its decision.

Can the business afford to improve its location?

Business cannot afford to improve location: if the business is small and has a limited budget, the cheapest location might be the most suitable.

Business is struggling: a saturated local market might mean that it is better for the business to try to move to a new country.

Is the business struggling in its domestic market?

Business is not struggling: if the answer is no, moving to a different country might not be suitable and choosing a more suitable local location might be better.

Analysis **Evaluation**

Working in small groups, choose a business and review the suitability of two different locations for this business. You can either choose two locations in your local area (one in a city centre and the other outside the city) or in two different countries. For each location, produce a fully annotated map that includes the following features:

- infrastructure
- proximity to raw materials
- cost of site (research the rent on some available properties)
- available space
- availability of labour (research local unemployment rates to help with this)
- proximity to customers.

If you choose locations in two different countries, consider the following in addition to the list above:

- minimum wage
- population (this indicates the potential for customers and employees).

Recommend one of the locations, justifying your choice. Present your findings to the group.

Knowledge check

1. **Consider two factors that might be important when deciding where to relocate. (4)**
2. **Consider two factors that might influence a business thinking of relocating overseas. (4)**
3. **Explain why a country with a low minimum wage might influence a business's decision to relocate. (3)**
4. **Other than minimum wage, identify three legal issues that might influence a business's decision to relocate overseas. (3)**
5. **Explain two factors that are important when relocating a manufacturing business. (4)**

Total 18 marks

Check your progress:

✓ I can outline the main influences on a business's location and relocation decisions.

✓ I can apply the relevant factors to the location decisions of a business depending on its sector and the relevant legal controls.

✓ I am able to recommend and justify an appropriate location for a business in given circumstances.

Exam-style questions: short answer and data response

1. Table 1 shows the production costs involved in making mountain bikes.

Fixed costs	$4500
Variable cost per bike	$60
Selling price for each bike	$240

Table 1

a) **Define** the term fixed costs. (2)

b) **Calculate** how many bikes would need to be sold to break-even. Show your working. (2)

c) **Explain** the impact on the break-even point if the selling price drops to $200. (4)

Figure 1 shows a break-even chart for making mountain bikes with a new selling price.

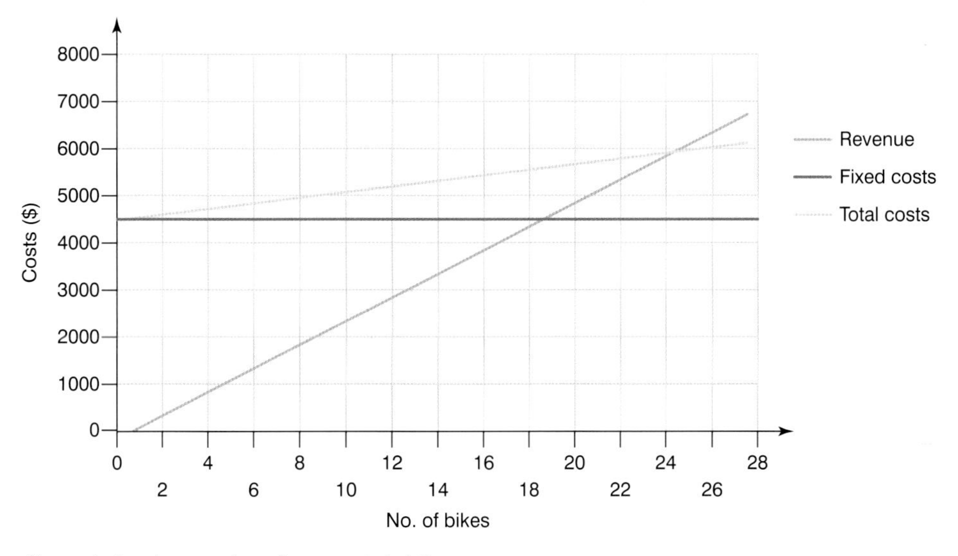

Figure 1: Break-even chart for mountain bikes

d) **Explain** two decisions that a break-even chart can help a business to make. (6)

e) The operations director thinks the best way to make more profit is to increase the selling price of the mountain bikes. Do you agree with her decision? **Justify** your answer. (6)

2. MG is an electronics business that makes televisions and other household goods. They currently batch produce their products. As they are growing in size, they are considering changing their production method to flow production.

   a) **Define** the term batch production. (2)

   b) **Identify** one advantage and one disadvantage of using batch production. (2)

   c) **Explain** two advantages of using flow production for a business like MG. (4)

   d) **Explain** three potential diseconomies of scale that might affect a business as it grows in size. (6)

   e) **Explain** three factors that a manufacturing business like MG might consider when deciding on a new location. (6)

3. General Vehicles (GV) is an international car company. Globally, demand for GV's new cars is falling, although sales have shown considerable growth in Brazil and China. In Germany, GV has introduced just-in-time stock control, has limited its factory hours to 40 a week and has reduced its workforce to 70.

   GV are considering relocating some of its manufacturing plants currently in Germany to Brazil or Poland. Table 2 shows some basic information on each location.

	Brazil	Poland
Average wage per hour	$2.50	$5.50
Transport costs per month	$5 000.00	$2 000.00
Rent per year	$15 000.00	$11 000.00

Table 2

   a) **Define** the term just-in-time. (2)

   b) **Identify** two factors that GV should consider when deciding where to locate its German manufacturing plants. (2)

   c) **Explain** two legal factors that might influence GV's decision on where to locate its manufacturing plants. (4)

   d) **Explain** three consequences of using just-in-time stock control. (6)

   e) GV's operations director thinks that the company should move its manufacturing plant to Brazil. Do you agree with her decision? **Justify** your answer. (6)

Note: The exam-style questions, answers and commentary in this book were written by the author; in examination the number of marks awarded to questions like these may be different.

Exam-style questions based on case studies

Fast and Frozen Foods

Fast and Frozen Foods (FFF) is a British manufacturer of frozen foods that supplies a variety of meals to retailers across the world. The company's sales data for the last year is detailed in Appendix 1.

Europe	70%
Africa	18%
Asia	12%

Appendix 1: Sales data for FFF

FFF are looking to expand their manufacturing and open up a new factory to produce a new product line. Product 1 is a frozen chocolate product that will be very popular in African markets, as it uses locally sourced cocoa beans from the Ivory Coast. Product 2 is a frozen ice-cream product that will be marketed to European customers and is expected to sell 1000 units in the first year. Appendices 2 and 3 show potential break-even data for both products.

	$
Selling price	4
Variable cost	1.5
Fixed cost	5500
Forecast sales per month	500

Appendix 2: Chocolate product forecast

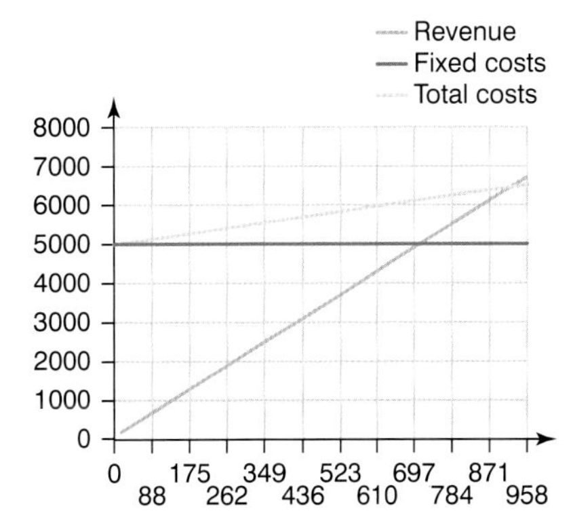

Appendix 3: Break-even graph – ice cream

> *We expect the chocolate product to sell more units, helping us generate more economies of scale; however, that is on the basis that we mass produce the item. I think if we batch produce, and produce a number of different flavours, we might be able to appeal to more customers. However, the variable cost will go up to $2.50 per item.*

Appendix 4: Extract from the operation director's report on the chocolate product

1. If FFF decide to manufacture Product 1:

a) Outline two advantages and two disadvantages to FFF if they used flow production. (8)

b) Justify which of the two products FFF should produce. Refer to Appendices 2, 3 and 4 in your answer. (12)

2. a) **Explain** four factors that FFF might consider when deciding where to locate their new factory. (8)

b) FFF have decided to produce Product 1. **Explain** whether FFF should use batch production or mass production. **Justify** your answer with reference to Appendices 2, 3 and 4. (12)

3. a) **Explain** four economies of scale that FFF might benefit from by increasing their product range. (8)

b) **Justify** a suitable method of ensuring high quality with the new product line. (12)

4. a) **Explain** two advantages and two disadvantages of using a break-even chart. (8)

b) Is a break-even graph a suitable decision-making tool when deciding whether to produce ice cream or the chocolate product? **Justify** your answer. (12)

Note: The exam-style questions, answers and commentary in this book were written by the author; in examination the number of marks awarded to questions like these may be different.

Exam-style questions based on case studies

Mystique Clothing Ltd

Mystique Clothing Ltd is a clothing manufacturer situated in the middle of the garment district in Mumbai, India. Mystique Clothing supply a number of top brands with clothes such as jeans, silk shirts, T-shirts and hand-stitched sequin dresses. Although Mystique Clothing have invested in some of the latest technologies to aid their manufacture, each garment still requires highly skilled humans to operate the machinery. Because of quick changes in fashion, Mystique Clothing often have very little time to produce the items, which can result in employees rushing the work to meet the order deadlines.

	Month 1	Month 2	Month 3
Output	500	700	600
Employees	50	55	58

Appendix 1: Mystique Clothing jeans production

Mystique Clothing have been trying to increase the level of production for all of their garments, as they believe it is more beneficial to them to produce large quantities of the goods, not only because it satisfies their customers but also because Mystique Clothing may benefit from reduced costs. Appendix 2 is an overview of the costs for the production of jeans for Month 2.

Output	Fixed costs	Variable costs
0	1000	0
100	1000	120
200	1000	240
300	1000	360
400	1000	480
500	1000	600
600	1000	720
700	1000	840

Appendix 2: Mystique Clothing jeans production costs, Month 2 (all figures in $)

1. a) With reference to Appendix 1, **explain** two benefits to Mystique Clothing of increasing the level of production of their garments, such as jeans. (8)

Mystique Clothing are considering using quality control or quality assurance in the manufacture of their clothing.

b) Outline whether quality control or quality assurance would be more suitable. **Justify** your answer. (12)

2. a) **Explain** two benefits that lean production could have for a business like Mystique Clothing. (8)

b) **Explain** three benefits to Mystique Clothing of using technology within their production process. (12)

3. a) **Explain** two factors that Mystique Clothing should have considered before locating their business in Mumbai, India. (8)

b) What is the most suitable method of production for Mystique Clothing to use? **Justify** your answer with reference to job, batch and flow production. (12)

4. Mystique Clothing are considering producing a new line of clothing. They are undecided as to whether to produce a range of cardigans or a range of jumpers. Cost and profit data is forecasted below.

	Jumpers	Cardigans
Expected demand	2000	1500
Selling price per garment	$12.50	$16.00
Variable cost of garment	$6.00	$8.50
Expected fixed cost per month	$2000	$3500

Appendix 3: Forecasted cost and profit data for Mystique Clothing's new product lines

a) **Outline** two variable costs and two fixed costs that Mystique Clothing might have to pay. (8)

b) Should Mystique Clothing produce the new cardigans or the new jumpers? **Justify** your decision. (12)

Note: The exam-style questions, answers and commentary in this book were written by the author; in examination the number of marks awarded to questions like these may be different.

Past Paper Questions

Paper 1

Section 4

1 Gomez is the manager of a small computer repair business. Table 1 shows some costs and prices for his business. As it is a competitive market, Gomez knows it is important to maintain customer loyalty and revenue. Gomez knows that a lower break-even point would help improve profits. He thinks the best way to lower the break-even point is to raise prices.

Price per customer	\$30
Variable cost per customer	\$20
Average number of customers per month	140
Monthly fixes costs	\$1000

Δ Table 1: Cost and price information

a) What is meant by 'revenue'?

____

____

____ (2)

b) What is meant by 'variable cost'?

____

____

____ (2)

c) Using the information in Table 1, draw a break-even chart for Gomez's business. (4)

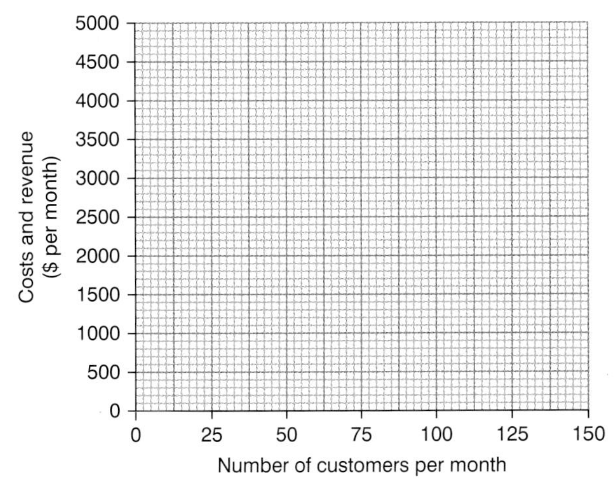

Cambridge International IGCSE Business Studies 0450 Paper 11, Q1 June 2015

Past paper questions

Paper 2

Section 4

The following case study is taken from past papers created by Cambridge Assessment International Education. We have only provided extracts of this case study, and it does not reflect the full case study that you may be provided with in your examination.

Gorgeous Gifts (GG)

George started GG ten years ago in country X. He could have bought an existing business for $50 000 but he wanted to start a new business of his own.

George formed a partnership with his friend Fred who did not want any management responsibilities. They each invested $15 000 into the business. GG now has six stalls selling gifts. The stalls are located in seaside towns which are visited by many tourists.

Now George wants to expand GG. He has the following two options.

Option 1

Open six shops in the seaside towns and sell his stalls. The shops are much bigger than the stalls and could sell a wider variety of gifts. George wants to buy the shop buildings and will need a loan to do this. He can sell each stall for $5000 but each shop costs $50 000.

Option 2

Keep the gift stalls but open gift shops inside city centre hotels. There is a chain of 20 hotels that has a shop available in each of their hotels across the country. George will have to make one payment of $20 000 to the hotel chain when he opens his shops. He will also have to give them 10% of his profits from the shops each year.

Appendix

Balance Sheet for GG for year ending August 2013 ($)

	2012	2103
Fixed Assets		
Market Stalls	30 000	30 000
Current Assets		
Stock	10 000	18 000
Debtors	0	0

	2012	2103
Cash at Bank	5 000	2 000
Total	15 000	20 000
Current Liabilities		
Creditors	10 000	10 000
Overdraft	0	0
Total	10 000	10 000
Working capital	5 000	10 000
Net Assets employed	35 000	40 000
Financed by:		
Partners' capital	30 000	30 000
Profit and loss reserves	5 000	5 000
Bank loan	0	5 000
Capital employed	35 000	40 000

1 a) **Identify** and **explain** two economies of scale GG might benefit from as the business expands. (8)

b) Do you think George should be happy with the financial position of the business? **Justify** your answer by calculating liquidity ratios and using other information in the Appendix. (12)

Cambridge International IGCSE Business Studies 0450 Paper 23, Q3 a & b, Nov 2013

Skills Builder

AO1: Knowledge

Using the glossary to help you, give a clear and concise definition of each of the key terms mentioned within each question. Ensure that you use key terminology throughout your answer and be especially careful that you do not confuse productivity and production.

AO2: Application

Application means using not just text and data from the case study but also the context. This means the setting of the case study. To do this, consider the following:

- What type of industry is the business in?
- What method of production does the business use?
- How can you use the data from tables or appendices to strengthen your answers?

AO3: Analysis

You will need to **analyse** if you are to go on to form a reasoned judgement (evaluation). For each point you mention, develop the consequence.
For example:

- 'The advantage of this is...'
- 'This may lead to...'
- 'However, this may mean that the following could happen...' (give a disadvantage).

Use paragraphs to form your analysis and always remember to make it clear how your points answer the question. For example, if a question asks for the benefits of lean production, you will need to develop your point to show why lean production is a benefit.

AO4: Evaluation

Evaluation requires you to give a judgement. This means that, once you have analysed the points you have mentioned, you should make a decision based on what you have considered.

- Overall, what is your verdict on the question?
- Is there one point that you think is more important?
- Do you have all the necessary information to make a judgement? If not, what other information do you require?

he role of the finance department is arguably the most important in any business, s whatever a business does, it will always have to balance the books. Poor financial management can result in businesses making massive losses yet still continuing to rade.

n this section, you will learn:

- about the main reasons for businesses needing finance both in the short and long term
- about the main sources of finance for businesses, both internally and externally, including the main factors they must consider in making a financial choice
- about the importance of cash flow and cash flow forecasting to help a business overcome a short-term cash flow problem
- how businesses manage, publish and interpret their financial information and where the money comes from
- how businesses make a profit and what they do with it
- to analyse accounts to judge profitability, liquidity and financial performance over time
- how financial accounts are used to publish information that investors can look at.

KILLS BUILDER

ood progress

nowledge: You show a sound nowledge of the key terminology.

pplication: You demonstrate good nderstanding of the key terms that ou use by explaining and applying hem to a business situation.

nalysis: You develop the onsequences of the points you have nentioned for the type of business n question, explaining the potential dvantages and disadvantages for he business.

valuation: You make judgements vhen they are required.

Excellent progress

Knowledge: You define and identify all the key terms relating to finance, and use this terminology within your written answers.

Application: You show a clear ability to apply your knowledge to a given business situation, using detail such as the legal ownership, the size of the business and the type of product/service they sell to help inform your answers.

Analysis: You develop the consequences of the points that you have mentioned for the type of business in question, explaining the advantages and potential disadvantages.

Evaluation: You make judgements and suitable recommendations, justifying your reasoning where possible with numerical data calculated from the case study.

ECTION CONTENTS

5 Financial information and decisions

Starting points

You have been invited to present a new business idea to a group of local business investors who have lots of money ready to invest in your idea. Before you make your presentation, you need to think about:

- what you would spend the money on
- the main reasons you need start-up capital
- whether you will need more money in the future.

Write your ideas down, ready to share with the class.

Business finance: needs and sources

The need for business finance

Aims (5.1.1)
By the end of this section, you should:

- Understand the main reasons why businesses need finance, for example, start-up capital, capital for expansion and additional working capital
- Understand the difference between short-term and long-term finance needs.

Why do businesses need finance?

Sources of finance (also known as funds or capital) are where and how a business gets the money it needs to trade, to grow and, ultimately, to survive. Businesses need money for **working capital** (the purchase of day-to-day items such as inventory), for expansion (opening a bigger factory, for example) and to get started in the first place (start-up capital).

At start-up	To manage daily operations	To expand
 Money will be used to pay for premises (buildings), new equipment and advertising, and so on.	 Money (known as working capital) is used to pay employee wages and to purchase inventory, and so on.	 Finance might be used to pay for a larger factory or office, or for new branches in a different city or country.
Research and development	**For takeovers**	**For new premises/technology**
 Finance is needed for research into new products, and to test and trial them.	 When one business buys another, it needs money to pay for the acquisition (purchase).	 As a business grows, it might need more space or new technology to keep up with competitors.

Use of finance in a business can be split into two categories:

- **Capital expenditure.** Money spent on purchasing fixed assets (buildings, machinery, and so on) that will be used in the business for a period greater than one year.
- **Revenue expenditure.** Money used to cover short-term day-to-day expenses and to help generate sales (inventory purchases, wages, advertising expenses, and so on).

CASE STUDY

Shrek in Shanghai

Dreamworks Animation, the Hollywood studio behind *Shrek*, *Kung Fu Panda* and *Madagascar*, opened a new theme park in Shanghai in 2016 because it is seeking to expand into China. Having hit its tight deadlines, it is now looking to find more money to start building another theme park in Beijing by 2021.

The money raised for building the park will be used for capital expenditure. Once the park is operating, money from items such as ticket sales will be used to fund revenue expenditure. Over time, any surplus (that is, retained profit) could be used as a source of finance to help develop the park (such as being used to fund a new ride).

Short-term and long-term finance needs

Sources of finance are often grouped according to the use of the funds and the time frame over which money is borrowed:

	Time frame	Examples
Short term	Less than one year	Purchase of inventory, payment of salaries
Long term	Five-plus years	New factory build, takeover of another firm

Following the principle of matching, the source of finance that a business chooses must be appropriate to the proposed use. For example:

- A new car factory would benefit Honda over many years. A bank loan that is repaid over an equivalent time period might therefore be the most appropriate source of finance (long-term use matched to long-term finance).
- A business selling fresh food will use its inventory almost daily. If it needs additional funds to buy this inventory, an overdraft might be most appropriate (short-term use matched to short-term finance).

Research whether any firms in your country have recently raised funds. Consider the following:

- Identify whether the money raised was used for capital or revenue expenditure.
- Identify whether the source of finance used was short or long term.

Present your findings as a simple table summarising the results.

Knowledge check

1. **Using examples, outline two reasons why a firm needs finance. (6)**
2. **Justify appropriate financial time frames (short or long term) for the following business activities: (12)**
   a) Nike builds a new retail store in India
   b) TGP Capital's (a financial investment company) takeover of Billabong clothing
   c) A small firm needs funds to pay salaries
   d) A factory in Vietnam installs a new production line system
   e) An African firm buys a new delivery vehicle
   f) The fashion retailer Zara buys material from Bangladesh.

Total 18 marks

The main sources of finance

Aims (5.1.2)

By the end of this section, you should:

- Understand internal sources and external sources, with examples
- Understand short-term and long-term sources with examples, for example, overdraft for short-term finance and debt or equity for long-term finance
- Understand the importance of alternative sources of capital, for example, micro-finance, crowd-funding
- Understand the main factors considered in making the finance choice, for example, size and legal form of business, amount required, length of time, existing loans
- Be able to recommend and justify appropriate source(s) of finance in given circumstances.

Internal and external sources of capital

Where a business gets its money from can be split into two main categories:

- **internal finance** – money obtained from within the business.
- **external finance** – money obtained from sources outside of the business.

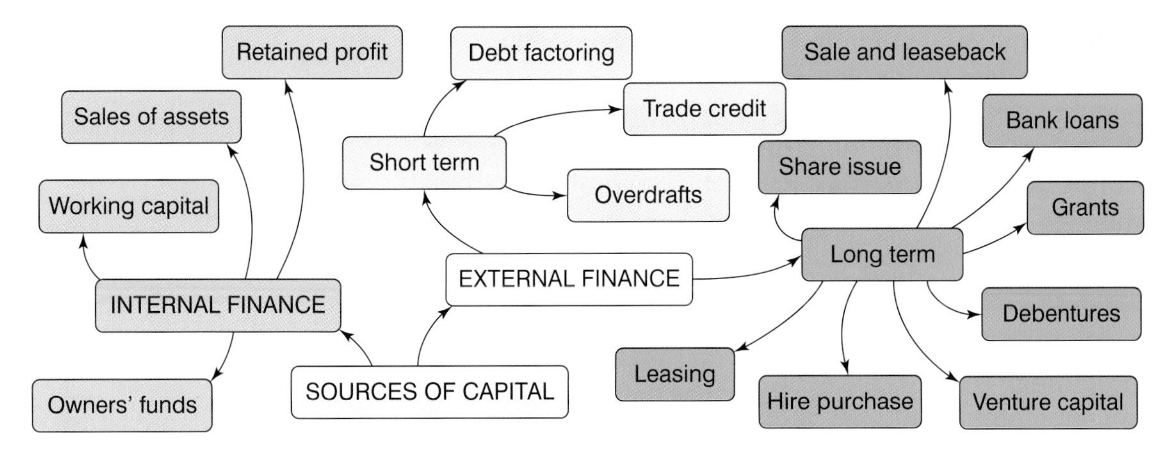

Debt and equity

Sources of finance can also be categorised as debt or equity.

- **Debt** – this involves using money that must be repaid, plus interest.
- **Equity** – this most commonly refers to raising money by selling shares in the company. It can also refer to owners' funds (known as private equity).

Whether a firm uses debt capital or equity will depend on the owners' willingness to share ownership of the business. Also, in some cultures, having debt of any form is considered socially unacceptable. Both factors will affect how much debt an owner is willing to take on.

This willingness also depends on the availability (how easy it is to get loans, and so on) and price of debt. The price of debt is determined by how much interest is charged on the loan.

Did you know?

Apple has nearly $250 billion in its cash reserves, ready to use for buying a rival, starting a new business or simply expanding its production of iPhones.

Debt	Equity
Advantages of debt compared to equity • Owner(s) retain full control of the firm • Profits are not shared with a lender • With fixed interest rates, monthly loan repayments are known and can be planned for • Relatively easy for most firms to set up bank loans	**Advantages of equity compared to debt** • Benefit from shared ownership and shared risk • No monthly repayments • Repayment often only necessary once firm is making profits
Disadvantages of debt compared to equity • Unlike equity, debt must at some point be repaid • Interest rates may be variable and thus repayments difficult to plan for • High interest costs during difficult financial periods might cause problems with repayment • Security (in the form of an asset) is required to secure the loan	**Disadvantages of equity compared to debt** • Owner must give up some control of the business • Owner must share profits • Usually only available to limited companies • Legally complicated and expensive to set up and manage

The extent to which a firm is funded by debt or equity is known as its debt-to-equity ratio (also known as **gearing**).

A $100 million company funded through a $40 million bank loan with the remainder in equity ($60 million) has a gearing ratio of 40:60 (debt:equity). A limited company with no debts has a ratio of 0:100 (low gearing); a company with a ratio of 80:20 (80% debt; 20% equity) is highly geared. The higher the gearing, the greater the burden (problems) of debt. If the interest rate goes up or the firm has cash flow problems, repaying the loan could become a problem.

For a business, evaluation of the debt versus equity question is key. For example, a growing partnership must ask itself whether it is better to raise funds through debt or by incorporating (the process of converting to public or private limited company status – see 1.4 Types of business organisation) and issuing shares. This question is one that only the owners themselves can answer. They will need to consider carefully the issues given here and, most importantly, their own attitude to risk and keeping control of the business.

CASE STUDY

Saving the firm

South African company Hwange Colliery has announced it is working with its trade payables (those it owes money to) to convert its short-term debt into longer-term debt, having suffered liquidity and debt issues in 2016. The business is, however, facing some resistance from its trade payables, who are unwilling to give additional time for payment. Hwange's main business features are mining and processing coal and associated by-products. Despite a drop below break-even, it is hoped the business will be back to being profitable in 2018, with profits increasing the year after.

Internal sources of finance

Internal sources of finance (capital) are those that are generated by the business itself. One example is profit.

Owners' funds

A sole trader or members of a partnership may inject (put in) more of their own money into a business.

Advantages of owners' funds	Disadvantages of owners' funds
✓ It provides a quick, interest-free source of funds.	✗ There is greater financial risk for the owners. ✗ Business owners can be willing to face considerable risks – some even use their personal credit cards to pay for business expenses.

Retained profit

Once a business starts to make a profit, it can use this profit as a source of finance. Ploughing back (putting back) profit into a business has the advantage of avoiding the costs (for example, interest charges) of external finance. It is, however, only available if the business actually makes a profit and if the owners do not want to keep the profit for themselves.

Advantages of retained profit	Disadvantages of retained profit
✓ It provides an interest-free source of funds.	✗ It is not always available. (A firm needs to make profits to reinvest them.) ✗ Owners receive less reward for their risk (lower return on money invested in the business).

Working capital

Working capital is money available for immediate use to fund day-to-day operations. Reducing inventory, delaying payment to trade payables, or encouraging trade receivables (individuals or firms, usually customers, that owe the business money) to pay on time can help to increase the amount of working capital available. A business can then use this money for other purposes. However, the business must be careful not to make itself vulnerable to a cash flow crisis. It must also make sure it has enough inventory to meet demand.

Advantages of working capital	Disadvantages of working capital
✓ Efficient management of cash is good business practice.	✗ Money is not always available. (A firm may need its working capital to cover immediate expenses.) ✗ A firm must ensure it still has sufficient inventory to meet customer demand.

Sale of assets

A firm could sell buildings, vehicles or even parts of its business as a way of generating funds. To help it reduce debts, ConocoPhillips, a US oil producer, has sold its assets in western Canada for $13.3 billion to Cenovus Energy.

Advantages of selling assets	Disadvantages of selling assets
✓ It can enable a business to release large sums of money.	✗ The firm loses the use of the asset. ✗ Finance is only available if an asset can be sold (which may take time).

External sources of finance

Internal sources of finance have the advantage of being inexpensive and convenient (easy and quick to access). Most businesses, however, have limited internal funds and need to seek external sources of finance. These external sources are usually grouped according to the time frame over which they are most often used.

Short-term finance

Short-term sources of finance are used to fund revenue expenditure and are usually repaid within one year.

Overdrafts

An overdraft is effectively a short-term bank loan. A bank allows a business to draw out of its accounts more money than it has deposited (put in). An overdraft is often used to cover cash shortages, and a business may only be overdrawn for a matter of days. Interest is only paid when the account is overdrawn. For example, if a firm was overdrawn by $10 000 for 30 days (at a typical average of 15% interest), it would cost the firm $116, plus a fee to the bank for the overdraft facility.

Δ Overdrafts help a business to cover cash shortages, although there are interest charges to pay.

Advantages of an overdraft	Disadvantages of an overdraft
✓ It is cheaper than a bank loan. ✓ It is a flexible way for businesses to borrow small amounts for very short periods of time.	✗ In return for flexibility, the banks charge high interest rates and fees – if used over the long term, this makes overdrafts very expensive.

Evaluation

Evaluate the overdrafts offered by different local banks. Which banks offer the best overall overdraft for small businesses? Why? Consider the following:

- What risks are involved with overdrafts?
- When might a firm need to use an overdraft?

Present your findings as a one-page information sheet aimed at young entrepreneurs setting up their first business.

Trade credit

Most business-to-business transactions are completed on a credit basis. A business does not pay immediately for the goods it purchases; instead it may be given 30, 60 or 90 days to pay. This credit period gives the firm time to sell the goods and therefore generate funds to pay the supplier.

Advantages of trade credit	Disadvantages of trade credit
✓ Trade credit is interest free and easily available. ✓ It is possible to secure early payment discounts if accounts are settled (paid) before the deadline – the firm benefits from the credit period and from a discounted price.	✗ Start-ups and young firms may not be offered credit unless they have proven their ability to pay. ✗ Trade credit needs to be carefully managed to avoid overtrading and cash flow crisis.

Debt factoring

This involves 'selling' a debt (money owed to a firm by its trade receivables) to a debt factoring company. These companies give the firm a percentage of the debt and will then attempt to recover the full debt for themselves. The business gets immediate access to cash but may forgo (give up) the full value of the debt. In return for the service, the debt factoring company retains a percentage of the recovered debt.

WORKED EXAMPLE

Debt owed	$100 000
Debt factoring firm recovers	$100 000
Firm receives	$80 000
Debt factoring firm's profit	$20 000 (20% of the debt's value)

Such services are also used to recover bad debts (money owed to a firm that is overdue).

Advantages of debt factoring	Disadvantages of debt factoring
✓ It provides businesses with quick access to funds. ✓ The firm does not have to worry about collecting the debt (and avoids the full impact of bad debts).	✗ The firm may not receive 100% of the debt. ✗ The riskier a debt is, the lower the percentage received.

Long-term finance

Long-term finance is used to fund capital expenditure and is usually repaid over a period longer than one year.

Leasing

By leasing (hiring) an asset instead of purchasing it, a business reduces the amount of finance it needs to raise. A business pays a set fee (usually monthly) to lease an asset for a period of time. After this period, the business returns the asset to the leasing company. The business might choose to renew the leasing contract and receive a new asset. Leasing companies also maintain the asset and replace it if it breaks.

Leasing is cheaper than outright purchase in the short term but more expensive over the long term. Despite the additional cost, leasing is useful for equipment such as computers that go out of date quickly.

Advantages of leasing	Disadvantages of leasing
✓ There is lower initial capital requirement (less money needed) to gain use of an asset. ✓ It spreads the impact on cash flow. (Instead of one large payment, the business makes smaller payments over time.) ✓ The firm does not have to worry about care and maintenance of the asset. ✓ The firm can replace the asset regularly.	✗ The total cost of leasing is usually higher than purchasing the asset.

Hire purchase

Hire purchase is similar to leasing, but gives a firm the advantage of owning the asset once it has made all the monthly payments. This makes hire purchase cheaper than leasing but without the benefits of flexibility.

∆ The types of asset suitable for hire purchase or leasing include business vehicles, IT equipment, office equipment and factory machinery.

Advantages of hire purchase	Disadvantages of hire purchase
✓ The firm owns the asset once all payments are made.	✗ The firm is usually responsible for maintenance (and replacement) of the asset. ✗ The total cost of hire purchase is usually higher than the cost of purchasing the asset.

Bank loans

Bank loans are usually repaid on a monthly basis over a number of years. The bank charges interest on the loan amount. Banks loans are a relatively safe source of finance, because they have a fixed interest rate so the business knows what the monthly repayment amounts are and can plan for them.

Advantages of bank loans	Disadvantages of bank loans
✓ Bank loans are quick and easy to arrange. ✓ They can be arranged for different amounts and time frames.	✗ Depending on the interest rate and amount loaned, bank loans can be expensive. ✗ Banks usually require some form of security on the loan (a business building or, in the case of a sole trader, a personal asset such as a house). ✗ If the business is unable to repay the loan, the bank will repossess (claim) the asset.

A potential difficulty with bank loans is the need for businesses to demonstrate their ability to repay. For new firms with no credit history (proof of repaying previous loans), this may be difficult. Larger businesses, with established credit records, may find access to bank loans easier and may be offered better interest terms. This is known as an economy of scale (see 4.2 Costs, scale of production and break-even analysis).

Sale and leaseback

Businesses use sale and leaseback to resolve short-term cash flow crisis (see 5.2 Cash flow forecasting and working capital). They can also use it as a way of funding long-term growth. The business sells an asset (usually a building) and then leases it back from its new owner. This generates an immediate inflow of cash at the expense of long-term lease payments.

Advantages of sale and leaseback	Disadvantages of sale and leaseback
✓ The firm gains a large injection of capital. ✓ The firm retains use of the asset.	✗ The cost of leasing the asset back will be high. ✗ The leasing arrangement may not include maintenance.

CASE STUDY

Sale and leaseback

NXT Energy Solutions is a Canadian firm offering airborne oil survey systems to reduce time, cost and especially risk in the oil and gas exploration cycle. It has recently reduced its capital by selling, then leasing back, its aircraft to Cessna Citation for $2.3 million.

Venture capital

Venture capitalists are specialist finance providers. Where a start-up or young business is unable to raise sufficient funds, it often uses venture capital. Venture capitalists invest in smaller, risky ventures and do not ask for security. Instead, they loan money in return for a share of business ownership or for a share of any eventual profits.

Venture capitalists may also wish to have a say in how the business is run and the right to influence its strategy. For inexperienced business owners, this support from venture capitalists can be very useful.

Advantages of venture capital	Disadvantages of venture capital
✓ It may be one of the few sources of finance available to a start-up business. ✓ Venture capitalists often offer management advice and consultancy as part of the loan.	✗ Firms have to share ownership and profit with the venture capitalists. ✗ Venture capital is usually only available to high-potential businesses with strong growth prospects.

Evaluation

A friend of yours runs a small company selling bespoke (made to order) artwork over the internet. Customers provide an example of the artwork required (perhaps a favourite family photograph), then professional artists copy the image and it is sent to the customer.

Over the past few months the service has become increasingly popular. Your friend needs to purchase a warehouse to store the artwork while it is processed for shipping (delivery) and a larger space for the team of artists to work. She would also like to promote the service in more countries.

The business is already set up as a private limited company, with ownership shared between your friend and her husband. To fund the expansion, she is considering using venture capital.

Evaluate the advantages and disadvantages of using venture capital and make a recommendation. Is venture capital the most appropriate source of finance in this context?

Debentures

Debentures are a form of long-term loan to a limited company. They have fixed interest rates and are repayable over a specified time period (often 15–25 years).

Advantages of debentures	Disadvantages of debentures
✓ Debentures provide a source of very long-term finance. ✓ Interest rates may be cheaper than bank loans.	✗ They are only available to large limited companies.

Grants

In many countries, governments offer grants to businesses. The amounts on offer can range from less than $100 to many thousands of dollars. Grants are available for businesses setting up in certain locations, producing certain products or for creating employment opportunities.

Advantages of grants	Disadvantages of grants
✓ Grants provide a cheap or free source of funds. ✓ Businesses do not usually have to pay back the grant.	✗ Grants are often only available for specific types of business or specific areas of a country.

CASE STUDY

Grants aid African communities

The United States African Development Foundation (USADF) offers grants to African businesses that promote economic development in Africa. The grants range from $50 000 to $250 000 and are offered to small and medium-sized firms (with a maximum of 100 employees) whose products or projects contribute positively to local communities.

Other sources of finance

As well as using direct sources of finance (such as a bank loan), a business might choose to reduce the amount of capital it needs to raise by getting other firms or other investors to provide some of the capital.

Joint ventures

Businesses often reduce the amount of finance they need to raise by engaging in **joint ventures**. A joint venture is where two or more businesses join forces to finance a new business venture or product. For example, the South Korean firm SK Innovation entered a joint venture with Germany's Continental, setting up a new company that sells car batteries. SK Innovation has a 51% stake in the new company and Continental has 49%.

Franchising

One other way of reducing the need for finance is for a business to grow through franchising (see 1.4 Types of business organisation). In return for an initial fee and a share of profits, the franchisor allows other firms (franchisees) to use its brand and sell its products. The franchisor is therefore able to grow its business without the need for significant capital investment. A famous example of a franchise is McDonald's.

Did you know?

McDonald's is globally famous for its franchise opportunities. The USA has the most restaurants (14 267), whereas Portugal has 148.

Share issue

For limited companies, a share issue is a way of generating large sums of money. Selling newly issued shares to investors raises more funds, but reduces the owners' stake in the business. German bank Deutsche Bank released 687.5 million shares so that it could raise $8.6 billion for additional investment. In order to do this, current large shareholders will have to give up a proportion of ownership in return for this additional capital.

Change in business status

A change in business status can be used to generate funds. For example, a sole trader might take on a partner who would bring additional funding. A partnership might convert to a limited company to benefit from the ability to sell shares.

Advantages of a change in business status	Disadvantages of a change in business status
✓ A change in business status can be a way of raising funds and spreading the risk of ownership. ✓ The original owners can benefit from new ideas and input.	✗ The original owners risk losing control of the business. ✗ Converting to a private or public limited company takes time and can be expensive.

Micro-financing

For firms in less industrialised countries, micro-finance has become an increasingly important source of finance. Micro-finance allows people on very low incomes to borrow small amounts of money to start up or expand a small business, often without the need to provide security (an item of value, which the lender can sell if the borrower fails to repay the loan).

Did you know?

'Lend with Care' is a micro-finance website that allows people all over the world the opportunity to invest in small start-up businesses in countries that are traditionally more agriculturally focused. The entrepreneurs then pay the money back over an agreed period of time.

Crowd-funding

Crowd-funding is a relatively new type of finance that is often used to generate money for micro-finance projects. Based on micro-donations (sometimes as low as $1), crowd-funding uses the social power of the internet to help small firms launch creative projects or environmentally friendly products. A good example of how such financing works is kickstarter.com, which has facilitated micro-financing for projects such as films, stage shows, graphic novels and video games.

CASE STUDY

Micro-loan funds education

Kiva.org, a popular micro-finance website, helped a small cosmetics business in Togo to secure a micro-loan for the purchase of supplies. The loan was for $725, which the business repaid within 14 months. The business owner needed the supplies so that she could use her profits to fund her children's education.

Factors affecting choice of finance

When choosing sources of finance, a business needs to evaluate:

Availability of internal funds

If a business has internal funds available, it must consider whether it is appropriate to use these funds. What will be the impact on working capital? How might shareholders react to lower dividends (the portion of a limited company's profit that is paid to shareholders)?

Length of time

The time frame (period) of repayments or exposure to debt must relate to the purchase the business is making. A fixed asset may pay for itself over many years and should be funded with long-term finance.

Cost

A business must obviously consider the cost of raising finance. Cost is closely related to time frame:

- Issuing shares is expensive, but can raise large amounts of capital for long-term use.
- Trade credit is usually interest free, but is only available for short periods of time.

Size and legal form of business

A sole trader may only have a limited range of financial options. A public limited company (PLC) usually has a wide range of sources of finance available. PLCs, due to the size of loans they undertake and the security they offer, are often able to negotiate lower interest rates on bank loans. Smaller businesses will often be limited in their sources of finance as banks and investors will want to see a proven track record. Larger businesses offer lower risk and often attract investors who want to gain a good return on their money.

Control

The degree of control that a business's original owners wish to maintain will affect their choice of finance. For example, if a firm's owners would prefer to keep control of the business, then venture capital or conversion to limited status may not be appropriate sources of finance.

Amount required

The source of finance will vary depending on the amount needed. A simple overdraft may be all that is required and this can be obtained from the bank. However, if a large business wanted $100 million to invest in a new joint venture in a new market, the source of finance would need to be able to offer this amount – for example, via investors or a share offering.

Δ A business may need to provide security in the form of an asset such as a building or vehicle to gain access to bank loans.

Existing loans

The level of current gearing can determine the sources of finance available. A business that already has several bank loans may find it difficult to secure another. In any case, a business that is already highly geared (a high debt-to-equity ratio) may put itself at risk if it takes on additional loans. Any increase in interest rates will have a significant effect on the firm's debt burden (the amount it must repay).

Security

Small businesses in particular may have little to offer as security on a bank loan and may find it difficult to get one. Larger, more established businesses will have proven track records and assets that they can use as security. Banks are potentially more likely to lend to large firms.

Above all, the source of finance chosen must be appropriate to the business situation and the motive for needing finance. Business growth requires both adequate short-term cash flow (working capital) and long-term finance for expansion. The two requirements may well be met by very different sources of finance.

Evaluation

Evaluate which factors affecting choice of finance are likely to be most appropriate in the following situations:

- A highly geared and very profitable manufacturer needs funds to build a new factory.
- A firm, such as Apple Inc, with significant cash reserves, wants to invest in research and development of new products.
- A writer (sole trader) who publishes books needs funds for a larger than usual print run. She is unwilling to use personal assets as security.
- A partnership of lawyers needs additional funds to expand the business. The current partners are reluctant to further share ownership.
- A profitable and well-established public limited company seeks financing for an expensive project at a time when interest rates are high.

In each case, recommend and justify an appropriate source of finance.

Present your findings as a mind map, linking each situation to an appropriate source of finance and the factors that affect that choice:

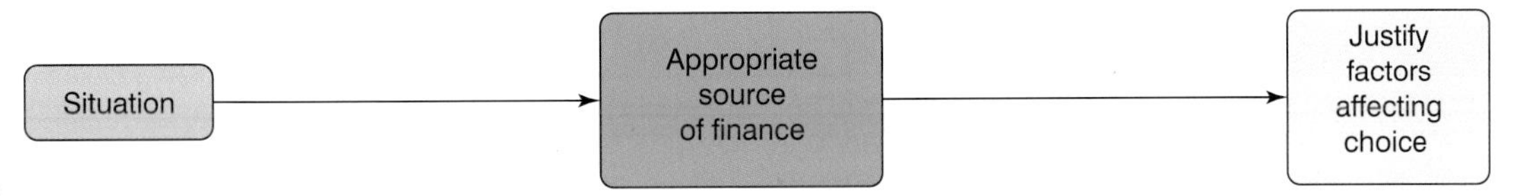

Knowledge check

1. **Explain when a business might prefer to use a bank overdraft rather than a bank loan. (3)**
2. **Explain the differences between equity and debt. (4)**
3. **Define the term debt factoring. (2)**
4. **Define the term venture capital. (2)**
5. **Explain the difference between leasing and hire purchase. (4)**
6. **Outline an example of when micro-finance may be an appropriate source of finance. (2)**
7. **Identify three factors a business might consider when deciding on sources of finance. (3)**

Total 20 marks

Check your progress:

✓ I understand the main reasons why a business needs finance.

✓ I can explain the main reasons why a business needs finance, and can give examples of internal, external, short-term and long-term sources.

✓ I can discuss the importance of alternative sources of capital and outline the key factors that should be considered.

✓ I can recommend and justify appropriate sources of finance in given circumstances.

Cash flow forecasting and working capital

The importance of cash and of cash flow forecasting

Aims (5.2.1)

By the end of this section, you should:

- Understand why cash is important to a business
- Be able to explain what a cash flow forecast is, how a simple one is constructed and the importance of it
- Be able to amend or complete a simple cash flow forecast
- Understand how to interpret a simple cash flow forecast
- Understand how short-term cash flow problems might be overcome, for example, increasing loans, delaying payments, asking debtors to pay more quickly.

What is cash and why is it important to a business?

Cash or cash flow is the term that businesses use to describe the money that they have available to plan the day-to-day running of the business. As you will see later in this section, it is very different from profit and far more important when it comes to running a business. Without sufficient cash, a business cannot pay its bills. If this is a long-term problem, then a business will eventually fail.

Cash flow is categorised as either an inflow or an outflow. In simple terms, this means money coming into the business (inflow) or going out of the business (outflow).

Δ Cash inflows can come from paying customers.

Δ Cash inflows can also come from other sources such as bank loans.

Cash inflows

Cash inflows can be defined as money coming into the business, which can come from a number of different sources and which the business can use for a variety of different reasons.

Type of inflow	Where it comes from	What it might be used for
Revenue/sales	This is the money that the business receives from its customers for the product or service that it provides them with.	Businesses normally use revenue to cover the costs of running the business, such as paying suppliers and bills.
Loan	This is a one-off inflow borrowed from a bank.	Businesses normally use loans to pay for a one-off item such as upgrading machinery.
Share capital	This is normally a one-off inflow from raising and selling more shares to shareholders.	Businesses normally use share capital to pay for business growth and investments.

Cash outflows

Cash outflows can be defined as money going out of the business to pay for bills, supplies or loan repayments. It is important that a business forecasts when their outflows take place to ensure that it has enough cash to cover the expected cost.

Type of outflow	What it means
Payment to suppliers	Suppliers are the businesses that sell raw materials to a firm. The firm then adds value to the raw materials. For example, the suppliers to a furniture manufacturer will supply the firm with the wood needed to make the furniture.
Payment of overheads	Overheads are the bills that a firm has to pay on a monthly or quarterly (every three months) basis, for example, electricity and water.
Wages/salaries	Businesses normally pay their employees on a monthly or weekly basis, depending on how they are paid.
Loan repayments	A business might need to pay back a loan that it has used to pay for a one-off item, such as new machinery.
Mortgage repayments/rent payments	Depending on whether a business owns or rents its premises, it will normally have monthly costs to pay for the property. These costs will either be mortgage repayments or rent payments.
Investments/growth	Businesses often invest in new premises or machinery in order to bring about growth. They need to plan their cash flow to ensure they have enough money to pay for the investment.

Cash flow forecasts

Cash flow forecasts are financial statements. They predict future cash inflows and outflows so a business can ensure that it has enough cash to cover the cost of its outflows. If it does not do this, the business will have cash flow problems. If the business then ignores or does not notice these problems, it could result in insolvency (the inability to pay its debts). This often results in the business failing.

The benefits of forecasting include:

- By forecasting the timings of its cash flow, a business can manage its cash so it does not have a shortage, resulting in the ability to pay its bills.
- Forecasting can help a business plan for the future and predict when it might have enough cash to afford growth or investment opportunities.

Cash flow forecasts normally have the following layout:

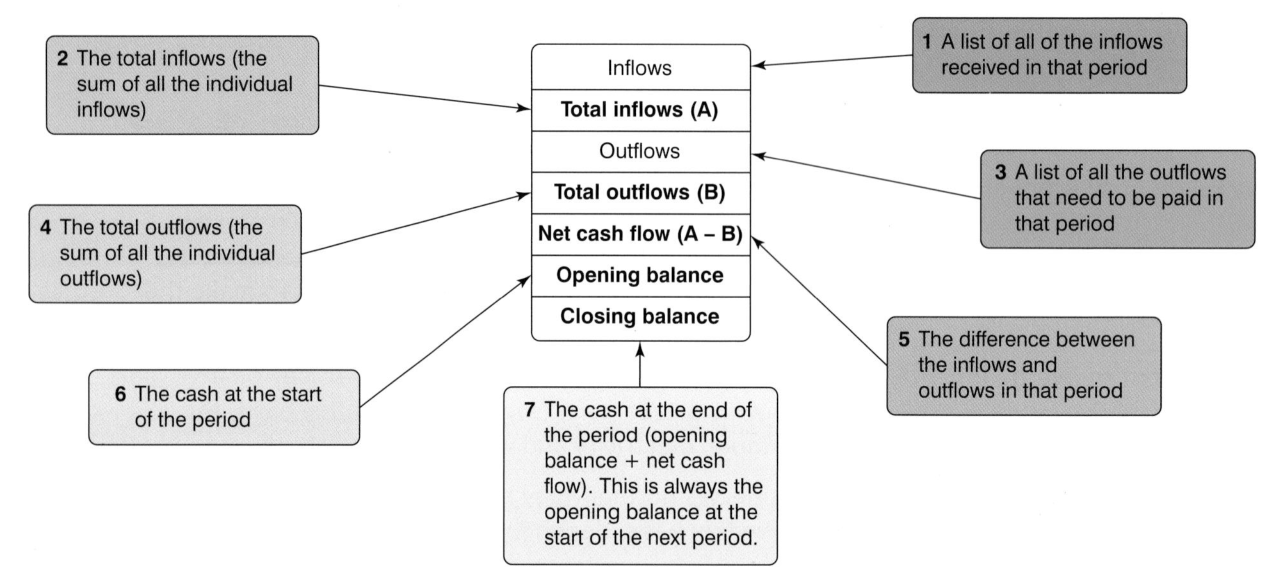

Δ The net cash flow is the most important figure to look at. If this is continually negative, it shows that the business has cash flow problems

WORKED EXAMPLE

In order to construct a cash flow forecast, it is important that you distinguish between the inflows and the outflows and then ensure that you look at the timings of the cash flows – for example, when the inflows will be received and when the payments (outflows) need to be made. The following is an example of how this can be done.

Hajar Hotels, Dubai, need to construct a cash flow forecast for the next four months, in order to manage their cash flow. They have forecast the following inflows and outflows for the period May to August:

Although the mortgage gives a short-term inflow, it needs to be paid back. However, as it is used to pay for more hotels, it should increase revenue.

	May	June	July	August
Inflows (000,000)				
Revenue	145	145	145	165
Mortgage		500		
Total inflows (A)	**145**	**645**	**145**	**165**
Outflows (000,000)				
Wages	130	130	130	145
Electricity & Water		20		
Suppliers	15	15	15	15
Repayments			40	40
Total outflows (B)	**145**	**165**	**185**	**200**
Net cash flow (A – B)	–	480	(40)	(35)
Opening balance	125	125	605	565
Closing balance	125	605	565	530

For the last two months, the outflows are more than the inflows, resulting in a negative net cash flow for the month.

The net cash flow is negative, which shows short-term cash flow problems. If this continues, the business will eventually run out of money.

Hajar Hotels, Dubai, expect revenue of 145 million (145m) United Arab Emirates dirham (AED) each month except for August, when they expect 165m AED (this is money coming in from paying customers).

In June, they take out a mortgage for 500m AED to pay for the 'purchase' of two new hotels. They will start to make monthly repayments of 40m AED in July.

They pay wages of 130m AED each month except for August, when they need to pay 145m AED.

Their electricity and water bills, which they pay each quarter (once every three months), are 20m AED.

They have suppliers that they have to pay each month, expected to cost 15m AED.

At the start of May, they have an opening balance of 125m AED.

Dealing with cash flow problems

Problems with cash flow or **liquidity** (see the next section in this topic on Working capital) exist when a business does not have enough money, or cash, in the short term to pay for its outflows. The business can take a number of measures to help it solve these problems.

Short-term methods

- Securing a bank overdraft will allow the business to have a negative cash balance for a while. However, this will normally cost, as banks charge finance costs (interest) on the overdraft (see 5.1 Business finance: needs and sources).
- Asking for credit on some of their outflows will allow the business more time to pay for their expenses. This often happens with bills – a business receives the product (for example, electricity), but then has two months before it has to pay for it.

- The business can ask its trade receivables (customers who owe the business money) to pay more quickly. Some businesses allow customers a certain period of time to pay for their product or service. This flexible payment can attract more customers but also leave a business with short-term cash flow problems.
- A bank loan will provide a business with a large inflow of cash. However, the business will have to pay this back with interest. Unless the business can use the bank loan to generate more inflows or to reduce outflows (through methods such as increased advertising or more efficient production methods), then it will only delay the business's cash flow problems rather than solve them.

Long-term methods

- For any large outflows, businesses need to ensure that there is an inflow to cover the cost before the outflow has to be paid. For example, a business wishing to upgrade its ICT facilities, which will cost a significant amount. The business needs to secure the funding before paying the cost.
- Businesses can try to increase their inflows or reduce their outflows. This should solve any long-term cash problems.

Top Tip

Use appropriate headings for your cash flow forecast, such as: Inflows, Outflows, Net cash flow, Opening balance, Closing balance.

CASE STUDY

Improving cash flow

Next PLC is copying its rival, ASOS, by increasing its sales online. It hopes that this increase in its online presence will help improve its cash flow. Next had recently announced its first profit fall for eight years, which sparked rumours that the company would change its strategy. By selling more garments online, Next can speed up transactions, improving its cash flow position overall.

Application **Analysis** **Evaluation**

Al-Rashid Clothing Ltd has made the following predictions for its cash flow for the months of January to June:

- The company predicts sales of $4 million each month for the months of January to March, increasing by $1 million for the next three months.
- It has labour costs each month of 50% of its sales.
- It also has rent to pay each month, costing $1.5 million.
- It has electricity bills to pay in March and June, each costing $0.5 million, and marketing costs of $1.2 million each month.
- In April, it is planning a $6 million advertising campaign, on top of its current marketing costs, to raise awareness of its new clothing lines.

Construct a cash flow forecast for the six-month period from January to June.

Identify any cash flow problems for Al-Rashid Ltd. You can do this on your cash flow forecast by annotating (labelling) your forecast or by using a series of bullet points underneath.

Recommend a method of improving Al-Rashid Clothing Ltd's cash flow. Consider both short-term and long-term improvements in your recommendation.

Knowledge check

1 **Define the following terms:**

a) cash inflow **(2)**

b) cash outflow. **(2)**

2 **Identify two possible inflows and two possible outflows that a business might have.** **(4)**

3 **Explain two reasons why it is important to produce a cash flow forecast.** **(4)**

For the month of March, a business has outflows of $130 000 and inflows of $140 000.

4 **Calculate the net cash flow for the month of March.** **(2)**

In April, the business's inflows remain the same, but its outflows are predicted to increase by 10%. The closing balance from March was $15 000.

5 **Calculate the closing balance for the month of April.** **(4)**

6 **Explain two ways a business could improve its cash flow.** **(6)**

Total 24 marks

Working capital and liquidity

Aims (5.2.2, 5.5.2)
By the end of this section, you should:
- Understand the concept and importance of working capital
- Understand the concept and importance of liquidity.

What is working capital?

The word capital is another word for money, and in this instance, it means the money that a business has to work with (use) on a short-term basis. Working capital is effectively the business's cash flow. Whereas capital expenditure is the money that a business obtains for purchasing assets, working capital is the money that is available to cover everyday expenses such as paying bills and suppliers.

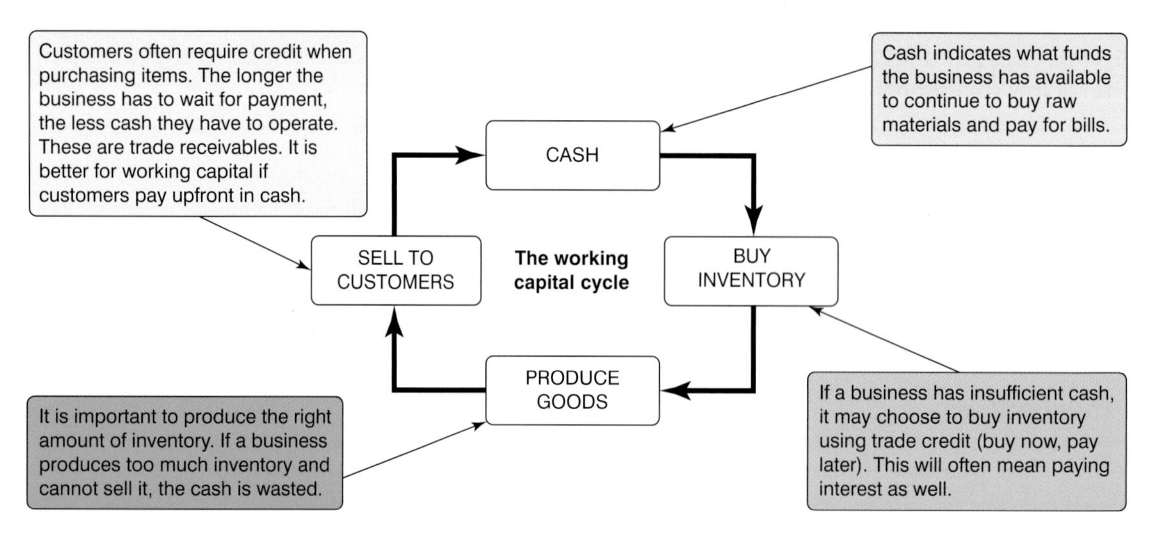

Δ The working capital cycle

What is liquidity?

Liquidity is the extent to which a business can meet its short-term liabilities (debts). In simpler terms, it is the extent to which the business can pay its bills. A liquid business will have enough cash to pay its bills on time and clear its debts.

Good liquidity	Bad liquidity
✓ The business has enough cash to pay its bills.	✗ The business has more bills to pay than it has cash coming in to pay them.
✓ The business has a positive net cash flow (see the previous section on The importance of cash and of cash flow forecasting).	✗ The business has a negative net cash flow for most months.

Liquidity problems

When a business has liquidity problems, there are a number of possible consequences. All of these are likely to damage the success of the business in the long term.

- Suppliers and bills are not paid on time, incurring late payment charges and interest on the outstanding amount owed (finance costs).
- Suppliers may not continue to supply a business if they consider it to be a 'high risk' (unlikely to be able to pay for the supplies).
- Banks are likely either to not lend or to charge a high rate of finance costs (interest), as they view the business as high risk.
- A business might be forced to use a long-term source of finance, such as a loan, to solve a short-term cash flow problem. This will result in bigger debt and will only delay any liquidity problems.

How to improve poor liquidity

Businesses rarely fail because of their long-term debt. Although having a high level of long-term debt is a problem, it is normally short-term problems and the inability to pay bills that cause businesses problems, as they will need immediate payment. It is therefore vitally important that, if a business has liquidity problems, it tries to solve these as quickly as possible.

Methods for improving a company's liquidity include:

- **Ensure trade receivables pay on time.** Having to wait to receive payment from customers means the business has to wait longer to pay its trade payables.
- **Avoid any further investment.** The business should use all the money it has access to to sort out the short-term liquidity problems.
- **Control costs.** Having cheaper costs, such as choosing a cheaper supplier, will help improve the amount of working capital available.
- **Increase inflows into the business.** The business could do this by increasing the selling price or attempting to sell more units.

CASE STUDY

Online liquidity

Indian online retailer Snapdeal is looking for additional investment from current shareholders, as well as new investors. Having lost its second place in the online retail market (to Amazon) last year, it has struggled with liquidity and is now looking for $100 million in new investment. It believes it can become profitable in two years, but will need to convince investors of this if it is to raise the capital.

Application

Using an appropriate search engine, research businesses that are having working capital or liquidity problems.

- For each business, research the reasons why it is having liquidity problems.
- Write a letter to the financial director of one of the businesses – summarise your findings and recommend a solution to its working capital problem.

Knowledge check

1. **Define the following terms:**
   a) cash payment (2)
   b) credit period. (2)
2. **Explain the meaning and importance of working capital. (2)**
3. **Explain one reason why working capital is important to a business. (3)**
4. **Explain why it is so important for a business to manage liquidity. (2)**
5. **Explain two potential short-term methods of improving liquidity. (4)**

Total 15 marks

Check your progress:

✓ I can explain why cash flow is important for a business and use a basic cash flow forecast.

✓ I am able to construct, amend and interpret a simple cash flow forecast.

✓ I can discuss the importance of cash flow shortages, outlining different methods to improve the flow in the short term.

✓ I can outline the reasons why liquidity is so important to the long-term success of a business.

Income statements

What profit is and why it is important

Aims (5.3.1)

By the end of this section, you should:

- Understand how a profit is made
- Understand the importance of profit to private sector businesses, for example, reward for risk taking/enterprise, source of finance
- Be able to explain the difference between profit and cash.

What is profit and how is it made?

Profit is the money that a business makes over a particular period of time. It is the difference between the selling price of a particular product or service and the cost of supplying that product or service. Profit is the main aim for private sector businesses, and is the end result of the process of adding value.

Profit is often considered to be the reward for entrepreneurs and businesses taking risks. When an entrepreneur has a business idea, they often have to devote a lot of their own time and put their personal money into the business before they have a chance to make any money, and with no guarantee. Profit is the reason why entrepreneurs want to start a business and the reason why established businesses continue to operate. In order to fully understand the concept of profit, you need to understand the elements that make it.

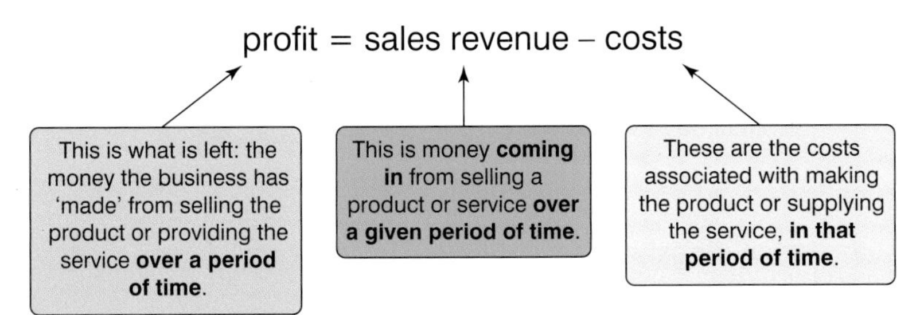

Sales revenue or turnover

'Sales revenue' and 'turnover' mean exactly the same thing: the money received from doing business – normally either selling a product or providing a service. Only the money received from this business activity can be classed as sales revenue and used when calculating profit. (Other cash inflows, such as bank loans, share capital or money raised from selling assets, cannot be used to calculate profit.)

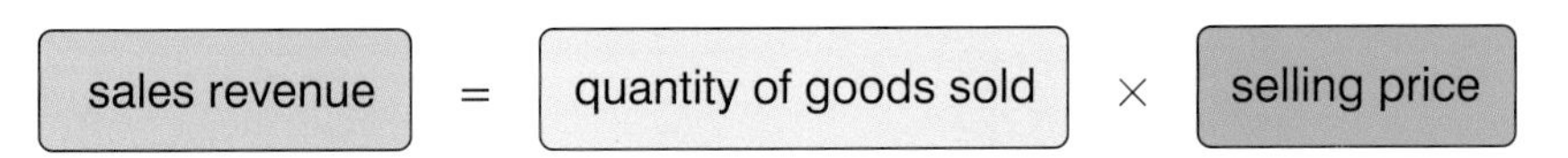

Costs

Similar to sales revenue, these are only the costs that are associated with providing the normal day-to-day business activity. These costs are therefore referred to as revenue expenditure. The cost of purchasing large, one-off items that are kept for a long time, such as vehicles, cannot be included when calculating profit made over time.

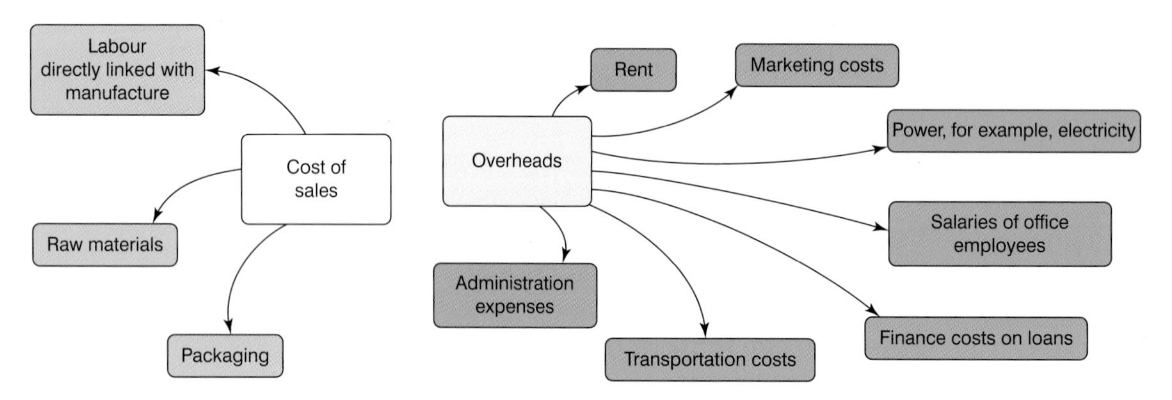

Δ Production employees' wages can be directly linked to manufacturing a product, so are sometimes classed as a cost of sale.

Δ Administration salaries are not directly linked to the making of a product and are therefore classed as an overhead.

Gross profit and profit

Profit is the money that a business has left after it has subtracted the revenue expenditure from the sales revenue that it receives from customers, within a given period of time.

Profit is normally split into categories: **gross profit** and profit.

Gross profit is the 'big' profit that shows the money made after only the cost of sales has been subtracted.

gross profit = sales revenue – cost of sales

Profit is the 'smaller' profit figure that shows the money made after all of the revenue expenses have been subtracted.

profit = gross profit – overheads

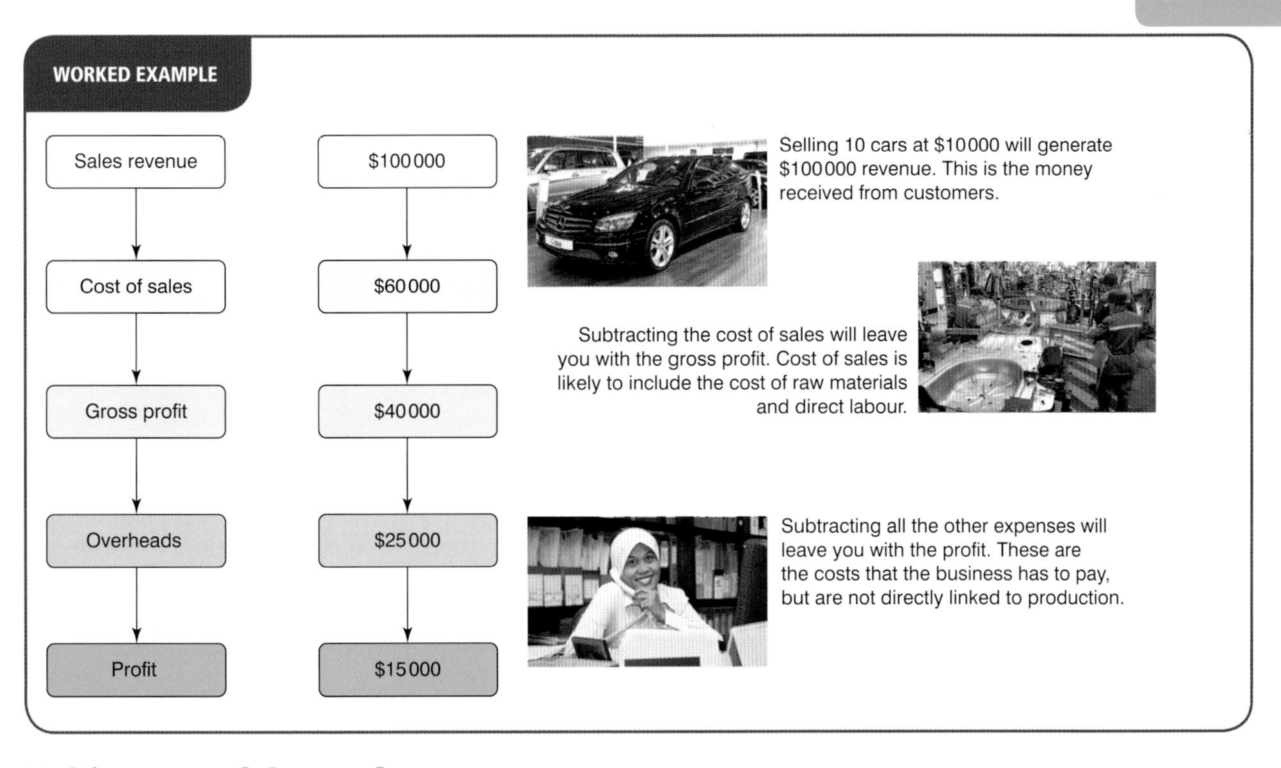

Making use of the profit

Profit is the most important figure that a business will look at, as this is the profit that it can keep. Except for taxation, there are no more costs that need to come off the profit figure. A business must now decide whether it wishes to retain the profit for later use or distribute it to shareholders through dividends, or do a bit of both.

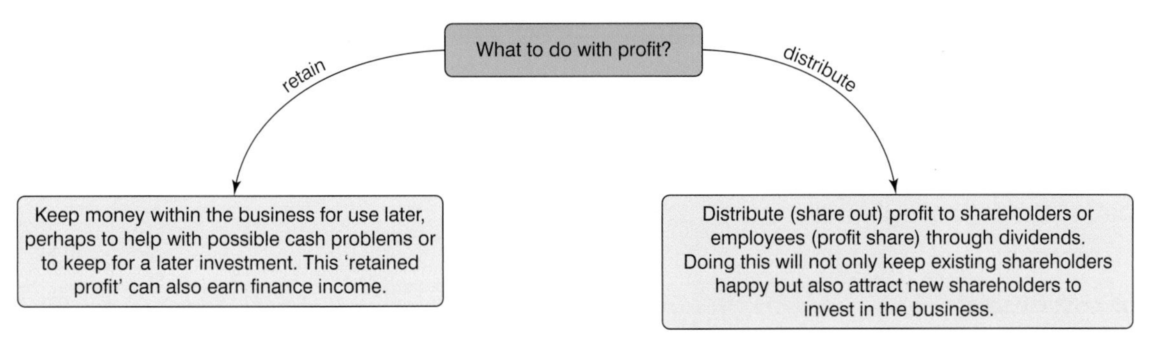

Importance of profit

Profit is important to private sector businesses, as it is a reward to the entrepreneur for taking the risk in setting up the business. The profit is often paid in the form of a dividend, but it can also be used to expand an existing business or start up a new business altogether. Profit allows these actions to occur and offers the owner a reward for the hard work and success of the business. Some private sector social enterprises see profit as important, as it provides money to invest in their specific cause or focus. For example, without profit from its charity shops, Oxfam would have less money to invest in its global aid projects. For all businesses, profit is an excellent source of finance for longer-term projects.

How are cash and profit different?

While cash is all the money coming in and out of a business, profit is a figure that is calculated over a period of time, only taking into account revenue and revenue expenditure. For example, a loan would appear on a cash flow forecast, but it is not revenue, so cannot be included when calculating profit. In addition, buying new premises would be included as an expense in the cash flow forecast, but would not be included as an expense when calculating profit, as it is not revenue expenditure. This is because premises are kept for a long period of time and therefore cannot be included as an expense in one particular period of profit.

CASE STUDY

TOHO achieves record profits

TOHO is a film distributor and studio that has been operating since 1932. It is famous for the Godzilla franchise and saw most success with its anime film *Your Name*, which is Japan's second most successful film of all time, only behind the Oscar-winning *Spirited Away*. Profits have jumped 23.4% in a year and the studio has new films on the horizon.

Evaluation

Research four businesses (either local or international companies) that have seen an improvement in profit over the past few years. Create a mind map for each business, with your ideas as to why its profit levels have improved. Make a judgement on which business you think will have the most long-term increase in profit.

Knowledge check

Al Hasawi International has recorded revenue of $5 million and has sales costs amounting to $2 million. Its overheads for the year are $1.2 million.

1. **Define the following terms:**
   a) **revenue** **(2)**
   b) **cost of sales** **(2)**
   c) **overheads.** **(2)**

Al Hasawi International manufactures air conditioning units.

2. **Identify four overheads that the business might have to pay.** **(4)**

In one year Al Hasawi International sold 40 000 units at an average selling price of $240 per unit.

3. **Calculate the business's revenue.** **(2)**
4. **If each unit cost Al Hasawi International $200 to make, calculate the business's gross profit for the year.** **(3)**

Al Hasawi International's overheads for the year were $1.4m.

5. **Calculate the business's profit for the year.** **(2)**

Total 17 marks

Income statements

Aims (5.3.2)

By the end of this section, you should:

- Understand the main features of an income statement, for example, revenue, cost of sales, gross profit, profit and retained profit
- Be able to use simple income statements in decision making based on profit calculations.

The main features of an income statement

The **income statement**, or profit and loss account, is a formal statement that details the profit a business makes over a particular period (usually a year). It is calculated by subtracting the business's revenue expenditure (both cost of sales and overheads) from its revenue (income). Potential investors and current investors use the income statement to see how much money the company is making and how much it is prepared to pay them, in the form of **dividends** (profit paid back to shareholders instead of being kept by the business).

Sole traders and partnerships also need to prepare an income statement, although it tends to be slightly different, as these types of organisation do not pay dividends.

The income statement follows exactly the same approach as calculating profit. However, whereas a business might calculate gross profit and profit for an individual product line or project, the income statement will show the whole business's profit (or loss) over a period from all their trading activity. This can be a complicated task for a large organisation with a lot of product lines that it sells in many countries.

Key Term

Sole trader: an unincorporated business owned by one person.

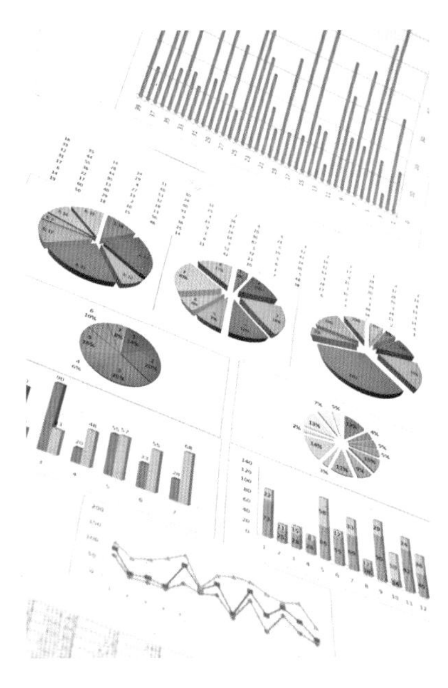

Δ Limited companies need to publish their financial statements each year.

A simple income statement for a sole trader

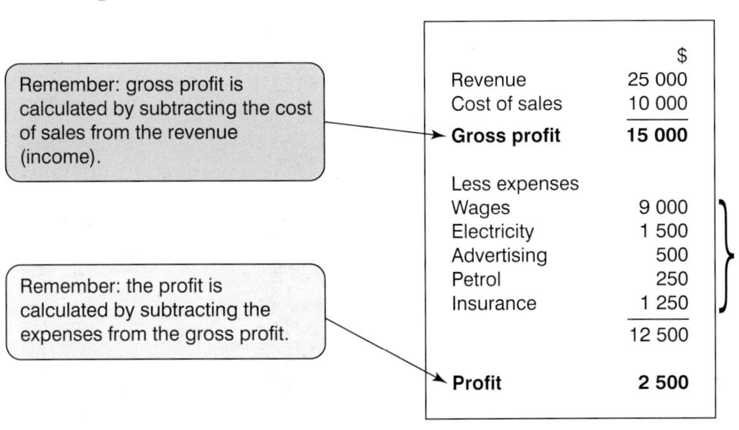

	$
Revenue	25 000
Cost of sales	10 000
Gross profit	**15 000**
Less expenses	
Wages	9 000
Electricity	1 500
Advertising	500
Petrol	250
Insurance	1 250
	12 500
Profit	**2 500**

A simple income statement for a PLC

A sole trader is a far smaller operation than a public limited company (PLC), so their accounts are normally a lot simpler. There are more stakeholders (groups or individuals who have an interest in the business's performance) involved with the running of a PLC, so its accounts must be slightly more detailed. It is a legal requirement that they publish these accounts on a yearly basis.

> **Did you know?**
>
> Apple holds the record for the largest ever quarterly (three months) profit figure – a staggering $18 billion.

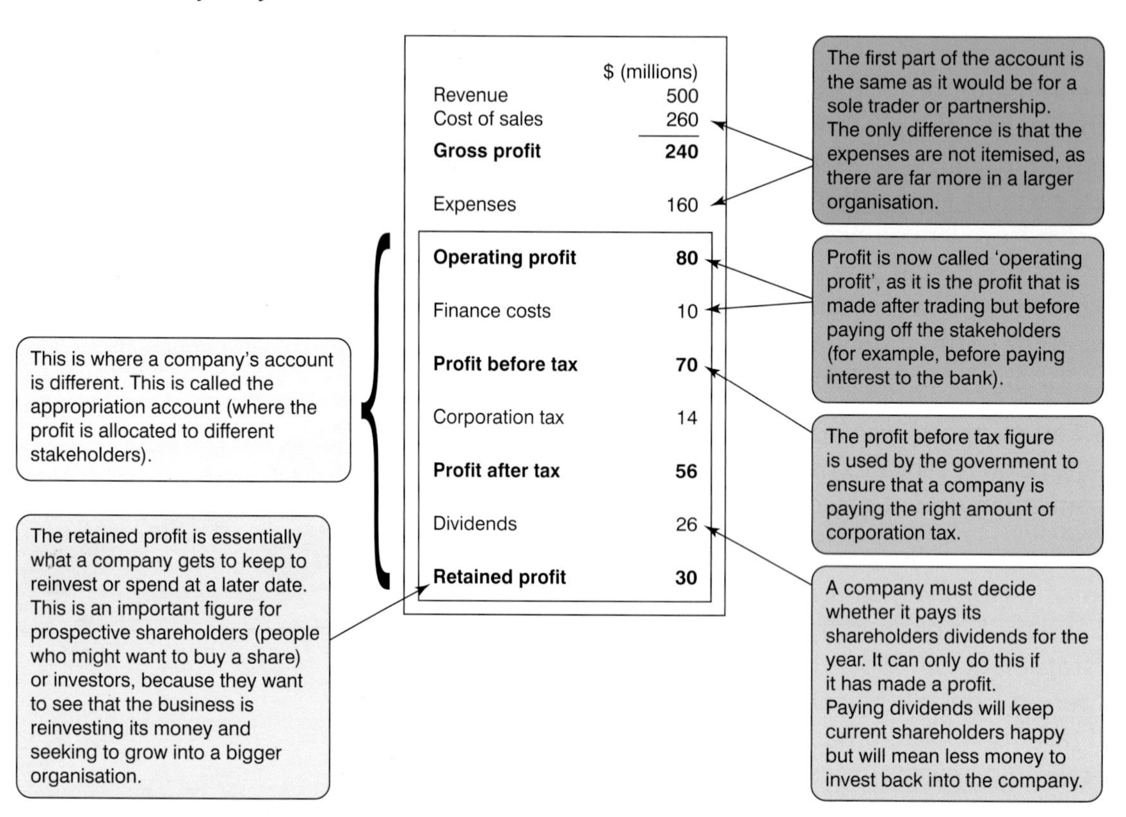

	$ (millions)
Revenue	500
Cost of sales	260
Gross profit	**240**
Expenses	160
Operating profit	**80**
Finance costs	10
Profit before tax	**70**
Corporation tax	14
Profit after tax	**56**
Dividends	26
Retained profit	**30**

CASE STUDY

Statement shows fall in profits

Carrefour Group is a French multinational retailer, with its headquarters near Paris. It has stores across Europe, South America and most of the Middle East. Carrefour Group is the world's second largest retailer and has to publish its financial statements each year. Last year, its profits fell for the first time in three years, with the blame put on increased competition in the market place. However, digital sales in food and non-food were €1.2 billion, and Carrefour projects that this figure will triple to €4 billion by 2020.

Using an income statement to make decisions

A business can make decisions and set targets for the next year by looking closely at its annual income statement. The target for all businesses is to improve their profit levels, or to maintain their profit levels if they anticipate a drop in revenue due to a potential recession or fall in demand.

Δ Advertising can help to increase demand for a product.

A business can make a number of decisions to help it achieve this:

- **Increasing the amount of revenue.** Increasing the amount of revenue should lead to higher levels of profit, providing that costs do not rise by the same amount. There are a number of ways a business can try to increase its revenue. Increasing the amount of advertising may help to increase demand for a product and therefore help sales grow. Alternatively, if the demand for the product is quite high, a slight increase in selling price will also increase the revenue.
- **Order raw materials in bulk.** Ordering raw materials in bulk should mean benefiting from lower costs (a purchasing economy of scale – see 4.2 Costs, scale of production and break-even analysis). This will reduce the cost of the raw materials the company uses, which should increase the amount of profit the company makes.
- **Use cheaper raw materials.** Using a cheaper supplier for raw materials will reduce the cost of sales. However, this may also mean that the quality of the final product is not as good, which could lead to fewer sales.
- **Improve production efficiency.** Improving production efficiency should cut down the level of waste, which is a cost to the business. The leaner the production (the less time and money that is spent on production), the lower the business's costs will be, therefore creating a larger amount of profit.
- **Cut down on overheads.** A company can cut down on overheads by simple procedures, such as choosing a cheaper electricity supplier, or by riskier strategies, such as reducing the amount spent on marketing and advertising. In addition, some businesses choose to reduce their workforce in order to cut costs. However, this is often considered to be the last resort, as cutting employees can limit the business's ability to grow in the future and may affect employees' motivation.

In addition to these profit-making decisions, a company may also decide to pay its shareholders more dividends for the year. This is likely to attract investment from new shareholders seeking a high dividend. Alternatively, it might decide to invest the year's profit into areas such as research and development or expansion, or to give its employees a bonus for the year.

Application **Analysis** **Evaluation**

Taste of Asia is a UK-based PLC that owns a series of Asian-themed restaurants across Europe. You have been asked to produce an income statement for last year's trading. The company has the following information available to help you construct the account:

- Its employees' salaries have cost £4 million over the year, and it has paid the same amount on rents for restaurants.
- It has paid £6 million on marketing across Europe and has to pay insurance of £1 million each year.
- It has received revenue across all of its restaurants of £80 million and ingredients have cost the company £45 million.
- Because the company has recently expanded, it has a loan of £100 million, which has finance costs of £5 million per year.
- It has agreed to pay its shareholders £10 million in dividends.
- The level of corporation tax in the UK is 20% for a business of this size.

Construct an annual income statement for Taste of Asia PLC.

Write a finance director's report that recommends a way that Taste of Asia PLC could achieve the management's target of £5 million retained profit. Try to consider the risks of your choices within your report.

Knowledge check

1 **Explain the following terms that might appear on an income statement:**

a) revenue **(2)**

b) retained profit. **(2)**

A hotel chain states that its gross profit before tax is $4.0m; its overheads for the year are $2.5m.

2 **Calculate the year's profit.** **(2)**

3 **Define the following terms:**

a) gross profit **(2)**

b) overhead. **(2)**

Total 10 marks

Check your progress:

- ✓ I can explain what profit is, why it is important and how it is made.
- ✓ I can outline the importance of profit to private sector businesses and explain the difference between profit and cash.
- ✓ I can describe the main features of an income statement.
- ✓ I can use simple income statements to help make decisions based on profit calculations.

Statement of financial position

The main elements of a statement of financial position

Aims (5.4.1)
By the end of this section, you should:
- Understand the main classifications of assets and liabilities, using examples.

Understanding a statement of financial position

Whereas an income statement is a record of how much profit a business makes over a particular period, the statement of financial position is a record of what a company owns and how it has paid for it at any given time. In simple terms, it is a record of what the business owns and the sources of finance it used to pay for it.

The statement of financial position focuses on three key elements: **assets, liabilities** and equitable funds (equity) (see 5.1 Business finance: needs and sources).

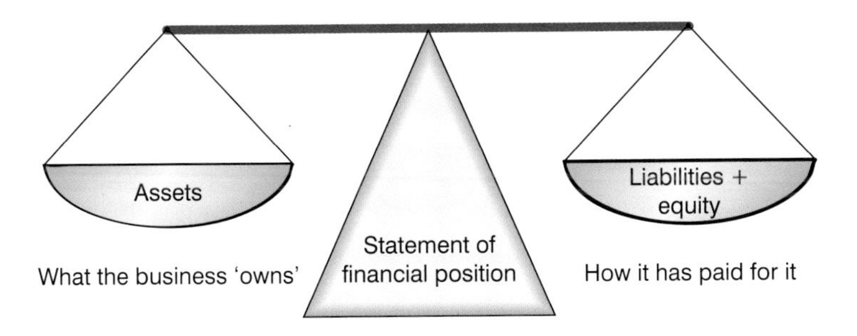

Assets and liabilities

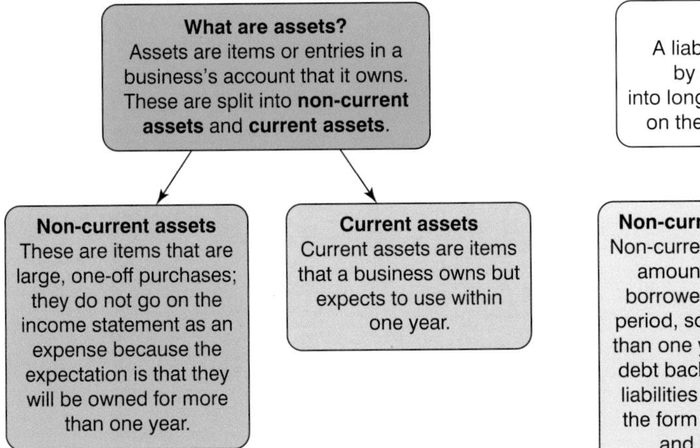

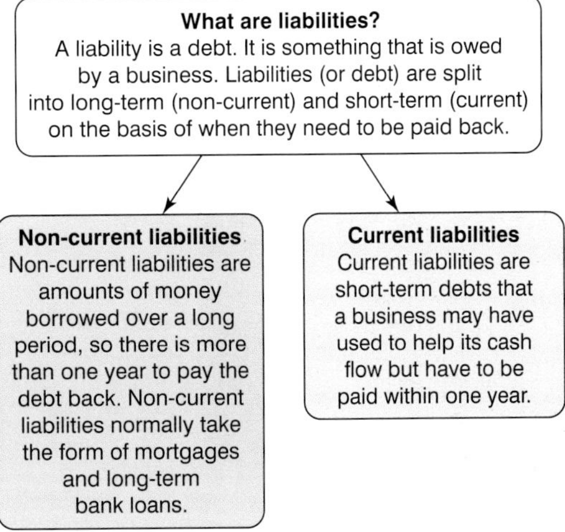

Classifying assets

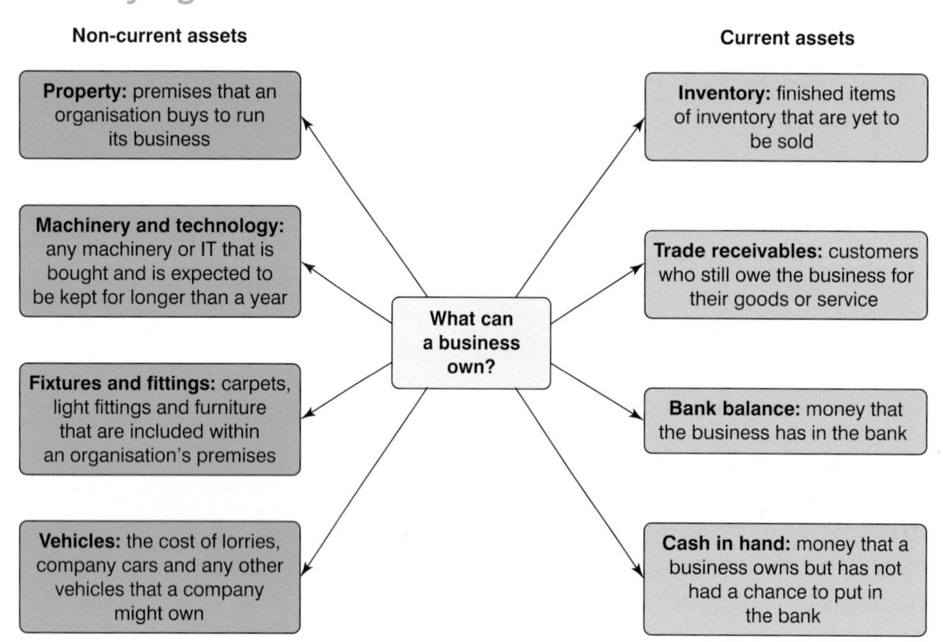

Classifying liabilities

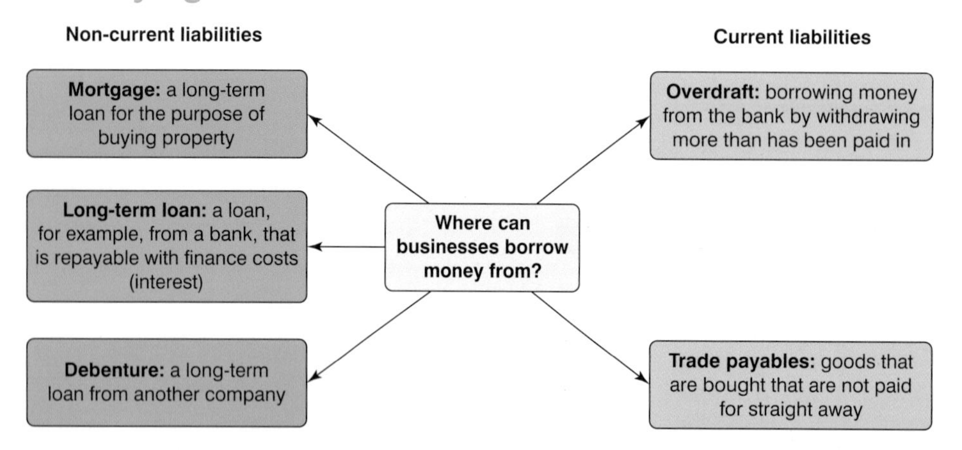

◁ The premises that an organisation buys to run its business is a a non-current asset; the mortgage on the property is a non-current liability.

◁ Current assets include items of inventory that are yet to be sold.

What are equitable funds (equity)?

A business does not always have to go into debt when it pays for assets, as there may be other sources of finance available to it – finance that is not borrowed, so does not have to be paid back. These funds include:

- share capital or owners' funds
- retained profit (money made by the business and kept for reinvestment).

Key Term

Share capital: a one-off cash inflow from raising and selling additional shares in a business.

CASE STUDY

Inflating figures

Tesco has agreed to pay a $161 million fine over its accounting scandal. It inflated its profits and assets on its income statement and statement of financial position, resulting in legal proceedings against the company that lasted two years. It is reported that Tesco increased its figures to help secure a higher share price and improve the attractiveness of its business for investment.

Application **Evaluation**

Look at the extracts from two statements of financial position. One is for a business that provides a service; the other is for a business that manufactures goods.

- Complete the statement of financial position for both businesses by filling in the missing figures (?).
- Which business do you think is a manufacturing business and which is a service business? Explain your reasoning.
- Which business do you think is performing better? What else might you need to consider to make your decision? Justify your reasoning.

	Business A	Business B
Non-current assets	$	$
Machinery	100	?
IT	?	100
Premises	70	40
	200	**150**
Current assets		
Inventory	15	2
Trade receivables	?	4
Cash	5	20
	35	**?**
Current liabilities		
Trade payables	(40)	(20)
Net current assets	?	?
Total	?	?

Knowledge check

1. **Explain the following terms using examples:**
   - **a) non-current asset** **(2)**
   - **b) current asset.** **(2)**
2. **Using an example, explain the term current liability.** **(2)**

Total 6 marks

Interpreting a statement of financial position

Aims (5.4.2)

By the end of this section, you should:

- Be able to interpret a simple statement of financial position and make deductions from it, for example, how a business is financing its activities and what assets it owns, sale of inventories to raise finance.

Statements of financial position and how to interpret them

The statement of financial position should always balance, for the simple reason that nobody ever gets anything for free. For every asset, whether current or non-current, a business must show how it has paid for it.

How the statement of financial position is laid out

It is important to remember that the statement of financial position does not tell you how profitable a business is, just how much it is worth – or how much it owns.

Top Tip

You will not be expected to put together a statement of financial position at this level. You will, however, be expected to interpret and understand a completed statement of financial position.

Non-current assets always go at the top of the statement of financial position. These should be listed at their current value, not their original cost.

A Non-current assets	$
Factory	100 000
Machinery	100 000
	200 000
B Current assets	
Inventory	50 000
Cash in the bank	25 000
	75 000
C Current liabilities	
Trade payables	(25 000)
D Net current assets (B – C)	50 000
E Net assets (A + D)	**250 000**
Financed by:	
Non-current liabilities (mortgage)	100 000
Shareholders' funds	150 000
F Capital employed (= E)	**250 000**

This is arguably the most important part of the statement of financial position and shows a business's short-term liquidity. A business should always have more current assets to cover its current liabilities. This shows the business's working capital.

Net assets (the business's total assets minus all of its current liabilities) shows how much the business is worth. It is the total sum of all of the business's assets.

The capital employed represents how much money has been invested in the business to pay for all of its assets. This includes long-term liabilities and equity. This figure will always balance with the net assets.

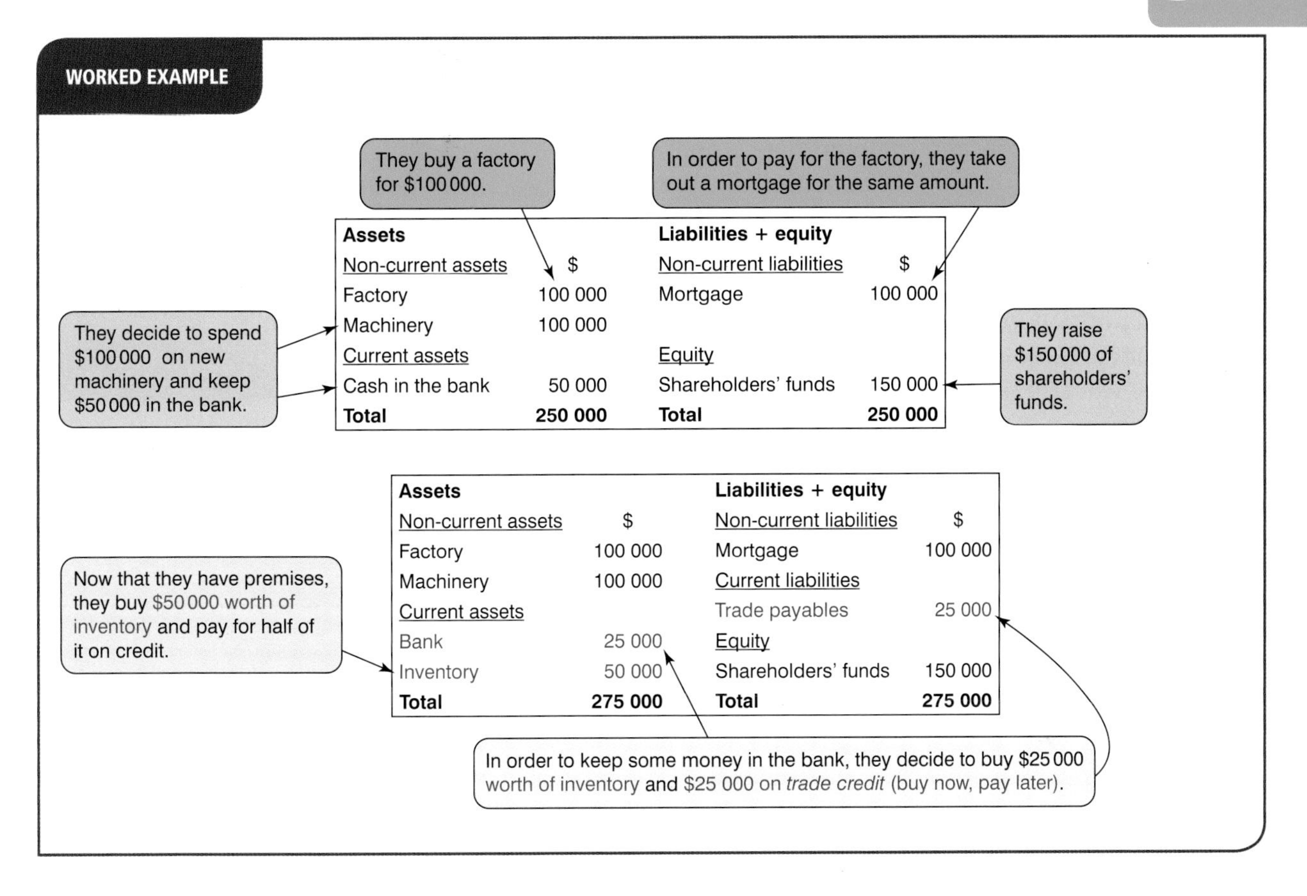

Assets		**Liabilities + equity**	
Non-current assets	$	Non-current liabilities	$
Factory	100 000	Mortgage	100 000
Machinery	100 000		
Current assets		Equity	
Cash in the bank	50 000	Shareholders' funds	150 000
Total	**250 000**	**Total**	**250 000**

Assets		**Liabilities + equity**	
Non-current assets	$	Non-current liabilities	$
Factory	100 000	Mortgage	100 000
Machinery	100 000	Current liabilities	
Current assets		Trade payables	25 000
Bank	25 000	Equity	
Inventory	50 000	Shareholders' funds	150 000
Total	**275 000**	**Total**	**275 000**

Capital employed

Capital is another word that accountants use for money. However, when using the term capital, they specifically mean large amounts of money. Capital employed is a figure that is calculated from the statement of financial position. It means how much money has been invested into a business and should include the total equity and the non-current liabilities.

△ The amount of money invested into a business is known as 'capital employed'.

CASE STUDY Enron investors tricked

In 2000, a USA energy and commodities company, Enron, reported revenues of over $100 billion. Over the next 16 years, Enron had grown to be the USA's seventh largest company, stretching across 40 different countries. However, they concealed massive debts from their statement of financial position in order to trick investors into parting with their money. Enron was eventually discovered and the company went bankrupt, causing a loss to shareholders of $74 billion.

Δ Protesters hold up an effigy (a model of a person) of Enron's chief executive officer (CEO), New York, 2002.

Application **Analysis**

Working in small groups or pairs, think of a business idea that you might like to start up. This can be as small or large an operation as you choose. Once you have your idea:

- List the assets that you think you might need for your business to operate and research the cost of these assets.
- Recommend a way to pay for these assets from a variety of current liabilities, non-current liabilities and equity.
- Compile a forecast statement of financial position based on your predictions. Try to use correct headings and lay the account out as shown in the example in this section.

Knowledge check

1. **Identify and explain two stakeholders that might be interested in a business's statement of financial position. (6)**
2. **Explain the difference between equity and non-current liabilities. (4)**
3. **Explain how a statement of financial position can show how a business has funded their assets. (3)**

Total 13 marks

Check your progress:

- ✓ I can explain the main elements of a statement of financial position, and give examples.
- ✓ I am able to interpret a simple statement of financial position and make deductions from it.

Analysis of accounts

Profitability and financial performance

Aims (5.5.1 and 5.5.3)

By the end of this section, you should:

- Understand the concept and importance of profitability.
- Understand how to interpret the financial performance of a business by calculating and analysing profitability ratios and liquidity ratios: gross profit margin, profit margin, return on capital, current ratio, acid test ratio.

How can we measure a business's performance?

You can measure a business's performance by analysing and interpreting the final accounts, the income statement and the statement of financial position. In order to see how well a business is doing, two methods of assessment can be used: **profitability** and liquidity.

- The profitability will show how much of the sales revenue the business turns into profit. You can do this by analysing the income statement.
- The liquidity will show how easily the business can pay off its short-term debts. This will give a good indication of its working capital or cash flow.

Δ Analysis of a business's accounts helps to measure performance.

The concept and importance of profitability

Profit is the measure often used to judge the success of a business or enterprise. Put simply, it is the money left when all costs are deducted from the revenue or sales of a business. However, its importance cannot be summarised so simply. Although a business can operate without making a profit for many years, profit is important to reward investors, for fund growth and to pay back borrowing. Profit is also important for securing longer-term investment, as investors will look for proven success and stability before parting with their money.

Measuring profitability: income statements

You can measure the profitability of a business using two simple formulas: the gross profit margin and the net profit margin. You can calculate these using figures from the income statement.

Gross profit margin

The gross profit margin is the percentage of sales that is turned into gross profit.

$$\frac{\text{Gross profit}}{\text{Sales revenue}} \times 100$$

Profit margin

The **profit margin** is the percentage of sales that is turned into profit. As this is the profit that a business can either keep (retain) or distribute to shareholders, it is a much better indication of how profitable the business has been.

$$\frac{\text{Profit}}{\text{Sales revenue}} \times 100$$

WORKED EXAMPLE

Summary of income statements for Buenos Aires Construction PLC ($ 000s)

	Year 1	Year 2
Sales revenue	1500	1000
Cost of sales	400	300
Gross profit	1100	700
Less expenses	900	550
Profit	200	150

From the income statement, you can see that the business made more profit in Year 1 than in Year 2. However, this does not mean that it was more profitable. In order to measure profitability, we need to turn the business's profit figures into a percentage of sales revenue:

	Year 1	Year 2
$\frac{\text{Gross profit}}{\text{Sales revenue}} \times 100$	$\frac{1100}{1500} \times 100 = 73\%$	$\frac{700}{1000} \times 100 = 70\%$

In Year 1 the business turned 73% of its sales into gross profit, or for every $1.00 sales it turned $0.73 into gross profit.

In Year 2 the business turned 70% of its sales into gross profit, or for every $1.00 sales it turned $0.70 into gross profit.

This would imply that Year 1 was more profitable for the business.

However, gross profit margin only shows the profit made on raw materials. The profit margin is a much better indication of profitability:

	Year 1	Year 2
$\frac{\text{Profit}}{\text{Sales revenue}} \times 100$	$\frac{200}{1500} \times 100 = 13\%$	$\frac{150}{1000} \times 100 = 15\%$

In Year 1 the business turned just 13% of sales revenue into profit, whereas in Year 2 it turned 15% into profit. This indicates that Year 2 was a more profitable year, despite the fact that the business made more profit in Year 1.

The business had a higher gross profit margin in Year 1, which implies that the business managed to reduce its expenses (overheads) in Year 2, helping it make more profit on each item sold.

Evaluation of profitability ratios

Turning the profit figures into a percentage of sales means that you can compare different businesses and year-on-year performance. The higher the percentage, the more profitable the business has been. Although the gross profit margin is important, the profit margin will interest shareholders more.

A figure on its own is of little use unless it can be compared against either another year or competitors.

Top Tip

When measuring profitability, for both the gross and profit margins, what you are actually calculating is a percentage: profitability = percentage.

Measuring liquidity: statement of financial position

WORKED EXAMPLE

Summary of statements of financial position for Buenos Aires Construction PLC ($ 000s)

	Year 1	Year 2
Non-current assets	1000	1200
Current assets		
Inventory	**400**	**100**
Trade receivables	100	200
Cash in the bank	200	250
	700	**550**

Current liabilities (trade payables)	**600**	**450**
Working capital	100	100
Net assets	**1100**	**1300**
Financed by:		
Bank loan	600	600
Shareholders' funds	400	450
Reserves	100	250
Capital employed	**1100**	**1300**

You can see that the working capital is the same for each year. This implies that the business's liquidity was no different in Year 1 and Year 2. By using a couple of liquidity ratios, we might be able to tell otherwise.

Top Tip

When analysing a statement of financial position, don't get bogged down with all the figures. The most important part to look at is the current assets and the current liabilities.

Current ratio

The current ratio is the ratio of the current assets to the current liabilities. It is always expressed as X:1.

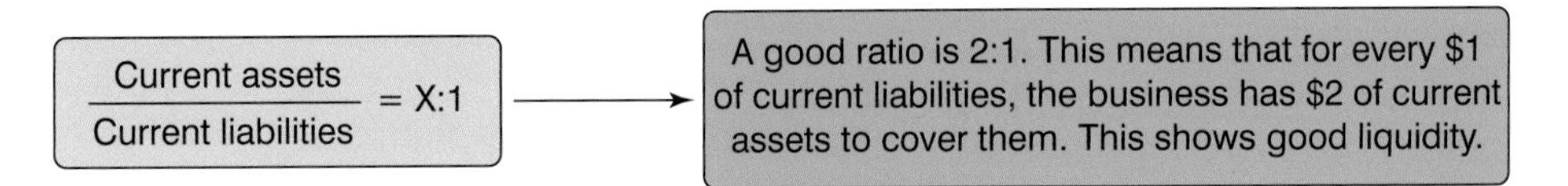

WORKED EXAMPLE

	Year 1	Year 2
$\dfrac{\text{Current assets}}{\text{Current liabilities}} = X{:}1$	$\dfrac{700}{600} = 1.17{:}1$	$\dfrac{550}{450} = 1.22{:}1$

Based on 2:1 as the benchmark (what the business is aiming for), both of these current ratios show that Buenos Aires Construction PLC has potential liquidity problems, as its cash flow is very tight. Year 2 was slightly better, as for every $1 of current liabilities the business had $1.22 of current assets to cover them, whereas in Year 1 it only had $1.17 of current assets to cover every $1 of short-term debt.

Acid test ratio

Like the current ratio, the acid test measures a business's liquidity, or ability to meet its short-term debt. However, the acid test is a more accurate indicator of liquidity as it removes inventory from the calculation, because there is no guarantee that a business will ever sell its inventory. You should use the acid test ratio when trying to assess a business's ability to pay its short-term debt:

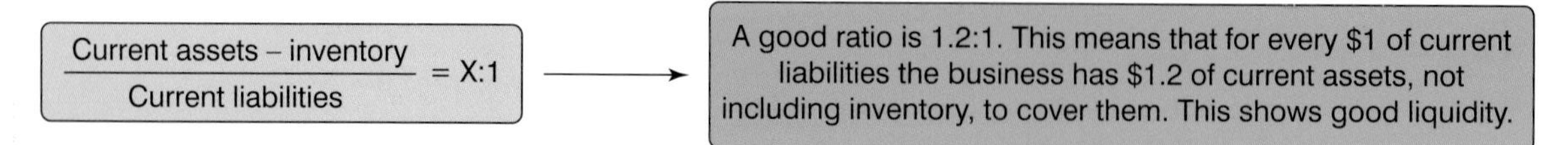

WORKED EXAMPLE

	Year 1	Year 2
$\dfrac{\text{Current assets} - \text{inventory}}{\text{Current liabilities}} = X{:}1$	$\dfrac{700 - 400}{600} = 0.5{:}1$	$\dfrac{550 - 100}{450} = 1{:}1$

In Year 1, the business had too much money tied up in inventory. This is risky, as there is no guarantee that it will sell the inventory. This means that in Year 1 it only had $0.50 of liquid assets to pay off every $1 of short-term liabilities.

In Year 2 its liquidity was much better. Looking at the statement of financial position, this is because the business had far less money tied up in inventory. In Year 2, for every $1 in short-term liabilities, it had $1 of liquid assets to cover them. Although 1.2:1 is the benchmark for good liquidity, 1:1 is much better than 0.5:1.

Evaluation of liquidity ratios

Although the current ratio is useful, the acid test is a much more accurate indicator of the liquidity of a business. Anything less than 1:1 suggests that the business has liquidity problems that need immediate attention.

However, it is important to look at the type of business in question. A supermarket is likely to have large amounts of inventory that will be sold, so it is of less concern. A fashion business that is coming to the end of a season with unsold inventory is in a far more worrying situation.

Δ When evaluating liquidity ratios, it is important that you consider the type of business in question.

Return on capital employed (ROCE)

The capital employed is the amount of money that has been invested into the business that includes both non-current liabilities and equity. The return (profit) on that capital employed is how much profit the business has made as a percentage of that capital employed. This ratio uses both the income statement and the statement of financial position.

WORKED EXAMPLE

	Year 1	**Year 2**
$\frac{\text{Profit}}{\text{Capital employed}} \times 100$	$\frac{200}{1100} \times 100 = 18\%$	$\frac{150}{1300} \times 100 = 12\%$

As with profitability ratios, the higher the percentage, the better. As the majority of capital employed has come from banks and shareholders, they will want to see that the business is using their money to good effect by turning it into profit.

Therefore, from the viewpoint of investors, Year 1 was the more successful year.

Overall evaluation of a business's performance

All of these ways of assessing businesses' performance are important. No single method is more important than another. However, a business can be profitable but go out of business if it has poor liquidity or takes on too much debt. So, if the acid test or current ratio highlights liquidity problems, this should be flagged up as a cause for concern.

CASE STUDY

Renewable energy returns look good

Potential shareholders are currently looking at investing in companies offering renewable energy sources such as DC21 Ltd in the UK, which installs wind turbines. This is because, once installed, the turbines have little or no running costs, so investors can expect a good return on their investment (capital employed).

Analysis Evaluation

Using a suitable internet search engine, research the accounts of three similar companies. These are normally included in the annual report for a particular company and are often found on their website.

- Once you have found each set of company accounts, analyse the company's financial performance by carrying out as many ratios (and profitability percentages) as you can.
- Choose one of the companies and write a report to be circulated to its shareholders, outlining its financial performance. The report should compare the company's performance with the other two businesses. Refer back to the sections on liquidity and income statement to help you advise the company on how it might improve its position.

Knowledge check

1 **Explain the following terms;**

a) profit margin **b) liquidity.** **(4)**

Imran Hussain is the financial director of a furniture manufacturer. Imran has the following information available to him:

- **revenue: $750 000**
- **gross profit: $300 000**
- **profit before tax: $100 000.**

2 **Calculate the following ratios using this information:**

a) gross profit margin **b) profit margin.** **(4)**

Explain what gross profit and profit margins will show Imran. **(4)**

3 **Imran has revealed that the capital employed into the business is $1.2m. He shows you the following extract from the statement of financial position:**

Current assets	$
Inventory	60 000
Trade receivables	30 000
Cash in bank	5000
Current liabilities	50 000

4 **Calculate the following two ratios, using the information from the table:**

a) current ratio **b) acid test.** **(4)**

Industry averages for the current ratio and acid test are:

- **current ratio 2:1**
- **acid test 1:1.**

5 **Explain whether Imran should be concerned about his business's liquidity.** **(6)**

Total 22 marks

Why and how accounts are used

Aims (5.5.4)

By the end of this section, you should:

- Understand the needs of different users of accounts and ratio analysis
- Be able to explain how users of accounts and ratio results might use information to help make business decisions, for example, whether to lend to or invest in the business.

Why use an income statement?

There are a number of stakeholders who have an interest in a company's income statement. This is why the company needs to publish its income statement so it is readily available.

We can see how different stakeholders will use the information provided in an income statement. Consider the example of Protea Furniture PLC, a home furniture producer based in South Africa.

Other companies' managers: Management from other companies might be interested in a competitor's financial performance. This might be to make decisions on their own product lines or as a measure of performance, to see how their profit levels compare.

Current shareholders: Current shareholders will want to see how much of the company's profit has been allocated to dividends. The more profit the business makes, the more likely it is to pay its shareholders a higher amount of dividends.

Year 1 income statement

	$ (000s)
Sales revenue	6500
Cost of sales	4500
Gross profit	2000
Overheads	1750
Profit	250
Taxation	50
Profit after tax	200
Dividend	25
Retained profit	175

Potential shareholders: Although potential shareholders will want to see that dividends are being paid, they will be more likely to want to invest in a company that is showing signs of growth, as it will be more profitable in the long term. Companies that have large amounts of retained profit are normally likely to be able to grow without the need for more borrowing.

Lenders: A bank might wish to see a company's income statement to ensure that the company can afford the finance cost (interest) and make the repayments on any future loans.

Government: Every year, a company's income statement is audited before it is published. This means that an independent group checks the company's accounts to make sure that the profit figures it publishes are accurate. Once the profit has been agreed, the government can see how much corporation tax the company is due to pay.

CASE STUDY Success leads to funding

In 2015 Michele Grosso set up DEMOCRANCE in the UAE, a platform designed to bring insurance to under-insured low-income earners in the Middle East. Initially Grosso used his own savings for the company, and borrowed money elsewhere rather than asking the bank for a loan. Now that the platform has demonstrated some successes, and looks like it could be profitable in the future, Grosso is able to start a round of early investment funding. Ensuring he kept clear accounts will have allowed him to do this.

Why use a statement of financial position?

The statement of financial position is quite a complicated document, so there are not many people who make use of what it shows. However, there is a small group of specialists who use the statement of financial position.

We can see how different stakeholders will use the information provided in a statement of financial position in the example from Protea Furniture plc.

Year 1 Statement of financial position	
Current assets	**$ (000s)**
Inventory	2000
Trade receivables	3000
Cash in the bank	2750
	Total = 7750
Non-current assets (Fixed assets)	10 000
Total assets	17 750
Current liablities	
Trade payables	3000
Working capital	3000
	Total = 6000
Long-term liabilities	
Long-term loan	8000
Share capital	2000
Reserves	1750
	Total = 11 750
Total liabilities (Capital employed)	17 750

Auditors: Auditors will look at a business's statement of financial position, to ensure that it has not exaggerated the value of its assets to try to attract investors.

Lenders: Banks are possibly the organisation that will have the most interest in an organisation's statement of financial position. They will want to see that the business has assets that it can use as security (something that a bank can take if repayments are not made) for any potential loans. In addition, they will want to see where its previous capital has come from. A business with high levels of borrowing is far less likely to be granted a new loan.

Trade payables: Trade payables might want to view a statement of financial position, to ensure that the business has enough cash or working capital to pay them back if they agree to allow them a credit period.

Investors: Anyone wishing to invest in the business will want to see what assets the business already has. A business with a lot of assets is generally a far more attractive investment than one that has few assets.

Using ratios to make decisions

By analysing financial statements, users of accounts can make a more informed (well-supported) opinion on the business's performance and can then make more informed decisions. Look at the example for Protea Furniture PLC here.

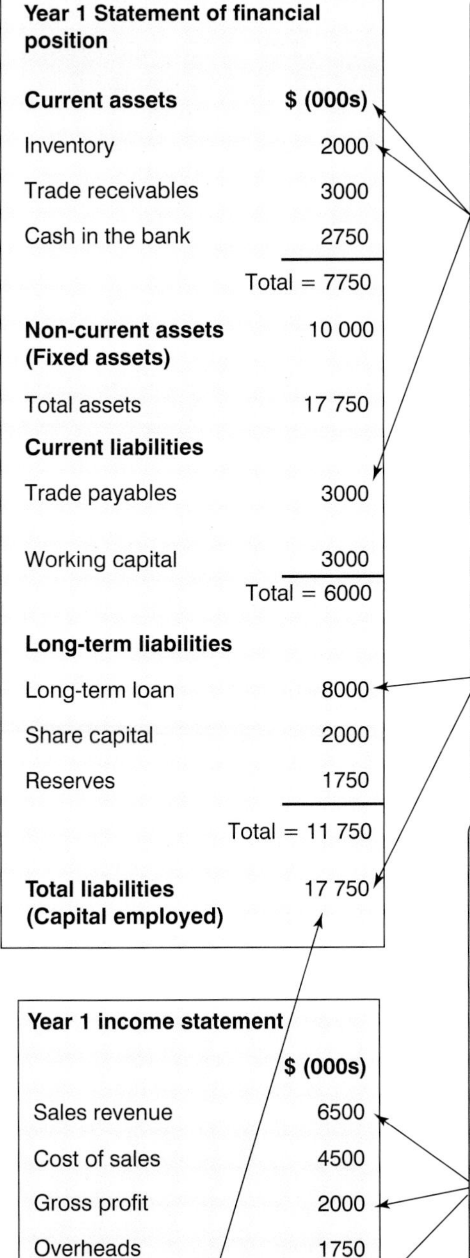

Year 1 Statement of financial position

Current assets	**$ (000s)**
Inventory	2000
Trade receivables	3000
Cash in the bank	2750
	Total = 7750
Non-current assets (Fixed assets)	10 000
Total assets	17 750
Current liabilities	
Trade payables	3000
Working capital	3000
	Total = 6000
Long-term liabilities	
Long-term loan	8000
Share capital	2000
Reserves	1750
	Total = 11 750
Total liabilities (Capital employed)	17 750

Year 1 income statement

	$ (000s)
Sales revenue	6500
Cost of sales	4500
Gross profit	2000
Overheads	1750
Profit	250

The current ratio and acid test

$$\text{Current ratio} = \frac{7\,750}{6\,000} = 1.2{:}1$$

$$\text{Acid test ratio} = \frac{7\,750 - 2\,750}{6\,000} = 0.83{:}1$$

Users' interpretation
Trade payables would be especially interested in these ratios, as they show Protea Furniture's ability to pay its existing trade payables. As the acid test shows that it only has $0.83 of liquid assets (not including inventory) to pay every $1 of trade payables, they would be unlikely to want to offer Protea Furniture any more goods on credit, as there is a risk the company might not be able to pay them back.

Users' interpretation
Banks would be interested to view Protea's statement of financial position, as it will show them how it has paid for its assets. Looking at the capital employed figure, it's clear that it has already taken out a loan for $8000. This could mean that banks are unwilling to lend more.

The gross and profit margins

Gross margin: $\frac{2000}{6500} \times 100 = 31\%$

Net margin: $\frac{250}{6500} \times 100 = 4\%$

Users' interpretation
Other companies' managers would be interested to view these figures, as they show how Protea Furniture's performance compares to their own. If Protea's margins are better, they can then investigate their own business to find out why. Comparing their margins with Protea's will help managers of other businesses to make a judgement on how well they have performed over the same period of time.

Return on capital employed

$$\frac{250}{11\,750} \times 100 = 2.13\%$$

Shareholders and potential investors would be interested in the return on capital employed, as it shows how much of their investment is being turned into profit. The figure of 2.13% is very low, meaning prospective investors are likely to look elsewhere for a more profitable investment.

Analysis **Evaluation**

You are a financial advisor and need to advise your client on what company to invest in. Your client is interested in three businesses in the construction market that are listed on Brazil's Stock Exchange (BM&FBOVESPA). Your client is expecting to keep the shares for several years.

Extracts from income statement, R$ (000s)

	Amadi Construction	ASM Buildings	Palmas & Balsas
Sales revenue	7500	9000	6000
Profit	3500	3000	3500
Dividends	3000	2000	500
Retained profit	500	1000	3000

Extracts from the statements of financial position, R$ (000s)

	Amadi Construction	ASM Buildings	Palmas & Balsas
Net assets	**10000**	**12000**	**15000**
Financed by:			
Share capital	4000	1500	7500
Loans	5000	10 000	2500
Reserves	1000	500	5000
Capital employed	**10000**	**12000**	**15000**

Prepare a presentation to deliver to your client, including:

- what a shareholder looking for a long-term investment wants
- any relevant financial ratios that you consider to be important for shareholders, and what they mean
- your choice of company, with full justification.

Knowledge check

1. **Identify and explain two stakeholders who might be interested in a business's income statement. (6)**
2. **Explain why potential shareholders might be interested in a business's profit margin. (2)**
3. **Explain how other businesses might make use of a competitor's gross profit margin. (2)**
4. **Explain how a bank might use a business's statement of financial position when deciding whether to lend the business money. (4)**

Total 14 marks

Check your progress:

- ✓ I can outline the concepts and importance of profitability and liquidity.
- ✓ I can explain the key ratios for profitability and liquidity.
- ✓ I can interpret and analyse the financial performance of a business by calculating profitability and liquidity ratios.
- ✓ I can explain why and how accounts are used by different stakeholders.
- ✓ I understand why and how account users might use information to help make decisions.

Exam-style questions: short answer and data response

1. Agrimario is a large Brazilian mining company. Figures 1 and 2 show their key financial data for the last year.

Δ Figure 1: Proportion of sales from import and export

Gross profit	$1.2m
Profit	$0.6m
Return on capital employed	20%

Δ Figure 2: Selected data from income statement and statement of financial position

a) **Calculate** the value of sales received from imports last year. (2)

b) **Define** the term return on capital employed. (2)

c) **Outline** the points of view of two stakeholders when considering Agrimario's return on capital employed. (4)

d) **Explain** whether you think shareholders will be happy with the profit margin of the business. (6)

e) **Explain** two ways in which Agrimario could improve their profit. (6)

2. Look at the following extract from Agrimario's statement of financial position for the last year (Figure 3).

Current assets	**$ (000s)**
Inventory	4500
Trade receivables	1000
Cash	30
Total:	**5530**
Current liabilities	**$ (000s)**
Trade payables	2500
Total:	**2500**

Δ Figure 3: Extract from Agrimario's statement of financial position

Agrimario's finance director is concerned about the business's liquidity.

a) **Define** the term current liability. (2)

b) **Define** the term liquidity. (2)

c) **Explain** two benefits Agrimario could gain from cash flow forecasting. (4)

d) Do you think the finance director is right to be concerned about Agrimario's liquidity? **Justify** your answer. (6)

e) **Outline** three ways in which Agrimario could improve their liquidity. (6)

3. a) Identify two sources of finance. (2)

b) **Define** the term dividend. (2)

c) **Explain** two reasons why a business such as Agrimario might need finance. (4)

d) **Explain** three benefits of Agrimario leasing new equipment. (6)

e) Agrimario's finance director thinks it's important for the company to hold a large amount of inventory and very little cash. Do you agree? **Justify** your answer. (6)

Note: The exam-style questions, answers and commentary in this book were written by the author; in examination the number of marks awarded to questions like these may be different.

Exam-style questions based on case studies

Santos Deporta Ltd

Santos Deporta Ltd (SDL) is a family-owned chain of sport retailers that has been operating for 25 years. For the first 15 years of trading, SDL was very successful in gaining a competitive market share. It established a brand around quality with average selling prices reflecting this quality image.

Over the past 10 years, SDL's market share has fallen significantly. This is because of increased competition from a number of national chains and the growth of online retailers selling similar products at a far cheaper price. Currently SDL only stocks its own brand, which is manufactured by a local supplier who has helped SDL establish its quality image.

Extracts taken from SDL's last two annual reports are given below.

Appendix 1: Extract from SDL's income statement for Year 1 and Year 2

Income statement	**% (000s)**	
	Year 1	**Year 2**
Revenue	450	400
Cost of sales	320	310
Gross profit	130	90
Expenses	100	80
Profit before tax	30	10

Appendix 2: Extract from SDL's statement of financial position for Year 1 and Year 2

Statement of financial position	**% (000s)**	
	Year 1	**Year 2**
Non-current assets	1000	1300
Current assets	320	550
Current liabilities	300	600
Working capital	20	(50)
Total assets	**1020**	**1250**
Financed by:		
Non-current liabilities	800	800
Reserves	150	160
Shareholders' funds	70	290
Capital employed	**1020**	**1250**

Carlos Santos, the current managing director and major shareholder, is concerned about the financial performance of the business, even though its assets have grown over the year. The company has recently refurbished (renovated) its top performing stores and he is concerned that SDL's falling revenue and its increasing amount of short-term debt is becoming a problem.

1. a) In Year 1, there was a drop in SDL's working capital. With reference to Appendix 2, **explain** two problems with having poor working capital. (8)

   b) Carlos believes that a drop in working capital is a bigger problem than the drop in profit. Do you agree with Carlos? **Justify** your answer. (12)

2. Carlos is considering refurbishing more stores by using a bank loan. The bank has asked to see the business's final accounts.

   a) **Identify** two reasons why the bank would want to see SDL's final accounts before deciding whether to lend the company any money. (8)

   b) Carlos has decided to apply for a bank loan of $1 000 000 to pay for the refurbishment. With reference to the appendices, **justify** whether you think the bank should lend SDL the money. (12)

3. a) **Explain** two features on SDL's statement of financial position and income statement that might interest potential investors. (8)

   b) Carlos believes that SDL's important stakeholders would find little interest in viewing the statement of financial position and income statement. Do you agree with Carlos's view? **Justify** your answer. (12)

4. a) **Explain** two reasons why it is important for a business such as SDL to make a profit. (8)

   b) With reference to Appendix 1, **outline** three decisions that would help SDL to improve its profits. (12)

Note: The exam-style questions, answers and commentary in this book were written by the author; in examination the number of marks awarded to questions like these may be different.

Exam-style questions based on case studies

The Crown Place Hotel

The Crown Place Hotel Ltd is a chain of hotels in the Sharm El Sheikh region of Egypt. Set up 10 years ago when tourism in the area started to boom, The Crown Place Hotel Ltd has been steadily profitable each year.

	Year 1	Year 2
Profit margin	12%	12.5%
Return on capital employed	16%	20%
Current ratio	1.1:1	0.8:1

Appendix 1: Key financial ratios for past two years

However, although the hotel chain is profitable, the financial director, Elliot Brazier, is concerned with the hotel chain's cash flow position, as illustrated in Appendix 2.

	All figures in $					
	May	**June**	**July**	**Aug**	**Sept**	**Oct**
Income						
Cash sales	5000	6000	14000	22000	16000	7000
Credit sales	2000	3000	5000	6000	4000	2000
Total inflow	7000	9000	19000	28000	20000	9000
Outflows						
Mortgage	10000	10000	10000	10000	10000	10000
Wages	7000	7000	7000	7000	7000	7000
Inventory	2000	2000	2000	2000	2000	2000
Electricity		1500			1500	
Marketing			3000	3000		
Total outflow	19000	20500	22000	22000	20500	19000
Net cash flow	−12000	−11500	−3000	6000	−500	−10000
Opening balance	45000	33000	21500	18500	24500	24000
Closing balance	33000	21500	18500	24500	24000	14000

Appendix 2: Cash flow forecast for May to October, Year 2

Elliot realises that most sales are made in July and August and he wishes to make changes to help improve the company's cash flow. He has changed the marketing for the hotel chain and the way its manages its employees throughout the year.

One way he has already considered is to open a new hotel, which would cost $200000. Given the current cash flow situation, he is unsure how to pay for the hotel.

1. a) **Explain** two suitable sources of finance to pay for the proposed new hotel. (8)

   b) Do you think opening a new hotel is the most effective way to improve cash flow? **Justify** your answer. (12)

2. Shareholders are users of a business's financial information.

   a) With reference to Appendix 1, **explain** two ways they might use a business's income statement. (8)

   b) For Year 2, the finance director has set an objective of achieving a 14% profit margin. **Outline** three methods that will allow The Crown Place Hotel Ltd to achieve this. (12)

3. a) **Explain** two limitations when preparing a cash flow forecast. (8)

   b) Financial statements, such as the income statement, statement of financial position and cash flow forecast, are very important to a business's success. Which of these three types of financial statement is the most important when managing a successful business? **Justify** your answer with reference to the benefits of each type of financial statement. (12)

4. a) **Explain** two differences between profit and cash. (8)

   b) Would The Crown Place Hotel Ltd's important stakeholders view the business as a success? **Justify** your answer. (12)

Note: The exam-style questions, answers and commentary in this book were written by the author; in examination the number of marks awarded to questions like these may be different.

Past Paper Questions

Paper 1

Section 5

Muammar sells boxes of spices to markets. Workers in Muammar's business are paid on a piece rate basis. Table 1 gives financial details of the business in 2012.

Fixed costs per month	$10 000
Employee wages	$2 per box
Raw materials	$3 per box
Marketing costs	$1 per box
Selling price	$8 per box
Sales per month [average]	9000 boxes

△ Table 1

a) Identify two examples of fixed costs for Muammar's business.

Example 1: ________________________________

Example 2: ________________________________ (2)

b) Identify two reasons why sales may vary from month to month.

Reason 1: ________________________________

____ (2)

Reason 2: ________________________________

____ (2)

c) Calculate the annual profit that Muammar made in 2012.

____

____

____

____

____

____

____

____ (4)

Cambridge International IGCSE Business Studies 0450 Paper 11, Q2 Nov 2013

Paper 2

Section 5

The following case study is taken from past papers created by Cambridge Assessment International Education. We have only provided extracts of this case study, and it does not reflect the full case study that you may be provided with in your examination.

Ted's Tools (TT)

TT is a chain of shops which sell tools such as hammers, screwdrivers, electric drills and saws. The business was started 20 years ago as a partnership between 2 friends, Ted and Mustafa.

TT has 10 shops. There are 2 shops in each main city in country A. The business has grown by reinvesting profits and opening a new shop every 2 years. Each shop employs a shop manager and 5 shop assistants. The shops open 10 hours a day for 6 days a week.

Most of TT's customers are people who are building or repairing their own houses. The tools and equipment TT sells are cheap but low quality. As a result of this, few building firms and construction companies buy from TT. Most building firms only buy high quality tools and equipment that will last a long time.

Appendix 1

Competitor's Advertisement – Ed's Equipment

Tools and equipment for home and business use – we sell or rent!

Tired of buying tools that you only use a few times? Tired of buying tools which break after using them a few times? Then here is the answer.... For all your needs when building or repairing your house come to **Ed's Equipment**.

- Rent the tools you need for half the cost of buying them.
- All high quality tools as used by construction companies.
- Tools are reliable and high quality.
- Trade credit is available to business customers.
- Large range of tools in our big shop.

Visit us at our shop on Main Road, New City, 3210997.
Telephone: 377228665

Appendix 2

Cash flow forecast for TT ($000s) for the second half of 2013

	July	August	September	October	November	December
Opening bank balance	1000	1100	1650	1550	1350	y
Cash inflows						
Cash sales	1000	1100	400	300	300	500
Credit sales	100	100	100	100	100	100
Total cash inflows	1100	1200	500	400	400	600
Cash outflows						
Stock	600	250	200	200	300	500
Wages	100	100	100	100	100	100
Overheads	300	300	300	300	300	300
Total cash ouflows	1000	650	600	600	700	900
Net cash flow	100	550	x	(200)	(300)	(300)
Closing bank balance	w	1650	1550	1350	1050	z

Figures in brackets are negative

1 Ted and Mustafa want to increase the sales revenue from TT shops. There are three options listed below. Consider the advantages and disadvantages of each of these options and recommend which option you think Ted and Mustafa should choose. **Justify** your answer. (12)

i) Rent tools to customers instead of selling the tools

ii) Sell high quality tools to construction businesses

iii) Start to also sell paint and decorating equipment in the shops

Recommendation

2 Refer to the cash flow forecast in Appendix 2.

i) Calculate the values of **w**, **x**, **y** and **z** and write your answers below. (4)

ii) Comment on two ways the cash flow position could be improved. Recommend the best way for Ted and Mustafa to improve the cash flow over the next 6 months. **Justify** your answer. (8)

Cambridge International IGCSE Business Studies 0450 Paper 21, Q2b & Q3b June 2013

Skills Builder

AO1: Knowledge

With finance questions, avoid using the word 'money'. You should always be able to use the correct terminology, such as revenue, cash flow (working capital), liquidity, capital or profit.

AO2: Application

Application means using the case study, not just the text and data from the case study but also the context (the setting for the case study). In addition, you might want to consider the following:

- What type of industry is the business in?
- What type of legal ownership does it have?
- Can you use any data from the case study to help justify your answers?

AO3: Analysis

To form a recommendation properly or provide a judgement you will need to **analyse** the information you have been given. Do this by developing your points and manipulating the data to provide information. If you can, work out some of the financial performance ratios to help you **analyse**. For example:

- profit margin
- return on capital employed
- current ratio
- acid test.

To gain the highest grades, you need to know how to calculate these and explain what they mean. Use paragraphs to form your analysis and remember to link your points back to how they answer the question.

AO4: Evaluation

Evaluation requires you to give a judgement. This means making a decision after you have considered all the possible options.

- If you have used any data to explain your choice, include this as a way of justifying your decision.
- Link your choice back to the type of business in the case study. What would be most suitable for this business?

As with all finance questions, **use the data.** Don't be afraid of maths.

There are daily reports about the state of the economy in most newspapers. The reason for this intense (concentrated) media coverage is the impact the economy has on business growth, and in turn the importance of business growth on unemployment and consumer spending – things that affect us all.

In this section, you will learn:

- about the main stages of the business cycle and the impact this has on employment, inflation and gross domestic product (GDP)
- how government control of taxation, spending and interest rates can affect business activity
- how companies manage ethical concerns and environmental pressures
- how environmental concerns and ethical issues represent both opportunities and constraints for businesses
- how and why businesses might respond to environmental pressures and opportunities
- about the importance of globalisation, and the opportunities and benefits it brings to businesses
- about the reasons for the importance and growth of multinational companies (MNCs)
- about the impact of exchange rate changes and the effect they can have on businesses as importers and exporters of products.

SKILLS BUILDER

Good progress

Knowledge: You demonstrate knowledge of different external influences and a sound ability to define the concepts.

Application: You apply knowledge of external influences to different business contexts, using terms, concepts, theories and methods appropriately to address problems and issues.

Analysis: You develop the consequences of the points that you have mentioned for the type of business in question.

Evaluation: You make judgements and recommendations when they are required.

Excellent progress

Knowledge: You define and identify all key terms relating to external influences, using this terminology accurately and appropriately.

Application: You apply detailed knowledge of relevant external influences to a given business situation and form suitable conclusions.

Analysis: You analyse how different external influences affect businesses and make judgements about the extent to which external influences affect a business.

Evaluation: You evaluate the strategies a business might use to manage external influences, and recommend which strategies might be most relevant to a particular firm.

SECTION CONTENTS:

6 External influences on business activity

Starting points

The government spends money generated from taxation on various services within the country. Working on your own, or in pairs, create a list for:

- the ways in which the government raises funds from taxation, such as income tax
- the areas in which the government spends money – for example, education.

Economic issues

Business cycle

Aims (6.1.1)

By the end of this section, you should:

- Understand the main stages of the business cycle, for example, growth, boom, recession, slump
- Understand the impact on businesses of changes in employment levels, inflation and gross domestic product (GDP).

The stages of the business cycle

Economies do not always grow steadily. Economic growth tends to move up and down in semi-regular patterns, as this graph of GDP growth for Brazil shows:

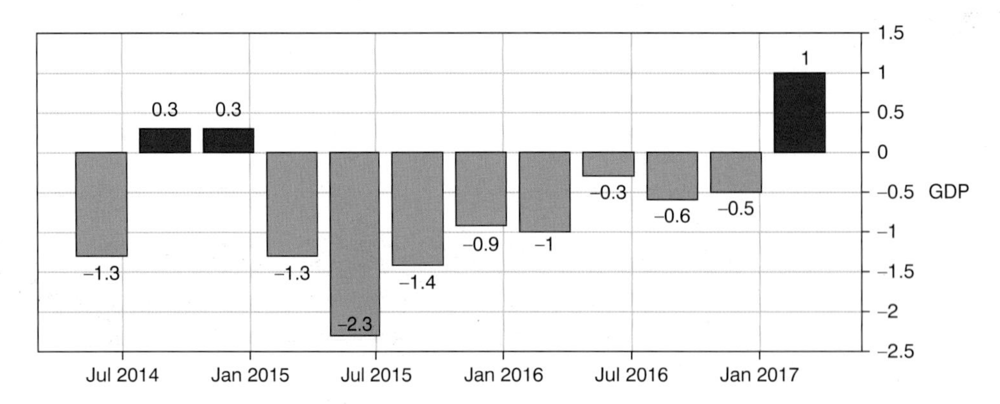

△ GDP Growth for Brazil (1960–2017)
Source: Trading Economics

The way in which economic growth fluctuates (varies) over time is known as the **business cycle** (or **trade cycle**). These fluctuations (variations), while not occurring at regular time intervals or for defined time periods, do display a pattern. These patterns can be simplified as growth (recovery), boom, recession and slump.

Key Term

Business cycle (or trade cycle): the cyclical movement of economic growth characterised by recovery, boom, recession, slump.

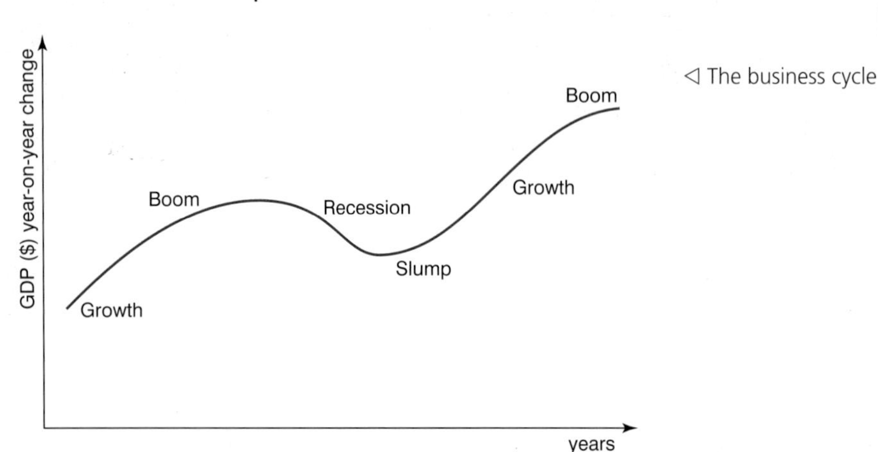

◁ The business cycle

Growth

During economic growth, the following economic conditions may exist:

- increasing sales
- increases in employment
- small increases in production
- businesses begin to consider investment
- growing business confidence, although still some uncertainty.

Business uncertainty can prolong the period of **recovery** and add to economic worries. Businesses may be reluctant to invest in new products/assets or to employ new employees if the economic outlook is uncertain.

Boom

Eventually, a recovery may result in an economic **boom**. This is a period of significant economic growth characterised by:

- high capacity utilisation (full use of business facilities)
- low **unemployment**
- high levels of demand (with increasing prices), possibly leading to **inflation**
- wage increases due to labour shortages
- significant business investment and expansion
- an increase in new business start-ups
- high confidence.

Key Term

Inflation: a general rise in prices over time.

A disadvantage of booms is overconfidence (too much confidence) and the potential for a subsequent downswing (fall) in economic growth. During booms, businesses often overextend themselves, borrowing heavily to finance growth and perhaps taking unnecessary risks. Any change in economic conditions can have a significant impact on such firms. Investors will be quick to demand money back and suppliers are likely to offer less favourable credit terms (see 5.1 Business finance: needs and sources). It is possible for a small fall in consumer and business confidence to quickly grow into a **recession**, as businesses are suddenly faced with a very different economic situation than that which they had planned for (as was the case during the global banking crisis in 2008–09).

CASE STUDY **Impact of change**

During the 2008–09 recession, all business sectors and sizes were negatively impacted in the UK. Transport firms Honda and British Airways laid off employees, oil firm Shell delayed many new projects and over 208 000 small businesses closed.

Recession

An economy is officially considered to be in recession after two consecutive (continuous) quarters of falling GDP. (A quarter is three months, so an economy will be in recession after six months of falling GDP.) In a recession, the following economic conditions may exist:

- falling demand
- businesses will cut output
- unemployment will rise
- businesses will cut back on investment
- business closures will increase
- there will be a fall in business confidence.

Business responses to recession

In order to survive a recession, a business may:

Stimulate demand	Minimise costs	Production	Investment
Cut prices Increase promotion Introduce special offers	Find cheaper raw materials Reduce employee levels Introduce flexible working practices Increase productivity Stop unnecessary expenditure Stop hiring new employees	Reduce spare capacity (sell assets) Cancel overtime/ reduce the working week Find cheaper production methods	Cancel planned investment

Slump/downturn

Economic **slumps** or **downturns** are characterised by:

- falling demand
- low production
- little, if any, business investment
- high unemployment
- high number of business closures
- low business confidence.

A slump represents the lowest point of economic activity before recovery begins.

The impact of the business cycle on business

The extent to which economic growth affects any one business depends very much on the nature of the business. Different businesses are affected in different ways at different stages of the business cycle. Some of the possible impacts are listed in the following table:

Stage of business cycle	Negative impacts	Positive impacts
Recession	✘ Producers of luxury goods may find that demand falls	✓ Accounting firms (dealing with bankruptcy), businesses selling cheaper goods and second hand stores may benefit from an increase in demand
Slump/ downturn	✘ Construction businesses may suffer as demand for new buildings falls	✓ Companies selling essential goods, such as pharmaceutical firms, are likely to be relatively unaffected
Recovery	✘ Discount retailers may experience a fall in demand	✓ Demand for a wide range of products will be high ✓ Recruitment agencies may see an increase in demand for temporary employees as businesses seek cautiously to increase production
Boom	✘ Businesses that rely on a small pool of skilled labour may find it difficult and expensive to recruit	✓ Luxury goods producers enjoy healthy sales

Impact of changes in business

Changes in employment levels

If sales fall, businesses may reduce the workforce to help reduce their overall costs. This increases the supply of labour for businesses to choose from if they need to fill a vacancy, which can mean that businesses recruit better candidates because of the increase in labour supply. If the economy is in a boom phase, a business may find it very difficult to recruit, as unemployment will be very low, with relatively fewer employees out of work. Businesses may react by increasing wages or offering additional benefits for their employees.

Changes in inflation

If inflation increases, this can mean that suppliers' prices to businesses also increase. This may mean the costs for businesses increase, employees demand higher wages and a new set of prices needs to be designed. For businesses that have a price list, such as a restaurant, this can be quite an expensive change to make, as they need to reprint all their menus. Low inflation means that businesses will see costs remain stable, with wages also staying low, as employees do not need additional pay to compensate for price increases.

Changes in gross domestic product (GDP)

If the GDP of a country is decreasing, this can indicate that overall spending on goods and services will decrease for businesses. The reduction in consumer spending can mean businesses will have to increase promotion, reduce prices or think about how they can continue to attract customers. If GDP increases, businesses may see sales increase and larger profits follow.

How government control over the economy affects business activity and how businesses may respond

Aims (6.1.2)
By the end of this section, you should:

- Be able to identify government economic objectives, for example, increasing gross domestic product (GDP)
- Understand the impact of changes in taxes and government spending
- Understand the impact of changes in interest rates.

Government economic objectives

When talking about the economy we are, in simple terms, referring to the financial health of a country – how much money the country has, how much money its people have, and how much money a government has to invest, for example, in education, roads, railways and hospitals.

The governments of most countries have four main economic objectives:

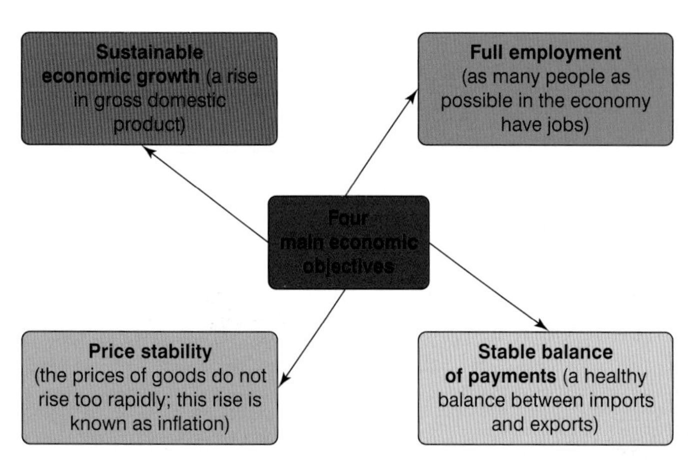

The most important of these objectives is sustainable (long-lasting) economic growth.

Economic growth

Central to a government's control of the economy is a desire for steady and predictable growth. Too little growth and the country will struggle with low demand, unemployment and a low or static (not improving) standard of living. Too much growth is like running before you can walk: the growth rarely proves to be sustainable and the economy quickly slows down again (often causing many business **bankruptcies** in the process).

Key Term

Bankruptcy: the legal process by which a company (or, in the case of unlimited firms, an individual) is declared financially unable to continue with the business.

The diagram illustrates these different rates of growth:

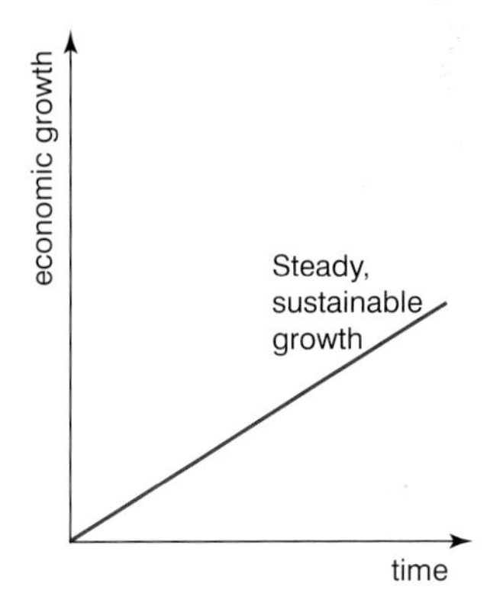

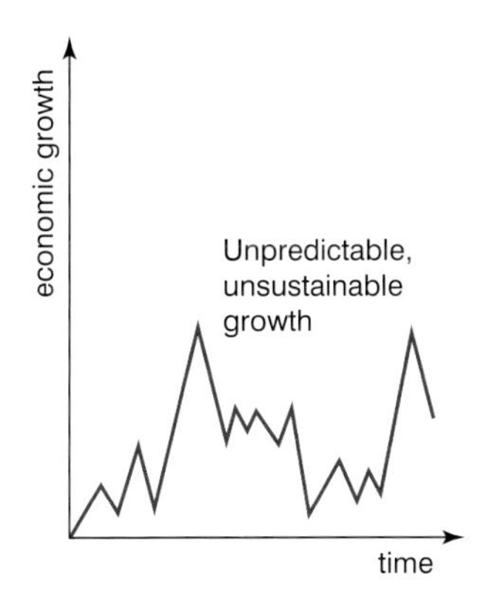

Economic growth is an important government objective, because with it comes improvement in standards of living, employment opportunities and prosperity (wealth). For businesses, economic growth means the potential for improved sales, expansion and more profit.

Factors affecting economic growth

With sustainable economic growth as the primary aim of most governments, the following factors affect the ability of a country to meet that objective:

- **Labour.** The larger the working population of a country, the greater the potential for growth. The more skilled employees a country has, the greater the potential for businesses to succeed and the economy to grow. The UK, for example, is well known for its expertise in the financial/banking sectors, so banking services are an important part of the UK's economy.
- **Natural resources.** The more natural resources a country has, the greater its ability to sell these resources to other countries. This fuels economic growth. Australia, for example, has enjoyed strong growth in recent years by exporting large quantities of iron ore and coal.
- **International trade.** If a country can **export** (sell to other countries) more goods than it **imports** (buys from other countries), its economy will grow. Japan, for example, is a country known for its technology products and exports more goods than it imports.
- **Technology.** New technologies can increase a business's ability to produce goods (perhaps lowering costs or increasing productivity). Improved telecommunications has, for example, contributed significantly to India's economic

△ Australia has large quantities of natural resources. The country has enjoyed strong economic growth by exporting these resources.

growth. New technology also offers new ways of making profit (recent growth, for example, in the sale of hybrid cars).

- **Government impact.** Through taxation, government spending and business regulation, governments attempt to control the rate at which an economy grows or shrinks. Indonesia, despite the global economic slowdown, is able to use **government spending** (the building of roads, railways, schools and hospitals, and so on) as one way of helping its economy to enjoy continued growth of 5% and above.
- **Confidence.** The confidence a business has in the future of the economy has a significant impact on its willingness to invest. If a business is confident about the future (predicting good future sales), it is more likely to invest in expansion or new products. This investment, in turn, helps the economy as a whole to grow. The reverse is also true: a lack of confidence reduces willingness to invest and causes a reduction in economic growth. Since the UK voted to leave the European Union in 2016, business confidence in investing or expanding has been reduced. Uncertain about the future, firms have delayed new projects, stopped hiring new employees and are looking at alternative locations for their offices.

Δ Many multinational companies have located customer-support call centres in India to benefit from India's low labour costs and good English language skills.

Measuring economic growth

In order to measure economic growth, a country's gross domestic product (GDP) is used. GDP is a measure of the value of all goods and services produced by an economy over a certain period. An increase in GDP represents an increase in economic activity and thus economic growth.

Economic growth can be measured relative to the performance of other countries, as the graph indicates:

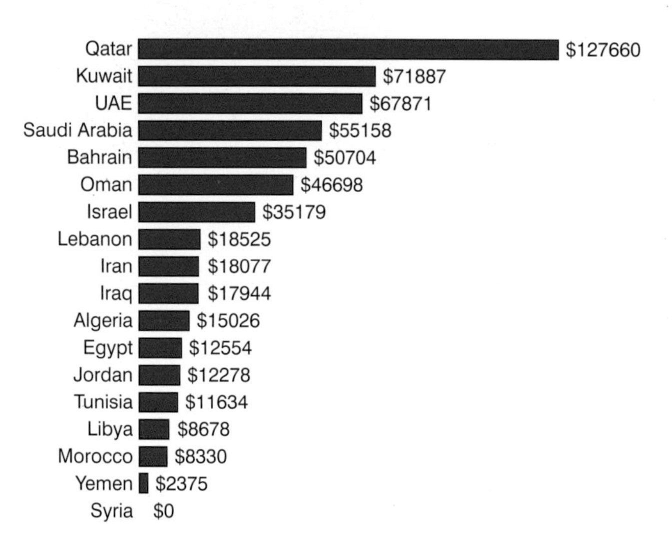

Source: IMF

◁ Gross domestic product per capita (GDP) is national economic output divided by the population, expressed in US dollars per person.

Analysis

With a partner, investigate the GDP of your own country. Consider the following questions:

- Has GDP grown or fallen in recent years?
- If it has fallen, has growth slowed (positive GDP but a lower figure than previous years) or has the economy actually shrunk (negative GDP figures)?
- What is the main contributor to the GDP of the country?
- How does the rate of GDP compare with neighbouring countries or with competing countries?

Extension: Consider how the government of the country has attempted to control economic growth (GDP). What policies have they used? Have these policies been successful?

Present your findings as a report for a business newspaper.

The consequences of economic growth

While overall economic growth leads to an improvement in living standards, employment opportunities and prosperity (wealth), it does have a downside. In countries with rapid economic growth, pollution, overcrowding and environmental damage are often very high (see 6.2 Environmental and ethical issues).

Δ India: rapid economic growth at the expense of overcrowding?

Economic growth also has a negative effect on the cost of labour. In a growing economy, unemployment is likely to be low and labour therefore scarce and expensive. Businesses may have to offer very generous salary and benefit packages to attract or retain employees, thus increasing costs.

Economic growth can also lead to business inefficiency. When demand is growing and profits are high, there may be little incentive (need) to control costs. Management attention is often focused on external growth (making more sales) rather than internal efficiency (keeping costs down). Businesses that can remain efficient during times of economic growth (keeping costs low and growing sales) will enjoy long-term success. These companies are often 'fitter' and 'leaner' and therefore much better prepared to cope with changeable economic conditions.

How changes in interest rates can affect business activity

In order to meet their objective of steady, sustainable growth, governments can use a variety of economic tools. The first of those tools is the **interest rate**.

The interest rate is essentially the price of borrowing money or the return for depositing (putting) money in a bank. The **central bank** (in essence, the government's bank) or the government itself can use interest rates to control the price

Key Term

Interest rate: the price of borrowed money – either the cost of lending money or the rate of return for depositing money in a bank.

of borrowing money and therefore control how much money people and businesses spend or save.

Interest rates affect economic growth (and therefore can help a government to meet its objectives) in two main ways:

Interest rate rise	Interest rate fall
If interest rates are high, it is more expensive for businesses and consumers to borrow money. High interest rates also encourage people to save money. Both of these factors can reduce business and consumer spending and will therefore slow the economy down.	If interest rates are low, it is cheaper for businesses and consumers to borrow money. Low interest rates also encourage people to spend rather than save. Both of these factors can increase business and consumer spending and will therefore help the economy to grow.

WORKED EXAMPLE

The data here show the impact of a rise in the interest rate (known as the **base rate**) from 0.5% to 1.25% and 2.75% on home loan (mortgage) repayments.

Mortgage amount ($)	Current monthly payment ($)	New monthly payment ($) with base rate at 1.25%	New monthly payment ($) with base rate at 2.75%
$100 000	556	602	691
$150 000	834	899	1036
$200 000	1112	1198	1382
$250 000	1390	1498	1727
$300 000	1667	1798	2073
$350 000	1945	2097	2418
$400 000	2223	2397	2764
$450 000	2501	2697	3109
$500 000	2779	2996	3455

As the data show, whatever the loan (mortgage) amount, as the base rate (interest rate) rises, so do the repayments. Even relatively small changes in interest rates can have a significant effect on a consumer's spending power (how much money they have to spend on other things once mortgage payments are made). It follows, then, that:

- higher interest rates reduce consumer spending on non-essential items, which slows down economic growth
- lower interest rates increase consumer demand and can help to stimulate economic growth.

A government (or central bank) can, therefore, use interest rates to control the level of demand (consumer and business spending) within an economy and meet its objectives. If, for example, the government objective is to slow down the economy, it may well increase interest rates. On the other hand, if the government's objective is economic growth, they may lower interest rates to help stimulate (encourage) demand as has been the case in Thailand, Brazil and Australia.

Not all businesses (or consumers) are affected by interest rates to the same extent. For example, businesses with low gearing (few loans) may be relatively unaffected. Similarly, a firm selling a price inelastic product may be able to put its prices up in an effort to offset lower demand. A firm might also respond to rising interest rates by launching lower-cost versions of its products.

Interest rate	Impact on business	Impact on consumer
Low	Reduces cost of borrowing/loans Exchange rate falls, aiding exports (sales of goods overseas) Consumer demand increases	Cost of debt falls, increasing ability to spend Consumer confidence will increase, as will the willingness to take on more debt (increasing demand for products)
High	Increases cost of borrowing Strong currency makes exports less attractive (harder to sell goods to foreign markets) Consumer demand falls	Mortgage costs rise, reducing ability to spend Consumers delay or cancel large purchases, as credit costs are high Consumers may save rather than spend

CASE STUDY

Managing the money

It is important to note that in many countries the interest rate is managed not by the government but by the central bank. In the United Arab Emirates, for example, the Central Bank of the UAE decides on a monthly basis what the interest rate should be.

Governments give control of the interest rate to central banks to reduce the impact of political interference. In theory, the bank should be better at managing the economy and less likely to use economic policies as a way of winning votes before an election.

Changes in taxation and government spending

Another tool that governments can use to control the economy is **taxation**.

Taxation can be split into two main categories: direct and indirect.

Direct taxes	Taxes on a business's profits or an individual's income
Indirect taxes	Taxes on goods and services

The level of taxation in an economy can affect spending and therefore can be used to control demand (and growth).

Direct taxes

- **Corporation tax.** This is a direct tax on the profits of businesses. The higher the tax, the less profit a business will keep. Lowering corporation tax can encourage businesses to expand, as the rewards for greater profits are higher. The Republic of Ireland, for example, charges corporation tax of 12.5% (compared with 29% in Germany, 19% in the UK and 33.3% in France). This low rate of tax has made the Republic of Ireland a very attractive place for multinationals to locate their European head offices, in turn helping the economy to grow.
- **Income tax.** This is a tax on an individual's earnings. The higher the level of income tax, the less money people have to spend on goods and services. As a result, demand will fall and economic growth will slow down. As the bar chart shows, different countries have very different rates of income tax (personal tax) and corporation tax. These differences are the reasons why some individuals (and some firms) move overseas in order to benefit from lower taxation.

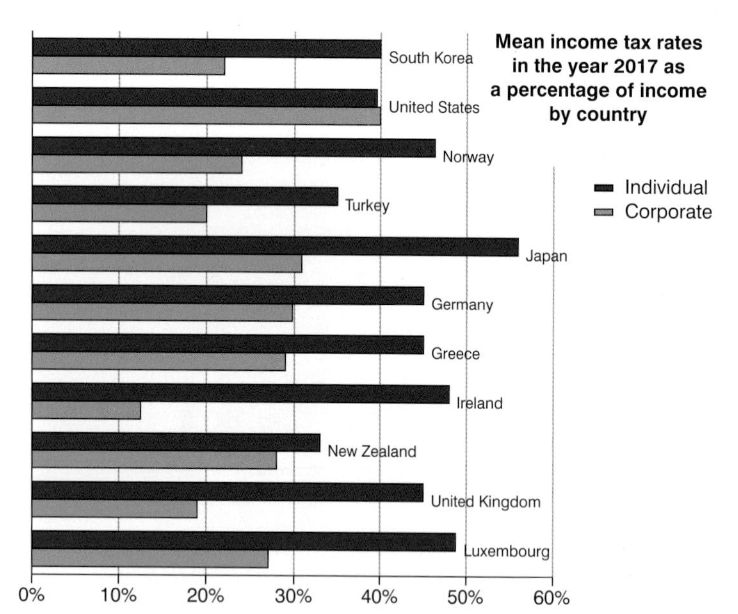

◁ In Dubai, for example, no income tax is charged on salaries, whereas in Sweden, Denmark, the Netherlands, Austria, Belgium and the United Kingdom the top tax rate is 45% or over. Therefore, in financial terms this makes Dubai a very attractive place to work.

Source: KPMG

While direct taxes can be used to control economic growth (helping a government to meet its objectives), the government must be careful not to make taxes too high. If corporation tax is considered too high, firms often move their operations to countries with more favourable (better) tax systems. Similarly, if income tax is too high, individuals may move overseas to work, benefiting from lower taxes in other countries. The net result of this for the government might be a significant and long-term decline in economic growth. The challenge is to increase taxes enough to control the economy but not enough to create disincentives (significant disadvantages) for firms and individuals.

Top Tip

Remember that all businesses are not affected equally by economic controls. A tax on cinema tickets (price elastic) is likely to have a much greater impact than a tax on products such as petrol (price inelastic).

Indirect taxes

The government also controls the level of **value added tax (VAT)**, which is a tax on goods purchased. The level of VAT affects the price consumers and businesses pay for goods and therefore affects demand (and, in turn, economic growth). For example, if a business sells a product for $100 and VAT is 10%, the final selling price to customers will be $110 ($10 of which goes to the government).

Other indirect taxes include the duty (another word for tax) paid on alcohol and cigarettes.

The impact of taxation on businesses, and how businesses might respond to different types of tax, is summarised here:

Type of tax	Item taxed	Impact on business	Possible business responses
Income tax	Income	Higher income taxes reduce consumer spending power Higher income taxes reduce the incentive to work	Reduce price of goods; focus promotion on 'value'; increase price inelasticity
		Employees receive less pay for additional work and, therefore, may be less willing to do overtime	Increase fringe/ non-financial benefits (see 2.1 Motivating employees)
Value added tax (VAT)	Spending	An increase in VAT lowers consumer spending (as goods are more expensive)	Maintain prices (absorbing VAT increase in profit)
		Higher rates of VAT force firms into price wars or require non-price competition (such as branding)	Focus promotion on branding; differentiate product; find new markets for product
Corporation tax	Business profits	A decrease in corporation tax may encourage firms to invest (to achieve and retain larger profits)	Open new branches; pursue expansion
		Higher corporation tax reduces profits and therefore limits the ability of the business to invest in expansion/growth	Cancel expansion plans; move operations overseas to a country with lower corporation tax

Government spending

In an effort to control the economy, and depending on its objectives, a government can increase or decrease the amount of money it spends (in a similar way to changing taxes and interest rates). Government spending on public services such as railways, roads, hospitals and schools helps to stimulate (increase growth in) an economy – for example, by providing jobs for public employees such as teachers and nurses, and by helping to create opportunities for firms that provide supplies for those services. The more money a government spends, the greater the stimulus for economic growth. In contrast, if the objective is to slow down the economy, a government could reduce its own spending (therefore reducing overall demand in the economy).

Did you know?

Malta has the highest corporation tax rate in the EU, with 35%. Bulgaria has the lowest, with 10%.

Δ Government spending on public infrastructure, such as road building, helps to stimulate economic growth.

Knowledge check

1. Identify one government objective. (1)
2. Explain how economic growth is measured. (3)
3. Outline the four main stages of the business cycle. (4)
4. Explain two strategies a business might use to survive a recession. (4)
5. Explain the difference between direct and indirect taxes. (2)
6. Outline how interest rates affect business profits. (2)

Total 16 marks

Check your progress:

- ✓ I can explain each of the main stages of the business cycle.
- ✓ I can describe the impact on businesses of changes in employment levels, inflation and gross domestic product.
- ✓ I understand how government control over the economy affects business activity and how businesses may respond.
- ✓ I can outline government economic objectives and the impact of changes in taxes, government spending and interest rates.

Environmental and ethical issues

Environmental concerns and ethical issues as both opportunities and constraints for businesses

Aims (6.2.1)

By the end of this section, you should:

- Understand how business activity can impact on the environment, for example, global warming
- Understand the concept of externalities: possible external costs and external benefits of business decisions
- Understand sustainable development; how business activity can contribute to this
- Understand how and why businesses might respond to environmental pressures and opportunities, for example, pressure groups
- Understand the role of legal controls over business activity affecting the environment, for example, pollution controls
- Understand the ethical issues a business might face: conflicts between profits and ethics
- Understand how businesses might react and respond to ethical issues, for example, child labour.

Introduction

No business stands alone. Business depends on society for its customers and its workforce. Firms depend on the environment for natural resources. In turn, society depends on business to meet the needs and wants of the population.

In simple terms, society and the environment present firms with both opportunities and threats. A business's success or failure may depend on its ability to understand and manage both of these.

The concept of externalities

The effects a business has on its wider environment are known as **externalities**. These externalities are the impact a firm's activities have on people not directly associated with its operations (such as the impact of a firm on the local community, not all of whom may be customers of the firm). In other words, externalities are the impact on people and things external to the firm.

These externalities can be both positive and negative. A **positive externality** might be, for example, the building of a road link for deliveries to a factory: local residents who can also use this road may actually get more benefit from the road than the firm. An example of a **negative externality** could be the congestion (traffic) caused by the factory's delivery vehicles.

When making decisions about its external impact (the impact of externalities), a business must consider the interests of the different groups or stakeholders that are affected by its actions, including shareholders, employees, the local community and suppliers.

When deciding which externalities are most important, a business must choose to whom it is ultimately responsible. That is, in whose interests it is acting and whose needs it should be placing first. There are two opposing views as to what this responsibility means:

- The '**shareholder view**': the most important priority of business is to make a profit for its shareholders. Shareholders have risked their money by investing in the company and so it is the duty of the business to reward them. The 'right' course of action is therefore, within the law, to maximise profits.
- The '**stakeholder view**': business has a much wider responsibility than just to its shareholders (who are only one group of stakeholders). The 'right' course of action is the one that balances the needs of many different groups. A business must consider the needs of employees, consumers and the community.

Δ Mobile phone mast: great phone reception for those living nearby (positive externality), but at a cost to the environment (land use and visual pollution) plus possible health risks (negative externalities).

Despite the possible impacts on profits (and therefore threats to long-term survival), many businesses today – such as Hewlett-Packard and Santander – are committed to acting in environmentally friendly and socially acceptable ways. For example, a business may:

- increase production costs in order to minimise pollution or improve working conditions
- turn down sales opportunities because they are considered socially unacceptable (unethical)
- make charitable donations out of business profits.

The reality is that not acting in an environmentally or socially responsible way can be more damaging to profits (through **negative publicity**, lost sales and government fines). Being socially and environmentally responsible is not just a good thing morally – it also makes good business sense.

How businesses can impact on the environment

The activities of a business can impact on the environment in a number of ways:

Energy use	Some businesses, such as paper manufacturers or oil refineries, use large amounts of energy. The production of this energy contributes to the use of **fossil fuels** (coal, gas and oil). Burning fossil fuels for energy produces carbon dioxide gas, and this is seen as a major factor in causing **global warming**.	
Waste	The large amounts of waste generated by business, as well as the amount of packaging that is used, have been criticised in recent years. While businesses must meet legal packaging requirements and must ensure consumer safety, packaging has to be disposed of. Many countries have large landfills (areas where waste is stored) that are environmentally damaging and very unpleasant for people who live near to them.	
Congestion	As economies grow, so too does the number of cars on the roads. The more businesses there are, the more deliveries that are made, and the more people who commute (travel) to work. Not only does congestion increase pollution, it also lowers the quality of life for people living in heavily congested areas.	
Pollution	Business activity causes noise, air and water pollution. The more businesses there are in an area or country, the greater the different types of pollution. In extreme cases, oil or chemical spills can cause significant harm to local wildlife and inhabitants, as in the case of the recent oil spill in Sharjah, United Arab Emirates.	
Land use	In many countries land is very scarce (limited). Business activity and the **infrastructure** (roads, rail links, and so on) needed to support business operations use up land. In many cases, this land may previously have been fields, forests or agricultural land. The use of land for business both contributes to global warming and reduces the natural habitat for wildlife.	

One major environmental concern is the issue of global warming (also known as climate change). Global warming is the slow but steady rise in global temperatures. Many scientists believe that global warming is caused by increases in greenhouse gases, such as carbon dioxide, which is released from burning fossil fuels. The increase in business activity, the destruction of forests (to profit from the sale of timber) and the conversion of green land into industrial areas, are all believed to contribute to global warming.

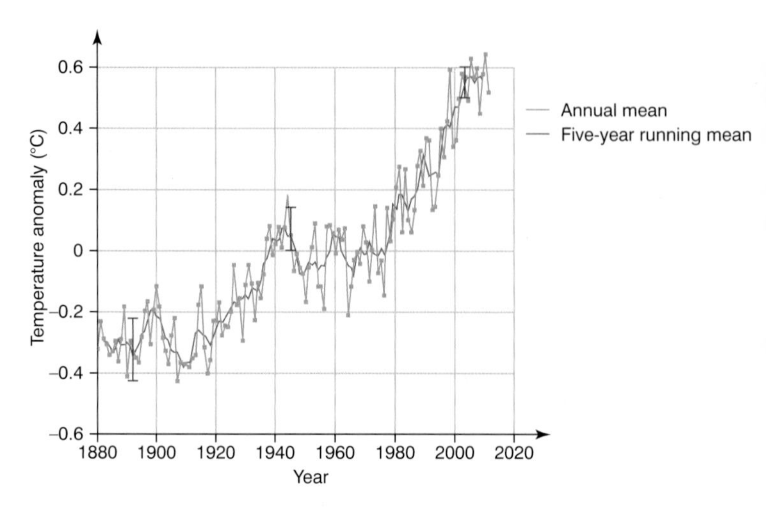

Δ Global land–ocean temperature index
Source: Public domain/NASA

Legal controls

In order to control the environmental impact of firms, many governments use laws to constrain (control) business activity. These laws might restrict a business by:

- stating where a business can locate (for example, many governments identify areas of 'greenbelt' and prevent businesses from locating there)
- setting strict limits for the amount of pollutants (harmful chemicals) a firm is allowed to release (and fining firms who break these rules)
- insisting that new factories and offices use a proportion of energy from renewable sources (such as wind farms or hydroelectricity)
- taxing firms for the disposal of waste (therefore encouraging them to reduce the amount of waste they produce)
- setting regulations that control what materials can be used in new buildings – stating, for example, that a percentage of all new building materials must come from sustainable (renewable) sources.

Did you know?

On 22 April 2017, the UK had its first day without using coal energy since the 1800s. Coal, the largest polluting fossil fuel, is slowly being phased out as a source of energy.

CASE STUDY

Smog control in Shanghai

The practice session for the 2017 Formula One Chinese Grand Prix was cut short due to poor visibility caused by heavy rain and smog (clouds made up of pollution and chemicals). The Chinese city of Shanghai struggles with smog and has recently had to issue public warnings, closing down schools and asking people to remain in their homes, as smog clouds descended on the city. The Chinese government has now promised to tackle the issue, focusing first on energy production, such as coal plants and car usage.

Application

Investigate an environmental issue in your country. Write a short summary of the issue and a brief analysis of the impact from the point of view of the following stakeholders:

- a manager of a business involved in the issue
- a member of the local community
- a politician working for the government.

Remember to consider how each of the stakeholders may react differently to the issue (some may react positively, others negatively).

How a business might respond to environmental pressures

In response to environmental concerns, some businesses base much of their marketing on their care for the environment. Firms are under pressure from consumers and exposed in the media (negative publicity) if it is discovered that their activities are damaging the environment. Firms do not want to suffer from the falling sales that this would cause. This fear in itself is often enough to encourage firms to act in socially and environmentally responsible ways. The US firm Best Buy, for example, offers free in-store recycling for any brand of electronics and claims to use sustainably produced materials in as many of its products as possible. Best Buy is currently ranked the third 'greenest' company in the USA, so in this way it has used its environmentally friendly nature as a source of competitive advantage.

CASE STUDY Oil damage

In 2012 a group of Nigerian farmers took the oil giant Shell to court for damage caused to their farms by leaking oil pipes. The local farmers claimed the oil spill polluted fish ponds, farmland and forests in Oruma in the Niger Delta. They claim it took Shell 12 days to seal the leaking pipe and blame the spill on a corroded (worn out) underground pipe.

In 2017, the National Human Rights Commission (NHRC) assured the farmers and communities of the Niger Delta region that it will continue to investigate and seek compensation and action from those involved.

Shell and other companies operating in the area have been heavily criticised and have suffered negative publicity for what many believe is poor environmental practice.

Opportunities offered by doing business in an environmentally friendly way include:

- **New business opportunities.** Environmental issues have presented many firms with a range of business opportunities. For example, many new businesses have opened up to offer recycling services and to sell recycled products. In Africa one business even offers a service that turns human waste into compost (fertiliser) for agricultural usage.
- **Lower costs.** The need to reduce packaging, waste and pollution can force a business to look again at its production processes and the amount of packaging it uses. Cutting down on waste can lower costs.
- **Customer loyalty.** Customers may be more willing to continue buying from a firm that is helping the environment rather than one that is damaging it.

There will also be a reduction in potential conflict with **pressure groups** that campaign on a range of social causes and try to influence business behaviour. A firm's employees may also be more motivated and labour turnover lower if employees feel that their work contributes to environmental sustainability (maintaining the environment for others).

△ There are many advantages to a business of acting in environmentally friendly ways.

Sustainable development

For businesses, modern thinking about environmental issues focuses on **sustainable development**. In simple terms, this means development that meets today's needs without damaging the ability of future generations to meet their needs.

In practice, sustainable development involves actions such as:

- replanting trees where land has been cleared for building projects
- only using energy or resources from renewable sources (such as solar power or renewable wood sources)
- rotating crop growth between different fields to avoid using chemical fertiliser
- minimising water use in buildings through efficient water management
- using 'brown' (recycled) water where possible
- incorporating green spaces into urban developments.

The advantages for businesses of sustainable development are the marketing benefits of 'being green' and, for example, the long-term cost savings associated with recycling. By sustaining the environment, they are also sustaining their own ability to do business for years to come.

△ Building rainwater collection systems for business premises is one way that businesses can support sustainable development.

It is now standard practice for a business to consider its impact on the environment. Most managers know that showing environmental concern is vital to a firm's positive image and, ultimately, to its long-term profitability.

CASE STUDY

Earth.Food.Love

Former professional footballer Richard Eckersley and his wife have set-up their very own zero waste shop. After quitting football, they decided that they wanted to help reduce environmental damage across the world by opening their very own 'bring your own packaging' store. Customers can buy a whole range of goods, from tea to cereal, but they must bring the containers each time.

Ethical concerns

Ethics refers to the rights and wrongs associated with behaviour. It relates to the moral judgements that businesses make about their behaviour, and the way they operate and interact with their stakeholders. For example, a business knowingly damaging the environment could be considered to be operating in an unethical manner.

Because what is considered 'right' and 'wrong' differs between countries, cultures and even within families (how many times have you disagreed with your parents/guardians about what is right or wrong?), ethics is a very complicated topic.

For example, is a business that pays overseas employees a wage that is lower than its own national minimum (but that is perfectly legal in the overseas country) operating ethically or unethically? If the law of a country allows firms to employ children as young as 14, but the laws of the firm's home country do not, is it unethical to employ 14-year-olds in the host country?

These are the types of questions **multinational companies (MNCs)** have to ask themselves as they do an increasing amount of business in countries all over the world.

Δ Ethical dilemmas: what is considered wrong in one country may be acceptable in another. For example, legal working hours differ between countries. Should a firm follow the laws of its own country or of its host country?

CASE STUDY

Environmental and ethical concerns

In the UK, a large proportion of seafood imports come from Asia. Countries such as Indonesia, Thailand and Vietnam sell large quantities to Europe each year. However, the ethical practices of these firms have come into question, with concerns raised over poor working conditions, low wages and the use of child labour. With severe pressure placed on the fishermen to maintain orders, ethical standards have declined. Organisations such as Oxfam have now raised significant concerns about long-term destruction of the ocean if this continues.

At the centre of tensions over **business ethics** is the need to make profit. For example, many American and European companies have moved production bases to South East Asian countries, where they can benefit from lower labour costs and therefore make more profit. Are these firms acting unethically by pursuing profit in this way?

Without these lower labour costs, the firms might struggle to compete and could go out of business. If that happens, both the US and South East Asian employees lose their jobs. Some people would argue that the firms are operating unethically by 'exploiting' lower labour costs, while others would argue that they are benefiting people in both the USA and South East Asia by providing employment.

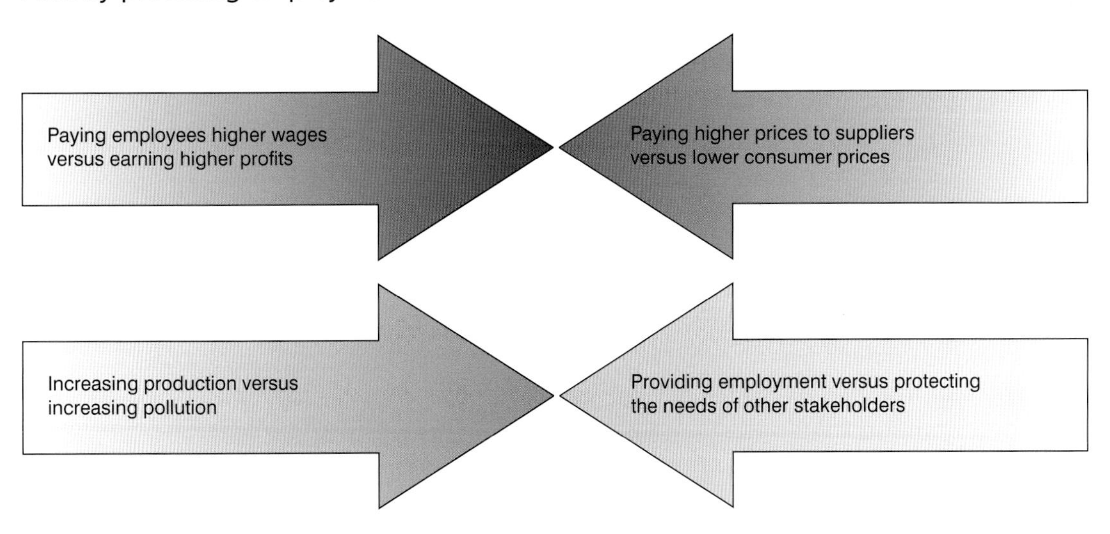

Δ Some of the tensions for businesses caused by ethical concerns

Evaluation

Working in pairs or small groups, conduct a debate based on the following scenario:

A multinational company operating in your country employs a large number of unskilled employees. The standard working day is 12 hours, but many employees at the company work 14 hours per day. While employees are paid for the extra hours, managers are quick to dismiss anybody not willing to work the extra hours. All employees work six days per week, but when the company has a big order to fulfil the employees are required to work seven days per week. Working conditions at the factory are good by local standards but poor compared with factories in the multinational's home country. Employees are paid the legal minimum wage.

Unemployment is high in your country, with few job opportunities for unskilled people.

One half of your group should argue that the business is operating ethically, while the other should claim that it is operating unethically.

In order to address ethical issues, many firms have adopted a 'code of ethics' that states what they will and will not do in whatever country they operate. Gap clothing, for example, has a Code of Business Conduct that outlines principles of fairness, dignity and respect in its dealings with its numerous global suppliers.

CASE STUDY

Ethical banking code

The banking group Santander has a very strict code of ethics. Not only does the business promise to act ethically itself, it also insists that its customers act in ethical ways.

To open a bank account with Santander, business customers have to complete a questionnaire detailing their business activities. If any of these practices do not conform with Santander's code of ethics, the bank will guide them towards more sustainable/ethical practices before approving loans, and so on.

As with environmental concerns, many firms use ethical behaviour as a way of promoting the business to potential customers. Starbucks, for example, promotes heavily its use of fair trade (ethically traded) coffee beans. Similarly, a business failing to act in an ethical manner risks facing significant negative publicity and damage to its sales.

Did you know?

Having started as a small group of volunteers in 1971, Greenpeace now has offices in over 40 countries, including Senegal, the Democratic Republic of the Congo and South Africa.

Pressure groups

In response to environmental and ethical concerns, businesses often face challenges from pressure groups about their activities. Pressure groups seek to influence government and business policy to protect or advance a particular cause or interest.

A pressure group may exist to focus on one very small local issue (such as the loss of woodland due to the building of a road) or, like the pressure group Greenpeace, they may focus on global issues such as overfishing or deforestation (removal or destruction of forests).

Pressure groups attempt to bring about change by, for example:

- drawing media attention to an issue (encouraging newspapers and TV news to report on the issue)
- **boycotting** (stop buying) a firm's products (and encouraging people to do the same)
- **petitioning/lobbying** (encouraging) government to change the law to stop a particular activity
- protesting outside a business or near to an area of concern (perhaps against the building of a road).

By engaging in these activities, the pressure group will be aiming for one of two outcomes:

- the business (or government) cancels its plans or changes it practices due to falling sales/public pressure
- the government changes the law to make the activity in focus illegal.

For an individual business, being the focus of pressure group activities can be extremely damaging to its reputation. The most successful tactic for pressure groups is to expose a firm to negative publicity, and therefore cause damage to its sales.

CASE STUDY Greenpeace changes policies

As a result of pressure from Greenpeace, numerous companies and many governments have changed their policies. A few of Greenpeace's successes include:

- food companies being stopped from buying forest-destroying palm oil
- the technology industry phasing out toxic chemicals
- a ban on dumping radioactive waste at sea
- the end of commercial whaling
- the introduction of a greener refrigeration technology.

All of these changes cost firms money in the short term, but, taking into account the possible damage to their reputations, the costs of changing are often smaller than the cost of lost sales.

Knowledge check

1. **Define the term externalities.** **(2)**
2. **Identify three constraints a government may place on a firm's activities to reduce its environmental impact.** **(3)**
3. **Explain, using a suitable example, the term sustainable development.** **(3)**
4. **Explain two possible ways in which a business might respond to environmental pressures.** **(4)**
5. **Outline what is meant by the term business ethics.** **(2)**
6. **Explain, using an example, two possible impacts of pressure group activity on a business.** **(4)**

Total 18 marks

Check your progress:

- ✓ I can explain why environmental concerns and ethical issues can be both opportunities and constraints for businesses.
- ✓ I can explain how business activity can impact on the environment, for example, global warming.
- ✓ I can explain how business activity can contribute towards sustainable development, and identify how legal controls help to achieve this.
- ✓ I can outline the ethical issues a business may face, and give examples of how a business might react and respond to ethical issues.

Business and the international economy

The importance of globalisation

Aims (6.3.1)
By the end of this section, you should:
- Understand the concept of globalisation and the reasons for it
- Understand the opportunities and threats of globalisation for businesses
- Understand why governments might introduce import tariffs and import quotas.

Globalisation

Have you ever visited another country on holiday and been relieved to find familiar brands and similar shops to the ones you have at home? Do you have friends of different nationalities who share similar views, interests and hobbies to you? If the answer to these questions is 'yes', then what you are experiencing is **globalisation**.

As more businesses trade across international boundaries, and as more people live or travel abroad, countries (and people) are becoming more similar.

Globalisation is essentially a process of increasing social and economic integration (coming together) that involves:

- an increase in **international trade** between countries
- the sale of **homogeneous** (similar) products by multinational companies (MNCs) across many countries
- the adoption of a common business language (often English)
- the movement of production from more industrialised countries to less industrialised countries
- an increasing exposure to global media that affects tastes and fashion (making them more similar).

One impact of globalisation is that countries are becoming increasingly interdependent. This means that countries rely on each other for their economic health. Taiwan, for example, has built its economic growth on technology manufacturing and is dependent on exports of technology to other countries. The countries it exports to rely on the import of this technology for their own economies.

Top Tip

Make sure you are able to identify and explain the effects (positive and negative) that increasing globalisation is having on all types of business, from small domestic firms to large multinational corporations.

Analysis

Have a look around you. Where were the clothes you are wearing made? Where was the furniture you are sitting on produced? If you have a computer, an MP3 player or a mobile phone, where were they manufactured?

Conduct a small survey among your friends. How many of the products you use on a daily basis were produced locally (within your country) and how many were produced overseas?

Present your findings (and those of your friends) as a series of images placed onto a world map. Analyse what the map tells you about the extent of globalisation.

CASE STUDY

Lack of drive cuts profits

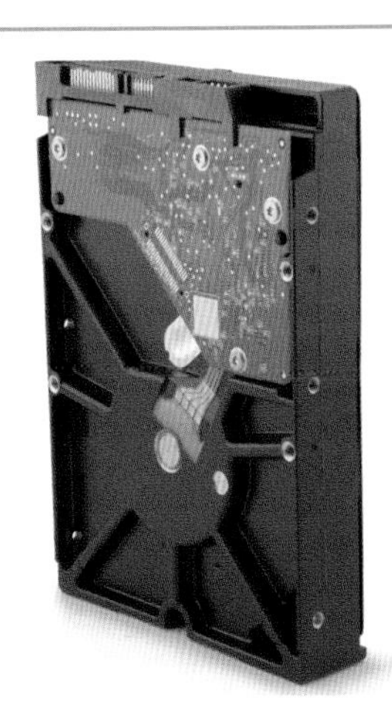

Thailand is one of the world's largest exporters of electronic hard drives. When Thailand's capital, Bangkok, suffered severe flooding in 2011, factories across the country temporarily closed. This caused hard drive production almost to stop. During the closures, world hard drive output fell by 30% and, due to restricted supply, prices rose. This provides a clear example of global **interdependency**.

The US firm Dell Computers was particularly affected by the fall in hard drive production. With no surplus hard drive stock, Dell was unable to meet customer orders and suffered a short-term dip in profits.

Globalisation is occurring for a variety of reasons:

- Improved communication and transport systems have made international trade and international travel faster and cheaper.
- Increased **labour migration** (movement) has encouraged cultural integration of people of many different nationalities living within one country, and has spread demand across the globe (for example, halal food is now found in many countries).
- **Economic trading blocs**, such as the European Union (EU), the African Union (AU) and the Arab League (AL), have made cross-border trade easier (for example, by lowering or removing import **tariffs** on certain products).
- Recession in more industrialised countries combined with rapid economic growth in many less industrialised and **emerging economies** has encouraged businesses to set up new branches in these growing countries. The supermarket chain Tesco, for example, has benefited from growth in Asia, with an annual 3.3% growth in Thailand and Malaysia, and 3.2% growth overall in Asia.

Key Term

Tariffs: a specific form of tax charged on imported goods.

- MNCs have taken advantage of lower **labour costs** in less industrialised countries. The location, for example, of factories producing goods for Western markets in China has contributed to Chinese economic growth.

There are both advantages and disadvantages to globalisation:

Advantages	Disadvantages
✓ **Globalisation allows countries to specialise and therefore increase GDP**. For example, many African farmers specialise in coffee growing. This specialisation allows for economies of scale, higher profits and, ultimately, economic growth.	✗ **The benefits of globalisation favour rich countries**. It is argued that developed countries benefit from lower labour costs while the developing countries get little benefit. However, globalisation is also blamed for causing unemployment in developed countries, as many businesses have moved their factories to countries with cheaper labour.
✓ **Consumers get a much wider variety of products to choose from.**	✗ **Globalisation does not benefit everyone equally**. In places such as Africa, the population does not have access to the technology or education to benefit from globalisation – so Africa fails to develop while other countries get richer.
✓ **It promotes understanding and goodwill among different countries** (improved relationships between, for example, the USA and China as a result of international trade).	✗ **Globalisation leads to financial problems that affect not just one country but many**. The global banking crisis of 2008–09 started in the USA and the UK, but quickly spread to affect many countries across the world.
✓ **Inward investment by MNCs helps countries by providing employment for local people**. MNCs also buy local resources, products and services. The money from these purchases contributes to economic growth.	✗ **There are no guarantees that the wealth from MNC investment will benefit the local community**. MNCs often send profits back to their home countries and global brands often force small, local firms out of business. MNCs are also quick to move production to even cheaper locations if wage costs rise.
✓ **Globalisation makes people more aware of, and more likely to find solutions to, global issues such as deforestation and global warming**. Global resources (such as food) can be used most efficiently, as countries can share resources.	✗ **It can be argued that globalisation has led to an increase in environmental and ethical problems**. A company may, for example, want to build factories in other countries because environmental laws are not as strict. MNCs may also impose poor working conditions and low wages on local employees, who have little power to resist.
	✗ **Some people view globalisation as a threat to global diversity**. Local traditions and languages are lost as the world adopts similar practices and a smaller number of languages.

Δ Globalisation: access to employment, access to products and services . . . but does everybody benefit equally?

Evaluation

In small groups, debate the benefits and drawbacks of globalisation. Identify one member of your group to take the role of 'judge' and present to them arguments for globalisation and arguments against.

Once you have concluded your debate, the judge should evaluate your arguments and should present a justified decision to the whole group on whether globalisation is a good or bad thing.

The opportunities and threats of globalisation for businesses

For a business, the main opportunities of globalisation are an increase in potential sales (it can sell its products in multiple countries) and the opportunity to benefit from lower labour costs (it can move production to countries with lower wages). Both of these advantages mean the firm can gain more profit.

Other advantages include:

- the cost of advertising campaigns can be shared across countries
- being known as a global brand may make the product more desirable
- economies of scale can be gained in production
- An economic downturn in one country (and a fall in sales) might be offset by economic growth (and rising sales) in other countries.

The main disadvantage to a business of globalisation is increased competition. Whereas, large multinational companies often benefit from globalisation, smaller firms often do not. For example, as a result of the growth of restaurant chains such as McDonald's and Starbucks, many local cafés and restaurants have been forced to close.

▷ One sign of the increasing power of globalisation is the rise in demand for coffee in China, a country not known for coffee consumption. Coffee consumption in China is now higher than in Portugal, a country where coffee drinking is part of the culture.

Reducing the impact of globalisation

To reduce the impact of globalisation, many countries use polices known as **protectionism**. This involves setting laws and regulations that aim to protect local firms from competition from overseas businesses.

Governments seek to protect domestic firms from international competition in order to:

- safeguard (protect) domestic jobs
- prevent foreign countries 'dumping' cheap imports into the country (which damages domestic sales)
- prevent the import of harmful or undesirable goods (especially where cultural sensitivities are involved).

The two most common forms of protectionism are tariffs and quotas.

Tariffs

A tariff is a specific form of tax imposed (charged) on imported goods. Israel charges a tax on the import of milk to protect domestic milk producers.

The rate of tariff usually varies according to the type of product. For example, luxury goods often face a higher tariff charge than essential goods. China, for example, charges a tariff of between 21% and 30% on the import of cars from the USA; the higher tax is charged on luxury vehicles.

By making products more expensive, the tariff makes imports less attractive to consumers and so lowers demand. Local products are cheaper in comparison to the imported products and therefore benefit from higher demand.

Δ Mexico uses import quotas for sugar as a way of protecting domestic sugar producers. Imported sugar is more expensive and, as it is available in smaller quantities, harder for consumers to find.

Quotas

An import quota is a limit on the quantity (amount) of a particular good that can be imported into a country. The restriction in supply both increases the price of imports and ensures that consumers are more likely to buy domestically produced products.

Knowledge check

1. **Define the term globalisation.** **(2)**
2. **Identify three reasons why globalisation is occurring.** **(3)**
3. **Explain the differences and similarities between tariffs and quotas.** **(4)**
4. **Identify three advantages and three disadvantages of globalisation.** **(6)**

Total 15 marks

The importance and growth of multinational companies (MNCs)

Aims (6.3.2)
By the end of this section, you should:

- Understand the benefits to a business of becoming a multinational and the impact on its stakeholders
- Understand the potential benefits to a country and/or economy where an MNC is located, for example, jobs, exports, increased choice, investment
- Understand the potential drawbacks to a country and/or economy where an MNC is located, for example, reduced sales of local businesses, repatriation of profits.

Multinational companies

Multinational companies (MNCs), also known as **transnational corporations**, are those that operate production or sales bases in more than one country. Examples include Colgate, Shell, Ford and the hotel chain Hilton.

CASE STUDY

Mothercare has mixed success

Mothercare PLC has seen mixed fortunes in the 21 different countries it operates in. The retailer, which specialises in products for expectant mothers and children up to age eight, said international sales in China, Indonesia and Russia all saw growth, whereas conditions in the Middle East remained challenging for the business. Although the company has seen its number of stores increase, it is still experiencing mixed growth around the world as different economies offer different challenges.

The benefits and disadvantages to a business of becoming an MNC

A firm may become an MNC in order to boost its profits by increasing sales and lowering costs. It can do this by:

- expanding sales beyond its own country (increasing profits)
- spreading the risk of operating in only one country (sales may be falling in one country while rising in another)
- benefiting from the economies of scale related to large-scale production
- benefiting from lower costs (particularly lower labour costs) in host countries
- accessing **raw materials** (particularly fossil fuels) not available in its own country
- locating branches and factories within a country to avoid protectionist barriers such as import tariffs and quotas
- localising products (adapting them to local markets) and reducing transport costs and delivery times.

Did you know?

The most recognised global brands are:

1. Apple
2. Google
3. Microsoft.

CASE STUDY Local car benefits

In order to avoid heavy import tariffs, both Mercedes and BMW have built factories in countries across South East Asia. By locating within countries that are members of the Association of Southeast Asian Nations (ASEAN), the car companies are able to avoid import tariffs that are sometimes as high as 300%. This ensures that their cars are affordable in these locations and they can achieve healthy sales and profits.

For the countries where these factories are based (Indonesia and Malaysia, for example), this means more job opportunities, a greater choice of cars and improved infrastructure in regions where the factories are located. Additionally, many of the smaller parts that go into car manufacture are often produced by locally owned firms. These firms benefit significantly from large orders made by companies such as BMW and Mercedes – the local firms make more profit and they employ more people, so the whole economy benefits.

There are, however, drawbacks to a firm of becoming an MNC:

- cultural and language differences can make operating internationally very challenging
- the business may need to adapt its products to suit local markets, which can increase costs and reduce profit margins
- the business may require large amounts of capital to set up overseas branches
- the business may find it difficult to compete against local firms that have local knowledge and loyal customers
- exchange rate changes may affect the business's profits (see the next section in this topic on the impact of exchange rates).

International competitiveness

International competitiveness refers to how well an MNC can compete on a global scale. Does it have the skills, resources and knowledge to be a successful multinational company? The international competitiveness of a business is influenced by:

- **Exchange rates.** Exchange rates can have a direct effect on the price of goods in different countries (see the next section in this topic on the impact of exchange rate changes). The impact of this on a business will depend upon price elasticity of demand (see 3.3 Marketing mix).
- **Cost of production.** The lower the unit cost of a product, the more price flexible a firm will be. Price flexibility may allow a firm to lower prices to ensure its products can compete with locally produced goods.

- **Product.** The type and nature of the product may determine success. A unique product that is not produced locally may enjoy healthy sales.
- **Brand.** The extent to which a brand appeals to people in different countries will affect international success. Businesses that can adapt their product to local needs are likely to enjoy much higher sales. McDonald's sells slightly different products in many of its different markets – for example, the popular Maharaja Mac is an adapted version of the Big Mac sold only in India.
- **Free trade agreements.** Political relations between countries can affect how successful international trade is likely to be. For example, trade agreements between European Union member states remove legal barriers to trade.

Benefits and drawbacks to the country where the MNC is located

Many governments offer **subsidies** (a reduction in taxes or money given as grants) to attract multinationals. There are, however, both advantages and disadvantages for a country of having MNCs located there:

Advantages	Disadvantages
✓ Increased job opportunities	✗ MNCs may offer low wages and poor working conditions for employees
✓ Increased exports from a country (helping to strengthen its currency)	✗ The jobs created are often low-skilled, manual jobs that offer little opportunity for long-term development and future economic growth
✓ Increased consumer choice	✗ Profits from MNCs often go back to the MNCs' own countries (**repatriation of profits**) and may not be spent in the host country
✓ Investment by the MNCs in infrastructure (roads, rail links, and so on) and in training/education	✗ Increased competition for local business often forces local firms to close
✓ Increased funds available to the government from taxes paid by the MNCs	✗ MNCs use up a country's resources and may contribute to environmental issues
	✗ MNCs often use complex accounting rules to avoid paying tax in the host country
	✗ MNCs often have significant power with local governments and may be able to affect decision making in their favour (possibly disadvantaging local firms)

Even multinationals that promote values of fairness are often criticised for their overseas activities. Common complaints include:

- allegations of labour exploitation (abuse) in 'sweatshops'
- sale of unsafe products
- damage to local environments
- the use of working practices that would be illegal in home markets.

CASE STUDY

Fair play failure

Many consumers, especially in Western countries, have protested against and boycotted MNCs that they believe are exploiting the benefits of globalisation and making profits while local people suffer. In response, many MNCs have signed anti-sweatshop or 'fair play' agreements that outline what they will and will not do in overseas countries. However, reports of companies failing to comply with (follow) the terms of these agreements are all too common.

Evaluation

Investigate the role of MNCs in your own country. Use the internet to research which, if any, MNCs are located in your country. See if you can find any information on their business activities.

Now imagine you work for one of these companies. Using your research findings and your knowledge of the advantages and disadvantages of MNCs, write a web blog evaluating the impact of your chosen MNC on your country. Your blog should present a justified position on whether you (as an employee for a MNC) believe that the MNC benefits or harms you and your country.

Knowledge check

1. **Outline what is meant by the term multinational company.** **(1)**
2. **Identify two reasons why a business may wish to become a multinational.** **(2)**
3. **Explain, using suitable examples, two ways in which multinationals might damage the countries in which they operate.** **(6)**
4. **Identify three advantages for a country of attracting multinationals to locate there.** **(3)**

Total 12 marks

The impact of exchange rate changes

Aims (6.3.3)

By the end of this section, you should:

- Understand depreciation and appreciation of an exchange rate
- Understand how exchange rate changes can affect businesses as importers and exporters of products, for example, prices, competitiveness, profitability.

Imports and exports

International trade between countries involves importing and exporting different goods:

- **Imports** are goods and services brought into one country from another (for example, Brazilian mangoes imported into France).
- **Exports** are goods and services sold from one country to other countries (for example, Vietnamese rice exported to New Zealand).

Exchange rates

International trade (the process of importing and exporting goods) requires businesses to convert (change) one currency into another. For example, in order for French firms to pay for imported Brazilian mangoes, they must convert euros into Brazilian real. The value of this conversion is based on the **exchange rate** between the two currencies.

The exchange of currency is just like any other transaction: one good is traded for another. In the case of international money transactions, the good being traded is currency – one currency is traded for another.

An exchange rate is, in essence, the price of one currency expressed in another (the value, for example, of the Emirati dirham against the US dollar).

△ Currency from different countries

WORKED EXAMPLE

If US$1 = 3.75 Emirati dirham, the price to an Emirates citizen of purchasing 1 US dollar is 3.75 dirham.

What determines an exchange rate?

The more of a currency that is supplied, the weaker (lower) a currency will be relative to others – its value is said to have depreciated (fallen).

Whether a currency appreciates (rises) or depreciates (falls) relative to other currencies will depend upon:

Imports/Exports	The difference between a country's imports and exports (its **balance of payments**) determines how much foreign currency a country buys. If, for example, a country has a greater proportion (amount) of imports (currency supply) than it does exports (currency demand), its exchange rate will depreciate (fall) relative to other currencies.
Interest rates	If interest rates are high in a particular country (relative to other countries), this will attract people to deposit money in the country's banks. In order to make these deposits, people need to buy the country's currency. This increases demand for the currency and causes its prices to appreciate (rise) relative to other currencies. If interest rates fall (relative to other countries), the result will be that investors move their money to the other countries. To do this, they must sell the original currency, increasing its supply and depreciating (lowering) its price relative to other currencies.

How do exchange rates affect businesses?

Changes in exchange rates can affect:

- the price a business charges for its goods in overseas markets
- how competitive in terms of price those goods are
- how profitable the company is.

In simple terms, importers and exporters are affected by exchange rate changes in the following ways:

Did you know?

The world's largest exporter of oil is Saudi Arabia. Last year it was responsible for 17% of the world's oil supply. Saudia Arabia holds the largest amount of oil reserves, so it doesn't look as though it's going to lose the number one spot any time soon.

	Importer	Exporter
Exchange rate appreciates	☺ Costs less to buy imported goods/ raw materials	☹ Their goods are more expensive overseas – sales may fall
Exchange rate depreciates	☹ Costs more to buy imported goods/ raw materials	☺ Their goods seem relatively cheap overseas – sales may increase

CASE STUDY Shrinkflation

A large number of businesses, including brands such as Doritos crisps, have reduced the size of their products in response to the impact of Brexit (the UK leaving the EU) on exchange rates. Rather than increase the price of the products, the businesses have decided to reduce the size, thereby keeping the same profit margins. Kellogg's have reduced the size of some of their larger cereal boxes from 800g to 720g. The changes in exchange rate have increased the price of some imported ingredients, making it more expensive to produce the products. The response of reducing the size of products in response to increased prices is known as shrinkflation.

The effect of exchange rate changes on price

Changes in the exchange rate between two currencies affect the price of goods imported from or exported to the respective countries. For example, the diagram summarises the possible impact on prices caused by exchange rate changes between the UK and the USA:

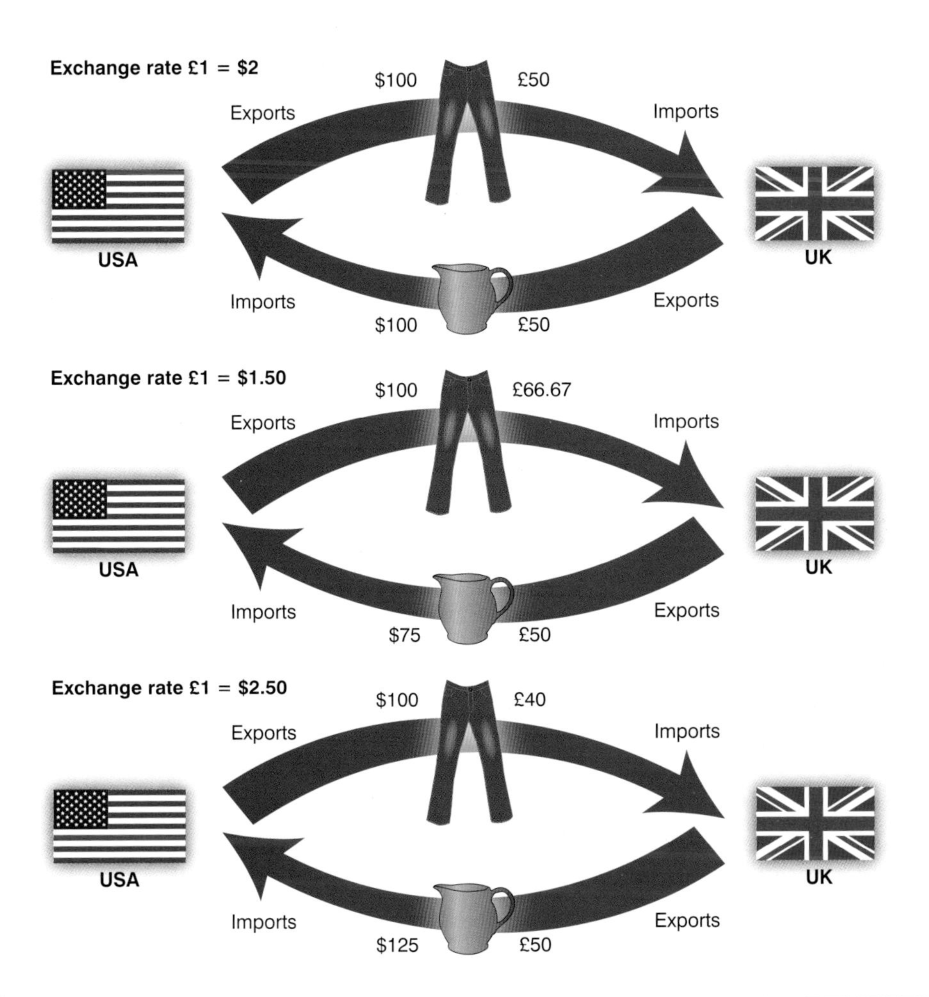

As the diagram on the previous page shows, a product's price depends on the exchange rate. For example, when the US dollar depreciates against the UK pound, the price of US jeans falls in the UK (meaning that US exporters are likely to sell more jeans in the UK).

However, in practice, firms do not usually change their prices every time the exchange rate changes. They may be forced to keep prices the same to remain competitive. If, for example, US pottery firms charge about $100 per item, then the UK pottery exporters will need to keep prices at a similar level (that is, $100 in the USA).

If the price is fixed, any change in the exchange rate will therefore increase or reduce the amount of profit a firm makes per sale (its profitability).

Effect of exchange rates on profitability

Let's say that the US jeans firm decides to keep UK prices at £50, perhaps because of competition from UK jeans manufacturers and to maintain brand image. If we assume cost of production is $25 per unit (per pair of jeans), the exchange rate changes in the table would have the following impact on profitability for the US firm:

Exchange rate	Price	Revenue	Cost (per unit)	Profit (per unit)
£1 = $2	£50	(£50 × $2) $100	$25	$75
£1 = $1.50	£50	(£50 × $1.50) $75	$25	$50
£1 = $2.50	£50	(£50 × $2.50) $125	$25	$100

In this example, at £1 = $1.50, a stronger (appreciating) US dollar reduces the US jean manufacturer's profitability. Despite the price remaining the same in the UK when converted into US dollars, every pair of jeans sold in the UK earns the US firm relatively less money. The reverse is also true: when the US dollar weakens against the pound (£1 = $2.50), even at the same UK price, the US manufacturer makes more profit (in dollars) per pair.

Effect of exchange rates on competitiveness

Businesses can use various strategies to minimise the impact of exchange rate changes. For example, an exporter that wishes to remain competitive may successfully choose to focus on non-price factors (such as brand or product differentiation), and therefore be less significantly affected by exchange rate changes. Luxury brands such as Hermès do not compete on price. With customers willing to buy their goods whatever the price (demand is price inelastic – see 3.3 Marketing mix), Hermès has the strategic flexibility to put prices up if exchange rates force it to do so. Or, because of its very high profit margins, Hermès can afford to maintain prices and (for a short period of time) bear the relatively small drop in overall profitability.

Δ Pedestrians walk past a Hermès store in Tokyo, Japan. Luxury brands such as Hermès are less affected by exchange rate changes.

CASE STUDY

Export success for Costa Rica

After entering into a free trade agreement with the United States, Costa Rica saw an increase of 1.4% in exports to the USA. Much of this success was the result of a **stable exchange rate** between Costa Rica and the United States. Costa Rican exporters could set prices in the USA and did not have to worry about the impact of exchange rate changes on their profitability – any changes were small and easily manageable.

It is also important to remember that not all businesses will be affected by exchange rate changes to the same extent. For example, a Bangladeshi clothing manufacturer that usually imports cotton from Kazakhstan may switch to purchasing cotton from a Ukrainian supplier until such a time that the exchange rate changes in its favour. It may also be able to use surplus stocks of cotton and therefore delay new imports until exchange rates are more favourable.

For businesses with few connections to overseas trade, and in industries with few competing imports, there may be little impact of exchange rate changes. In addition, if a business is both an importer and an exporter, the two sides of exchange rate effects may essentially cancel each other out.

Analysis

Investigate the exchange rate for a currency of your choice. Consider the following questions:

- Examine whether the currency has appreciated or depreciated over recent years.
- Analyse what caused this exchange rate appreciation/ depreciation.
- Discuss what the government did (if anything) to 'protect' (manage) the exchange rate?
- Explain how importers and exporters have been affected by any changes. If possible, give examples.

Using appropriate presentation software, present your findings in the style of a TV news report and show this to the rest of your class.

Knowledge check

1. **Define the term exchange rate. (2)**
2. **Identify one impact on an exporter of an appreciation of its country's currency. (1)**
3. **Identify one impact on an importer of a depreciation of its country's currency. (1)**
4. **Explain one way in which exchange rate changes might affect a firm's profitability. (4)**
5. **Explain how exchange rate changes might affect competitiveness. (3)**

Total 11 marks

Check your progress:

- ✓ I can outline the importance of the concept of globalisation.
- ✓ I can explain the opportunities and threats of globalisation for businesses, and why governments might introduce import tariffs and quotas.
- ✓ I can outline the reasons for the importance and growth of multinational companies (MNCs).
- ✓ I can explain the potential benefits to a business of becoming a MNC, and the benefits and drawbacks of MNCs to a country.
- ✓ I can explain depreciation and appreciation and the impact of exchange rate changes on importers and exporters.

Exam-style questions: short answer and data response

1. The economy of Busiland is experiencing an economic boom. The government has increased interest rates as a way of controlling the business cycle.

a) **Identify** any two stages of the business cycle. (2)

b) **Identify** two features of an economic boom. (2)

c) **Explain** two likely consequences for a clothing retailer of a rise in interest rates in Busiland. (4)

The government of Busiland is considering increasing taxes in an attempt to control economic growth.

d) **Identify** one tax the government of Busiland might choose to increase. **Explain** why raising this tax might be an appropriate control on economic growth. (6)

e) **Explain** one tax that firms pay and one tax that individuals pay in Busiland. (6)

2. BigHomes is a construction company that operates in Busiland. It specalises in building large residential homes for wealthy families. BigHomes is concerned about pressure groups and tries to be as ethical as possible in all its operations.

a) **Define** the term business ethics. (2)

b) **Define** the term pressure group. (2)

c) **Explain** two ways in which BigHomes might operate ethically. (4)

d) **Explain** two ways in which a pressure group might try to influence the behaviour of BigHomes. (6)

The government of Busiland has introduced a new law stating that construction firms must become 'more environmentally responsible'.

e) **Explain** two changes that BigHomes might make in order to act in a more environmentally responsible manner. (6)

3. To benefit from globalisation, BigHomes wants to become a multinational company. It is looking for new countries where it could start to build residential homes.

a) **Define** the term multinational company. (2)

b) **Identify** two factors that might influence BigHomes' choice of country in which to operate. (2)

c) Changes in exchange rates can cause problems for any business that trades globally. **Consider** one way in which exchange rates might affect BigHomes. (4)

d) Explain two ways in which BigHomes might benefit from globalisation. (6)

e) Identify and **explain** two possible externalities of BigHomes operations. (6)

Note: The exam-style questions, answers and commentary in this book were written by the author; in examination the number of marks awarded to questions like these may be different.

Exam-style questions based on case studies

Multinationals in India – the end of the general store?

For one day in 2017, 50 million Indians went on strike. They were protesting against controversial government reforms that will allow multinational supermarkets – like CostSavers or BigMart – to start selling in India.

In India, most shops are small general stores called kiranas. These small family-run businesses stock a wide variety of products and are found in most neighbourhoods. They are also an important focus for the community and a source of employment for 220 million Indians.

Critics argue that multinational supermarkets would put an end to the small community kiranas. With global economies of scale, CostSavers and BigMart can offer prices so low that local firms would never be able to compete.

CostSavers has performed poorly in the UK in recent years and much of its growth has come from emerging markets. In 2017, UK sales grew by 2.2%, whereas sales in Asia grew by 6%. In the USA, the 10 biggest supermarkets account for 51% of sales; in China, the top 10 comprise only 11%. With so much market potential, countries such as India, with a population of 1.25 billion, represent an opportunity for huge profit.

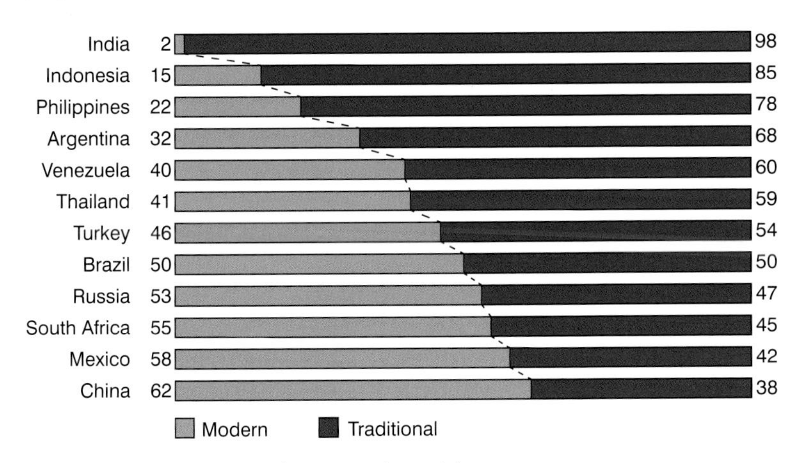

Source: Euromonitor, a market research provider

Appendix 1: Proportion of modern (supermarket style) retailers in various emerging markets versus more traditional, smaller retailers

Continuing operations 26 weeks ended 25 August 2017 (unaudited)	2016–17	Change from 2015–16
Group sales (inc. VAT)	£36 010 million	1.4%
Group revenue (exc. VAT)	£32 311 million	1.6%
Group trading profit	£1587 million	(10.5%)

Appendix 2: Summary of BigMart's results for the 26 weeks to 25 August 2017

	International results*	
	Actual rates	
	£ million	% growth
International sales	£11556	(0.2)%
International revenue (exc. VAT, exc. impact of IFRIC 13)	£10426	(0.2)%
International trading profit	£278	(17.1)%
International trading margin (trading profit/revenue)	3.63%	(73)%

Δ *Exc. Japan

Appendix 3: Summary of BigMart's financial results for its international markets in the 26 weeks to 25 August 2017. Figures in brackets represent negative numbers. Percentage growth is expressed year on year.

1. a) The Indian economy has grown rapidly in recent years. With reference to suitable appendix data, **explain** two advantages and two disadvantages for BigMart of operating in such a rapidly growing market. (8)

b) Considering the advantages and disadvantages that multinational companies create and, with reference to the appendices, do you think that a government should seek to attract these companies to its country? **Justify** your recommendation. (12)

2. As well as locating stores within India, BigMart will also source and produce goods locally. Local production will enable BigMart to avoid trade barriers.

a) Outline two different types of trade barrier and the impact of those barriers on a firm wishing to import goods to India. (8)

b) BigMart operates in 14 countries across Europe, Asia and North America. **Identify** two possible impacts of changes in exchange rates on multinational companies such as BigMart and **outline** suitable strategies to reduce this impact. (12)

3. With such rapid growth, the Indian government is concerned about the economy.

a) Explain two policies the government could use to control economic growth. (8)

b) Governments often help small businesses. **Outline** four ways in which the government could help the small kiranas. (12)

4. a) Explain two ways in which pressure group activity might affect CostSavers. (8)

b) To avoid pressure group activity, CostSavers is thinking of introducing a 'code of ethics'. Do you think this is a good idea? **Justify** your answer. (12)

Note: The exam-style questions, answers and commentary in this book were written by the author; in examination the number of marks awarded to questions like these may be different.

Exam-style questions based on case studies

AirStream

AirStream is a large company that manufactures and constructs wind farms. The company already has six wind farms located in unpopulated areas of Country X.

AirStream has plans to build a new wind farm on the coast to supply electricity to a new commercial and residential development called New Town. New Town has been growing rapidly over the past 10 years as new businesses have set up, existing businesses have grown and people have moved to the area in search of jobs.

The new wind farm will be located in an area that is popular with local walkers and is well populated with a variety of animal species, including rare birds.

Both the building of the wind farm and its ongoing maintenance will provide jobs for residents of New Town. The additional electricity supply will enable New Town to grow even further.

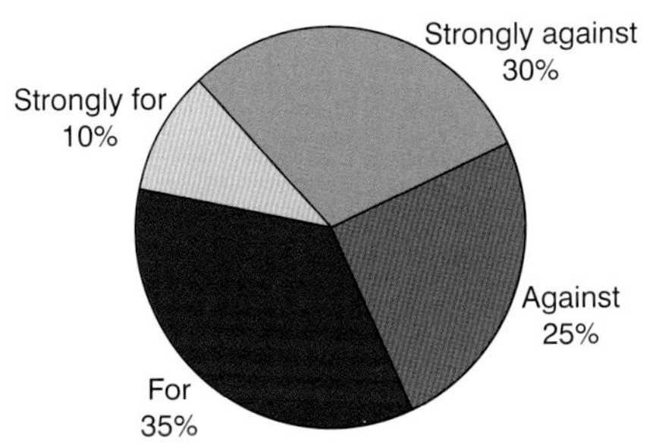

Appendix 1: Results of a research survey conducted by AirStream

Economic measure	Data	Change from previous year
Economic growth	3%	Down
Unemployment	7%	Up
Business closures	1256	Up
Business start-ups	100	Up
Population	4120000	Up

Appendix 2: Economic data for New Town

1. a) **Identify,** using appropriate information from the appendices, two possible social costs and two possible social benefits of the decision to build the wind farm. (8)

   Governments often pass laws to protect consumers and to protect the environment.

   b) **Outline** the possible implications of one form of consumer protection and one form of environmental protection for a company like AirStream. (12)

2. AirStream is a multinational company.

a) Explain the possible challenges that AirStream may face as a result of operating in many different countries. (8)

b) Airstream buys parts from Country Z. **Explain** how changes in the exchange rate with Country Z and the introduction of a tariff on these parts might affect the business. (12)

3. The government of Country X is concerned about its economic situation.

a) Governments often help local businesses. **Explain** why the government of Country X might help AirStream. (8)

b) Using the appendices, **explain** three possible economic concerns and how businesses in New Town might be affected by these concerns. (12)

4. The government of Country X wants to encourage all firms to follow the principles of sustainable development.

a) Explain two ways in which AirStream may operate in a sustainable manner. (8)

b) Do you think that all firms in Country X will benefit from sustainable development? **Justify** your answer. (12)

Note: The exam-style questions, answers and commentary in this book were written by the author; in examination the number of marks awarded to questions like these may be different.

Past paper questions

Paper 1

Section 6

Table 2 gives data about the economy of country C.

	National income Year per person ($)	Inflation (%)	Unemployment (%)
2010	650	5	10
2011	640	3	12
2012	600	1.5	18

Δ Table 2

The economy of country C is in recession. The Government wants to create more jobs by encouraging more businesses to start up. However some pressure groups are against this because they think that more businesses will cause more external (social) costs.

a) What is meant by 'recession'?

____

____

____

____ (2)

b) Identify two possible reasons why national income per person has fallen between 2010 and 2012.

Reason 1: __________________________________

____

Reason 2: __________________________________

____ (2)

c) Identify and explain two ways that a Government could help new businesses to start up.

Way 1: __________________________________

____

Explanation: ________________________________

____

Way 2: __________________________________

____

Explanation: ________________________________

____ (4)

Cambridge International IGCSE Business Studies 0450 Paper 11, Q4 Nov 2013

Paper 2

Section 6

The following case study is taken from past papers created by Cambridge Assessment International Education. We have only provided extracts of this case study, and it does not reflect the full case study that you may be provided with in your examination.

KK Cars

KK Cars is a sole trader taxi business owned by Trunal. He set up the business two years ago after he moved to New City in country X and could not find a job.

His taxi service usually has three types of customer:

- private customers who are local people without a car
- tourists who are visitors to the city
- businesses wanting documents (letters) delivered quickly.

Trunal's business made a slow start with very low profits. However, last year the business became well known for being reliable. The number of customers has increased and Trunal's taxi is now always fully booked. There are many other small taxi firms in New City and it is a very competitive market. Trunal has written for advice from a Government business advisor about how to expand his business.

Appendix

Information about the types of customers for KK Cars

Type of customer	Price of average journey	Average number of journeys per day	Variable cost per journey	Information about demand
Private customers	$10	40	$5	Mainly at weekends
Tourists	$20	30	$10	Seasonal
Businesses	$30	15	$15	During business hours
The fixed costs for the taxi are $20 per day.				

1 a) The rate of economic growth in country X fell from 4% to 0% in the last year. **Identify** and **explain** two effects this might have on KK Cars. (8)

b) **Consider** the effects on Trunal's business of each of the following legal changes. (12)

i) Higher standards of safety for taxis

ii) Shorter working hours for taxi drivers

iii) Lower speed limits for taxis

Cambridge International IGCSE Business Studies 0450 Paper 22, Q5 Nov 2012

Skills Builder

External influences impact on business activities in many ways. It is important to remember, though, that in Business Studies it is the **impact on business** that is important and not necessarily the economic theory itself. Understanding how exchange rates may have different impacts on different firms is more important in Business Studies than being able to link together economic theory. With this in mind, you should consider the following when studying external influences:

AO1: Knowledge and understanding

Get used to data. It is important that you are comfortable interpreting and using data about the economy that has been presented in a numerical or graphical form. Use newspaper articles, online resources, past papers and the questions in this book to develop your **knowledge and understanding** of the economy. Little mathematical ability is required and having a 'feel' for the economy will often be enough – remember that it is **understanding** how the economy affects a business that is important, not the economy itself.

One key point to remember is that a slowdown in economic growth, for example, does not mean that the economy is shrinking, just that it is growing more slowly (perhaps 1% GDP growth instead of 2%). Only a negative GDP number represents a shrinking economy.

AO2: Application

Very often you will need to consider the extent to which external influences will affect a firm. Remember that not all firms are affected to the same extent – you must be able to **apply** your knowledge to context. For example, a business that sells luxury goods will be more significantly affected by a fall in consumer income than a business that sells food.

AO3: Analysis

Understanding external influences is, of course, only one half of the picture; you must be able to **analyse** how a firm might react to those influences. The ability of a firm to react to external influences will be determined by internal factors. For example, a firm with a highly skilled, flexible and highly motivated workforce may respond much better to external influences than a firm with low-skilled and unmotivated employees.

AO4: Evaluation

You need to understand and be able to **recommend** and **evaluate** strategies that may make it possible for firms to protect themselves from external influences. For example, a firm with strong ethical and environmental policies is less likely to find its reputation damaged by poor practice. Pick a company (or several) that you are familiar with, and for every bit of economic news you hear, consider if/how it will impact on that firm. If you do this regularly, you should be in an excellent position to analyse and **evaluate** the external influences facing a company used in a case study.

Glossary

absenteeism the proportion of working days lost due to employee absence (through illness or accidents, and so on) – usually expressed as a percentage
accountability when employees, especially managers, are held responsible for their actions
added value the amount added to the value of a product through the production process. This is calculated by subtracting the original costs from the selling price. These costs could include wages
assets items that a business owns; those used up within a year are current assets, those kept longer than a year are non-current assets
autocratic leadership a style of leadership where the manager makes all decisions. Subordinates are given little say in what is done and how it is done. The leader gives instructions and expects them to be followed
average cost the average cost of producing one item – the total cost of production divided by the number of items produced
balance of payments in simple terms, the difference in value between imports to a country and exports from that country – a positive balance of payments means the country exported more than it imported; a negative balance of payments means the country imported more than it exported
bankruptcy the legal process by which a company (or, in the case of unlimited firms, an individual) is declared financially unable to continue with the business
base rate the interest rate set by a country's central bank, used as the basis for the interest rates of all other banks
batch production a production method where similar items are produced together – a whole batch moves through the different stages of production together
blog a website on which an individual or group presents and promotes opinions, information, and so on, on a regular basis (usually in written form)
boom a period of economic prosperity and economic growth
boycott to stop buying a product or engaging in a particular activity as a form of protest
brand image the personality given to a product through marketing activities
branding the use of a name, symbol or design to identify a particular product
brand loyalty the regular purchase of one brand of a product by a consumer
break-even a common business objective: to sell enough products so that its revenue covers its total costs – the business makes no profit but no loss
break-even point the point at which a business sells enough products to cover all of its costs: sales revenue = total costs
business cycle (or trade cycle) the cyclical movement of economic growth characterised by recovery, boom, recession, slump
business ethics the moral judgement about the rights and wrongs associated with business behaviour
business to business (B2B) a situation where one business makes a commercial transaction with another
business to consumer (B2C) business or transactions conducted directly between a company and consumers
cash flow the level of money that a business has at any one time – insufficient cash will lead to the inability to pay bills on time
central bank the bank responsible for overseeing and managing monetary systems within a country – in particular, many central banks control a country's interest rate
chain of command the path that instructions are passed along within an organisation
collective bargaining the process of a union negotiating with employers on behalf of its members
commission a percentage of the sales revenue from selling a product, which is paid to the salesperson
communication the two-way traffic of messages in verbal, written, visual or electronic form, internally within an organisation and externally with its stakeholders
company an organisation that engages in business activity and is a separate legal entity from the owner; either a private limited or public limited company
competitive advantage the source of a firm's advantage over competing firms – excellent customer service can, for example, be a source of competitive advantage
competitive pricing when the price of a good is set at the same level as other products in the market and at a level customers expect or are willing to pay
computer-aided design (CAD) using computers to help produce better designs for products
computer-aided manufacture (CAM) using computers to aid the manufacturing process – this allows for consistent quality in the production of goods
consumer to consumer (C2C) a form of commerce in which products are traded directly between consumers – usually via an intermediary such as eBay
contingency plan a plan that a business prepares in case anything goes wrong with a particular strategy or to help respond to unexpected events
continuity having more than one business owner so that the business will be able to continue when one of the owners dies
corporation tax a direct tax on the profits of business – this is the business version of an individual's income tax. The higher a business's profit, the more corporation tax it will pay

cost-effective a measure (often informal) of how much value for money a purchase is
cost leadership a strategy where a firm seeks to be the lowest-cost seller in a particular market
cost per unit the cost of producing one item
customer loyalty see brand loyalty
customer satisfaction survey a form of primary market research intended to find out how happy customers are with a firm's services
deed of partnership a legal document that joins the members of a partnership – it includes details of the partners, their financial investment and profit sharing
de-layering an act that removes a layer or level from the organisational chart, normally to cut costs
delegation when a manager gives authority to another employee to complete a task, although the manager retains the ultimate responsibility for the completion of the task
democratic leadership a style of leadership that involves employees in the decision-making process – the leader seeks and considers the opinions of employees before making decisions
departments organisational charts are normally organised by departments, for example, operations or marketing
desk research the process of gathering secondary data
developing economy a country with a low standard of living and low industrialised base, but with rapid growth in certain areas of the economy – Kuwait is considered to be a developing economy
differentiation the features of a product, its price, its place of sale or the way in which it is sold that make it different to competitors' products. Ensuring that products are different to those offered by competitors – often this means adding or altering features that make the product appeal to specific market segments
direct tax tax paid directly by businesses or individuals, in other words, income tax and corporation tax
discriminatory pricing different prices are charged to different groups of people at different times – cinemas, for example, charge different prices for daytime and evening showings
diseconomies of scale the disadvantages of a business growing too large that result in an increase in its costs per unit
disintermediation a move towards direct distribution – reducing the stages a product must pass through to reach the consumer by 'cutting out' intermediaries
dismissal where an employee is told to leave the job because of poor behaviour or unsatisfactory performance
disposable income the proportion (%) of a person's (or family's) income available for them to spend on non-essential purchases
distribution channel the method used by a business to get its product(s) to consumers
dividends a share of the profits given by the business to shareholders
division of labour when work is divided up between different groups or individuals within a workforce. This is usually done based on the skills or the specific responsibilities of the departments. In this way, employees become specialists at one particular task
downsize to reduce the number of employees in an organisation in order to reduce costs and increase efficiency
downturn see slump
e-commerce trade undertaken using electronic means, usually the internet but increasingly mobile technology
economic growth an assessment of economic activity within a country, measured by GDP
economic trading bloc a group of countries that have entered into legal trading agreements with one another, removing barriers to trade (such as tariffs) – examples include the European Union (EU), the African Union (AU) and the Arab League (AL)
economies of scale the advantages a firm gains as it grows in size that reduce costs per unit – such as discounts for buying in large quantities
efficiency the comparison between the output produced and the actual amount that could be made – the more efficient a person or business is, the higher its production
elasticity how responsive a good or service is to a change in price
emerging economy a country with a low standard of living and a low industrialised base but with very rapid economic development – Brazil is considered to be an emerging economy
employment contract a legal contract that a firm gives to an employee, setting out the basic terms and conditions of employment (such as place of work, working hours and salary)
empowerment giving employees the power to make the decisions that affect their working lives and improve the production or service process
enterprise a willingness to take on a new project, idea or business venture, for example, a new start-up business
entrepreneur an individual who starts his or her own business – this person often shows initiative and a range of skills, including determination, energy and hard work
environmental impact the effects business activity can have (both positive and negative) on the environment
equal pay the concept of employees, regardless of age or gender, being paid equally for undertaking the same job with the same level of expertise
exchange rate the price (value) of one currency expressed in another currency (for example, $1 = €0.75)
exchange rate appreciation a currency's value rises against another – the currency is stronger
exchange rate depreciation a currency's value falls against another – the currency is weaker
export the sale/transference of goods from one country out to another

extension strategy a marketing strategy designed to extend a product's life and (hopefully) prevent sales from declining
externalities the impacts a firm's activities have on people not directly associated with its operations – such as the impact of a firm on the local community, not all of whom may be customers of the firm
factors of production the resources needed to produce a product or service – these include labour, land, enterprise and capital
fair trade agreement an agreeement signed by a company that states it will purchase supplies only from sources that offer 'fair' prices to manufacturers or growers
field research the process of gathering primary data, using observation, experimentation or asking questions
first mover advantage the benefits a firm gains, such as brand loyalty, from being the first to launch a new product or service in a market
fixed cost a cost that is not directly linked to production – it will therefore stay the same regardless of how productive a business is
flow production when an item is mass produced using a production line – large quantities of an item can be made
focus group a small group of consumers who are asked in-depth (qualitative) questions about a product and how they use it
focused marketing see niche marketing
fossil fuels a natural carbon or hydrocarbon fuel such as coal or gas, formed in the geological past from the remains of living matter
franchise an arrangement in which an established and popular business allows another individual to use its business name, products and logo—for example, branches of McDonald's
franchisee a new business that enters into an arrangement with a franchisor to trade under its name and sell its products
franchisor an existing business that allows new businesses to trade under its name
fringe benefit a form of non-financial reward, such as a company car or discounts on company products, offered as part of an employee's basic package
gearing the proportion of a company's finance that is funded from debt (loans) against equity (shares)
globalisation the increasing trend for businesses to trade across international boundaries and for people to live or travel to countries that are not their own – in the process, countries (and the people within them) become more similar
global warming a sustained increase in the Earth's temperature, which is linked to climate change
government spending government money (from taxation) spent on public services (schools, roads, railways, hospitals, and so on)
gross domestic product (GDP) the monetary value of all goods and services produced by an economy during a specific time period
gross misconduct when an employee breaks an important company rule. Examples include stealing or failing to follow safety procedures
gross profit revenue minus the cost of production only
headcount the number of employees within a firm
homogeneous the same – in business terms, this refers to similar, if not identical, products being sold by multinational companies (MNCs) across many countries
import the sale/transference of goods (or services) from one country into another
income statement a document that summarises the financial performance of the business in a given time period
income tax tax on an individual's earnings
incorporation the process of turning an unincorporated business (a sole trader or partnership) into a company
indirect tax taxes on goods and services, for example, VAT
induction training received when an employee first joins an organisation – the training may cover basic elements of the job, safety and an introduction to company systems
industrial action the range of activities (work-to-rule, strike, and so on) that trade unions use as a way of increasing their bargaining power with firms. Trade union members usually only engage in industrial action when negotiations have failed to give them an acceptable result
inflation a general rise in prices over time
infrastructure the network of roads and access to basic amenities that a business needs in order to succeed in a particular location
interdependency the trading relationships between countries that mean countries rely on each other's products (exports) for economic wellbeing
interest rate the price of borrowed money – either the cost of lending money or the rate of return for depositing money in a bank
intermediary a stage in the distribution channel. Intermediaries are the stages a product must pass through in order to reach the end consumer (retailer, wholesaler, and so on)
international trade trade with a country beyond a company's own national borders
job description a description of the tasks, role and responsibilities of a particular position
job design the design of an employee's job, which takes into consideration how motivating that job is – the job design might introduce job enlargement or job enrichment
job enlargement when employees take on a wider range of tasks as part of their job but maintain the same level of responsibility
job enrichment an attempt to make a job more challenging or rewarding through greater variety, scope, training and/or decision-making power
job production when one-off or handmade items are produced, normally to meet the needs of the customer's specification

job rotation the process of switching an employee between tasks or jobs over a period of time
joint venture an agreement between two businesses to work together on a particular project – this will involve sharing the profits and joint decision making
labour cost the cost – most significantly the salary/ wage costs – of using employees
labour migration the movement of employees from one country to another, or from one region of a country to another
labour productivity how much production an individual employee has completed
labour retention the desire for a firm to keep labour turnover as low as possible
labour turnover the proportion of employees who leave a firm compared with the total employed during a given time period (usually one year) – usually expressed as a percentage
laissez-faire leadership a style of leadership that supports employees in achieving targets at the same time as allowing them the freedom to decide how to meet the targets – laissez-faire leaders empower employees and may provide guidance only when required
lean production a philosophy that a business uses to try to reduce the time, resources and labour involved in production, to make it more efficient
liabilities debts that a business owns; those paid within a year are current liabilities, those paid over a period of years are non-current liabilities
limited liability as a company is a separate legal entity, its owners are not liable (responsible) for the company's debts – this means the owners can lose what they have invested, but not their personal possessions
liquidity the amount of capital available for a business
lobbying putting pressure on the government, a company or other body to change its behaviour/ decision in some way by seeking to influence the opinion of those making the decision
lower order needs the physiological, safety and security needs that form the foundation of Maslow's Hierarchy of Needs
market where buyers and sellers meet to exchange goods and services, usually for money – this can be an online, a black or a normal shopping market
market challenger a firm that is competing with a strong market leader for market share
marketing an approach to business that seeks to identify, anticipate and satisfy changing customer needs in order to add value to products or services
marketing mix the combination of product, price, promotion and place (distribution) (also known as the 4Ps) that determines how a firm markets to its customers and potential customers
marketing strategy the particular balance of a firm's marketing mix; its focus on a niche or mass marketing approach and its methods for managing relationships with customers and potential customers
market orientation a business that is customer-driven, finding out what customers want before making decisions about product, price or promotion
market research the process of collecting and interpreting data about customers, the market and competitors
market segment a clearly defined section of a larger market
market share the percentage of total sales that a firm achieves in a market
mark-up the difference between the cost of a product or service (to the producer) and its selling price (to the consumer)
mass market a large market containing lots of customers buying similar products
mass marketing promoting a similar product in similar ways to a very large, usually international, market
merger when two or more businesses, often voluntarily, join together to form a new legal entity
minimum wage many countries specify a legal minimum wage, which is the lowest amount that a business can pay an employee (usually expressed per hour or per day)
motivation the desire to achieve a certain result or outcome – the more an individual desires a certain outcome, the harder they will work (the more motivated they will be) to achieve that outcome
multinational company (MNC) a business that operates production or sales bases in more than one country – also known as a transnational corporation
multiskilling training an employee so that they can perform a variety of jobs within the organisation
nationalisation takeover of privately owned businesses by the government – often occurs in energy markets
negative externality a negative impact of a firm's activities on its wider stakeholders
negative publicity media reporting of a business's activities in a potentially damaging way
niche marketing promoting and selling a product to a small, clearly identifiable segment of a larger market
off-the-job training training that takes place away from the place of work and that involves things such as conferences, courses and online learning
on-the-job training training that takes place at the place of work – usually the person does the actual job while an experienced employee observes and guides him or her, making corrections as required
opportunity cost a benefit, profit or value that a firm has to give up in order to achieve or have something else
organisational chart a chart that shows the roles and responsibilities of all of a business's employees, including the level of authority that they have
output the total number of products produced over a period of time
outsource to use other (external) companies to provide services within a firm – firms often outsource services such as security, cleaning and catering

overtime employees are paid more for working additional hours – the rate of pay is more than the employees earn during normal hours
partnership an unincorporated business that has more than one owner – in the UK, until 2002, partnerships were limited to 20 partners, but now they can have as many partners as they wish
penetration pricing a product is launched into an established and competitive market at a low price in an attempt to attract customers – the firm usually increases the price once it has gained market share
performance-related pay (PRP) a type of bonus scheme that provides a financial reward to employees for meeting agreed, individual targets
person specification a description of the type of person, their skills, qualifications and experience, required to fill a particular vacancy
petitioning the presentation of a formal letter, usually with multiple (often many thousands of) signatories, requesting a particular action or outcome
physiological needs the essentials of human survival, such as food, water, shelter and rest
piece-rate a system that pays employees for each unit of output (each product) they produce
piece-rate bonus an additional payment for each unit produced by an employee over a certain target
pop-up store a temporary, and often small, outlet that appears ('pops up') for a short period of time, often as part of a promotional campaign or to sell seasonal products
positive externality a positive impact of a firm's activities on its wider stakeholders
pressure group a group that campaigns on a range of social causes and tries to influence business behaviour (for example, Greenpeace)
price amount charged for a good or service
price elastic demand for a product is responsive to changes in price
price elasticity a measure of how sensitive (responsive) demand for a product is to changes in its price
price inelastic demand for a product is not very responsive to changes in price
price skimming a product that is first to market or has a significant unique selling point may be launched at a high price
primary data information collected first-hand, that did not already exist
primary sector the sector that generates raw materials, for example, coal or wood, which the tertiary sector then uses to make a product
private limited company a registered company that is not permitted to sell shares to the general public
private sector organisation a business such as a sole trader, a partnership or a company that is owned by a private individual(s)
production see output
productivity a measure of efficiency – units of output are compared to units of input. The measure that is most often used is labour productivity: the number of units produced by an employee in a given time period
product life cycle a graph showing the average stages a product goes through from launch, through growth, maturity/saturation and eventually decline
product recall when a firm requests that customers return products – usually for safety reasons
profit the financial gain of a business once all the costs have been paid using revenue
profitability the amount of sales revenue (or selling price for a single unit) that is turned into profit – expressed as a percentage
profit margin the percentage of a product's final selling price that is profit
profit share employees are offered a share in the annual profits of an organisation
protectionism laws and regulations that aim to protect local firms against competition from overseas businesses
publicity a method of marketing that attracts public attention to a product, service or company through the use of special events and media focus
public limited company (PLC) a company that sells its shares to the general public through a stock exchange – because the company can sell shares to anyone, it can raise massive amounts of money
public sector organisation an organisation that is owned by a government, rather than private individuals
qualitative data information gathered from a small group of people, using detailed discussions and interviews to explore the attitudes of consumers in depth
quality ensuring the standard of a product or service meets the expectations of customers
quality assurance a method of improving quality by trying to prevent mistakes happening in the production process
quality control a method of systematically checking the quality of a number of products at different stages during the production process
quantitative data data from a large group of respondents showing numbers, proportions or trends within a market, such as how many people buy a particular product
quota a limit on the quantity (amount) of a particular good that can be imported into a country
raw materials the unprocessed ingredients or materials that are needed to produce a product – these are a variable cost of production
recession a period when the economy is growing more slowly than previously
recovery a period when an economy starts to grow after a slump
recruitment the process of hiring new employees to fill vacant positions in a business
redeployment moving an employee from one part of the business to another
redundancy pay a one-off payment received by an employee when they lose their job due to redundancy (also known as severance pay)

redundant when a firm has too many employees for its current needs, or when the skills of an employee are no longer needed, the firm will make some employees redundant (it will ask the employees to leave)
relationship marketing a focus on long-term relationships with customers (rather than being satisfied with a single sale) – firms often use social media and the internet to keep customers up to date with new products, news and special offers
repatriation of profits the return of profits to a company's home country – rather than those profits remaining in and being spent in the host country
research and development (R&D) the use of a combination of science, imagination and marketing in order to generate new ideas, invent completely new technologies, make prototypes or test products with consumers
robotics the use of computerised arms to help production – normally cheaper, more accurate and more productive than using human employees
royalties a percentage of the yearly profit made by a franchisee that they pay to the franchisor
safety needs the human need for security, freedom from stress and a sense of permanency in their lives
salary employees on a salary system are paid an agreed sum for a year's work
sample a smaller group selected from a bigger population to be representative of the attitudes and characteristics of the total population
sampling a small research group is selected from a larger population
scarcity the lack of a product or material, for example, gold and diamonds are scarce resources
scientific management (F. W. Taylor) the principle of scientific observation, experiment and calculation designed to arrive at one 'best way' of completing a task – Taylor believed that money motivates and that firms should pay employees well but expect them to act as 'part of the machine'
secondary data information that has already been collected or published
secondary sector the secondary sector uses manufacturing to transform the raw materials generated in the primary sector into a product
self-actualisation the ultimate sense of achievement—a feeling a person has that they have achieved something with their life
self-esteem when a person feels good about themselves, proud of something they have done or when they experience a sense of achievement
selling price the amount that a product is sold for – this should normally be more than the average cost per item
separate legal identity when a business is a separate entity to its owners in the eyes of the law – the business's owners and employees are therefore not responsible for the business's actions and debts (limited liability)
severance pay see redundancy pay
share capital a one-off cash inflow from raising and selling additional shares in a business
shareholder an individual, group or business that owns one or more shares of a business – shares are exchanged for money
shareholder view the view that shareholders' interests (as the owners of the company) are the most important and should be protected
shares a company can be owned by shareholders. The ownership of the company is allocated to its owners using shares. The more shares an individual owns, the more of the business they own and control
silent partner sometimes called a sleeping partner – someone who invests in a partnership but does not take part in the day-to-day running of the business. It means that their liability is limited to their investment and no more
slump economic conditions defined by falling demand, falling output and rising unemployment
social enterprise a business that seeks to raise income, which it invests in a specific social or environmental issue
social needs the need to interact with other human beings, to belong to groups and to benefit from friendship
sole trader an unincorporated business owned by one person
span of control the number of subordinates someone has within their authority
specialisation focusing an individual or group on one particular skill or process that they are suited to or for which they possess the correct skills
stable exchange rate when the value of a currency changes very little against other currencies
stakeholder anybody who has an interest (direct or indirect) in what a business does and how it does it (for example, employees, suppliers, the local community)
stakeholder view the view that the interests of a firm's wider stakeholders should be protected, even where this conflicts with the interests of shareholders
subordinate an employee who is under the authority of another
subsidies money granted by the state or a public organisation to help an industry or business keep the price of a product or service low
sustainable development business and economic development that meets today's needs without damaging the ability of future generations to meet their needs – what we do today should not harm our future
systematic random sampling random sampling based on a system, for example, choosing every tenth person who walks into a store
takeover when one business or group of people buys a majority stake in another business, so that it owns the business
target market the particular market segment at which a business aims its product(s)

tariffs a specific form of tax imposed (charged) on imported goods
taxation money charged by a government on, for example, individual earnings (income tax), company profits (corporation tax) and consumption (VAT)
tertiary sector businesses that sell goods or services that have been made in the secondary sector
test marketing launching a product in a specific, usually small, geographic area to test customer reaction
total cost the total cost of producing a certain number of goods: variable costs + fixed costs
trade credit credit extended by one trader to another for purchasing a good or service
trade union an organisation that exists to provide workplace support for its members
transnational corporation a company with operations or sales bases in more than one country
two-factor theory (Herzberg) the theory that two factors (motivators and hygiene factors) are both important in motivation – the hygiene factors must be in place for motivators to be effective
undifferentiated marketing see mass marketing
unemployment the proportion of working age people in a country out of work – usually expressed as a percentage
unfair dismissal when an employee is dismissed (they lose their job) for reasons other than gross misconduct, consistently poor performance or a breach (break) in the terms of their employment contract, for example, in most countries, dismissal due to a one-off illness is considered legally unfair
unique selling point (USP) a feature of the product, its image, its price, its promotion or its distribution that is different from and superior to the competition
unlimited liability a key feature of unincorporated businesses – the owners are personally liable (responsible) for the debts of their business
value added tax (VAT) a tax on goods purchased
variable costs costs that are directly linked to production – these increase as the business's level of production (output) increases
wage money paid for completing a set number of hours – usually expressed per hour
working capital the money available to a business to pay for its day-to-day expenses and short-term debts

Index

Glossary terms are in **bold** type

Acknowledgements

The publishers wish to thank the following for permission to reproduce photographs. Every effort has been made to trace copyright holders and to obtain their permission for the use of copyright materials. The publishers will gladly receive any information enabling them to rectify any error or omission at the first opportunity.

(t = top, c = centre, b = bottom, r = right, l = left)

p6–7 Dann19L/Shutterstock, p8 Max Earey/Shutterstock, p10 Konstantin Stepanenko/Shutterstock, p11 catwalker/Shutterstock, p12t Diego Cervo/Shutterstock, p12tc Kosarev Alexander/Shutterstock, p12bc Sipa Press/Rex/Shutterstock, p12b huyangshu/Shutterstock, p14 Clynt Garnham Food & Drink/Alamy Stock Photo, p15 vovan/Shutterstock, p17t eyeidea/Shutterstock, p17c TTstudio/Shutterstock, p17b Monkey Business Images/Shutterstock, p18 CommerceandCultureAgency/Getty Images, p19 Agencja Fotograficzna Caro/Trappe/Alamy Stock Photo, p22t Joseph Sohm/Shutterstock, p22b ostill/Shutterstock, p24 Photosani/Shutterstock, p25 Cyberstock/Alamy Stock Photo, p28 Barone Firenze/Shutterstock, p30 Frank Romeo/Shutterstock, p33 Suhaimi Abdullah/Stringer/Getty Images, p34 mrmohock/Shutterstock, p35 Andrew D. Bernstein/Contributor/Getty Images, p38 Steve McWilliam/Shutterstock, p40 Tashatuvango/Shutterstock, p41 jps/Shutterstock, p43 Comstock Images/Getty Images, p44 Fer Gregory/Shutterstock, p47 1000 Words/Shutterstock, p51 ricochet64/Shutterstock, p52 gary718/Shutterstock, p53t Monkey Business Images/Shutterstock, p53b Muellek Josef/Shutterstock, p54l BasPhoto/Shutterstock, p54r travellight/Shutterstock, p58 hagit berkovich/Shutterstock, p60 Dean Drobot/Shutterstock, p62 JOHAN ORDONEZ/AFP/Getty Images, p63 ton koene/Alamy Stock Photo, p65 Keith Homan/Shutterstock, p66t BartlomiejMagierowski/Shutterstock, p66b frans lemmens/Alamy Stock Photo, p76–77 Mark Yuill/Shutterstock, p78 Philip Date/Shutterstock, p80t paul prescott/Shutterstock, p80c paul prescott/Shutterstock, p80b AVAVA/Shutterstock, p81t wavebreakmedia/Shutterstock, p81b Greg Epperson/Shutterstock, p83 Blend Images/Shutterstock, p87 Bloomberg/Contributor/Getty Images, p89 oticki/Shutterstock, p90 Zurijeta/Shutterstock, p91t Iakov Filimonov/Shutterstock, p91b Monkey Business Images/Shutterstock, p93 Stuart Jenner/Shutterstock, p98 Bloomberg/Contributer/Getty Images, p100 Xinhua/Alamy Stock Photo, p102 stefanolunardi/Shutterstock, p103 sirtravelalot/Shutterstock, p104t Diego Cervo/Shutterstock, p104b wavebreakmedia/Shutterstock, p105t MANPREET ROMANA/Stringer/Getty Images, p105b baranq/Shutterstock, p106 David Paul Morris/Stringer/Getty Images, p113 Feng Yu/Shutterstock, p114 Stuart Jenner/Shutterstock, p115 Milkovasa/Shutterstock, p117 JOHN MACDOUGALL/AFP/Getty Images, p119t Goodluz/Shutterstock, p119b Monkey Business Images/Shutterstock, p120 Pressmaster/Shutterstock, p121 Bloomberg/Contributer/Getty Images, p125 IrinaK/Shutterstock, p127 opla/Getty Images, p128 Diego Cervo/Shutterstock, p129 Andrey_Popov/Shutterstock, p130 iofoto/Shutterstock, p132 Ant Clausen/Shutterstock, p133 gresei/Shutterstock, p135 Rawpixel.com/Shutterstock, p137 Petinov Sergey Mihilovich/Shutterstock, p142 Daniel M Ernst/Shutterstock, p143t Kristi Blokhin/Shutterstock, p143b think4photop/Shutterstock, p144 DaLiu/Shutterstock, p145 Daniel Fung/Shutterstock, p158–159 littlesam/Shutterstock, p161 s_bukley/Shutterstock, p162 Emilio100/Shutterstock, p164 Kenishirotie/Shutterstock, p167 A. Aleksandravicius/ shutterstock, p168 Zhang Peng/LightRocket/Getty Images, p169 JuliusKielaitis/Shutterstock, p171 Tony Latham/Loop Images/SuperStock , p173 Patti McConville/Alamy Stock Photo, p176t cobalt88/Shutterstock, p176c Pixsooz/Shutterstock, p176b Junial Enterprises/Shutterstock, p177 Aaron Amat/Shutterstock, p178 RAGMA IMAGES/Shutterstock, p179 Golden Pixels LLC/Shutterstock, p186 Leszek Kobusinski/Shutterstock, p187 MAHATHIR MOHD YASIN/Shutterstock, p188 Directphoto/age fotostock/SuperStock, p192 Takashi Usui/Shutterstock, p193 Zzvet/Shutterstock, p196 Augustine JUMAT/Shutterstock, p197l artemisphoto/Shutterstock, p197r dean bertoncelj/Shutterstock, p201 Michael Halberstadt/Alamy Stock Photo, p202t omphoto/Shutterstock, p202b Shestakoff/Shutterstock, p205 République Beirut: www.republiquebeirut.com, p207 Jon Feingersh/Getty Images, p208 Gil C/Shutterstock, p209 Iain Masterton/Alamy, p210 Stokkete/Shutterstock, p211t Rebecca Sapp/WireImage/Getty Images, p211b Robert Harding Picture Library/SuperStock , p215t Fotos593/Shutterstock, p215b Annette Shaff/Shutterstock, p219t Nieuwland Photography/hutterstock, p219b Valentin Valkov/Shutterstock, p222t Iryna Rasko/Shutterstock, p222b Tanasan Sungkaew/hutterstock, p224 Zhukov Oleg/Shutterstock, p225 leonori/Shutterstock, p227 Bloomberg/Bloomberg/Getty ages, p229 Monkey Business Images/Shutterstock, p232 Felix Mizioznikov/Shutterstock, p242–243 Albert rimov/Shutterstock, p245t servantes/Shutterstock, p245b Monkey Business Images/Shutterstock, p247 sHelen/Shutterstock, p249 Ken Wolter/Shutterstock, p250 Robert Cianflone/Getty Images Nes/Getty Images, 1t Kzenon/Shutterstock, p251b alterfalter/Shutterstock, p252 MongPro/Shutterstock, p253 Yalcin Sonat/tterstock, p254t RAGMA IMAGES/Shutterstock, p254b Kim Steele/The Image Bank/Getty Images, p255t Rainer

Plendl/Shutterstock, p255b Oldrich/Shutterstock, p257 Blend Images/Shutterstock, p258 indianstockimages/Shutterstock, p261t nikkytok/Shutterstock, p261b Stephen Coburn/Shutterstock, p262 r.nagy/Shutterstock, p265 yakub88/Shutterstock, p269 Kaesler Media/Shutterstock, p271 Bloomberg/Bloomberg/Getty Images, p273 BWAC Images/Alamy Stock Photo, p275 NAN728/Shutterstock, p276 xieyuliang/Shutterstock, p290–291 Wara1982/Shutterstock, p292tl Dusan Petkovic/Shutterstock, p292tc kurhan/Shutterstock, p292tr RAJ CREATIONZS/Shutterstock, p292bl Stuart Jenner/Shutterstock, p292bc diez artwork/Shutterstock, p292br terekhov igor/Shutterstock, p293 cozyta/Shutterstock, p296 Bloomberg/Bloomberg/Getty Images, p298 Michaelpuche/Shutterstock, p300 michaeljung/Shutterstock, p302 Andrey Yurlov/Shutterstock, p304 Joseph Sohm/Shutterstock, p305 wanpatsorn/Shutterstock, p306 Benjamin Haas/Shutterstock, p308l Tyler Olson/Shutterstock, p308r 2xSamara.com/Shutterstock, p312 Casimiro PT/Shutterstock, p318l BartlomiejMagierowski/Shutterstock, p318r ESB Professional/Shutterstock, p319t DDCoral/Shutterstock, p319c Vasily Smirnov/Shutterstock, p319b erwinova/Shutterstock, p320 Kyodo News/Contributor/Getty Images, p321 S.Dashkevych/Shutterstock, p322 pcruciatti/Shutterstock, p323 cdrin/Shutterstock, p326l Olexa/Shutterstock, p326r Champiofoto/Shutterstock, p327 Chris Warham/Shutterstock, p329 Juthamat8899/Shutterstock, p330 Anthony Correia/Shutterstock, p331 Monkey Business Images/Shutterstock, p335t Denys Prykhodov/Shutterstock, p335b WDG Photo/Shutterstock, p338 ZouZou/Shutterstock, p352–353 sdecoret/Shutterstock, p355 gorkem demir/Shutterstock, p359 Tom Grundy/Shutterstock, p360 Dennis Owusu-Ansah/Shutterstock, p361 Mikadun/Shutterstock, p363 Paul Cowan/Shutterstock, p366 Vadim Ratnikov/Shutterstock, p368t Karl R. Martin/Shutterstock, p369t airphoto.gr/Shutterstock, p369tc Huguette Roe/Shutterstock, p369c chuyuss/Shutterstock, p369bc xpixel/Shutterstock, p369b VanderWolf Images/Shutterstock, p370 atiger/Shutterstock, p371 Leonid Ikan/Shutterstock, p372t DAVID HECKER/DDP/Getty Images, p372b Steven Frame/Shutterstock, p373 Sergey Nivens/Shutterstock, p374t Angelo Giampiccolo/Shutterstock, p374b Tran Qui Thinh/Shutterstock, p376 Tupungato/Shutterstock, p377 LOUISA GOULIAMAKI/AFP/Getty Images, p378 Kovalchuk Oleksandr/Shutterstock, p381l wizdata/Shutterstock, p381r Barna Tanko/Shutterstock, p381b TonyV3112/Shutterstock, p382 wen mingming/Shutterstock, p383 Bloomberg/Contributor/Getty Images, p384 Nataliya Hora/Shutterstock, p386 Glynnis Jones/Shutterstock, p387 vinnstock/Shutterstock, p389 Keith Homan/Shutterstock, p391t USJ/Shutterstock, p391b MyImages - Micha/Shutterstock.

We are grateful to the following for permission to reproduce copyright material:

Statistics on p18 from The World Factbook, © Central Intelligence Agency; Figure on p84 'One more time: How do you motivate employees' (2599-PDF-ENG) by F. Herzberg, Exhibit 1. Reproduced by permission of Harvard Business Publishing; Figure on p109 based on data from OECD Employment Outlook 2017, OECD Publishing, Paris, http://dx.doi.org/10.1787/empl_outlook-2017-en. Reproduced with permission; Definition of Marketing on p160 from American Marketing Association, www.ama.org. Reproduced with permission; Definition of Marketing on p160 from The Chartered Institute of Marketing, www.cim.co.uk. Reproduced with permission; Figure on p165 'Monthly spend by Category, India' from, Emerging Consumer Survey, 2016 Credit Suisse, www.credit-suisse.com. Reproduced with permission from Credit Suisse Research Institute; Figure on p354 from GDP Growth for Brazil (1960–2017), Trading Economics, www.tradingeconomics.com. Reproduced with permission; Figure on p360 based on 'Gross domestic product (GDP) per capita data' in World Economic Outlook Database, International Monetary Fund, April 2017. http://www.imf.org/external/pubs/ft/weo/2017/01/weodata/index.aspx, © IMF 2017; Figure on p365 reprinted from Tax Rates Online, © 2017 KPMG International Cooperative (KPMG International), a Swiss entity. Member firms of the KPMG network of independent firms are affiliated with KPMG International. KPMG International provides no client services. No member firm has any authority to obligate or bind KPMG International or any other member firm vis-à-vis third parties, nor does KPMG International have any such authority to obligate or bind any member firm. All rights reserved. All information provided is of a general nature and is not intended to address the circumstances of any particular individual or entity. Although we endeavour to provide accurate and timely information, there can be no guarantee that such information is accurate as of the date it is received or that it will continue to be accurate in the future. No one should act upon such information without appropriate professional advice after a thorough examination of the facts of a particular situation. For additional news and information, please access KPMG's global Web site on the Internet at http://www.kpmg.com; Figure on p370, Public domain/NASA; and Figure on p395 'Proportion of modern (supermarket style) retailers in various emerging markets versus more traditional, smaller retailers', © Euromonitor International, www.euromonitor.com. Reproduced with permission.